# AGGRESSION

# McGRAW-HILL SERIES IN PSYCHOLOGY

HARRY F. HARLOW, *Consulting Editor*

---

# AGGRESSION:
## A Social Psychological Analysis

**Leonard Berkowitz**
*University of Wisconsin*

McGraw-Hill Book Company
New York   Toronto   London   San Francisco

AGGRESSION: A Social Psychological Analysis

II

04870

*Dedicated with love to my parents*

# Introduction

As indicated in the title, this book will present a social psychological analysis of aggressive behavior. The intended meaning of the phrase "social psychological" should be clear so the reader can have some idea of the scope of the following discussion. Expectations for a work of this sort are bound to vary. Hostile behavior is all too familiar to every one of us, but we do not employ the same theories or conceptions in trying to understand such actions, and our needs in dealing with aggression are not the same. For many reasons, then, the considerations that are important to one reader are not necessarily significant for another.

The emphasis here will be on the actions of the individuals in social (i.e., interpersonal) settings. Social psychology is often defined as the study of human behavior in response to stimuli associated with other people. However, although the present focus is on factors governing hostility in human beings, some of the information pertaining to these determinants comes from research with animals. These latter investigations will be described briefly, along with the more usual (for social psychology) studies employing children, adolescents, college sophomores, and older adults. Animal research can contribute a great deal to our knowledge of the origin and course of aggression in the individual human being. Surely at least some of man's emotional reactions stem from his biological heritage (cf., Hebb & Thompson, 1954; Freud, 1959d; Scott, 1958).

But it is necessary, of course, to go well beyond these animal investigations. Man, possessing language, is greatly susceptible to symbolic influences. He can inhibit his aggressive tendencies when overt hostility would be a serious departure from his own internalized moral code and/or the behavioral standards of other people important to him. He also engages in aggressive actions in order to win the approval of others. Comprehensive analyses of aggression obviously must include consideration of these social determinants of behavior. The findings of social psychological research must be brought to bear upon the study of hostile interactions if these interactions are to be understood adequately.

Many different kinds of studies are gathered together under the banner of social psychology, however, and the writer's professional bias should be anticipated. All sciences seek to develop general propositions that are capable of relating one phenomenon within its realm to another phenomenon. Later on in this book, for example, I will discuss the proposition that the intensity of the emotional state, anger, produced by a frustration is a direct function of the degree to which all the goal-oriented responses the individual is capable of making in a situation are blocked. Laboratory experimentation is the procedure par excellence for the development of such abstract principles. Hypotheses can be formulated on the basis of observations made in a clinic or "real-life" situation, but unless there is control of other factors that could possibly account for the relationship between the variables of concern, the statement of this relationship is at best highly tentative. Control over such possibly confounding factors is best achieved in the laboratory. For this reason, many of the investigations cited in this book were conducted in the psychological laboratory. Their procedures generally are only a pale reflection of real-life hostile interactions; the frustrations they employ usually are relatively mild, and the aggressive reactions typically are fairly tame. Nevertheless, such experimentation enables us to control extraneous variables and permits the development of ever more precise theoretical propositions.

There would be many serious omissions, however, if we were to confine ourselves exclusively to laboratory investigations. Among other things, this book attempts to deal with the behavior of people in lynch mobs and in air raids. These hazardous situations, needless to say, have not been replicated in the experimental laboratory. Observations made in such important naturalistic situations must also be employed here. We will generally be concerned with almost the full range of human aggression (although extremely little will be said about pathological cases, such as the extreme sadist or masochist or the insane murderer, of interest largely to the psychiatrist). The material covered ranges from hostile reactions to an insult, through social prejudice, intergroup rivalries, and wars. Experimental findings will be resorted to whenever possible in analyzing these hostile encounters, but the results of less controlled observations will also be emphasized.

The primary purpose in all this is to develop a set of theoretical statements about aggressive behavior. The hypotheses to be presented here in the pursuit of this aim will necessarily be fairly abstract, possessing few of the rich, dramatic details inherent in the psychiatric case report, the newspaper story, novel, or movie. The above-mentioned principle regarding the relationship between anger intensity and degree of thwarting illustrates such an omission of details. Nothing is said of the exact form of the aggressive response to the anger state, or of the nature of the actions that are blocked by the frustration, or of the previous life history of the individual. These considerations are largely irrelevant as far as this hypothesis is concerned. The abstract propositions, however, may aid us in understanding the origin, course, and outcomes of the hostile interactions portrayed by the reporter, clinician, and writer and, hopefully, may someday contribute to the reduction of violence in interpersonal relations.

In developing these theoretical statements I will lean heavily on the foundation constructed by a team of psychologists working at Yale University in 1938 and 1939: John Dollard, Leonard Doob, Neal Miller, O. Hobart Mowrer, and Robert Sears. The result of their collaboration was an overly sketchy but, nevertheless, extremely helpful monograph entitled *Frustration and Aggression,* which provides what is still the best theoretical framework for the analysis of social aggression. As I will point out in the following chapters, modifications and extensions have to be made in this framework, but the foundation, I believe, is extremely sound.

Among the difficulties faced by the Yale psychologists were insufficient and inadequate data. All too frequently they had to rely on nonsystematic observations and inadequate measures, such as their subjects' statements of what they had done, or would do, in frustrating situations. The succeeding chapters of this book will demonstrate that today, approximately twenty-two years after the publication of *Frustration and Aggression,* many of the data available for hypothesis development in the area of aggression are still inadequate. In many instances hypotheses and analyses will be presented for which there is at best only relatively slight proof. Perhaps the major reason for the paucity of adequate data stems from the absence of clear-cut hypotheses based upon a systematic analysis of aggression to guide the investigations in this area. Recognizing the inevitable, the writer does not mind formulating hypotheses that other investigators will prove to be incorrect. There will be compensations if his analyses aid in the more rapid accumulation of systematically important information, knowledge that "adds up." It is hoped that at the very least the present book will point to problems requiring additional research.

Many of the concepts employed here are defined more or less as they were by Dollard and his colleagues. These definitions can be summarized briefly. Generally speaking, a *frustration* is said to be any interference with some ongoing goal-directed activity. Such thwartings usually (if not always) produce an emotional reaction, *anger,* the intensity of this emotional state being a function of certain aspects of the frustration. Anger, in turn, is regarded as an internal condition making aggressive responses relatively likely to occur. Anger, we can say, heightens the probability of hostile behavior. However, the anger "drive state" generally produces aggressive responses only in the presence of relevant cues, stimuli having some association with the anger instigator. The strength of the aggressive reaction to a frustration is in direct ratio to the intensity of the resulting anger and the degree of association between the instigator and the releasing cue. The aggressive reaction may not, of course, be displayed in overt behavior; other responses elicited in the situation can inhibit the hostile actions. *Aggression* and *hostility* are synonymous terms in this book and denote behavior aimed at the injury of some object.

The use of the Dollard et al. approach to aggression does not mean this book is committed to employ only those theoretical concepts favored by the Yale group. In actuality, the present work is conceptually eclectic. The terms used will be the ones that seem most appropriate for the given problem being discussed. Thus, the language of S-R learning theory will be utilized in analyzing hostility generalization, but cognitive concepts will be employed when referring to interpretations, belief systems, and the like. There is no real incompatibility between these theoretical constructs; all can contribute to our understanding of aggression.

The contents of this book are as follows:

The nature of the instigation to aggression is discussed in the first two chapters. Instinct conceptions of aggression are reviewed in Chapter 1. A distinction is made between those analyses (e.g., Freud's) maintaining that instinctive behavior is impelled by a constantly driving force within the organism whose energy must be expressed in some manner, and other views (e.g., McDougall's) contending that aggression is the innately determined response to some appropriate but not ever-present stimulus. Evidence bearing upon each of these positions is presented. The frustration-aggression hypothesis is discussed in Chapter 2. The concepts are defined, and several objections to this formulation offered by various writers are analyzed. In general, the frustration-aggression formulation is supported.

Chapter 3 is concerned with situational determinants of the strength of the instigation to aggression. The hypotheses initially proposed by Dollard et al. are essentially supported, but they also are modified somewhat in order to incorporate the operation of interpretations and expectancies.

Factors affecting the inhibition of aggression are discussed in Chapter 4. Where the Yale psychologists confined themselves to the effects of anticipated punishment, the present analyses also emphasize the role of guilt feelings. Social conditions governing the strength of the inhibitory tendencies are given particular attention.

Chapter 5 deals with determinants of the nature and target of aggressive responses to frustrations. Neal Miller's inner-conflict model (Miller, 1948) forms the basis of this discussion, and data generally consistent with this model are cited. The analysis is then extended to instances of intergroup conflict in Chapter 6, particularly cases of hostility displacement and scapegoating.

Other factors involved in intergroup conflict are reviewed in Chapter 7. Aggressive tendencies aroused by opposing belief systems and competitive situations are discussed, along with various conditions reducing the level of hostility between groups.

Chapter 8 is concerned with the catharsis hypothesis. A distinction is drawn between those versions of the catharsis doctrine contending that hostile behavior reduces the strength of the remaining instigation to aggression, and formulations maintaining that aggressive behavior is tension reducing, resulting in the aggressor "feeling better" after he makes his attack. This tension reduction seems to come about, according to empirical data, when the angered individual believes his frustrator has been aggressively injured by himself or an acceptable substitute.

Chapter 9 deals with the effects of violence in television, movies, and comic books. The characteristics of the audience for media aggression are considered. It is suggested that frequent portrayals of hostility in the mass media can affect the audience's attitude toward aggression and that under certain specified conditions the media violence may even evoke as well as shape hostile responses. There seems to be a greater likelihood that media violence will increase the probability of subsequent aggression than provide a cathartic lessening of hostile energies.

The characteristics and development of aggressive personalities are discussed in Chapter 10. Highly aggressive people are regarded as having strong aggressiveness habits, not a constantly active aggressive drive. The habit must be activated by a relevant cue. Frustration and modeling influences in the formation of hostile personalities are considered.

Finally, Chapter 11 is concerned with antisocial acts of aggression in the form of crime, suicides, and homicides. Attention is given to the role played by frustrations and a variety of social conditions.

The present book is, in a very real sense, a cooperative venture. It certainly would not have been possible without the thinking and efforts of countless research scientists. I am greatly indebted to them for the facts they have accumulated and the theoretical conceptions they have advanced. A good many psychologists have generously contributed their time to reading and criticizing early drafts of individual chapters, and I would like to express my appreciation to all of them. But particular thanks are due to Profs. Albert Bandura, Robert Singer, John Thibaut, and M. Brewster Smith for their comments on major parts of the manuscript. In acknowledging my gratitude to all these gentlemen, the least I could do is to absolve them of whatever shortcomings the present work might have. My thanks also go to Profs. Robert Sears and Leon Festinger for making it possible for me to spend a profitable and stimulating year at Stanford University, where much of this book was written, and to my colleagues at the University of Wisconsin for creating an almost ideal research environment.

The contributions to this book came in many forms. The research reported here could not have been possible without the cooperation of thousands of subjects, human as well as animal. I thank them for whatever indignities and insults they may have suffered, and trust that our advancing knowledge provides some measure of compensation. My own research benefited greatly from the skillful and invaluable help given by my students and research assistants, particularly Mr. Douglas S. Holmes, Mr. James A. Green, Dr. Jack E. Hokanson, Mrs. Jacqueline R. Macaulay, Miss Louise Daniels, Mrs. Edna Rawlings, Mr. Woodrow W. Call, and Miss Isabelle Birnbaum. This research was conducted under a grant (M1540) from the National Institute of Mental Health, United States Public Health Service. Finally, and certainly not least, I would like to thank my wife and daughters for their constant encouragement and patience.

*Leonard Berkowitz*

# Contents

# chapter I

# Instinct Conceptions of Aggression

Some years ago a group of boys in New York City attacked and brutally murdered a youngster because, as a member of a rival gang, they felt he should not have been in their area. This was only one of thousands of illegal aggressive acts committed in American cities each year, but the extreme nature of the crime and the youth of the individuals involved brought it nationwide attention. By reviewing our present knowledge of the causes and consequences of aggression—behavior whose goal is the injury of some object[1]—this book, in one way or another, will attempt to provide some possible reasons for this and other acts of brutality.

Aggression is a complex problem, whether the hostile acts are performed by the average American or by juvenile gangs such as the one mentioned above. Much has yet to be learned about the factors determining the likelihood of an aggressive outburst. Shortly after World War II a former mental patient went berserk and killed thirteen innocent passersby, including five women and three children, with a war-souvenir pistol. How could this tragedy have been prevented? Is anyone able to predict such violent outbursts? Certainly the psychiatrists who had released the patient from the mental hospital had not been able to foretell what he would do. What stimuli incite aggression? A recent news story from Hollywood reported the case of a confessed triple slayer who said he had killed his second victim after taking her to see a movie about a deranged murderer. Had the movie played any part in inducing the man to kill? Some say yes and others no. It is difficult to provide a clear and unequivocal answer.

But despite this uncertainty about the causes of violence, many people in preceding ages (and even today) would be content with a simple explanation for the murders. If asked about the boys in New York City,

---

[1] The terms "aggression" and "hostility" are employed synonymously in this book to denote behavior aimed at the injury of some object. "Anger" refers to the emotional state, presumably resulting from frustration, which, in the presence of a suitable cue, instigates aggressive responses.

these people would say the youngsters, coming from ethnic minority groups, had committed the crime "because this is the way they are." Aggressive behavior supposedly is inherent in their "nature." This conception is not necessarily a manifestation of prejudice. Rather, more often, it seems to be an expression of a general tendency to explain a person's actions by referring to some category in which he can be placed. Classify an object, such "Aristotelian thinking" would maintain (Lewin, 1935, p. 4), and we explain its behavior. A person is aggressive simply because he is a Negro, Puerto Rican, or Irishman, much as he might be assertive, ambitious, and unscrupulous merely as a direct consequence of his being a Jew.

This view of causality obviously is inadequate to account for the behavior of organisms. The ideal psychological formulation should specify the antecedent conditions leading to particular actions. In this case, what gives rise to hostility? The present chapter will consider some of the more prominent analyses of aggressive behavior that are based upon the doctrine of instincts.

There are a number of reasons for such a discussion. One is historical. Before the advent of behaviorism around the time of World War I, many observers of the hostile tendencies in man and other animals, whether in psychology, political science, philosophy, or literature, assumed, practically as a matter of course, that these tendencies were biologically determined. Moreover, these views have not disappeared from the contemporary scene. Somewhat similar beliefs are still held today in psychology, largely by several followers of the psychoanalytic movement. This is not merely an ivory-tower controversy. The notion of instinctive hostility has important implications for governmental and educational policies. Lax and permissive law enforcement regulations may be unrealistic if people are born with an urge to attack others, while harsh and restrictive discipline may only make matters worse if hostility is a learned reaction to frustrations. The citizen of a democracy concerned with the problem of controlling aggression through legal and educational institutions must have some awareness of the nature of aggression.

## Approaches Taken

The nest-building behavior of birds can serve as a fairly well agreed upon illustration of instinctive behavior. At the proper time in their life, robins, for example, will build the nests characteristic of their species even if they have been reared in isolation from other robins. Since this nest building is found universally among the members of the species and appears without opportunity to learn, there is little dispute that the behavior pattern is determined genetically. All who would explain hostility as an analogous process, then, contend that aggressive tendencies also are unlearned responses to some excitation. (However, they would also say the exact form of these responses in man and the higher animals can be modified through learning.) Nevertheless, even though they share this fundamental assumption, advocates of the notion of innate hostility differ in important ways in their conception of the actual operation of instincts.[2] These differences will be emphasized in the course of the following discussion, but they can be anticipated briefly here. Some writers, such as Freud and several of his disciples, view hostile actions as impelled by constantly driving forces whose energy must be released in one manner or another. In contrast, other people have taken the position that aggression has to be elicited by an appropriate stimulus. Like the above psychoanalysts, they regard instincts as innately constructed stimulus-response patterns, but unlike them, hold that the stimuli to aggression are not ever-present.

Since many instinctivists based their belief in innate aggression on the high frequency of wars in human history, our discussion of the instinct doctrine will begin with the problem of international conflict. We realize today that the question, "Why war?" is exceedingly complex (*cf.* Q. Wright, 1942), but it is one that has always attracted attention and has caused many to regard man as being born with a drive to injure or destroy. Following this, empirical evidence bearing on these instinct doctrines will be reviewed.

## Why War? Freud on the "Aggressive Instinct"

In the last fifteen or so years man has developed the capacity to eliminate all forms of life, including his own, from major portions of this planet. War seems unthinkable in the face of this horror, a nightmare easily shaken off in the more rational light of day. Who would risk war when a single hydrogen bomb could kill and maim millions in a crowded metropolitan area?

But yet, the fear of international conflict is not so easily dispelled. Certainly history provides little reason for confidence. At one time some people thought the invention of dynamite had made war too horrible for civilized nations to engage in. We have become accustomed to the

[2] Some of the instinctive-aggression formulations have been the result of Aristotelian thinking. One of the essential qualities in this mode of thought is the application of labels or category names to events as the explanation of these events. Thus, to say that an animal is a wolf presumably accounts for its strong proclivities to attack other species. ("Wolves are like that.") Similarly, other labels are employed in stating why the object category possessed the properties attributed to it. A wolf supposedly is aggressive because he has a strong aggressive instinct, and here the explanation stops. This analysis does little more than say that the animal behaves this way because this is the way he is.

idea that weapons may destroy tens, hundreds, and finally, hundreds of thousands of people in one blow, and through this adaptation the nightmare becomes somewhat less terrible. Nevertheless, this adaptation process alone obviously is inadequate to account for war. It perhaps may help explain why weapon development per se does not lead to the outlawing of war, but not why international conflicts take place. Other explanations are needed, involving economic, sociological, ideological, and probably psychological factors as well.[3]

Several of the most eminent minds of the twentieth century have sought the causes of war in human nature. In 1932 an agency of the League of Nations asked Prof. Albert Einstein to invite any person he chose to a frank exchange of views on some important problems. The problem Einstein selected was, "Is there any way of delivering mankind from the menace of war?" and suspecting that the roots of conflict could be found in man's makeup, he wrote to Sigmund Freud (Einstein, 1933). How is it, he asked, that propaganda devices succeed so well in rousing men to war? Training in the complexities of one science does not necessarily preclude giving oversimplified solutions to the problems in other disciplines. To Einstein "only one answer is possible." Man had within him, he felt, a "lust for hatred and destruction" which ordinarily was latent but could easily be aroused and raised to "the power of a collective psychosis" (p. 18).

Freud agreed with him. Einstein's proposition was consistent with his most recent interpretation of aggressive behavior. He believed in the existence of "an active instinct for hatred and destruction" in man, he replied, and then went on to outline briefly his conception of human instincts (Freud, 1959c). It is worth considering this conception in some detail because Freud's formulation is one of the few attempts to provide a theoretical underpinning for this "instinct." Careful examination of his views will help demonstrate the shaky foundation upon which this account of aggressive behavior was built.

But aside from its theoretical significance, Freud's hypothesis has some important implications for human conduct. An innate aggressive drive cannot be abolished by social reforms or the alleviation of frustrations. Neither complete parental permissiveness nor the fulfillment of every desire will eliminate interpersonal conflict entirely, according to this view. Its lessons for social policy are obvious: Civilization and moral order ultimately must be based upon force, not love and charity. Freud himself was of this opinion in his reply to Einstein. Law for him was the might of the community. But it also was violence "ready to be directed against any individual who resists it," and it supposedly worked

[3] One of the most comprehensive discussions of the causes and conduct of war has been presented by Quincy Wright in *A Study of War* (1942).

the way any violence worked (Freud, 1959c, p. 275). Pessimistically, he believed there was no use trying to do away with men's aggressive inclinations. Rather, the most we could hope for is to divert these destructive impulses "to such an extent that they need not find expression in war."

⇛ *The "Death Instinct."* [Before World War I Freud maintained that human behavior was largely governed by the interplay of two main instincts, sexual and ego instincts [He believed neurotics were ill because of their repression of experiences associated with their sexual desires. This repression came about because of their anxieties which were motivated by the ego instincts serving the purpose of self-preservation.] Their pleasure strivings had to be altered, postponed, or inhibited altogether because of the demands of the external world. The ego instincts operating under the "reality principle" were said to have countered the "pleasure principle." At this time Freud did not conceive of aggression as a primary drive. Rather, he felt that aggressive impulses resulted mainly from frustrations. These views were altered somewhat during World War I. For one thing, he now began to emphasize what previously had only been touched upon: hostile as well as sexual tendencies could be repressed. But more than this, by about 1920 he no longer believed that aggression was necessarily a product of the frustration of the sexual (pleasure-seeking) impulses (Thompson, 1950).

➙ His new theory again was based upon the assumption of two opposing instincts. This was the fundamental contrast of life (Eros) and death (Thanatos) drives, the former resulting in the continuation of life, the latter having death as its aim [Freud, however, did think of all instincts as having an important property in common: all sought the lessening of stimulation. [Libidinal strivings brought relief from sexual tension, and the death instinct the elimination of the tension of life itself]

[This supposed pursuit of tension reduction is a central notion in Freud's motivational theory as well as in his more specific formulation of the aggressive instinct] A full understanding—and evaluation—of this interpretation of aggression first requires a brief review of the psychoanalytic approach to motivation. Freud did recognize that pleasurable feelings sometimes accompany increases in internal stimulation, as in the case of sexual excitement (Freud, 1959a, p. 256). Nevertheless, for him the dominating tendency of organic life in general was the effort to control stimulation. The primary function of the nervous system presumably was either to abolish stimuli or to reduce excitation to the lowest possible level; it was "an apparatus which would even, if this were feasible, maintain itself in an altogether unstimulated condition" (1959b, p. 63).

The pleasure principle was readily thought of in these terms. The attainment of satisfactions seems to be followed by a lessening of tension, so it must be, he reasoned, that all pleasure seeking basically was aimed toward tension reduction (1959d, pp. 107–108). For example, the sexual act was associated with an extinction of a highly intensified excitation. Therefore, in desiring sexual activity the individual ultimately pursued this lessening of internal stimulation. In fact, any behavior must be directed toward tension reduction to the extent that it was oriented toward the attainment of pleasure.

But what is death if not also the elimination of excitation? Freud believed the universal goal of all living substance was "to return to the quiescence of the inorganic world" (1959d, p. 108). In other words, all life sought the peace of death, for to die was to be free from stimulation. The pleasure principle would appear to serve the death instinct, according to this formulation, but this principle nevertheless was different, he argued. It must be a modification of the death instinct brought about by the libidinal life instinct (1959a, pp. 256–257), and presumably was especially on guard against increases in internal stimulation which would make the task of living more difficult (1959d, p. 109). How this modification comes about was not stated.

Freud, however, did have some conjectures as to how we manage to live in spite of our death wishes. The life instinct could alter Thanatos in two ways. In one of these the libido turned the death instinct toward the objects of the outer world (1959a, p. 260). Essentially, in describing this process Freud maintained that an organism's striving for the condition of "inorganic quiescence" not only would produce its own destruction but also necessarily involved active self-destruction as the primary means of achieving this condition. This self-annihilation, then, was prevented when the life instinct diverted the destructive drive from the self to others. Thus, in attacking others the individual found an outlet for pressures otherwise driving toward his own death. In the second process the libido merged with the forces of the death instinct, not only erotizing the drive (i.e., rendering aggressive behavior a source of sexual pleasure), but supposedly also making it actually less dangerous to life.

This fusion of the life and death instincts presumably was responsible for both masochism and sadism (1959a). According to Freud, masochism, the tendency to attain pleasure from hostility toward the self, resulted from a backward flow of the destructive forces. The diversion of the death instinct outward was opposed by the restraints of civilization. Hostility to others not only could not easily be expressed, but also was frequently repressed, and the outward release of the energy was incomplete. On top of this, a "residuum" of the death instinct naturally remained within the organism. This combined with the now returning destructive forces as an intensified masochism (p. 267). One expression of this, said Freud, was the moral form of masochism in which the person had an unconscious feeling of guilt, or to put it in other words, a need for punishment by some parental authority. [Even this type of masochism represented a fusion of the libido with the death instinct, for the individual not only wanted to be beaten by this parent, but apparently also desired "passive (feminine) sexual relations with him"] (p. 266). Freud argued that it was only through postulating this backward flow of the death instinct following its civilized inhibition that a particular clinical phenomenon could be explained: " . . . the more anyone refrains from aggressiveness towards others the more strict and sensitive his conscience becomes," while one might expect that the avoidance of the socially undesirable aggressions actually should result in a good conscience (p. 267). A "strict conscience" with accompanying frequent guilt feelings is widely regarded as indicative of inner-directed hostility. Assuming this to be true, however, another explanation for the phenomenon described by Freud has been advanced, and this will be discussed in Chapter 5.

[Sadism is a more obvious example of the conjectured merging of libido with the death instinct. Injuring others has sexual connotations for the sadist and, thus, at one and the same time is an expression of both erotic and destructive forces within him]

This is not to say that injury to others is the only possible outlet for these violent energies short of suicide. [There are some socially permissible ways in which the death instinct may be gratified, according to Freud. Here he thought of the term "aggressiveness" as it sometimes is employed in everyday life—for example, when we compliment a salesman for his aggressiveness. In this context, of course, the word is synonymous with "assertiveness." But Freud meant more than this, for he believed it actually was the libidinally modified destructive instinct that impelled a person's striving for mastery or his drive for power (p. 260). This type of behavior, in being driven by the death instinct, could also provide some satisfaction for it.]

Obviously, according to this analysis of motivation generally and aggression in particular, man's energies must continually seek release. If they did not find an outlet in one form, they supposedly would be expressed in some other manner. [Assertiveness and competition might drain some of his destructive force, but if they did not, less desirable outlets would be found. If the death instinct directed outward produced wars, a nation which did not fight and had no suitable alternatives must destroy itself. Thus, war could be seen as a needed safety valve, a country's attempt at self-preservation] (Alexander, 1941; Thompson, 1950, p. 51). A gloomy prospect: unless we can find morally acceptable forms of aggressiveness we are doomed either to intranational conflict and national suicide (literally or figuratively) or to war and radioactive extermination.

*Criticisms.* Very few psychoanalysts today accept Freud's hypothesis of a death instinct. Dramatic though it may be, the concept of an innate drive for destruction, as Freud has posited it, is scientifically unwarranted. Most of the otherwise orthodox adherents to this movement share the reservations voiced by such leading figures as Otto Fenichel (1945). There are a number of bases upon which the hypothesis can be attacked, some logical, others factual.

The difficulties in the logic of Freud's speculations concerning the death instinct to some degree also apply to the general body of psychoanalytic theory. No other large set of present-day scientific hypotheses reveals the influence of a single person to a similar extent, according to one of the foremost exponents of this theory (Kris, 1951, p. 333). Consequently, Freud's mode of thought, with all its strengths and weaknesses, still largely characterizes this discipline. Since a philosophical critique of psychoanalysis is beyond the intended scope of this book, only one logical error, pertinent to the notion of the death instinct, will be cited. This has to do with the teleological thinking in Freud's discussion of the functional value of psychological processes. Under the cultural influence of Darwinism, nineteenth-century biologists often stressed the functional aspects of an organism's structure or behavior, that is, the value it had for the organism's survival. For many writers of the period a functional description of a process served as its explanation. This is a teleological error, for it implies that the end state of some process was its cause. Cannon's "emergency theory" of emotions can be used as an illustration. When an animal is subjected to threatening stimuli, certain physiological processes take place, such as a slowing down of the activities of the digestive system, which at times are described as preparing the animal for emergencies. This end state, the readiness to respond to emergencies, however, is not the cause of the physiological changes. Rather, they are due to the preceding actions of the nervous system.

Freud's development of his death instinct hypothesis reveals just this type of teleological thinking. He had observed cases that seemed to go "beyond the pleasure principle"; people sometimes displayed a tendency to repeat earlier situations, even when these events were painful. For example, shell-shocked soldiers frequently would relive their traumatic experiences in their dreams. Part of Freud's explanation of this phenomenon is acceptable today. He proposed that this repetition of painful experiences was an attempt to master the dangers in the situations. But he then went on to conjecture that the behavior was caused by a "compulsion to repeat" inherent in organic life (1959d). This supposedly universal attribute of life, he suggested, would bring about the earlier state of inanimate quiescence, and thus the repetition compulsion could be regarded as a manifestation of the death instinct. Repetitive behavior was a special instance of a general tendency to return to an earlier state, with the basic impetus for this tendency being the strain to achieve the primitive inorganic condition of no stimulus tension. In other words, here is the notion that some future condition, such as reduced excitation, or even the complete absence of excitation, was the cause of the neurotic compulsion. Obviously, this cannot be; the cause is not in the future. Claiming that some mysterious force—calling it an instinct, compulsion, or drive does not help—seeking to attain a future state in some unknown fashion produces certain behaviors is only the application of "word magic." We may feel we now understand the phenomenon, when actually we know just as little as before. There are few, if any, specific predictions that can be made on the basis of such vague formulations.

Philosophical arguments aside, there are other reasons to doubt the validity of the basic motivational model upon which Freud's hypothesis was based. Psychoanalytic theory, in common with the views held by many experimental psychologists, generally employs a tension-reduction framework in accounting for purposive behavior. According to this line of thought, excessive stimulation arises within the organism as the result of some biological deprivation, e.g., of food, water, or sex, impelling the organism to reduce this excitation. (The death instinct is but an extreme formulation of this thesis.) Recent research, however, seriously questions whether this tension-reduction model can satisfactorily handle the wide variety of phenomena to which it has been applied by both psychoanalysts and experimentalists (R. W. White, 1959).

For one thing, organisms at times seek stimulation from the external environment (Harlow, 1953). This is seen, for example, in studies of exploratory behavior. In one of these, Montgomery (1954) placed his animals in a Y maze in which they had a choice between the short arm leading to a dead end and a longer arm which itself was a complex maze. If the animals primarily sought the reduction of novelty their best bet was the shorter arm which they could explore very quickly. Instead, they tended to prefer the longer arm, much as if they had deliberately chosen to receive an increase in the stimulation produced by the unfamiliar surroundings rather than a rapid lessening of such stimulation. Several experiments involving electrical stimulation of animal brains also support the present analysis. They demonstrated that animals will work to *receive* such stimulation (Olds & Milner, 1954; N. E. Miller, 1957). In the investigations conducted by Miller and his colleagues, the psychologists found that cats and rats will learn to make certain responses (either running down the correct arm of a T maze or turning a wheel) in order to escape electrical stimulation to their brains and then will learn to make other responses (such as bar pressing) that *turn this stimulation on again.* In other words, the animals show not only a rewarding effect from the termination of the stimulation to the brain (as the tension-reduction theory would imply), but also a rewarding effect from the onset of this stimulation. These results may seem paradoxical, but they at least are not entirely consistent with the tension-reduction model. Not *all* behavior apparently is oriented toward the lessening of excitation.) Other animal experiments have demonstrated that the arousal of a drive without subsequent reduction in this excitation can have a reinforcing effect upon learning. Sheffield, Wulff, and Becker (1951) utilized a learning task in which the reward provided for the animals, naïve male rats, was the opportunity to copulate with a female, but not enough times to produce ejaculation. This reward facilitated learning even though, in the absence of ejaculation, there was no need reduction and the animals were left in a state of heightened excitement.

Many other investigations yielding similar findings could also be cited. All essentially suggest that organisms frequently go out of their way to obtain additional stimulation from their external environment. But more than this, the experiments indicate that in seeking this stimulation both animals and humans often desire states of raised tension and mild excitation. Summarizing some of this research, Hebb and Thompson pointed out that people exhibit comparable phenomena in their liking for dangerous sports or roller coasters, in their desire for challenging but sometimes frustrating work.

Such behavior in man is usually accounted for as a search for prestige, but the animal data make this untenable. It seems much more likely that solving problems and running mild risks are inherently rewarding, or, in more general terms, that the animal will always act so as to produce an optimal level of excitation.[4]

It is true, as pointed out earlier, that Freud did recognize the existence of occasional strivings for increased stimulation, largely as "forepleasure." This exception to the general principle, however, was not adequately incorporated within his basic interpretation of motivation. The exception proves the rule, says the old maxim, but "proves" here means "tests" rather than "confirms." The animal research just mentioned indicates that this type of exception actually is fairly common and as such provides a severe test of the tension-reduction view of pur-

[4] From Gardner Lindzey (Ed.), *Handbook of Social Psychology.* Vol. 1. Reading, Mass.: Addison-Wesley, 1954, p. 551.

posive behavior. There simply are too many instances in which organisms, human beings as well as lower animals, work for a buildup in excitations for us to accept the general model upon which Freud's death instinct conjectures were based. Organisms seem to desire an optimal level of stimulation, and perhaps occasional variations in this level as well, but there is no evidence that they seek the complete elimination of excitation. Death is not necessarily the inherent aim of all organic life. We must agree with an otherwise sympathetic critic of Freud's motivational approach: Of all Freud's speculations, his interpretation of aggressive behavior is the one most removed from facts (Fletcher, 1957).

## Other Conceptions of "Aggressive Instincts"

*Hartmann, Kris, and Loewenstein.* Psychoanalytically oriented writers since Freud have taken three different positions regarding the nature of the aggressive drive. A few apparently still hold to the original notion of a death instinct (e.g., K. Menninger, 1942, p. 295); others maintain that the impetus to hostility arises primarily from frustrations of one form or another (e.g., Durbin & Bowlby, 1939; Fenichel, 1945); and a third group (e.g., Alexander, 1941; Hartmann, Kris, & Loewenstein, 1949) prefers to keep the orthodox psychoanalytic view of behavior, including hostility, as driven by instincts, but does not relate the aggressive instinct to a supposedly more basic drive toward death. The views presented by Hartmann et al. may be taken as somewhat representative of this latter line of thought.

Their formulation does not offer a radical departure from Freud even though it abandons the construct of a death instinct. Sexual and aggressive impulses are posited as the two mainsprings for behavior, with both seen as instinctive in man, and again, similar energic principles are said to govern the operation of each drive. Thus, both libidinal and aggressive tensions presumably may be discharged by motor activity, and the reduction of both kinds of tension is pleasurable if there are no other reactions such as guilt feelings or anxiety. More important as far as a general motivational theory is concerned, they maintained with Freud that the energy of the aggressive impulse may be neutralized, much as sexual energy is neutralized, so that both can power behaviors having no apparent connection to sex or hostility. Aggression as well as sex provides the steam making the world go 'round.

Since this energy is constantly operative, danger and frustration release rather than arouse the drive. These situations provide an opportunity for hostility to be discharged more than they create aggression. Aggression supposedly is somewhat similar to the sex drive in this respect. "The vicissitudes of aggression resemble those of sexuality to such a degree that the assumption of a constant driving power comparable to that of the libido seems appropriate" (Hartmann et al., 1949, p. 28). As an illustration, Hartmann and his colleagues discussed a child whose activities were interrupted (p. 30). This interference with his actions mobilized his hostility so it could then be released. Without such an outlet he probably would have turned naughty. If the interruption itself had been aggressive in nature, the child, of course, probably would have reacted with a great deal of hostility, but this reaction would have been due to the relatively strong appeal or attraction of the interruption in drawing out the destructive force. Obviously, the notion of a constant driving force also implies that the aggressive energy continually seeks outlets and will be expressed in one form or another. Objective danger invites the discharge of aggression, they proposed. However, if this energy is not released in fighting, it may be internalized and thus give rise to guilt feelings, that is, aggression directed inward against the self (p. 24).

*McDougall.* Psychoanalysts are not alone in proposing the existence of an aggressive instinct. "Instinct," as a motivational construct, has lost favor in American psychology since the advent of behaviorism. Before this time, however, the concept was frequently invoked by many writers in Europe and the United States, including William James, Lloyd Morgan, William McDougall, and even J. B. Watson prior to 1918, who believed that psychology must account for purposive behavior as well as conscious states, the dominant concern of most academic psychologists of the period. It was only through the use of the doctrine of instincts, they believed, that deliberate seeking, striving, and working to attain particular ends, whether in human beings or animals, could be satisfactorily explained. McDougall (1926) made perhaps the most ambitious attempt of those in this group to show that even the most complex social interactions of man ultimately were based upon innate motive tendencies.

An instinct for him was an inherited psychophysical process common to all members of a given species:

. . . which determines its possessor to perceive, and to pay attention to, objects of a certain class, to experience an emotional excitement of a particular quality upon perceiving such an object, and to act in regard to it in a particular manner, or at least, to experience an impulse to such action (p. 30).

This tendency in itself was not learned, he argued, but nevertheless, it could be modified by learning. The original instigating stimulus arousing "the instinct of fear or flight," for example, supposedly was "any sudden loud noise." However, if an animal had repeated experiences in which particular noises were never followed by harmful effects, the instinct of flight would not be aroused by these stimuli. The organism had learned to discriminate between these and other noises, implying that "the perceptual disposition, the afferent inlet of the instinct," had been altered by environmental events (p. 36). Similarly, as the result of other learning experiences, initially neutral stimuli repeatedly associated with the original instigators through temporal contiguity may have come to excite the instinctive process (pp. 36–38). Motor activity could also be altered through learning; the bodily movements in which the instinct was expressed could be modified and complicated in the course of an organism's interactions with his environment.

The total cognitive-conative-affective pattern was an important feature of the instinctive process for McDougall. He maintained that an emotional feeling specific to each of the principal instincts accompanied the other components of the process. These affective aspects were less susceptible to modification than the other parts of the pattern (an angered person could control his muscle movements to a greater degree than his physiological reactions) but in themselves did not supply the motive force for action. The impulse to activity, the conative aspect of the process, was part of the total instinctive pattern, and was aroused, as was the feeling tone, by the instigating stimulus. Pleasure and pain had a minor role in McDougall's motivational scheme. These feelings could "modify instinctive processes, pleasure tending to sustain and prolong any mode of action, pain to cut it short" (p. 44), but directly or indirectly, instincts were the prime movers of all activity. They determined the aim of each action or train of thought and provided the driving power sustaining it (p. 45).

Aggression (the instinct of pugnacity) was somewhat different from other instincts, according to McDougall. In contrast to the other motive forces, there was no specific class of objects whose perception constituted the first stage of the instinctive process. Rather, the instigating condition was some frustration, i.e., interference with an activity impelled by any of the other instincts. Along with other psychologists to be discussed below (Dollard, Doob, Miller, Mowrer, & Sears, 1939), McDougall proposed that the intensity of the excitement aroused by the frustration was in direct proportion to the strength of the obstructed impulse (McDougall, 1926, p. 62).

This outline of McDougall's views permits a comparison between his and the Hartmann et al. conceptions of aggression. Obviously, even though McDougall welcomed the psychoanalytic use of the instinct doctrine (pp. 465–467), the two formulations differ in several important respects. The Englishman was much less willing to erect an entire psychological system on the two pillars of sex and hostility and posited many more principal instincts. Further, starting from observations of "normal" animal and human behavior instead of psychopathology, he paid less attention to the individual's defenses against his disapproved impulses and somewhat more to the specific learning conditions under which instinctual processes could be modified. But most important of all for our present purposes, where the above-mentioned psychoanalysts saw aggression as a constantly operating force continually seeking release, McDougall argued that the inherited disposition to pugnacity had to be activated by some instigating frustrating condition. The consequence of this latter difference, of course, is that McDougall's outlook upon life essentially was somewhat more optimistic than that of Hartmann and his colleagues. Interpersonal and international conflict conceivably could disappear with the elimination of rivalry, competition, and other obstructions to the pursuit of individual and national goals. McDougall, however, might have objected somewhat to our labeling this an "optimistic" occurrence. He himself preferred to look at the bright side of conflict and maintained that a highly developed instinct of pugnacity led to the selection and survival of the best individuals and groups (pp. 285–302). The more combative males within any group were the ones who could win mates and survive to breed, while combative societies had to organize in order to fight other groups most effectively. European peoples have innately stronger aggressive tendencies than the people of India and China, he believed, and this made for the (supposedly) greater social organization, integration and "conscientiousness" in the former cultures (pp. 297–298). From his Darwinian viewpoint, pugnacity was probably the most important factor in the "selection of the fit and the extermination of the less fit (among both individuals and societies) resulting from their conflicts with one another" (pp. 301–302).

*Criticisms.* This is not the place to evaluate the scientific status of the instinct doctrine. (Some recent discussions of this concept can be found in Allee, Nissen, & Nimkoff, 1953; Fletcher, 1957; Thorpe, 1956; and Tinbergen, 1951.) A few remarks are pertinent, however. For one, there is little doubt that the term has frequently been employed in a vague and imprecise manner. The sociologist L. L. Bernard, reviewing the writings of some four hundred authors, counted about six thousand urges that had been called instinctive (cited in Allee et al., 1953, p. 295). Apparently, every time many of these writers felt an urge to explain some behavior they would invoke an "instinct."

This type of criticism seems to be more appropriate for the Hartmann, Kris, and Loewenstein conception than for that advanced by McDougall. The former were entirely vague about the roots of their so-called instinctive aggression. People fight, they told us, in order to satisfy some hypothesized need to fight that is not and cannot be traced to any physiological or even behavioral source. Until these sources can be identified, instinct must remain nothing more than a name applied to a class of actions. McDougall at least is somewhat more specific in his description of these antecedent conditions for aggression.

Research with animals conducted by ethologists and comparative psychologists is still more damaging to the formulation proposed by Hartmann and his colleagues. Man presumably possesses an aggressive instinct because of his biological heritage and his membership in the animal kingdom. His innate, biologically determined reaction tendencies should also be present in lower animals. Freud, the reader will remember, assumed that the death instinct existed in "organic life in general." It certainly is unreasonable phylogenetically to maintain that human beings would have these biological tendencies if the other animals did not. This being the case, the advocate of the instinctive aggression doctrine is hard-pressed to defend himself against the essentially negative evidence provided by biologists and psychologists.

## Fighting among Animals

Scott and Fredericson (1951) reviewed a number of studies of the causes of fighting in mice and rats, and many of their observations seem relevant to animal aggression generally. They established two main classes of instigations to hostility depending upon whether there was obvious competition between animals or not. Aggression incited by competition clearly does not stem from a constantly operative instinctive drive to hostility. This is primarily either instrumental aggression, in which the hostile acts are utilized as an attempt to achieve some goal, or a reaction to frustrations largely representing an attack upon obstructions to the attainment of this goal.

*Dominance.* There is one type of competitive fighting that may pose some problems, however: hostility instigated by strivings for positions of dominance. Conflicts over food, mates, or nesting sites can easily be defined as being in the service of these biologically necessary aims, but what about the fighting produced by competition for dominance? What impels an animal's struggle to control the other members of his species in his vicinity? There is little doubt that dominance hierarchies exist in many different animal groups or that the members of a wide variety of species compete for the dominant status in any assemblages they might form. Schjelderup-Ebbe's pioneering observations that chickens establish "pecking orders," in which hens can aggress against other hens in their flock who apparently are subordinate to them without receiving retaliatory aggression, but do not attack other hens above them in this "power hierarchy," have also been found to pertain to the social behavior of many different birds and mammals and even some lizards and fish (Collias, 1944, 1951; Scott, 1958b). In many of these species, when a number of organisms strange to each other are grouped together, there is a period of active fighting resulting in a dominating victor and subordinate vanquished. Peace then emerges with the structuring of the relationships among the organisms; in any potential competition the dominant ones fight or exhibit aggressive behavior while the others display defensive behavior or attempt to escape. These relationships, once established, are remarkably stable (Collias, 1944), but they are learned, and this learning follows regular principles (Scott & Fredericson, 1951).

We can only speculate about the conditions producing these struggles for rank. However, there are some very real benefits to be obtained through winning superior status, and the aggressive competition for dominance may well be instrumental to the pursuit of these goals. Dominant organisms, for example, generally have greater freedom of movement than do those subordinate to them, giving them greater access to food, mates, or desirable territory (Collias, 1944). There is additional evidence for the possible instrumental significance of dominance in the heightened competition for rank frequently produced by hunger and food shortages (Collias, 1944). The dominance struggle may even have a sexual function in certain species that is independent of competition for mates or nesting sites (Carpenter, 1960). Nevertheless, whatever the basis for the dominance strivings, whether they are instrumental to the satisfaction of other drives or are autonomous,[5] there is little reason to believe that they are the expressions of a constantly operative instigation to aggression.

*Noncompetitive Fighting and the Effects of Male Sex Hormone.* The second category of causes listed by Scott and Fredericson, noncompetitive fighting, on first glance would seem to offer more encouragement to the "constant force" doctrine. To illustrate this type of combat, Fredericson found that male mice who had been reared in isolation from the age of twenty-one days "spontaneously" began to fight with other males, when brought together with them, at about thirty-six days of age (cited in Scott & Fredericson, 1951, p. 277). While there is no obvious competition involved in this aggression, there are at least three other factors which affect the fighting: the male sex hormone, training, and pain. Of these, the hormonal influence upon apparently spontaneous aggression appears to be most consistent with the Hartmann et al. formulation; internal chemical processes intimately related

[5] H. F. Harlow has suggested (personal communication) that dominance patterns in monkeys normally develop out of their play patterns. He also has observed aggression developing in these animals in the course of their play, but this type of behavior may be expressions of exploratory or manipulatory drives or the result of pain produced in satisfying these drives.

to sexual functioning could serve as the ever-present stimuli to hostile acts. This might be inferred from Fredericson's study mentioned above. The age at which his male mice began to display aggression corresponds to the onset of the production of the male hormone. Further, females of many species generally fight less frequently or vigorously than the males (Collias, 1944; Scott & Fredericson, 1951).

Biologists and psychologists have amply documented the relationship between the male sex hormone and fighting in the absence of obvious competition. Beach, for example, castrated a male rat that had been an "unusually vigorous copulator when placed with animals in heat." There was no diminution of copulatory responses at first, but by eleven days after the operation there was a loss of both these responses and aggressiveness. Lessening the supply of the male hormone had decreased both sexual and aggressive behavior. When this supply was increased through injections of testosterone propionate, not only was copulation restored, but there was a revived aggressiveness as well (Beach, 1945). Beeman has conducted some of the more definitive experiments in this area in which she typically staged encounters between mice previously kept in isolation. Again, there were no readily apparent material gains to be obtained through fighting. Among other things, Beeman reported that male mice who were castrated either in adulthood or prior to this time and then kept isolated for at least twenty-five days failed to display the aggressive behavior characteristic of normal mice. Subcutaneous implantation of testosterone pellets revived these aggressive tendencies, which then generally subsided again when the pellets were removed (Beeman, 1947).

The question now is, what is the reason for this noncompetitive fighting? One likely possibility, of course, is that the animals actually were competing for something. The combat may have been instigated, in part at least, by struggles for social rank (Vandenbergh, 1960), and/or "undisturbed possession of living space [generally] rather than for any particular bit of space" (Calhoun, cited in Scott & Fredericson, 1951, p. 280). Scott and Fredericson also proposed as a cause of the aggression (somewhat teleologically) that the "fighting in rats and mice may also tend to prevent homosexual activity and to insure distribution of the sexes through the living space, so that fertile mating behavior is easily achieved" (p. 300). Thus we again see it is unnecessary to postulate the existence of a closed, entirely self-contained internal system impelling the organism to aggression. The behavior apparently has to be elicited by stimuli ultimately originating outside the organism. If the hostility were entirely self-stimulated we could not account for the fact that inexperienced mice do not attack their littermates "spontaneously" as they do strange mice, and that it is even difficult to train them to attack their brothers and sisters (Scott & Fredericson, 1951, p. 277).

The male sex hormone probably does not provide any direct stimulation to hostility. For one thing, there is evidence that other instigations or learning experiences can override the effects of the androgen. Bevan, Daves, and Levy (1960) gave some of their mice a series of successful fighting experiences, in essence teaching them that victory facilitated escape from electric shocks, while others were trained to be losers or were allowed no pretest fighting experience. There were both normal and castrated animals in each of the experimental groups. Encounters with other mice were staged after this initial phase, and it was found that the castrated mice receiving male sex hormone treatments appeared to fight about as vigorously as the normals and more strenuously than the castrates not receiving androgen therapy. Observation of the data suggested, nevertheless, that the previous fighting experience had a more powerful effect on the later fighting behavior than did androgen status. For all of the groups differing in male sex hormone level, those mice whose earlier aggressions had been successful fought longer and more energetically in the final encounters than the animals not given this pretest experience. Beeman also has shown that animals first trained to fight and become dominant generally tended to continue to fight even after being castrated (cited in Scott & Fredericson, 1951, p. 284).

Aggressive habits apparently do not require an adequate supply of male sex hormones for their continuation. Scott and Fredericson suggested (pp. 284–285) that once aggressive or defensive habits have been strongly established "organic changes have very little effect unless they are so serious as to threaten the life or cripple the functions of the animal." Fighting behavior is elicited in the inexperienced animal, they believed, by external stimuli, such as the presence of a strange animal or the sight of another running away, or by the pain of an attack (p. 288). Whatever the primary stimuli to aggression, fighting produces some pain (extreme pain supposedly would give rise to escape or defensive actions), and these writers hypothesized that the male hormone lowers the threshold of sensitivity to the painful stimuli (p. 285). Beach's analysis of the effects of the male hormone upon sexual arousal (Beach, 1942) can also be applied here. He maintained that this hormone increases the excitability of some hypothesized central excitatory mechanism and lowers the threshold of the motor responses. Each of these possibilities would imply that androgen does not itself directly stimulate aggression, but instead acts to lower the threshold for or otherwise increase the excitability of whatever instigating stimuli there may exist in the situation.

All in all, then, there is little empirical evidence in the animal research literature for the notion of an ever-active primary aggressive drive. One of the classical investigations of primate behavior throws more water on this conception. After observing the social life of a baboon colony in captivity (though in a relatively free state) at the London Zoo, S. Zuckerman (1932) noted that sexual rivalry was the sole cause of serious fighting among these animals. There was little really intensive fighting over food, perhaps because of the plentiful diet provided for them, and practically none for any other reasons. In other species even those animals who invade another's territory seem to be oriented basically toward goals other than aggression per se. They may be searching for food or a nesting site, and the encroachment upon another's defended area apparently is usually accidental (Q. Wright, 1942, p. 1199).

Fighting between animals of different species also is surprisingly rare. The eminent ethologist Tinbergen (1953) has remarked that the great majority of fights seen in nature involve individuals, usually males, belonging to the same species. According to his observations, there is no evidence of a general aggressive instinct in animals; actual fighting does not occur as often as people tend to believe, and in most cases the opponents display "threat ceremonies" rather than actually coming to blows.

There is one possible source of support for the Hartmann formulation in the work of Konrad Lorenz, one of the most famous of the modern students of animal behavior. He maintained that the mechanism of each instinctive pattern builds up an excitation in the particular instinctive center in the central nervous system which is dissipated by the performance of the action. If the pattern is not released by some appropriate situation the "specific action potential" or "action-specific energy" supposedly, to employ a hydraulic analogy, is dammed up. As a result, the threshold for stimuli capable of releasing the action pattern is lowered, or if the energy accumulation is great enough, the action pattern goes off by itself. This latter process is called "vacuum activity," and presumably is a case of autonomous or spontaneously generated behavior. We have here, in essence, a supposedly self-stimulating system in contrast to reflexes, which are responses to detectable stimuli (Ewer, 1957, pp. 601–602; Thorpe, 1956, pp. 18–19). Animals sometimes go through the motions of an instinctive pattern even though there is no obvious adaptational purpose to this activity. We are told the pattern is exhibited because there had been an overaccumulation of its action-specific energy, the "overflow" of this energy producing the instinctive movements.

To put words in their mouths, the psychoanalysts could argue that the aggression represents just this type of instinctive pattern. Specific action potential (energy) might build up, giving rise to the sudden and spontaneous discharge of hostility as a vacuum activity if sufficient release had not been obtained previously.

The investigations just cited, however, cast doubt on this possibility. Hostility in animals does not exhibit the characteristics of vacuum activity. As we have indicated, there are relatively few instances in which these organisms display "spontaneous" aggression not obviously instrumental in nature or stimulated by some obstruction, and even these infrequent cases may be accounted for by frustrations. For that matter, the very conception of vacuum activity is open to question[6] (Thorpe, 1956, pp. 22–26).

Other writers also have concluded that there is no empirical reason to postulate a general innate, constantly active tendency making for aggression in animals (e.g., Fletcher, 1957; Q. Wright, 1942). J. P. Scott, an experimental biologist, has provided a cogent summary of these views:[7]

There is no physiological evidence of any spontaneous stimulation for fighting arising within the body. This means that there is no need for fighting, either aggressive or defensive, apart from what happens in the external environment. We may conclude that a person who is fortunate enough to exist in an environment which is without stimulation to fight will not suffer physiological or nervous damage because he never fights. . . . We can also conclude that there is no such thing as a simple "instinct for fighting" in the sense of an internal driving force which has to be satisfied. There is, however, an internal physiological mechanism which has only to be stimulated to produce fighting.

Thus, Hartmann et al. have no real evidential basis for their conception of an instinctive urge toward aggression. These studies indicate that man is not born with a drive to fight. Nor is there any reason to believe he has a continually active destructive force within him that must be released in one form or another. The animal data do not necessarily invalidate the McDougall formulation in its entirety, however. This latter notion, it will be recalled, does not argue for a constantly operating biological tendency, but only for a motive force

[6] After reviewing much of the pertinent ethological literature, the psychiatrist John Bowlby strongly advocated discarding the "psycho-hydraulic model of instinct with its reservoir and accumulation of 'energy'" (1957, p. 234). He believed this model was now discredited, and would substitute in its place an instinct model "comprising a species-specific behavior pattern governed by two complex mechanisms, one controlling its activation and the other its termination" (pp. 234–235). Ethological discoveries increasingly emphasize the role played by exteroceptive stimuli in activating and terminating these instinctive actions, he maintained.

[7] From *Aggression*. Chicago: Univer. of Chicago Press, 1958, p. 62. Copyright 1958 by the Univer. of Chicago.

activated by obstructions to instinctive impulses. Fighting among animals stimulated by sexual rivalry, competition for food, or the invasion of home territory by other animals certainly could be regarded as aggression produced by frustrations.

*Instinctive Targets for Aggression.* Everyday versions of the aggression instinct doctrine sometimes contend that there is a built-in target for the hostility within particular animals. Cats, for example, supposedly are a dog's "natural" enemies. Research does not treat this contention too kindly; whatever hostility does exist between species can be modified by environmental events. Some thirty or so years ago a psychologist (Kuo, 1930) studied three groups of kittens: one group raised without ever seeing rats, a second group which was given the opportunity to observe their mothers killing rats, and a third group reared in the company of rats. After four months, 43 per cent of the cats in the first group had killed at least one rat, while 85 per cent of those who had watched their mothers kill rats had also done so. Learning had strongly affected the cats' behavior toward their supposedly instinctive target for aggression. But this is shown even more strongly by the actions of the cats in the third group. None of these animals raised with rats had killed any by the end of the four-month period. A similar modification has been observed even in organisms whose behavior patterns are more rigidly biologically determined. Allee (1931) has shown that ants will not attack other colonies, whether of the same or even different species, if they have been brought into the alien colony when young and placed in physical contact with all members of this colony for several days.

These last two studies strongly suggest that animals are not predetermined to aggress against particular objects by their genetic makeup. Learning of one kind or another apparently is involved in the selection of these targets, especially in the phylogenetically more advanced animals. Although the evidence is somewhat equivocal, it is likely that these targets are not attacked primarily because they are a "natural" or even a safe or available object for the release of some aggressive drive. Higher animals, such as carnivores, do not have an innate recognition of their usual prey (Thorpe, 1956, p. 407). Rather, the members of the attacking species seem to have learned that the other organisms either are desirable sources of food or are threatening to them. This learning can be altered. A mouse may be a succulent morsel to some cats but playmates to other felines who themselves have learned to prefer birds. (This also is consistent with McDougall's conception of aggression. He had explicitly noted that the combative instinct in any species did not involve the perception of any particular class of objects, and thus, any organism conceivably could arouse the impulse.)

*Neutralized Aggressive Energy.* One final troublesome point in the psychoanalytic interpretation of aggression concerns the assumption of neutralized energy. Hartmann et al., maintaining the essential structure of psychoanalytic motivational theory, had proposed that aggressive as well as sexual energies, diverted from their original instinctive action patterns (i.e., neutralized), provided the drive for other, nonsexual and nonaggressive behaviors. There are few outside the psychoanalytic movement who would subscribe to this notion. If anything, experimentalists are prone to go in the opposite direction. Instead of postulating only a few general urges, animal researchers tend to think of relatively many specific motive forces, each providing the impetus to only a limited range of behaviors (Allee et al., 1953; Thorpe, 1956, Ch. 2). Nissen pointed out, for example, that grooming, wrestling, and play-biting occur more frequently in chimpanzees after the reduction of the sex drive than before (Allee et al., 1953, p. 294). These actions must be motivated independently of sex. The conclusion is inescapable. There is no basis for assuming neutralized energy other than the desire to protect the conception of just one or two primary drives (R. W. White, 1959, p. 310).

*McDougall's Analysis of Wars.* So far, then, McDougall's model for aggressive behavior seems to be faring somewhat better than the Hartmann model. This does not mean his analysis is without serious flaws. His anthropological reasoning is particularly dubious. The reader will recall McDougall's contention that Europeans have a stronger aggressive instinct than Indians or Chinese. This presumably was inferred from a greater incidence of fighting and war among the former peoples, but even this observation can be questioned. American soldiers who fought the Chinese Communists in Korea probably would testify that Chinese are not low in pugnacity in comparison to Europeans. If the Chinese were relatively peaceful in McDougall's time (although they certainly were not lacking in aggression then—witness the Boxer Rebellion and other instances of intranational strife during that period), this undoubtedly was due to cultural factors rather than innate predispositions. Otherwise, we would have to assume that the genetic structure of the Chinese race had changed from the first years of the twentieth century to the early 1950s—an improbable occurrence.

Any attribution of international strife to biological characteristics also would predict that societies have relatively constant war rates over the generations. Their frustrations probably would not change too radically with time so that nations predisposed to conflict because of their supposedly strong instinctive drive to aggression should have a generally higher incidence of war through the years than those nations who are low in this impulse to pugnacity. However, Wright reported in his monumental *A Study of War* (1942) that this type of consistency did not exist for many national groups. There were about twenty-six hundred battles involving European states between 1480 and 1940. Dividing these into fifty-year periods, he found that France, Austria, Great Britain, and Turkey had a relatively constant rate of participation in battles, while the rates for Prussia and Russia increased and those for Spain, the Netherlands, Sweden, and Denmark decreased. Somewhat similar results were obtained when other indices of "warlikeness," such as participation in wars and the proportion of war years in the history of the states, were employed. Conflict with other nations obviously was more strongly related to the political and technological status of a country relative to that of the other European states than to any ethnological characteristic. Wright concluded that the general lack of consistency in these indices makes the attempt to correlate international strife with persistent national factors apparently unrewarding (pp. 220–221).

War among nations is a social phenomenon, not a biological one.[8] This certainly is strongly indicated by Wright's analysis of national differences in "warlikeness." Thus, if there is a correlation between the frequency of international conflict and cultural characteristics, this probably does not mean, as McDougall had believed, that the aggressive drive is one of the causes of social organization. While it is true that societies have to mobilize their resources for combat, social organization is more likely to shape war than be shaped by it. Witness Nazi Germany. Basically, McDougall's mistake was to propose an overly simplified analysis of an exceedingly complex problem. This error seems to be generally characteristic of those who would account for human behavior in terms of supposedly instinctive drives, whether for hostility, sex, gregariousness, or any of the multiplicity of urges people have listed.

## SUMMARY

Instinct conceptions of aggression agree in viewing hostile tendencies as basically unlearned responses to some excitation (although they also recognize that the exact form of these responses in the higher animals can be modified through learning). However, there are differences of opinion regarding the origin of the aggression-instigating excitation. Instinct doctrines can be divided into two types on this point.

Freud and his disciples regarded hostile actions as impelled by a

[8] T. M. Newcomb (personal communication) has quoted Norman Thomas as saying war is so instinctive that men have to be drafted or otherwise impressed into military service during wartime and be threatened with death before the firing squad if they desert.

constantly driving force (i.e., the causal condition is entirely within the organism) whose energy must be released in one manner or another. Freud believed this energy stems from the "death instinct," a fundamental tendency to return to the quiescence of inorganic matter supposedly inherent in all living organisms. Impulses toward self-destruction motivating the individual to kill himself will arise as he seeks the elimination of internal stimulation, according to this conception, but the self-destruction is prevented by the turning outward of the aggressive impulses. Attacks upon others, either directly or in substitute form as attempts to control or master others, are said to provide an outlet for the energy of the death instinct.

Research findings offer little support for this reasoning. A wide variety of studies demonstrate that not all animal behavior is oriented toward tension reduction. Human beings as well as lower animals frequently work for an increase in internal excitations, indicating that organisms desire an optimal level of stimulation, and perhaps occasional variations in this level, but not the complete elimination of excitation.

Other writers, such as Hartmann et al., have modified Freud's analysis by positing an innate aggressive force conceptually similar to libido that is somatically rooted but not based upon some hypothesized death instinct. According to this view, attacked objects invite the discharge of aggressive energy rather than instigating aggressive impulses. Hostile actions decrease internal tension and, therefore, can be pleasurable, but physiological processes supposedly will lead to an increase in the aggressive energy as time passes.

McDougall's formulation of aggressive behavior does not envision such endogenous impulses toward aggression and thus constitutes a second type of instinctive aggression doctrine. For him hostile behavior had to be elicited by an appropriate stimulus, namely, some frustrating event.

Investigations of fighting among animals generally provide stronger evidence for McDougall's analysis than for the Hartmann et al. conception. Animal aggression arising from obvious competition clearly does not stem from a constantly operative (i.e., entirely internally based) instinctive drive to hostility. Such hostility is primarily either instrumental aggression or a reaction to frustrations. Fighting originating from struggles for dominance may have the same bases since animals achieve very real benefits through winning superior status, and several biologists have maintained that there actually are competitive reasons for what seems to be noncompetitive fighting. Since "spontaneous" animal aggression is a relatively rare occurrence in nature (and there is the possibility that even these infrequent cases may be accounted for by frustrations or prior learning of the utility of hostile behavior), many ethologists and experimental biologists rule out the possibility of a self-stimulating aggressive system in animals.

One important lesson to be derived from these studies is that there is no instinctive drive toward war within man. Theoretically, at least, it is possible to lessen the likelihood of interpersonal conflict by decreasing the occurrence of frustrations and minimizing the gains to be won through aggression. McDougall's as well as Freud's interpretation of war can be criticized. Social rather than biological characteristics determine the aggressiveness and warlikeness of nations or other groups.

# chapter 2

# The Frustration-Aggression Hypothesis

*Frustration and Aggression*

Most authorities today regard aggression as originating ultimately in response to some frustration. As we already have seen, this idea is not new. Freud had maintained in his earlier writings that aggression was the "primordial reaction" to the frustration occurring "whenever pleasure-seeking or pain-avoiding behavior was blocked" (cited in Dollard et al., 1939, p. 21), and many psychoanalysts and psychiatrists prefer this view to his later formulation (e.g., Durbin & Bowlby, 1939; Fenichel, 1945; Saul, 1956). But before going any further into this, some definitions are in order. The concepts "frustration" and "aggression" have many meanings in everyday life, and we should be clear as to how these terms are to be used in this book.

The course we shall follow is to adopt the relatively widespread and precise definitions employed by Dollard et al. in their now classic monograph *Frustration and Aggression* (1939). This work, a milestone in the application of the methods and concepts of experimental psychology to important social problems, also provides a helpful systematic foundation for the study of aggressive behavior. A "frustration" for these psychologists is "an interference with the occurrence of an instigated goal-response at its proper time in the behavior sequence" (p. 7). To translate this technical terminology into simpler language, they present an illustration of a boy, James, who, on hearing an ice-cream vendor's bell, wanted an ice-cream cone (pp. 3–9). We can say that the boy is *instigated* to obtain this cone. A number of response sequences may be elicited as a result of this state of affairs. He runs toward his mother, thinking of the delights of the ice cream, and calls to her. When he reaches his mother he pleads for the cone, pulling her to the front door. These goal-oriented activities, or response sequences, will be terminated when James gets a cone (reaches his goal) and, making the goal response, eats the cone—that is, assuming the boy is not insatiable. The goal response is defined as the reaction reducing the strength of the instigation (p. 6).

But suppose that James does not get the ice cream. His mother may insist, for example, that he wait until dinnertime. The series of responses leading to the consumption of the cone is interrupted. There is an interference with the occurrence of the instigated goal response, and James cannot eat the ice cream. This interference is the *frustration*.

In this sense the term obviously refers to the condition or event bringing about the interruption in the response sequence and not to the emotional reactions resulting from this interference. The thwarting need not be caused by events outside the person, however. Responses from within the individual can produce this interference. Going back to our illustration (in so doing we depart from the letter but not the spirit of the Dollard et al. work), James's mother may have given him money from his allowance to buy the ice cream. But in going out of his house, James might have remembered that he was saving to buy a baseball glove. He is now in conflict, with his recollection of this other goal interfering with the sequence directed toward the attainment of the ice cream. These opposing responses can be regarded as frustrating to the extent that they do interrupt the other sequence.

Two phrases will constantly reoccur throughout the course of this discussion: *instigated response sequences* and *drives*. The former phrase more clearly implies an ongoing activity (which, however, may be internal to the organism), but both are meant to be synonymous here. When the writer speaks of a "frustrated drive" he generally refers to interference with some goal-directed activity, or the blocking of some response tendency that has been set into operation. It is important to keep this in mind because drives are not necessarily always active. The intensity of the sex drive in the adult, for example, probably is dependent upon both internal and external stimulation, with external cues doing much to activate and enhance the sexual strivings. If an individual does not attend to these cues, or if they do not have strong erotic significance for him, his sex drive will be at a relatively low level. Since this person has little sexually oriented activity, either internally or in overt behavior, any inability to have sexual intercourse would not interfere with many ongoing response sequences. Similarly, a man who has been without food for a number of hours will not necessarily become angry because he has missed a meal. He may be engaged in work—book writing, for example—and the activities involved in *this* work are not being thwarted. According to the present conception, anger would result only if goal-directed activity is blocked.

Brown and Farber distinguished among four kinds of frustrating conditions (although they preferred to define a *frustration* in terms of the hypothesized resulting internal state of an organism): (1) physical barriers; (2) delays "between the initiation and completion of the response sequence"; (3) "omission or reduction of a customary reward"; and (4) the eliciting "of a response tendency that is incompatible with the ongoing one." Although these conditions differ in several respects, Brown and Farber assumed all of them can arouse reaction tendencies that interfere with ongoing chains of responses. All presumably produce internal reactions capable of interrupting these response sequences. Thus, for them there is no useful distinction to be made between the production of a *conflict* and a *frustration* (Brown & Farber, 1951, p. 481). Both sets of events, in arousing incompatible reaction tendencies within the individual, are essentially similar.

The present writer agrees up to a point. Incompatible responses instigated within the individual can frustrate a particular course of action. There is, however, an important difference between these two concepts, at least as far as the aggressive reaction is concerned. If hostility is directed primarily toward the perceived locus of the frustration, as Dollard and his colleagues proposed (1939, p. 39), it matters whether the interfering responses have been aroused principally by events within or outside the organism.

Dollard et al. defined *aggression* as any "sequence of behavior, the goal-response to which is the injury of the person toward whom it is directed" (p. 9). The behavior, they pointed out, need not be overt, but may occur in thoughts and fantasies, symbolic or direct attacks on inanimate as well as animate objects, or for that matter, may not seem to be aimed at any target at all (p. 10). Nevertheless, as just mentioned, there is an implicit tendency to attack the frustrating agent. Assertiveness and accidental injury to others are deliberately excluded from the category of aggressive acts, and no assumptions are made of a general, free-flowing destructive energy impelling nonhostile responses in the vein of what G. W. Allport (1954, p. 356) has termed the "steam-boiler theory of aggression." This book generally employs the same definition of the term aggression.

In one way or another, then, practically all present-day observers of human hostility contend that frustrations can produce an instigation to aggression. This is not to say that this instigation (*anger* in the present book) will necessarily be revealed in overt behavior. The individual obviously will inhibit his hostile reactions if he is anxious about the display of aggression and fears retaliation or punishment. As it is most frequently worded, the frustration-aggression hypothesis usually maintains that frustration often arouses or increases the *instigation* to aggression. Whether this instigation leads to open hostility depends upon other factors to be discussed later. Nor is it proposed that there are no consequences of frustration other than aggression. A person who is thwarted in his attempt to reach some goal may engage in any one (or several) of a variety of behaviors. His goals may change to those pre-ferred at an earlier stage of life (goal regression); his ways of achieving the present goals may become more childlike (instrumental-act regres-sion); he may exhibit fixation and not alter his behaviors at all; anxiety may make his actions more primitive and crude but without producing instrumental-act regression; or to be most optimistic, he may attempt to solve the problem posed by the interference.

The differences of opinion that do exist concerning the frustration-aggression hypothesis generally center about two problems. Some writers argue whether all aggression is the result of frustration, but most of the disputes in this area involve the question of whether every frustration increases the instigation to aggression. To put it succinctly, we ask, is frustration the necessary and sufficient condition for the arousal of aggression? The Dollard et al. formulation will be modified somewhat in dealing with these questions.

## Is All Aggression the Result of Frustration?

*"Nonfrustration" Causes of Aggression.* Durbin and Bowlby listed three classes of "simple causes" of fighting, only one of which supposedly deals with frustrations. Drawing their evidence primarily from observa-tions of children and apes, they argued that fights break out because of (1) disputes over the possession of external objects and (2) resentment at the intrusion of a stranger into their group, as well as because of (3) frustrations (1939, pp. 7–10). Karl Menninger, an explicit critic of the frustration-aggression thesis, was vehement in his opposition, claim-ing that the proposition is "nonsensical." He stated, "anyone who has had his toe stepped on, *which is certainly not a frustration,* knows how inadequate such a formula is" [italics mine] (1942, p. 295).

Seward (1945b) objected to the Yale conception largely on the basis of animal data. Frustration, for him, is not the only condition insti-gating aggression. Fighting also is aroused, he noted along with Durbin and Bowlby, by "stimulation from a strange animal of the same species." But where Durbin and Bowlby maintained that the stranger is attacked because of "resentment" at his intrusion—implying a vague sort of terri-torial defense—Seward suggested the aggression was produced by dominance strivings. As pointed out in the preceding chapter, Scott and Fredericson (1951) have also mentioned the sight of a strange animal as a cause of fighting[1] (although they do not attempt to explain why this should be), along with the sight of an animal running away, and slight pain.

The difficulty here obviously lies partly in the definition of frustration,

[1] H. F. Harlow (in a personal communication) maintains this is a relatively rare occurrence.

and partly in a failure to consider instrumental aggression. The above writers clearly have a somewhat narrower conception of the term than do Dollard and his colleagues, and Brown and Farber. However, at the risk of losing rigor through an excessive broadening of the concept, all of the aggression-arousing conditions mentioned by these critics can be considered as instances of frustrations.

A child who fights with another over the possession of a toy undoubtedly is thwarted in his desire to possess the toy. This probably is so even if the child had not wanted it initially. Seeing the other with the toy could well have increased this object's attractiveness, or at least, by prompting the child to compare himself (not having a toy) with his peer (who has one), caused him to feel deprived relative to this other, producing resentment. Similarly, the stranger intruding into the group could be interfering with attempts (explicit and implicit) to attain either security in well-ordered relationships with familiar peers, or other goals, such as food, nesting sites, or dominant status. If there is resentment against a stranger, it probably arises because he is seen as a potential threat (i.e., potential obstacle to goal attainment). The organism, not being certain his goals can always be gained, may regard the stranger as another rival in a competitive world.

The objection raised by Menninger concerning the stepped-on toe has been brought up by others as well, and McDougall showed how this type of situation could be regarded as an obstruction to the gratification of an impulse (1926, p. 62). If a man suddenly struck him in an unprovoked manner, the blow might not openly interfere with any activity at that moment, he pointed out, but it could nevertheless interfere with his "impulse of self-assertion." The exact nature of this impulse, of course, is unimportant; what is relevant here is the *interruption of an internal response sequence or the blocking of some drive.* Similarly, a person who steps on our toes might also arouse anger if this action interrupted or interfered with the internal responses oriented toward the preservation or attainment of security and comfort. People probably differ in the extent to which they will react with overt hostility to their toes being stepped on. It is a reasonable guess that the greatest annoyance will be exhibited by those most concerned with keeping or gaining security and comfort, in other words, those suffering the severest frustrations. Mild pain, the third aggression-arousing factor listed by Scott and Fredericson, may act as a frustration in just this way providing it interferes with some instigated response sequence.

We see, then, that these supposed exceptions turn out not to be exceptions at all. They can be understood as variations of the frustrating conditions mentioned by Brown and Farber.

*Learned Aggression.* There *are* some aggressive acts, however, that are not necessarily directly instigated by frustrations. During World

War II, for example, many of our airmen participated in bombing raids against German and Japanese cities without feeling the slightest anger toward their civilian victims. (As a matter of fact, not a few of them felt better if they avoided thinking of the people living in the cities.) On the other side, Germans and Japanese inflicted injury and death in many instances toward those whom *they* did not hate. The aggression in this case was coldly and deliberately carried out as a matter of policy. It was *instrumental aggression* in the sense that the behavior was primarily oriented toward the attainment of some goal other than doing injury (such as winning the war). These actions supposedly would help the aggressors reach the goal. Competition in everyday life also produces this type of instrumental aggression. The businessman or politician who spreads lies about his rival believes that hurting the other (symbolically but nevertheless in a very real fashion) is necessary if he is to get what he wants. The rival may be hated in some cases, but such actions undoubtedly also are carried out at times in order to achieve certain noninjurious ends. Aggression in the service of dominance strivings also would be an instance of this instrumental aggression and therefore is not necessarily produced by frustrations.

The instrumental significance of hostile behavior is not always readily apparent. Bandura and Huston (1961) have demonstrated that children can acquire hostile modes of behavior merely by observing the aggressive actions of adults. They contend this is no "identification with the aggressor" (A. Freud, 1937), whereby the child supposedly adopts the attributes of an aggressive, punishing agent, transforming himself from the victim to the agent of aggression, in order to alleviate anxiety. Rather, the children seemed to have learned the aggressive acts by imitating the adult's behavior. The quality of the adult-child relationship did not affect this learning in the Bandura-Huston experiments; a nurturant adult was copied as often as a less nurturant one. Nevertheless, the adult, in providing a model for the children to imitate, may have helped define the appropriate or at least permissible modes of behavior. He may have told them, in essence, that these actions might help them obtain whatever satisfactions they wanted from the situation.

Dollard and his colleagues excluded this type of hostile behavior from consideration in their discussion of the frustration-aggression hypothesis. They said simply and legitimately that they would not be concerned with learned aggression in their work. The aggression they deal with "reduces only the secondary, frustration-produced instigation, and leaves the strength of the original instigation unaffected" (1939, p. 11). That is, the hostile responses that concern them have no purpose other than that of injuring the frustrater. Since this exclusion of learned aggression would also eliminate consideration of those people who have learned to employ hostility frequently as a way of achieving their goals, and since consideration of this type of hostility is necessary for a more complete understanding of aggressive behavior, instrumental aggression will be discussed in this book.

*Anger as an Intervening Variable.* A second criticism of the frustration-aggression hypothesis proposed by Menninger deals with the motive force behind the hostile behavior. Where does the aggressive energy come from that is provoked by the frustration, he asked? (1942, p. 295). The only answer, he believed, is that this behavior is impelled by an aggressive instinct. However, the above discussion showed that this is not a satisfactory solution to the problem, and some other explanation must be found.

The question does highlight one of the notable omissions in the Dollard et al. formulation. The Yale psychologists attempted to deal with aggressive reactions to frustration without referring to any emotional state, such as anger, intervening between the thwarting and the hostile acts. Mowrer, one of the original authors of *Frustration and Aggression,* later came to realize that the neglect of these emotional responses raises more problems than it solves. Even though the 1939 book drew its inspiration from psychoanalytic theory, he remarked,[2]

It was at the same time dominated, methodologically, by a strong behavioristic slant which required that frustration and aggression be treated in a simple stimulus-response framework, which had little or no place for the intervening variable of anger. . . .

Emotional arousal provides part of the answer to Menninger's question concerning the source of the aggressive drive. As Brown and Farber (1951) first proposed, the emotional state produced by some frustrating condition can be regarded as a motivational construct. Anger (which always refers in this book to the emotion) serves as a drive heightening the likelihood of aggressive behavior.

There does not seem to be any simple one-to-one relationship between anger intensity and aggressive response strength, however. Other factors intervene to affect the probability of aggressive reactions to frustration. Chief among these, I believe, is whether or not a suitable aggression-evoking cue is present in the situation.[3] In company with other writers (e.g., Berlyne, 1960, p. 167), I maintain that *drives such*

[2] Reprinted with permission from O. H. Mowrer, *Learning Theory and Behavior.* New York: John Wiley & Sons, Inc., 1960, p. 404.

[3] This formulation makes explicit what is only implicit in the *Frustration and Aggression* monograph. Thus, by suggesting that cues are necessary to elicit aggressive actions we can explain why the strongest hostile responses in the absence of inhibitions supposedly are directed toward the perceived source of the frustration (Dollard et al., 1939, p. 39), and why progressively weaker aggressive responses theoretically are evoked by objects having less and less similarity to the frustrater (N. E. Miller, 1948).

*as anger do not lead to the drive-specific behaviors* (aggression in this case) *unless there are appropriate cues or releasers.* These cues are stimuli bearing some degree of association with the anger instigator, but they need not be physically present, nor is the association created only by physical similarity to the instigator. The thwarted individual may display hostile behavior after thinking of his frustrater. This latter person, we can say, is present symbolically in the former's psychological environment and, as a symbolic cue, evokes the aggressive responses. Similarly, a disliked object may become the target for displaced hostility because the frustrated individual subjectively equates the substitute with his tormenter (Berkowitz & Green, 1962).

According to this conception, then, a frustration creates a predisposition to make hostile responses by arousing anger. Whether these responses are actually performed, however, depends in part upon the presence of suitable aggression-evoking cues. For the time being, I will propose that *the strength of the aggressive reaction to some thwarting is a joint function of the intensity of the resulting anger and the degree of association between the instigator and the releasing cue.* Extreme anger arousal may broaden the range of external objects capable of evoking aggression, perhaps because emotionality reduces the ability to discriminate among stimuli (Easterbrook, 1959) and therefore, in effect, enhances the association between the instigator and other available objects.

A study by Weatherley (1962) has yielded findings consistent with the present reasoning concerning the importance of aggression-evoking cues. College women whose mothers had been either high or low in permissiveness toward aggression either were deliberately angered by the experimenter or received a kindlier treatment from him. After this a second person, supposedly unconnected with the experimenter, administered two sets of Thematic Apperception Test (TAT) cards, one containing strong cues for aggressive themes and the other low in "picture pull" for aggression. Maternal permissiveness toward aggression probably leads primarily to relatively weak internal restraints against aggression rather than to a strong, constantly active "aggressive drive." Thus, it is not surprising that the permissively reared students in the nonaroused condition gave no more aggressive responses to the TAT cards than did the less permissively trained women in this nonangered condition. The two nonaroused groups did not differ in the strength of their instigation to make aggressive responses. It was not until the women were provoked that significant differences emerged. But here too, relevant cues were necessary to activate the arousal predisposition created by the experimenter's insults. The students whose mothers had permitted aggression exhibited reliably more fantasy aggression than did the less-angered permissively treated group only to the high cue cards. Their aroused hostile inclinations were not revealed, even though their inhibitions were fairly weak, unless aggressive cues were present.[4]

Learning, obviously, can affect an individual's reaction to frustrating situations. Anger and relevant cues may exist, but nonaggressive response tendencies may be stronger than the inclinations to hostile actions and thus prevent the occurrence of overtly hostile behavior (N. E. Miller, 1941; R. Sears, 1941). The strengths of these nonaggressive tendencies can vary with prior learning experiences and with the intensity and persistence of the frustration-produced emotions. Some people habitually react to thwartings with renewed effort, while others may attempt to withdraw or seek help. In each of these cases, furthermore, if the initial (or primary) frustration reactions should fail to remove the obstacle, other responses may occur (N. E. Miller, 1941).

The nature of the thwarting reaction depends, at least in part, upon the person's interpretation of the situation confronting him, and these interpretations can also be habitual responses. As will be discussed more fully later, the interpretation can govern which of the individual's instigations are blocked and the degree to which they are thwarted. He may or may not perceive another's criticism, for example, as an attack upon himself, and he may or may not judge this as a serious criticism or attack. The learned interpretation also can determine what emotions other than anger also are aroused. The individual may perceive some features of the frustrating situation as dangerous and thus believe he has to hide his hostility if he is to avoid punishment. Aggression anxiety is evoked in this situation, we might say. In other cases he may think any hostility on his part would be a violation of his moral standards, and consequently the aggressive reactions to any anger he feels also are inhibited, but this time by guilt feelings. Anger may be generated on each of these occasions arousing aggressive responses, but other emotional states evoked in these situations, such as anxiety or guilt, have produced stronger tendencies incompatible with aggression inhibiting overtly hostile behaviors.

Learning experiences probably also affect the nature of the responses made to anger. When angered, a seventeenth-century French nobleman might automatically reach for his sword, a nineteenth-century cowboy

[4] Research into the effects of electrical stimulation of chicken brains (von Holst and von Saint Paul, 1962), published after the present manuscript went to press, further highlights the importance of situational cues in evoking aggressive behavior. In these experiments stimulation of a certain region of the fowl brain led to organized patterns of aggressive behavior primarily when relevant cues ("an enemy, real or artificial") were present. An electrically stimulated rooster would attack a small stuffed predator or the rooster's keeper, but would exhibit "only motor restlessness" when "all substitutes for an enemy" were lacking.

for his gun, and a twentieth-century Englishman for a pen so that he could write a letter to the *London Times*. These stereotypes, of course, are not too accurate, but they at least illustrate how learning governs the exact form of the aggressive reaction. It also may be that if a person has been given the appropriate training experiences his anger alone could serve as the stimulus to other emotional states, which in turn, give rise to aggression-inhibiting tendencies. Thus, followers of certain religious movements may have learned to become ashamed of the anger they might feel in any situation.

The assessment of anger intensity from behavioral observations obviously requires the consideration of previous learning. A person who displays violently hostile actions upon being frustrated may do this because (1) he is in an intense emotional state, i.e., his anger level is very high, and/or (2) he has learned to perform violent actions in response to provocations. Some of his aggressive behavior, in other words, is due to acquired aggressive habits.

*Reassociation of Aggressive Responses with Stimuli Other than Those of Anger.* Brown and Farber (1951) did not insist that frustration reactions are the only source of aggressive behavior. They believed originally innate responses to anger may become "functionally connected to almost any stimulus" (p. 490). Certainly, this "reassociation" must account for the instrumental aggression mentioned earlier. Some children seem to get into fights with their peers in order to attract attention from their otherwise indifferent mothers. The aggressive actions they engage in apparently have become "functionally connected" to their acquired drive to gain love and attention from their mothers so that arousal of this nonaggressive drive gives rise to the hostile behavior (I would add: in the presence of a relevant cue—the mother or stimuli associated with her). A similar "reconnection" process may explain an observation published by Scott. He reported (1958a, p. 59) that mice trained to fight with a series of easy victories never showed the emotional reactions characteristic of fighting in their species, but instead, quickly leaped upon their next victim. The hair-fluffing and other fighting signs may be fear (epinephrine) reactions primarily rather than norepinephrine-anger responses. If so, all Scott's observation signifies is that the fear concomitants of fighting had diminished with continued victories. However, if these fighting signs are produced by anger, other emotional reactions, such as elation, elicited by the easy victories, could have become conditioned to the sight of other mice. These nonanger emotional reactions then may have been the drive conditions arousing the fighting behaviors. When another animal was introduced into the persistent victor's cage this emotional drive state was aroused, giving rise to the aggressive attacks.

Wurtz (1960) presented a hypothesis consistent with this line of thought in his reanalysis of data obtained by Sears, Pintler, and Sears (1946). The doll-play behavior of 150 nursery school boys and girls was scored for the intensity of aggression expressed by and to parent and child dolls (i.e., the dolls as either the fantasy agents or victims of aggression). For this sample more intense fantasy aggression was associated with the parent dolls, both as attacker and attacked, than with the child dolls. Wurtz accounted for these results by invoking the mechanism of classical conditioning. Supposedly because their hostile behavior had been punished relatively frequently by their parents, the instigation to aggression in these children presumably had come to be functionally connected with anxiety (anticipation of punishment), and both of these drive states, in turn, were associated with their parents. Arousal of the aggressive drive would activate the anxiety, but similarly, anxiety would be the stimulus to aggressive responses. Parents and their symbols, such as dolls resembling them, might evoke anxiety reactions in the children which then would elicit the fantasy aggression. More direct overt hostility, of course, would be inhibited by this anxiety, and Wurtz concluded: "In fantasy as compared with real life, anxiety functions more as a stimulus than as an inhibitor" (p. 136).

This interesting notion certainly merits further investigation. Other explanations of the Wurtz findings are also available. For one, if anxiety associated with parents does account for the differences in the doll-play aggression, this anxiety could have produced the intense hostility because it operated as a frustration more than because it had become functionally connected to aggression. Nevertheless, this study at least can illustrate how the "reassociation" of aggression with some drive other than anger might take place.

## Does Every Frustration Lead to Some Form of Aggression?

Dollard et al. (1939) stimulated controversy on the very first page of their classic monograph. Providing a preview of their theoretical model, the authors presented a sweeping two-part generalization as their basic postulate. The first part, stating that "the occurrence of aggressive behavior always presupposes the existence of frustration," has already been discussed. In the second half of the statement, the Yale psychologists proposed that "the existence of frustration always leads to some form of aggression" (p. 1). Needless to say, this latter phrase drew the fire of many critics (e.g., Levy, 1941; Maslow, 1941).

Two years after the publication of the book, in a symposium on the frustration-aggression hypothesis, Miller admitted that the basic generalization "was unclear and misleading." There was an implication, he pointed out, strong enough to override later statements in the book to the contrary, that "frustration has no consequences other than aggression." He suggested that a better phrasing was: "Frustration produces instigations to a number of different types of responses, one of which is an instigation to some form of aggression" (1941, p. 338). Nevertheless, this rewording did not alter the basic supposition that every frustration increased the likelihood of overt hostility. The specific nature of any one frustration was important only with respect to the intensity of the drive that was blocked and the degree of interference with the response sequences. Both of these factors supposedly were positively related to the resulting instigation to aggression. Otherwise, no distinctions were made among qualitatively different forms of frustration. It was this point that several critics attacked.

Many of their criticisms will be discussed in the following pages. Surprisingly, though, few questions were asked about one of the more obvious problems in the Yale thesis. If every frustration increases the probability of aggression, what are the characteristics of those situations producing stronger fear than aggressive reactions? These situations also can be defined as obstructing drive satisfaction, but in what way do they differ from the frustrations eliciting relatively strong anger? Another modification of the Dollard et al. formulation will be proposed in attempting to answer these questions. To anticipate, it seems likely that the conditions arousing fear are perceived and interpreted differently from the situations producing anger. Another set of intervening processes omitted by the 1939 group, the individual's *interpretation* of the situation confronting him, therefore must be considered.

*Types of Frustrations and Aggressive Behavior.* Many of the critics believed it was necessary to differentiate among various classes of frustrations if aggressive reactions were to be predicted. Not every thwarting, they argued, necessarily arouses anger. Rosenzweig (1944) proposed a fairly elaborate classification scheme, implying that each category would produce a different reaction. Frustrations were divided into *primary* and *secondary* frustrations, the former referring only to the existence of an active need, such as hunger, the latter involving obstructions in the path to a goal, and thus coming closer to the present definition of frustration. These secondary frustrations were further differentiated in terms of the nature of the obstacle. The obstruction might be *passive*, representing "impassibility without itself being threatening" (as an illustration of this, Rosenzweig cited the case of a hungry man confronting a locked door to a room containing food when he has no key), or the obstacle might be *active*, in which there is not only an obstruction to need satisfaction, but also a threat "to the immediate security of the organism." Finally, the obstacle may be *external* or *internal*, either within or outside the individual (pp. 381–382).

Rosenzweig looked at frustration primarily from a clinical viewpoint and therefore was most concerned with active internal obstacles to need satisfaction. Frustrations of this sort were involved in the conflict situations emphasized by psychoanalytic theory (p. 382). *Ego-defensive* reactions, including hostility, presumably occur only in response to threats to the ego, i.e., only as a reaction to active secondary frustrations. His threefold division of ego-defensive reactions is well known and forms the basis of the Rosenzweig Picture-Frustration Study, a widely used (though with uneven success) projective test. When the individual is frustrated there may be (1) *extrapunitive* responses in which he "aggressively attributes the frustration to external persons or things"; (2) *intropunitive* responses in which he "aggressively attributes the frustration to himself"; or (3) *impunitive* responses which "avoid blame altogether."

Maslow (1941, 1943) also argued that distinctions should be drawn among qualitatively different kinds of frustrations. Like Rosenzweig, he felt *deprivations* (Rosenzweig's primary frustrations) must be differentiated from other forms of thwarting. However, unlike this other writer, he set up only one other category, *threats,* frustrations of the organism's "basic needs." The psychologically harmful effects usually attributed to frustration in general, he maintained, are really due specifically to threats. Deprivations alone supposedly are less likely to produce aggressive reactions.[5]

The words may be different in the Rosenzweig-Maslow line of thought, but operationally, their arguments and those of Dollard et al. seem to yield essentially the same predictions regarding aggressive behavior. The Yale group hypothesized that the strength of the instigation to aggression varies directly, among other things, with the "strength of instigation to the frustrated response" (1939, p. 28). The stronger the drive whose satisfaction is being blocked, the more intense the aggressive reactions and, consequently, the greater the likelihood that some hostility will be revealed openly. This continuum of "strength of instigation to the frustrated response" is involved in Maslow's distinction between threats and deprivations. He defined threats in terms of obstacles to the satisfaction of the organism's basic needs, drives presumably of greater intensity than those involved in deprivations. Thus, if investigation shows that threats do provoke aggressive actions where

[5] Most writers actually are in agreement on this point. Deprivations, as defined by Maslow and Rosenzweig, do not seem to involve the frustration of ongoing goal-directed activities. Dollard et al. (1939) and the present writer stress the importance of considering whether the response sequence has been "activated," i.e., set into operation or instigated. As discussed earlier in this chapter, a man who has been without food for some time is not angered if he is engaged in non-food-related activities and does not want food.

deprivations do not, this may well be due to the interference with the stronger instigations. Since the resulting anger is more intense in this case, the hostile responses are more likely to be manifested in overt behavior.

*Dimensional Aspects of Frustrations.* The basic difficulty with the Rosenzweig-Maslow (and similar) formulations is that they have established discrete categories where, in actuality, there is a continuous dimension. "Threats" vary in degree; "basic needs" vary in the urgency with which they must be satisfied. To go back to Rosenzweig's illustration of the hungry man confronted by a locked door to a room containing food, the extent of threat represented by the door is a function of his degree of starvation. Not only can privations be threatening, but this is no dichotomy of either "threat" or "no threat." What is central here, clearly, is the intensity of the frustrated drive, rather than the qualitative nature of the frustration. It is not necessary to multiply concepts by differentiating among frustrations in some absolute and arbitrary manner. Drive strength or other aspects of the thwarting can be abstracted out and treated as a continuous variable in predicting aggressive responses.

This procedure, which of course is the one employed by Dollard and his colleagues, is more parsimonious, and logically more defensible, than the type of theorizing that invokes several concepts where only one can do. We can see this advantage in the analyses of several studies. The Yale group, for example, has reported that relatively minor deprivations can provoke aggressive reactions if they are repeated often enough (1939, p. 31). Instead of resorting to the argument that the hostility arose when the deprivations became threats (since there are no a priori specifications of the operations defining these constructs, the argument can be tautological), Dollard et al. accounted for this finding with only one concept. They contended that the instigational effects summated with repeated frustrations (pp. 31–32). In another investigation, Graham, Charwat, Honig, and Weltz (1951) found that physical attacks directed against the individual were more likely to produce strong aggressive reactions in him than were less direct attacks. The researchers pointed out that the former direct attacks may be regarded as threats, while the latter indirect hostility supposedly is not in this category of frustration. However, rather than arbitrarily dividing a continuum of frustrations into discrete classes, as this scheme implies, they also proposed an alternative and preferable analysis. In line with the Yale model, Graham and her coworkers suggested that the different forms of hostility directed against the subject varied in the degree to which they interfered with such strivings as the drive for self-enhancement. The person receiving a physical blow suffered a greater interference in satisfying these drives than the person receiving indications of mild dislike. Their interpretation, then, is a special case of the more general supposition regarding the relationship between degree of interference with the response sequence and the strength of the instigation to aggression (Dollard et al., 1939, pp. 30–31).

*The "Arbitrariness" of Frustrations.* Some attacks on the contention that every frustration increases the instigation to aggression are not based on a distinction between threats and deprivations. These objections still differentiate among classes of frustrations, however. In one of the studies employed to buttress the Dollard et al. formulation, Doob and Sears (1939) had presented their subjects with written descriptions of sixteen frustrating situations they supposedly had previously encountered. The subjects were asked to say what their reactions had been. Examining these situations, Pastore (1952) concluded that the frustrations were unreasonable or arbitrary. He felt it was the arbitrary nature of the thwartings that had produced the frequently reported aggressive reactions. To test this hypothesis, Pastore repeated the investigation by giving some of his subjects descriptions of arbitrary frustrations (e.g., "You're waiting on the right corner for a bus, and the driver intentionally passes you by."). Other subjects were told of frustrations that judges agreed were nonarbitrary (e.g., "You're waiting at the right corner for a bus. You notice that it is a special on its way to the garage."). As expected, significantly stronger aggressive reactions were indicated by the subjects in the arbitrary frustration condition. Pastore proposed on the basis of this that the arbitrariness of the frustration was an important determinant of the intensity of the resulting aggression. Frustration per se did not necessarily arouse hostility. A. R. Cohen (1955) more recently has obtained the same findings, using a similar procedure.

These studies, nevertheless, do not unequivocally demolish the Yale contention for a number of reasons. The subjects receiving the nonarbitrary treatment may have inhibited their aggressive reactions, as Pastore himself suggested (1952, p. 731), because they had learned that society frowns upon hostile responses to "reasonable" frustrations. Rothaus and Worchel (1960) reported data apparently supporting this possibility. Employing the same type of questionnaire descriptions, their subjects were asked to indicate not only how they themselves would respond to the frustrations, but also how another person, identified only by initials, would react. This latter question was designed to be a "projective" measure of aggressive tendencies within the subject himself. The results showed, as Pastore had found, significantly stronger manifestations of hostility after arbitrary than after nonarbitrary frustrations. However, there also was a significantly greater number of hostile feelings reported in response to the projective than to the nonprojective items following the nonarbitrary frustrations, presumably indicating inhibited aggression in the "reasonable" frustration condition.

One of the difficulties with this conclusion, though, is that the above investigators utilized only questionnaire descriptions of hypothetical situations. As I noted elsewhere (1958, p. 269), the procedure employed in these studies is particularly susceptible to the intrusion of the subjects' own psychological theories and to verbal control over behavior. They may have responded to the questionnaires in terms of what they believed their reactions *should* be, or (as in the Rothaus and Worchel study) the way they *thought* most people would behave, but not necessarily the way they and others actually would react. Definitive investigations of the possibility that qualitatively different classes of frustrations produce different reactions must utilize real (though experimentally controlled) frustrations, not hypothetical ones presented in questionnaires.

But perhaps the most important flaw in Pastore's criticism of the Dollard et al. thesis has to do with his conception of the frustrating situations. He assumed that the response sequences in the arbitrary and nonarbitrary frustration conditions were blocked to an equal degree objectively but that there were differences in the subjects' interpretation of the thwartings. This assumption is not necessarily correct. I will try to show later that the subjects in the arbitrary frustration condition actually may have had more of their response sequences blocked (assuming this study represents what would happen in real life), perhaps because they had not expected the interference.

*Cognitive Factors in Frustrations.* These variables, the extent to which an obstruction is arbitrary and/or unexpected, do point, however, to a notable area of omission in the Yale formulation. Dollard and his colleagues, it will be recalled, were strongly behavioristic in their approach, and as such, were reluctant to consider the individual's inner state in their theorizing. They believed it was preferable scientifically to develop hypotheses utilizing only variables that could be observed directly. As a consequence, explicit references to emotions were omitted, as we already have seen, and so were any considerations of thought processes. Modern behavior theory can accommodate these factors, but their omission in 1939 resulted in several gaps in the study of hostility. Perhaps the most striking of these "holes" was left by the failure to regard man as a thinking animal whose perception and understanding of his environment could affect his reactions to it.

Suppose, to take Pastore's illustration, a person who has been waiting on a street corner for a bus sees one pass him by. His reaction to this frustration will depend partly upon his interpretation of the situation.

A paranoid, believing himself persecuted, might take this as a personal affront, while another man, knowing the driver on this route, could attribute his failure to stop to some good reason. The Yale group had postulated a relationship between the intensity of the instigation to aggression and the strength of the thwarted drive. Since a strong drive (for self-esteem) is blocked in the case of the paranoid, relatively intense anger should result. The paranoid's perception of the situation had determined which of his drives were thwarted, and thus affected the operation of the principles specified by Dollard and his collaborators.

Consideration of individual differences in these intervening cognitive responses, of course, is unnecessary for predicting frustration reactions when there are unambiguous obstructions to the satisfaction of drives most people possess, such as drives for self-enhancement or self-preservation. News of an impending atomic bomb explosion in their city coming from a very reliable source undoubtedly would disturb (to say the very least) nearly everyone living in it. We could predict that people would flee the city without inquiring into the way different groups understand the news. Most people undoubtedly would interpret the information in much the same manner. On the other hand, in order to anticipate reactions to a man running down the street carrying a gun in his hand, we would have to foretell the interpretations elicited in the passersby. Will they think he is a policeman, criminal, or lunatic? Taking the intervening cognitions into account significantly improves predictions primarily when the stimulus situation is so complex and/or ambiguous that a great variety of interpretations is possible. Since many social situations are fairly ambiguous, it is not unusual to find widely discrepant reactions in them; they are understood differently by the people involved.

*Frustrations Producing Fear.* One of the above examples raises a very important problem bearing on the question of whether all frustrations evoke anger. It also documents the desirability of considering cognitive and emotional responses to frustrations before predicting the behavioral outcome. An atomic bomb attack must be regarded as a frustration to the people who survive (assuming we can view this type of situation merely as psychologists). According to investigations made following the Hiroshima and Nagasaki atomic bombings (Janis, 1951, pp. 4–66), the dominant reaction among survivors shortly after the attack was acute fear rather than anger against the United States. These people had suffered very serious interferences with their drives, but instead of responding with extreme hostility toward those directly responsible for these thwartings, most of the victims displayed strong signs of anxiety and depression. These fear reactions persisted in a sizeable proportion of the populace of the two cities for many days after the bombings. Janis's valuable review of the effects of air warfare reveals that German and British civilians subjected to very heavy bombing raids apparently reacted in a somewhat similar fashion, so the actions of the Japanese cannot be attributed to their unique characteristics (pp. 98–125).

Evidence from England, Germany, and Japan does indicate there was a rise in aggressive attitudes after air attacks. But much of this feeling seems to have been directed against other people in the victims' own country, particularly their leaders and other authorities, and not as much as we might expect toward the enemy (pp. 126–152). This last seemingly paradoxical set of findings concerning the target of aggression will be discussed more fully later. The most important matter for the present concerns the reasons for the strong fear. The relationship between frustration and aggression cannot be fully understood without knowledge of the conditions determining whether the dominant reaction to a frustration is fear rather than anger.

As the remaining section of this chapter will attempt to show, there are at least two important aspects of fear-producing situations. Fear is stronger than anger in such situations because of two qualities of the obstruction: (1) *fearful events signify noxious consequences,* and as a result of these events the individual anticipates either physical or psychological damage to himself; (2) *the frustrated individual sees himself as having low "power" relative to that of the frustrating agent.* The more vulnerable or less powerful he feels, i.e., the less able he is to control the frustrating agent or punish it for the injury he has received, the more fear predominates over anger.

As mentioned earlier, Scott and Fredericson (1951) have proposed that slight pain produces aggressive responses in mice and rats, while severe pain presumably gives rise to escape and avoidance behaviors. This hypothesis can serve as a takeoff point, but it must be altered somewhat. Physical pain is not absolutely necessary for the arousal of fear. Anticipation of severe pain or serious loss can have the same effect. An observer of the bombing attacks upon England (MacCurdy, cited in Janis, 1951, p. 103) has singled out the "experience of suddenly facing danger in the immediate vicinity" as the most critical determinant of an air raid's emotional impact. People who had undergone "near misses," who had faced but narrowly escaped death, for example, seemed to show the most acute and persistent fear symptoms. More fortunate individuals not directly witnessing the destructive fury of an air attack, who had seen danger only from afar, sometimes exhibited anxiety when the signs of potential danger became apparent. They became afraid when the warning siren sounded or the enemy planes were heard overhead, but this emotion usually did not persist after the raid had ended. Typically, they then experienced relief and a feeling of successful escape. Other independent observations tend to support this emphasis upon direct exposure to grave danger as a major cause of fear reactions, particularly when these extremely threatening experiences are relatively unfamiliar and unexpected (Janis, 1951, pp. 98–125).

*Noxious Stimulation and Fear.* This elaborate discussion leads to an obvious and fairly simple point. *The intensity of the fear produced by a frustrating situation is a direct function of the intensity of the noxious stimulation experienced in the situation or anticipated because of it.* Moreover, we can suggest tentatively, *the noxious stimulation is frustrating, producing anger as well as fear.* However, *as the intensity of the noxious stimulation increases, either directly or in the perceived likelihood of its occurrence, fear rises more rapidly in intensity than does anger.* The relatively rapid increase in fear can be seen in the previously cited relationship between the pain inflicted on mice and the intensity of their aggressive acts. Anger was the dominant emotional state when the frustration was mild pain, but fear became dominant as this pain was increased.

A somewhat similar explanation can be used to account for the strong persistent fear reactions in people narrowly escaping danger during World War II. Very heavy bombing attacks and many "near misses" would naturally have aroused a good deal of fear. These responses then could have become strongly conditioned to a wide variety of cues: the thought of the enemy, the sound of airplane engines, the time of day at which air raids generally commenced, etc. As a consequence of this conditioning, these cues alone would have elicited strong fear reactions upon some later occasion. From the point of view of the people just missing death, *further injury or even death would have seemed all too likely.* Those who had not had these narrow escapes, on the other hand, did not have strong fear responses conditioned to environmental stimuli, and later, they could easily have disregarded thoughts of future harm. Danger became subjectively less probable. The sound and sight of air raids, or the anticipation of these attacks, did not "hurt" as much. Along these lines, Janis hypothesized that many people have learned to alleviate their fears of death, injury, and severe personal loss "by developing, to varying degrees of inner conviction, a feeling of personal invulnerability" (1951, p. 173). Narrow escapes from extreme dangers apparently seriously weaken, if not eliminate entirely, this protective mechanism. The feeling of invulnerability is broken down, and as a consequence, the individual now consciously faces the imminent prospect of harm.[6]

[6] The present formulation has the advantage of explaining why many frightened people also report experiencing some anger. Kardiner and Spiegel (1947) main-

This theme of fear and helplessness was continued in Janis's later analysis of stress reactions in surgical patients (1958). On the basis of psychoanalytic observations supported by a questionnaire survey, he suggested that patients provided with adequate preoperative information are stimulated to rehearse the danger situation mentally (setting into operation the "work of worrying"), which then causes them to find effective reassurances with which to control their fear. Anticipating the dangers, but also thinking of the reassurances, the adequately prepared patient presumably is less likely to feel helpless and extremely vulnerable when he actually enters the danger situation than the patient not having this information or the one who before this had defensively cloaked himself with "blanket immunity." As a consequence, the prepared patient apparently is less inclined than the others to develop either extreme depression and anxiety or a hostile resentment against those (e.g., doctors and nurses) whom he believes have let him down.

Frustrating situations also would "hurt" if they deprived the individual of a strongly held value or threatened the imminent loss of this value. A person who develops "stage fright" just before he is to make a speech, for example, probably expects this behavior to result in negative evaluations of him. His speech may not come up to his own standards, and/or the audience may think he was inept. The frustrating situation threatens harm to the value, a favorable self-concept.

The major feature of this analysis, then, is its emphasis upon the degree of harm the individual actually suffers or anticipates. However, a qualification of sorts may be necessary. Whether fear becomes the dominant emotion, at least in some situations, may not depend entirely on the absolute amount of hurt the person experiences. Rather, *the extent to which this emotion is stronger than anger may be a function of the individual's perceived power to control or hurt his frustrater relative to the frustrater's power to control or harm him.* He is more strongly afraid than angry when he believes he can receive serious harm from the frustrating agent, but is relatively unable to hurt him in return.

This reasoning seems to be consistent with observations of mob behavior. The usual explanation given for lynch mobs, such as the one that terrorized the Negro community in Leeville, Texas, in 1930 (Can-

---

tained that all the war trauma cases they observed not only had strong fear and anxiety, but also aggression "with or without the accompanying affect of rage." But where they contended that aggression and rage arose in an attempt to master the danger situation, the present view argues that both fear and anger may be results of the frustrations inherent in the danger situation, with fear increasing more rapidly in intensity as the noxious, harmful nature of the frustration increases. The fear may also be frustrating, further increasing anger.

tril, 1941), is that frustration-produced hostility in the whites was vented against the minority-group members. By striving for increased social status, by competing with the whites for jobs, the Negroes presumably threatened, and hence frustrated, the dominant group. But not only did the Negroes arouse hostility, it also was safe to attack them; the lynch mob members probably felt, for one reason or another, that they were fairly immune from punishment for any aggression they might express. They saw themselves as having more power than the Negroes and as being relatively invulnerable to any dangers associated with attacking them. Thus, overall, while the Negroes may have been threatening, they did not have too much ability to hurt the whites in retaliation, and anger was stronger than fear in the whites.

A mob in panic obviously has an altogether different relationship to the frustrating agent. In this case, the mob members perceive themselves as less powerful than this agent, and therefore, feel extremely vulnerable to the dangers the agent represents. He can hurt them more than they can hurt him. They can lose their lives and most valued possessions, but cannot seriously threaten the frustrater in return. Fear becomes stronger than anger and people flee. Cantril has described just this state of affairs in his analysis of the panic reactions to Orson Welles's famous 1938 broadcast, "The Invasion from Mars" (Cantril, 1958). Those who accepted the broadcast as news, and ran from what they believed to be the oncoming Martians, apparently thought these monsters were endangering their lives and everything they held dear. Their highly cherished values were threatened and no certain elimination of the threat was in sight (p. 300).

## Conclusions

Our general conclusion, then, is to support the essential validity of the Dollard et al. formulation with some modifications. These alterations are largely brought about through the introduction of two classes of variables held to intervene between the objective situation and the individual's reaction to it: *anger* and *interpretation.*

There are some obvious advantages to considering the emotional state, anger, when dealing with the question of frustration reactions. Research has indicated that the physiological concomitants of anger can perhaps be differentiated from those of fear (Ax, 1953; Schachter, 1957). Thus, physiological indices of these emotional states could be employed as dependent variables in testing hypotheses concerning the effects of various types of thwarting conditions upon emotional responses. (This is one way of assessing, for example, whether fear actually rises more rapidly in intensity than does anger with increasing severity of noxious stimulation, as was hypothesized earlier.) Going further, the emotion could be manipulated and "held constant" by means of direct physiological measurements of this state in determining how other factors affect the degree to which anger leads to open hostility. Clearly, observations of these emotional reactions will increase our understanding of the nature of the frustration-aggression relationship.

The present view of this relationship is fairly similar to that advanced by Dollard and his colleagues, on one hand, and by McDougall, on the other. In common with these writers, I should like to propose that every frustration increases the *instigation* to aggression, but this instigation is here termed *anger*. It also may be, as an up-to-date reinterpretation of McDougall's formulation would maintain, that anger is the primary, inborn reaction to thwarting.

Many critics have disputed this point. Learning experiences undoubtedly can influence the nature of the reactions to obstructions, as Brown and Farber have stressed, and N. E. Miller (1941) and R. R. Sears (1941) acknowledged. Some ways in which frustration reactions could be altered through learning have been described earlier. Briefly, it was suggested that these prior experiences can determine whether there are any response tendencies that are stronger than the frustration-produced aggressive inclinations, and if so, the nature of these non-aggressive reactions. One of the ways in which learning might operate to alter the response probabilities is through affecting the individual's interpretation of the thwarting situation. Earlier training, of course, also can affect the form of the person's responses to his emotions, for example, whether he will curse his instigator, try to invoke a magic spell, punch him in the nose, or challenge him to a duel. Aggression may be the innately determined response to anger, but the exact form of this aggression, and perhaps even its vigor and intensity, may be affected if not molded entirely by past experiences. This previous learning also will govern the form and strength of the behavioral reactions to the nonanger emotions elicited in the frustration situation.

Whiting (1944), a colleague of the authors of *Frustration and Aggression* at the Yale University Institute of Human Relations, came close to my theoretical inclinations in his description of the behavior of the Kwoma of New Guinea. This anthropologist noted that the members of this tribe customarily exhibit four different patterns of reaction to frustration: submission, dependence, and avoidance, as well as aggression. Which pattern is displayed seems to vary with the age of the individual. Young children, for example, supposedly characteristically respond to thwarting with increased dependence upon their elders. Nevertheless, Whiting's observations suggest that the primary emotional response to frustrations in the newborn is a general bodily reaction resembling what Sears, Maccoby, and Levin (1957) termed *rage* or *anger*. Along with these later writers, he contended that this is the innately dominant response to frustration and that it is modified by later learning. The present approach would suggest that later learning experiences (1) affect the individual's definition of the situation, and so determine which, if any, goal-directed actions are blocked, (2) determine whether any other response tendencies are aroused that are stronger than the elicited aggressive acts, and (3) affect the exact nature and intensity of these acts.

The following chapters also will have more to say about the nature of aggression. This is particularly true in the discussion of "hostility catharsis." Our understanding of the instigation to aggression obviously is incomplete without consideration of the conditions decreasing the strength of this instigation. Furthermore, the frustration-aggression model leaves the problem of "aggressive personalities" unsettled. How do they get that way, we want to know? Do they continually experience frustrations or is their anger hidden (repressed) but still active? On the other hand, is their aggression, as we already have suggested, not necessarily always impelled by anger, and if so, what role does anger have in their behavior? These and other questions concerning the "aggressive drive" remain. Before they can be dealt with there must be a more comprehensive discussion of the factors affecting hostile reactions to frustration.

## SUMMARY

Most authorities today regard aggression as originating ultimately in response to some frustration. The term "frustration" here, as in the classic work by Dollard and his colleagues, refers to an interference with ongoing goal-directed activity. Although internal conflicts can produce such an interference, as Brown and Farber have noted, it may be advisable to differentiate between self- and non-self-induced frustrations; Dollard et al. have hypothesized that hostility is directed primarily toward the perceived locus of the frustration.

Criticisms of the frustration-aggression hypothesis have been leveled against both aspects of this hypothesis. Writers have pointed out that not all aggression is the result of frustration, and some have insisted that every frustration does not increase the instigation to aggression.

There can be little doubt that there are nonfrustration causes of aggressive behavior (although some discussions of this thesis seem to employ an unduly restricted definition of frustration). Aggression may arise as instrumental behavior in which the hostility is primarily oriented toward the attainment of some goal other than doing injury. Instrumental aggression was excluded from consideration by the Yale psychologists; in essence, they said they were not interested in such behavior. Dollard and his collaborators confined their attention to reactive aggression, hostility stemming from the thwarting of instigated response sequences. Deviating somewhat from the letter (but not the philosophy) of the 1939 monograph, the present writer holds that frustrations produce an emotional state, *anger*, which heightens the probability of occurrence of drive-specific behaviors, namely aggression. However, whether aggressive responses actually are performed—even in the absence of restraints against hostility—depends upon the presence of suitable cues or releasers, stimuli associated with the anger instigator. The strength of the aggressive responses arising from a frustration is said to be a joint function of anger intensity and the degree of association between the instigator and the releasing cue.

This is not to say that learning experiences do not influence the nature of the reactions to obstructions. Prior experiences can (1) affect the individual's definition of his immediate situation and, thus, determine (a) whether he perceives frustrations, and if so, (b) which of his drives are thwarted; (2) determine whether any other response tendencies are aroused that are stronger than the elicited aggressive responses; and (3) govern the exact nature and intensity of the aggressive and nonaggressive responses.

Most of the controversy surrounding the frustration-aggression hypothesis concerns whether *every* frustration increases the instigation to aggression. The critics (e.g., Maslow) generally maintain that only particular types of thwarting, the blocking of the "basic" or more important drives (usually termed "threats"), breed hostility. Mere "deprivations" supposedly give rise to nonhostile reactions. There are several objections that might be raised against such a contention:

1. It argues for qualitatively different kinds of frustrations when there actually are only events varying in degree along certain continua. Drives vary in importance to the individual. An instigation that may be unimportant or weak on one occasion can be stronger and more important in other situations. At just what point does a "deprivation" suddenly become the supposedly qualitatively different "threat"?

2. The above-mentioned attacks upon the frustration-aggression hypothesis lead to an unparsimonious proliferation of concepts. Instead of arbitrarily establishing several different concepts to be used in different situations (and which at present can be invoked only after the fact), Dollard et al. can employ the same concepts in all frustration situations. These concepts refer to dimensional aspects of the frustration, and the effects to be predicted from a given thwarting depend upon the location of that frustration on the theoretical dimensions. Thus, one

of their dimensions refers to the strength of the thwarted drive. "Deprivations" would be low and "threats" high on this dimension. The stronger the instigation to the obstructed goal-directed activity, the Yale psychologists maintained, the stronger the resulting instigation to aggression. This would be the reason why "threats" are more likely to produce overt hostility than are "deprivations."

Pastore has introduced a variation of the Maslow thesis by insisting that the Yale studies made use of arbitrary or unexpected frustrations and that less arbitrary frustrations are not as likely to lead to aggressive responses. This criticism has the value of emphasizing the important part played by cognitive factors. A person's reactions to a frustration depend, to some extent at least, upon his interpretation of the thwarting situation. But here too, there is no need to establish a frustration typology. Assuming arbitrary frustrations are unexpected and that these have given rise to relatively strong aggression, such a phenomenon can be explained (as is discussed in the next chapter) by hypothesizing that the individual, in not expecting to be thwarted, either (1) was in the midst of some ongoing goal-directed activity, or (2) interpreted the frustrating event as being relatively severe, or (3) felt less of a need to inhibit his hostility. Arbitrary frustrations may also be regarded as a personal attack.

Dollard and his collaborators had not faced the important theoretical problem of "fear." Fear-producing situations are frustrations according to their (and our) definition of this latter term, but what is there about these obstructing situations that yields stronger fear than anger reactions? The answer is, fearful events signify noxious consequences; in such circumstances the individual anticipates either physical or psychological damage to himself. It is hypothesized that fear increases more rapidly than does anger as these anticipated noxious consequences increase in magnitude. The low "power" of the frustrated individual relative to that of the frustrating agent is another important aspect of the fearful situation. The more vulnerable or less powerful he feels, i.e., the less able he is to control or punish the frustrater for the injury he has received, the more fear predominates over anger.

# chapter 3

# Situational Determinants
## of the Strength of the
### Instigation to Aggression

The monograph *Frustration and Aggression* provides a useful framework for our discussion of conditions affecting the likelihood of overtly aggressive reactions to thwarting. Much of the psychological research bearing on the instigation of hostility can easily be summarized in terms of the factors listed by Dollard and his colleagues. This is not to say their list is complete, however. Other variables will be added in the course of the discussion that have been minimized or neglected entirely in the earlier work. Some of these, particularly expectancies and interpretations, have already been introduced in the preceding chapter.

To summarize the present analysis (based on the views of Dollard et al.), the strength of the instigation to aggression is a positive function of three factors: "(1) the strength of instigation to the frustrated response, (2) the degree of interference with the frustrated response, and (3) the number of frustrated response-sequences" (1939, p. 28). Available evidence indicates that these classes of determinants significantly affect the intensity of aggressive responses, and hence, the likelihood of overt hostility, but there also is reason to believe the original Yale propositions should be modified somewhat to incorporate the operation of expectancies. The present chapter will discuss some of the research findings bearing on these principles of hostility instigation. In this discussion I will assume that the Dollard et al. concept "instigation to aggression" is equivalent to the present term "anger," and that suitable aggression cues capable of evoking hostile responses were present in the studies assessing the strength of the instigation to aggression by means of questionnaire or other behavioral observations. But even given such aggression cues, the anger that is aroused is not necessarily expressed in overt hostility, and this chapter will be followed by a consideration of factors affecting the inhibition of aggression.

51

*Strength of Instigation to the Frustrated Response*

*Original Proposition.* The first Yale hypothesis posited a direct relationship between the strength of the initial drive whose satisfaction is blocked and the strength of the resulting instigation to aggression. *Interference with a strongly instigated striving toward some goal* supposedly *produces a more intense hostile reaction than does the thwarting of a weaker drive.* Two questionnaire studies and an experiment were cited as evidence for this proposition.

One of the questionnaire studies has been mentioned earlier. Doob and Sears (1939) asked college students to indicate what their responses had been to various frustrations described to them but which they supposedly actually had encountered within the preceding few months. They also were asked to rate how strongly they had wanted to do the thing that was blocked by the frustration. The stronger this rated desire, it was found, the greater the proportion of aggressive responses listed, and the less the subjects said they had performed substitute, nonaggressive acts. In a somewhat similar vein, Miller (cited in Dollard et al., 1939, pp. 30–31) had his subjects rate the degree of annoyance they would feel if various people whom they liked to different degrees had snubbed them and also how bothered they would be by being "off form" in a number of sports of different degrees of importance to them. Comparable results were obtained in both cases. If satisfaction was not obtained in dealings with a highly liked person or in the performance of a highly liked sport, there was greater annoyance than if the individual or sport was less well liked. Since the degree of liking for a person undoubtedly is in direct ratio to the strength of drive to have pleasant relations with him, being snubbed by a close friend implies the frustration of a stronger drive than being snubbed by an acquaintance or stranger. Similarly, failing to do well in an attractive sport probably involves the frustration of a stronger drive to do well than does inept performance in an unimportant activity.

It is, of course, difficult to say just what is involved in the annoyance reported by Miller's subjects, but a reasonable conjecture is that this feeling includes at least some anger, with other emotions probably present as well. The intensity of this complex emotional pattern appears to be a positive function of the strength of the thwarted drive. This relationship also is shown in the experiment conducted by Sears and Sears as part of the Yale program (cited in Dollard et al., 1939, pp. 28–29). A five-month-old baby's feeding was systematically interrupted by removing the bottle from his mouth after he had taken varying amounts of milk. Their data demonstrated that the time from bottle removal to outburst of crying lengthened as the child became more nearly satiated with the ingestion of a greater amount of milk, i.e., as his hunger drive slackened. In other words, the latency period for the emotional reaction was longer—the child did not cry as quickly—the weaker the instigation to the interrupted response sequence.

Sears and Sears assumed in 1939 that the immediacy of the crying reaction could be taken as an index of the strength of the instigation to aggression. They might not make this inference today, however. Sears more recently has differentiated between rage or anger on one hand, and the intent to injure on the other (Sears et al., 1957, pp. 221–222). He considered the former emotion as largely an innate response to thwarting, while learning supposedly is greatly involved in focusing and channeling this reaction into the intent to injure. Since it is this latter component that comes closest to the 1939 construct "instigation to aggression," the baby's emotional outburst probably would be taken as more of an indication of rage than of aggressive tendencies.

The present approach is sympathetic to the earlier interpretation. We here regard anger (or rage) not only as one of the primary innate reactions to frustration, but also as creating an inborn readiness to attacks upon the thwarting agent. This may well be a constitutionally determined linkage between stimulus and response, which nevertheless, is not too clear in the newborn human for two main reasons: (1) his failure to discriminate the source of the frustration, and (2) the diffuse and uncontrolled nature of his actions. The crying reaction to frustration, mainly indicative of the emotion of rage or anger in the infant, according to this analysis, could serve as an index of what would be in the older individual the predisposition to aggression. But whatever the interpretation, the Sears and Sears findings show that the intensity of the emotional reaction to frustration varies directly with the strength of the drive whose satisfaction is blocked.

*Later Evidence: Assuming Differences in Drive Strength.* Several recent investigations seem to corroborate the notion of a direct relationship between the strength of the frustrated drive and the intensity of the resulting emotional state, whether there are aggressive responses to this emotion or not. These later studies, then, would appear to be of interest primarily because of their demonstration of the variety of situations in which the relationship holds. However, considerations to be discussed below suggest that the original proposition may have to be modified to some extent. These studies, therefore, can denote conditions which should be incorporated in any revisions of the Yale hypothesis.

Haner and Brown (1955) reported an experiment in which drive strength was increased by the familiar "goal-gradient" principle: The strength of a tendency to approach a goal increases the closer the organism is to this goal (see, for example, N. E. Miller, 1948, 1951). Thirty elementary school children individually played a game in which marbles had to be inserted into holes. The experimenter terminated the trials at various distances from the goal of game completion, with each termination causing a buzzer to be sounded until the child pushed a plunger to stop it. The closer the child was to ending the game, and presumably the more intense his desire to reach this goal, the greater was the pressure he exerted against the plunger in response to the raucous, frustration-signaling buzzer. Haner and Brown assumed the child's pressing against the plunger was a hostile act, but it may have been merely a frustration-induced tendency to exert more vigorous responses in general (Marx, 1956). In either event, however, the degree of pressure against the plunger probably was directly correlated with the intensity of the child's internal emotional responses. Frustration-induced emotional reactions apparently increase in strength the closer the person is to the goal of his activities, presumably because the strength of the thwarted tendency also increases with nearness to this goal.

Miller's previously cited study of annoyances suggests that signs of hostility from those we like can be more upsetting than similar actions from people we care less about. This supposedly is the result of the frustration of a stronger drive for harmonious and pleasant relationships in the former instance.[1] Essentially the same type of phenomenon has been observed in experimental investigations of behavior in small-group settings. Festinger and his colleagues (Festinger, 1950) have noted that differences of opinion in groups whose members are highly attracted to the group (i.e., in cohesive groups), for example, because they have a great deal of personal liking for the others, seem to be more disturbing to the members than disagreements among people who are less attracted to each other. Thus, upon perceiving differences of opinion, members who strongly like the others in their groups (and who apparently are somewhat confident they are correct) make more of an effort to change the others' views in the early stages of their discussions than do people who are less concerned with maintaining pleasant relations with the others. Furthermore, if the differences persist so that it is clear that one or two opinion deviates will not change their attitudes, the tendency for the majority to reject them is directly proportional to the degree of attraction the group has for the majority. Instead of there

---

[1] However, people we like or respect can be important to us for a great many reasons, in addition to their satisfying affiliative needs. They also may provide emotional support, information, access to important groups, etc. Hostility from these people, therefore, also may imply the thwarting of a greater number of needs than hostility from a stranger; i.e., there is interference with a greater number of response sequences in the former case.

being a greater tolerance for divergent opinions with an increase in group cohesiveness, the opposite seems to be true.

A number of reasons can be advanced for these results. On the basis of his most recent theorizing (1957), Festinger would contend that there is greater discomfort (dissonance) produced by disagreement with attractive people than by differences with less attractive people. The communication and rejection behaviors supposedly are motivated by the desire to reduce this discomfort, by either getting the support of the deviates or removing them from consideration.

The present line of thought offers a somewhat different interpretation. The group members could well regard the divergent beliefs as potential signs of conflict, or perhaps as a mild rebuff from the others. A difference of opinion with someone liked or otherwise important, therefore, implies a threat to relatively strong drives for affiliative satisfactions (i.e., the possible disruption of an important relationship). As a consequence, there is a stronger emotional reaction in the former situation. Anxiety that the drives may not be satisfied could give rise to the attempt to convince the deviates, but the emotional state would increase as these attempts fail, or perhaps anger becomes the dominant emotion, and this elicits the aggressive rejection of the deviate.

This explanation obviously is similar to the reasoning employed by Dollard et al. in their discussion of the annoyances study. Disagreements with attractive or important people may be akin to rebuffs from a close friend. In both instances, relatively strong instigations are thwarted, and there is a fairly intense emotional reaction. The Yale psychologists suggested that the "violence of lovers' quarrels is probably a consequence of this same principle" (1939, p. 29). Arguments between lovers presumably involve interference with stronger instigations, such as for affectional behavior, than do disputes between nonlovers.

*Absolute or Relative Strengths of the Thwarted Tendencies.* Where the above discussion has been entirely in terms of the *absolute* strength of the frustrated drive, Brown and Farber (1951) maintained that the emotional intensity resulting from the blocking is a function of the strength of the original drive *relative* to the strength of the competing or interfering tendencies. They proposed the following formula to express this relationship (p. 484):

$$\text{Intensity of emotional reaction} = \frac{E_w{}^n}{E_s{}^{n-1}}$$

where $E_w{}^n$ is the weaker of the competing response tendencies within the individual, and the denominator refers to the stronger tendency. Note that for these writers the interfering responses always are internal to the organism. Frustrating situations supposedly give rise to these inner blocks either by arousing inhibitory tendencies opposing the completion of the instigated response sequence or by eliciting competing excitatory tendencies.

The anecdote of James and the ice-cream cone mentioned in the preceding chapter can be used in translating this terminology into everyday language. His frustration could have been created through the arousal of inhibitory tendencies in him, internal responses countering the desire for the cone but without establishing a substitute goal. These inner restraints may have been evoked, for example, by his mother's statement that he should not eat until dinnertime. As another possibility, the interference may be the result of cues eliciting a competing instigation. His mother may have reminded him that he was saving his money for a baseball glove. According to Brown and Farber, James would be upset and annoyed by his frustration, not simply to the extent he wanted the cone, but rather by how much he wanted it *relative* to the degree he felt he should not or could not buy a cone.

One interesting derivation from this formula yields a prediction actually opposite to that made by Dollard and his colleagues. Brown and Farber (1951) pointed out that any increase in the difference between the strengths of the two tendencies results in a *decrease* in the intensity of the emotional reaction even if the instigation to the stronger response tendency is *increased* (p. 486). Thus, James, who wanted a cone very much, but who also was only slightly instigated to save his money for other purposes, presumably would have a weaker emotional reaction than another boy who did not want ice cream too much, but who also had a weak but equal opposing desire to spend his money in another way.

Some (but certainly not all) of this may be implicit in the Dollard et al. formulation. Increasing the strength of an instigation generally will lessen the degree to which some opposition or obstruction can interfere with the drive. It takes more opposition to stop a hungry man from gobbling up food in front of him than would be necessary to prevent a less hungry person from doing this. The degree of interference can be kept constant only by bringing about a corresponding increase in the strength of the opposing tendencies. What this means, then, is that the Yale proposition should be modified slightly by making explicit what probably has been assumed. The strength of the emotional reaction to frustration, and of any resulting aggressive tendencies, is a direct function of the strength of the drive whose satisfaction is blocked *only if the total interference with this instigation is not lessened.*

But Brown and Farber say more than this. In accounting for the heightened emotional state apparently resulting from increases in the strength of the frustrated drive, their formula requires an *increase* in the intensity of the obstructing tendencies. If there is any merit to their hypothesis, *the frustrated individuals in the previously cited studies who were placed under relatively strong instigating conditions must have experienced subjectively greater interference with their desires than the subjects under the weaker drive conditions.* This seems to be a reasonable assumption in at least some of the above experiments. The strongly instigated people in these studies conceivably had a more definite expectation their drives would be satisfied than did the less strongly driven subjects. Nonfulfillment of the definite expectations could be a more severe frustration than failure to realize a goal the individual had not expected to attain.

*The Frustration of Expectations.* The Haner and Brown subjects, for example, who came close to ending the game were more likely to have expected to reach this goal than the children who were frustrated at the beginning of the trial. Similarly, the operations establishing high cohesiveness in the group experiments could have produced the belief that the group members had common views, particularly when the attraction to the group was based upon personal liking for the other members. In creating this attitude, the experimenters generally told their subjects they would like their partners and their partners would like them, implying they had comparable personalities and opinions. Certainly, similarity of values and opinions often is correlated with friendship, with these shared beliefs sometimes the cause and sometimes the result of interpersonal attraction (Newcomb, 1959). At any rate, the members of the cohesive groups, whatever the basis of this attraction, may have come to believe that the others in their group had similar points of view, and these expectations would have been frustrated by the expressions of disagreement. Miller's hypothetical annoying snubs from a close friend also could be more unexpected than rebuffs from a casual acquaintance. Most people seem to regard "liking" relationships as symmetrical (De Soto, 1960). "If I like him," we tell ourselves, "he probably will like me," and thus, since we presumably would not snub a friend, do not expect him to snub us.

Subjects operating under relatively strong drives in each of these instances, therefore, could have expected at least some drive satisfaction. Research to be described more fully later indicates that the blocking of activities involving strongly held anticipations leads to more intense hostility than does the nonfulfillment of weaker expectations; the former frustrations, in being unexpected, may perhaps be judged as more severe (Berkowitz, 1960b). If this is the case, the people in the high-drive conditions would have experienced a subjectively greater interference with their striving than the less strongly instigated subjects, as the Brown and Farber formulation requires. Indeed, *the rela-*

*tively strong emotional reaction apparently resulting from interference with strong instigations in these studies actually can be due, in part at least, to the degree of thwarting experienced by the subjects.* More research obviously is needed in which the strength of the frustrated drive and the experienced interference with this instigation are manipulated independently of each other. For the time being, however, it seems reasonable to conclude that the strength of the drive whose satisfaction is blocked is one of the parameters affecting the intensity of the emotional reactions to the thwarting.

### Degree of Interference with the Frustrated Response

*Original Proposition.* Where the first principle involved the strength of the instigation to a response sequence, the next principle deals with the degree to which it is thwarted, and reads: *The greater the degree of interference with some response sequence, the stronger the resulting instigation to aggression.* Dollard et al. illustrated this with the case of a golfer who was slightly distracted at a crucial moment in his swing. The distraction produced relatively little interference, and he was only mildly annoyed. A stronger distraction, resulting in greater interference, would have brought about a much more violent outburst. As another example, an employee who was very late to a scheduled meeting with his boss would interfere with his employer's drives to a greater extent than if he had been only a few minutes late, and undoubtedly would be reprimanded relatively severely (Dollard et al., 1939, p. 30).

Correlational findings are the only data cited in support of this important proposition. Hovland and Sears (1940) assumed that bad economic conditions generally should produce relatively strong interference with many of the drives possessed by the citizens of some community or area. In comparison with more prosperous times, the people would not have as much money to buy the things they desired and, in addition, would face more serious threats to their status and future security. The poorer the state of the economy, the more severe this thwarting, and consequently the stronger the resulting instigation to aggression. Since the prosperity of the Southern states until recently was largely dependent upon the money brought in by "King Cotton," the annual per acre value of cotton could serve as a general index of the economic well-being of the area. Hovland and Sears computed trend lines for the value of cotton between 1882 and 1930, and also the trend lines for both the total number of lynchings and the number of lynchings of Negroes in the same period in these states. These trend lines, in a sense, represented the long-range changes in these indices due to broad economic and sociological patterns. However, there of course were year-by-year deviations from these over-all trends; the value of cotton might have increased in any one year because of a poor crop or might have fallen because of a surplus or decreased demand that year. Deviations from the general trend in cotton value were found to be negatively related to deviations from the trend in the number of lynchings. This may indicate that unexpected financial losses, producing relatively severe *and unanticipated* interference with economic actions, determined whether there would be an unusually high number of lynchings in the South.

Mintz (1946) has questioned the stated magnitude of these correlations. According to his calculations, apparently based on more adequate statistical procedures, the correlation between cotton value and lynching deviations was of the order of $-.3$ instead of the reported $-.6$. Nevertheless, there seems to be relatively little doubt that unusual changes in the value of cotton bore *something* of an inverse relationship to unusual changes in the number of Negroes lynched in the South prior to the 1930s. Other researchers have obtained comparable results. Raper, for example, reported a correlation of $-.5$ between similar indices of lynchings and cotton value in nine Southern states for the first three decades of this century (cited in R. W. Brown, 1954, p. 849; and in Henry & Short, 1954, p. 187). The relationship between these two measures, of course, does not unequivocally support the Yale thesis. Other factors could have accounted for the fluctuations in the number of lynchings during this period, and certainly not all lynchings are caused, even indirectly, by economic hardships. But even admitting this, it is difficult to construct sensible alternative explanations for the correlations (assuming the relationship is reliable). Since the lynchings almost always were of Negroes by whites (R. W. Brown, 1954, p. 849), the data suggest hostility was engendered in the Southern whites by their economic frustrations, or perhaps by *unexpected* frustrations, with the degree of aggression being a direct function of the severity of the unusual interference with their drives. This hostility could have been directed against Negroes because they represented an increased threat to their jobs and status superiority during the times of business depression in the South.

Miller's study of annoyances also was cited in support of this second hostility-instigation hypothesis. His subjects indicated they were "much more irritated at being completely 'off form' in their favorite sport than at being only slightly 'off form'" (p. 31). There was a greater thwarting of their drive to do well in the former instance, giving rise to a stronger emotional reaction.

*Later Evidence.* Findings in two more recent investigations also can be cited as evidence for this second principle if we first assume strongly hostile attacks upon a person represent more severe blockings of his desires than only mildly aggressive acts against him. Strong aggression conceivably produces greater interference with a number of drives, such as those for physical comfort and self-enhancement. Graham et al. (1951), in a study mentioned in the preceding chapter, explicitly made this assumption in explaining their results. They gave their subjects fifty incomplete statements describing five types of hostile actions, ranging from a physical blow to mild indications of dislike, that various instigators had taken against a person. The subjects, 106 adolescents, were to indicate what they thought would be the "most likely way for a person to act in such a situation." According to their answers, there was a direct relationship between the intensity of the hostility received and the strength of the aggression likely to be returned. The Old Testament principle of "an eye for an eye" apparently was a more accurate description of human behavior in these situations than the New Testament admonition to "turn the other cheek" to those who strike us. A person who was hit or slapped probably would react more violently than one who, say, received a "nasty look." Taking these results at face value, the aggressive response to aggression undoubtedly stems from the degree of thwarting produced by the instigating attack and not from any moral code governing retributions.

In a more adequate test of the Yale proposition, McClelland and Apicella (1945) demonstrated experimentally that strong hostility directed toward an individual often provokes relatively intense anger. Twenty-eight male college students, working separately on a card-sorting task, were subjected to frustrations by causing them to fail on two out of every three trials. In addition, the experimenter, an undergraduate supposedly "of low prestige value," was extremely hostile and derogatory toward half the group and only moderately insulting to the others. The students' remarks were recorded and later classified according to the functions they seemed to serve. Approximately 30 per cent of the verbal reactions were coded as denoting anger or aggression under the moderate frustration conditions, while over 50 per cent of the remarks were so classified in response to the strong frustrations.

McClelland and Apicella, however, maintained that anger must be differentiated from aggression, making a distinction somewhat at variance from that drawn in this book. They defined aggression as attacks upon the frustrating agent or a substitute. Anger responses, in contrast, supposedly are not aimed *at* anything, and should be regarded as "substitute" actions since their main function may be to relieve tension or anxiety.

The distinction between *anger* and *aggression* does seem worthwhile. But instead of making inferences regarding the "functions" served by anger, we could say, simply, that the intense reactions observed by the psychologists (and not classified as attacks) were indicative of a complex emotional state, probably consisting largely of what is here termed *rage* or *anger*.[2] The McClelland-Apicella data indicate that these emotional rage reactions may be more closely related to the degree of interference with some drive than are the direct, overtly hostile responses to the anger. Rage responses are somewhat independent of the more focused, openly aggressive acts aimed at injuring another. The average frequency of direct aggression rose only slightly in response to the more intense hostile attacks: 18.5 per cent direct aggression after strong provocation, as against 16 per cent aggressive acts in the low insult condition. However, there was a much greater difference between these two conditions for those reactions classified as denoting anger: 32 per cent in the "strong" condition, but only 14 per cent in the low provocation treatment. The severity of interference with an individual's drives presumably bears a direct relationship to the intensity of his anger, but heightening this emotion does not necessarily increase the frequency and intensity of overt aggression. Indeed, as will be discussed more fully later, under some conditions increased anger may lead to a *decrease* in the intensity of the hostile actions expressed openly (Berkowitz & Holmes, 1960).

An experiment utilizing groups of subjects provides somewhat more direct support for the present thesis of a positive relation between degree of interference and the strength of the resulting instigation to aggression. French (1944) sought to determine whether organized groups (people who had known each other and worked together previously) would react differently to frustrating situations than would unorganized groups composed of people who had never seen each other before. In one part of the study he compared the interactions of the group members on a task in which they were highly interdependent with their behavior on two other tasks in which the members could function somewhat more independently of the others in the group. The comments of the observers and the subjects themselves strongly indicated that the other group members interfered with the behavior of any one individual more frequently on the interdependent task than in the other situations. Consistent with the Yale hypothesis, there was more aggression per minute directed against the other members of the group on the former task than during the problems in which the members could proceed to their goals relatively unaffected by the others. As further confirmation,

[2] These anger responses also may be manifestations of "aim-inhibited" aggression. The subjects may have shown they were "angry," but nevertheless suppressed their hostility to the instigator. McClelland and Apicella assumed there was little inhibition of hostility in their situation since the experimenter had little authority over the students. However, research has demonstrated that many middle-class college students inhibit socially disapproved responses, such as aggression, even in the type of situation employed by the researchers (R. A. Clark, 1955).

the observers' ratings of the degree of group interdependence, i.e., the extent to which the members worked together and affected each other, was found to be highly positively correlated with the rating of overt aggression in the group. Thomas (1957) has obtained similar findings in an experiment in which the degree of interdependence among the group members was manipulated directly. Inadequate performance by any one member was more likely to provoke hostility from the others when the individuals were highly dependent upon each other for goal attainment than when they could reach their goals somewhat independently of the others in the group. Any one person's poor perform-ance resulted in a greater degree of interference with the others' goal-directed activity, the more independent the group.

French also reported some observations in line with the findings by Graham et al., and by McClelland and Apicella. He noted there was a general tendency for those people who were the target for most of the aggression in the group to initiate most of the hostility displayed. His explanation for this was based upon the Dollard et al. formulation. "Presumably those who receive aggression from others perceive these aggressors as interfering agents" (1939, p. 286) and thus, those who were attacked most often were more likely to see themselves as severely thwarted than were the people who were attacked less frequently.

While the above evidence is not as unequivocal as one would desire, the general trend of the findings is clear. There seems to be litttle doubt that the degree of interference with some striving is directly related to the intensity of the resulting emotional reaction, anger.

## Number of Frustrated Response Sequences

*Original Proposition.* The third proposition concerning the strength of the instigation to aggression pertained to the number of frustrations an individual had experienced. Dollard and his colleagues hypothesized that *the instigation to aggression produced by each frustration summates with repeated thwartings.* Consequently, successive minor frustrations (particularly when close together in time) would produce an aggressive response of greater strength than would be expected from any one inter-ference alone (1939, p. 31). The only evidence given for this is anecdotal in nature. The investigators had employed a number of their subjects in several frustration situations. The last tasks in the series sometimes produced strong hostile reactions out of proportion to the objective degree of frustration in these tasks. In one case, a man who previously had been a willing subject in several very trying experiments seemed to "blow up" when asked merely to give free associations to fifty words (p. 32).

N. E. Miller (1941) presented a somewhat different hypothesis two years later yielding essentially the same predictions regarding the effects of repeated thwartings. He first clarified what he and his colleagues at Yale had conceived to be the relationship between frustration and aggression. Frustrations can have consequences other than aggression. Even though the instigation to aggression (i.e., anger) will be aroused by any given obstruction to a response sequence, Miller pointed out that other responses to this situation may be dominant, inhibiting the actual occurrence of the aggressive acts. Frustration, in other words, "produces instigations to a number of different types of response," and the instigation to aggression can occupy any position in the hierarchy of frustration reactions (p. 338). John Smith may have learned to respond to thwartings primarily with increased problem-solving activity. The instigation to this behavior is stronger than the instigation to aggression and cloaks this anger. If these other, nonaggressive responses remove the frustration, the strength of the instigation to aggression of course will be reduced, and hostile behaviors may not occur at all in this situation. However, *if these first responses do not somehow reduce the strength of the frustrated drive,* such as by overcoming the interference to goal attainment, *the instigations to these first frustration reactions "will tend to become weakened through extinction." The next most dominant response, which may or may not be aggression, will then tend to be elicited.* Eventually, any stronger and competing responses in John Smith's response repertoire will be extinguished with continuing frustrations, and aggression will occur, though it initially may have been an unlikely reaction to thwarting.[3]

These two formulations obviously can be combined fairly readily. Both predict an increased probability of overt hostility with continued obstructions to drive satisfaction. This heightened likelihood of aggres-

---

[3] Some empirical and theoretical considerations insist the *immediate* result of a frustration is to *strengthen* the instigation to the obstructed response sequence. Thus, Brown and Farber hypothesized that the emotional effects produced by the thwarting increase the strength of the operative drive. Mowrer (1960) also has discussed this possibility and has presented some supporting evidence. Consistent with this notion, Beller and Haeberle (1959) reported that the frustration of dependency behavior in nursery school children produced increased dependent behavior. This increase, however, probably is limited to the immediate effects of thwarting. *Persistent* and repeated frustrations may well have the effects proposed by Miller (1941). We would predict on the basis of the Miller formulation, for example, that people whose dominant, nonaggressive frustration reactions are only weakly learned (or weakly held) would give up these nonaggressive reactions relatively quickly under persistent thwartings. Such seems to be the case. Beller and Haeberle, in the previously mentioned study, found that children rated low in dependency habits showed an initial rise in dependent behavior after dependency acts were frustrated by an adult, but then reverted to other types of behavior more quickly than did the children rated as being greatly dependent.

sion may come about because of (1) the summation of anger effects and (2) the weakening of competing tendencies.

*Later Evidence.* The McClelland-Apicella experiment referred to earlier contains some data bearing upon this prediction. The subjects receiving either mild or intense anger provocations were each frustrated on ten trials, and the experimenters compared their behavior during the first five trials with their reactions to the last five frustrations. They found no evidence of an increased proportion of "anger-aggressive" reactions in the later trials in either condition. Instead, the subjects seemed to engage in more intense and unusual trial-and-error behavior with repeated blockings.

In contrast to these negative results, Otis and McCandless (1955) have provided some support for the Yale propositions. Nursery school children individually played a game in which a toy was to be moved down a "road" made of school blocks. This movement was obstructed by the experimenter in each of eight frustration trials, and the child's re-actions were recorded. Analyses of the data showed statistically signifi-cant increases in the frequency of "aggressive-dominant" actions and decreases in the number of "submissive-complaisant" actions (behaviors shown to be incompatible with aggression) from the first four to the last four trials. While the investigators regarded this finding as consistent with Miller's hypothesis, they also suggested another interpretation: The increase in aggressive behavior may be due to the "reinforcement of aggression provided by 'winning over the adult.'" Aggressive actions may have increased because this behavior helped the child win the game.

*Repeated Frustrations and Degree of Interference.* Some of the differ-ences between the McClelland-Apicella and Otis-McCandless results probably can be traced to differences in the task and the ages of their subjects. Because of these factors, the younger children (three to five years of age) in the latter study could have experienced a greater degree of thwarting than the college students employed in the former investiga-tion. (The children probably also had weaker inhibitions against ex-pressing hostility.) Their task and age provided them with relatively few alternative responses, other than aggression, to the acts blocked by the frustrating experimenter. Miller's 1941 analysis of the frustration-aggression relationship suggests hostile acts do not occur until the indi-vidual's stronger alternative, nonaggressive reactions to the obstruction have been weakened by nonelimination of the obstacle. McClelland elsewhere (1951, pp. 504–505) has advanced a somewhat similar hy-pothesis in proposing that emotional (or, to use his word, "defensive") responses to a situation do not arise until problem-solving actions are no longer possible. In essence, both writers seem to be maintaining that *the probability of emotional reactions is a function of the degree to which all possible[4] nonaggressive responses are blocked,* more than to the interference with any *one* response sequence. From the point of view of the thwarted individual, this would mean he responds emotionally to obstructions when he feels he no longer can cope with the situation. His repertoire of problem-solving behaviors has been exhausted.

The preschoolers could have "run out of" coping behaviors more rapidly than the college students. For one thing, the game played by the Otis-McCandless children probably did not permit as wide a range of alternative means of dealing with the frustration as the task given the McClelland-Apicella subjects. It also may be that the former children, being younger, did not see too many other possible courses of action. A greater proportion of their total repertoire in the situation was obstructed with continued thwartings, and they were quicker to exhibit emotional reactions. Strongly motivated youngsters may have had even fewer alternative actions available to them, perhaps because their strong drive state had narrowed the range of their cognitive "scanning" (Bruner, 1957, pp. 53–57). If this analysis is correct, one consequence of repeated interference with ongoing activities is to increase the range of behaviors shown to be ineffective in removing the obstruction. Thus, *the number of frustrated response sequences may be related to the intensity of the instigation to aggression, in part at least, because repeated thwartings heighten the degree to which all of the actions available to the individual are blocked.*

This does not mean that anger effects do not summate with repeated frustrations. Berkowitz (1960b) reported an experiment in which members of the same-sex pairs (either male or female college students) supposedly exchanged written communications with each other at two different times. Unknown to the subjects, these notes were intercepted, and other, previously constructed, communications were substituted which were either friendly or hostile in tone. Those subjects receiving the series of two unfriendly messages from their partners became significantly more hostile to them, as is indicated by the descriptions made of these partners at the end of the experiment, than the students receiving only one or no provocations in the communications. The anger effects of the two attacks apparently had accumulated in the former subjects. Some such cumulative process may account for the burst of temper often observed in people after they had experienced a series of minor annoyances. The frustrated children in the Otis-McCandless investigation also may have exhibited this accumulation of anger effects.

---

[4] Responses that are low in the person's response hierarchy, to use Miller's (1941) terminology, have a small likelihood of occurring and thus may be regarded as relatively nonpossible ways of acting.

Dollard et al. pointed out (1939, p. 31) that the time factor is of great importance in this cumulative process. There may be a buildup of only weak emotional reactions if the repeated frustrations are separated by relatively long intervals. Anger aroused by an obstruction can dissipate with time. Furthermore, a long delay before the onset of the second frustration also may permit the individual to think about the unpleasant event, giving him an opportunity to feel guilty or anxious about any aggression he might have displayed, or may even lead him to anticipate the reoccurrence of the thwartings.

We have now come to another effect of repeated frustrations: the development of expectations. Whatever the length of time between them, *thwartings may be anticipated if they are repeated. Such expectations can lessen the likelihood of an aggressive reaction.*

*Repeated Frustrations and Expectations.* The McClelland-Apicella college students probably differed from the nursery school children in their understanding of what the experimenter was doing. The men undoubtedly developed some guesses as to what the experiment was about or how the experimenter would behave throughout the course of the session. Consequently, as the trials went on, many of these students may have come to expect the repeated insults, causing them to react with indifference to the provocations.

A number of writers have mentioned the possibility that anticipated frustrations give rise to only mild reactions. Pastore (1952), for one, has suggested that arbitrary frustrations may produce relatively intense aggression because they involve interference with activities the individual had expected to complete. If a person had believed he would get on the next bus and then saw it pass him by "arbitrarily," he probably would be more strongly annoyed than if he had anticipated the bus's failure to stop. Bateson (1941) also argued that learning to expect frustrations can modify reactions to them. He believed that the frustration-aggression hypotheses advanced by Dollard and his colleagues would not apply to the Balinese. These people learn not to expect strong satisfactions in life and thus presumably would be less upset by any one thwarting. Balinese mothers apparently tease their children very frequently, holding pleasures of one sort or another before them like a carrot on a stick, and then unexpectedly taking them away. As a result, the Balinese child supposedly does not anticipate climaxes in his acts. He takes his pleasures where and when he can—in small, preliminary doses as the activity continues—rather than in some clearly defined distant goal.

Several different reactions to repeated frustrations must be differentiated here. On one hand, we may have a direct effect of expectation on the interpretation of the interference, and on the other, anticipations may determine whether or not a given goal-directed response sequence is blocked. If Bateson's observations are to be accepted at face value, this latter effect may take place among the Balinese children. They respond to their continuing frustrations with a shift in their goals. Instead of learning to expect satisfactions primarily at the end of a definite sequence, they presumably obtain pleasures from minor goals distributed throughout the sequence. Eventually, they become subjected to fewer and fewer actual frustrations even though the objective situation is repeated in a fairly constant manner. *Through anticipating obstructions in the path of certain actions or goals they learn other courses of action or other goals.*[5] Something similar may have occurred in people experiencing frequent air raids during World War II. Their anticipation of the air attacks enabled them to cope with the danger and thus minimized the degree of frustration. The individual expecting an air raid every night at nine o'clock could schedule his important activities for other times and be prepared to enter the bomb shelter before this time.

Generally, then, a person receiving an expected (or "nonarbitrary") frustration actually may suffer less interference with his actions than the individual who had not anticipated the obstructions. Going back to our overworked bus rider, suppose he had not noticed the sign on the approaching bus indicating that it was returning to the garage. The sight of the bus under these circumstances might well be a cue setting off a chain of preliminary response sequences; he readjusts his packages, reaches into his pocket for the fare, and begins to think of the martini awaiting him at home. This response chain, which had been activated by the expected imminent event, then is suddenly disrupted when the bus passes by. A similar set of response sequences would not have been in operation in the man who had not expected the bus to stop, and therefore this latter person would have been subjected to less thwarting.

This type of analysis can be extended to social situations in which people respond to each other in terms of structured role relations. There are many instances in which a person is expected to behave in a certain manner because of his particular role in a group or because of the rules of conduct existing in the situation. As a result, if this behavior frustrates other members of the group there may be relatively little hostility directed toward him. The others may believe he was obliged to act that way; he is seen as not having chosen to obstruct their endeavors, and thus, the frustration is not interpreted as a personal affront. But more than this, the other group members also may have expected

[5] This again highlights the importance of *degree of interference* as a factor affecting the strength of the instigation to aggression. The greater the degree of interference, the more the individual's alternative courses of action are blocked, and the less he can circumnavigate the obstruction.

him to act in this frustrating manner, since they were aware of the norms guiding his behavior, and may have shaped their responses accordingly. Their response sequences actually may have been subjected to less thwarting than if they had not had this anticipation. Horwitz, Goldman, and Lee (1954) have shown that people are less strongly annoyed with someone who frustrates them when this frustration arises from the individual's appropriate performance of his role than when they had expected him to act differently.

*Contrast and Assimilation.* Expectancies also may affect an individual's judgment of the severity of the frustrations he encounters. Psychophysical studies of weight judgments can be used to illustrate this process. (This may seem far removed from aggression, but there is reason to believe the same factors governing an individual's judgment of inanimate objects, such as lifted weights, also can influence his evaluation of other people.) The subject in many of these experiments first is given experience with a limited range of weights (the standard stimuli) and then is presented with another weight somewhat out of this range. Judgments of the latter weight involve a comparison between it and the standard. Typically, the judgment of the critical weight is found to vary with the discrepancy between it and the standard stimuli on the relevant judgmental dimension. If this difference is relatively small there usually is an *assimilation effect* in which the difference is minimized, while a *contrast effect,* exaggerating the discrepancy between the standard and critical stimuli, generally occurs when this difference is relatively great (Peak, 1958). Judgmental effects such as these have their counterparts in many different social situations (Berkowitz, 1960d; Sherif & Sherif, 1956).

Holmes and Berkowitz (1961) showed how contrast effects could influence an individual's evaluation of another person. Their subjects, college students, listened to a tape-recorded interview between a psychologist and a female student. In half the cases the psychologist acted in a very belligerent manner toward the girl, while he was very friendly and supporting in the interview heard by the remaining students. After listening to this tape the subjects were asked to rate the personality of a male student from a very brief recording of his voice. We can assume that the first recording (the interviewing psychologist) served as the comparison standard in the judgment of the student. The evaluation of the male student clearly varied with the nature of the person with whom he was compared. He received the most favorable evaluation when the subjects had previously listened to the "aggressive" psychologist and was regarded most unfavorably when he was preceded by the "friendly" psychologist. There was a great difference between the standard (the psychologist) and the critical stimulus person (the male student) in both conditions. The resulting contrast effect apparently exaggerated this difference, displacing the judgment of the student in the direction away from the psychologist.

Several other experiments involving reactions to aggressive behavior also seem to be susceptible to the same type of interpretation. In the first of these investigations (Berkowitz, 1960a), pairs of college students, both male or both female, who did not know each other, were brought together ostensibly for a study of "first impressions." The pair members made an initial rating of each other and then withdrew to separate rooms from which they wrote notes to each other. These were intercepted by the experimenter, who substituted previously constructed messages so that half the subjects received relatively friendly notes supposedly from their partner and the others received more hostile communications consisting of direct attacks upon them. Ratings made at this time indicated that these messages were very effective in shaping the subject's impression, or expectancy, of what the sender was like as a person. Following this, the subjects received another communication, supposedly from the partner, telling them what the partner thought of them, and again, these were either friendly or unfriendly in manner. If we assume that the expectancy formed on the basis of the first communication ("My partner is friendly" or "My partner is hostile")—or perhaps this initial note itself—served as the judgmental standard by which the second communication was evaluated, the reactions to this second communication can be readily understood. A contrast effect should have occurred in the judgment of the later message to the extent that this second information set differed from the first in degree of friendliness. The greatly discrepant second communication, as a consequence of its extreme evaluation, therefore should have had a greater impact on the final evaluation of the sender than the second communication which was consistent with the first message. The results bear this out. A significantly greater proportion of the subjects changed their evaluations of their partner following the second communication in the direction consistent with this latter message when it differed from the first in tone than when it was in accord with the first note. If the later message was hostile, more subjects became unfriendlier to the sender if it presumably was unexpected on the basis of the first note than if its tone could be anticipated from the earlier message. A similar process operated to affect reactions to the second friendly communication; more subjects became friendlier after receiving this note if it presumably was unexpected.

In a later study, Berkowitz (1960b) manipulated his subjects' initial expectancies regarding their partners by providing each subject with a fictitious personality diagnosis of his partner. The subjects then exchanged written messages with their partners, and as before, they received either friendly or hostile notes. As in the preceding study, these communications had the greatest impact when they differed from the initial expectation. Another experiment reported in this later paper indicated that the magnitude of this impact is a direct function of the discrepancy between the prior expectation and the later actual behavior—as would be expected from the notion of a contrast effect.

These findings also can be interpreted in a somewhat different fashion. It may be simpler to say merely that the effect of the second communication was proportional to the degree of new information it provided. This new information would be greatest, of course, when the second message was inconsistent with the first. However, this type of explanation cannot account for the above-mentioned contrast effect in the judgment of the male student following the experience with the psychologist. The student's voice could not yield any information about the psychologist. Rather, the latter's behavior seemed to provide a standard with which the student could be compared. The behavioral sequence in the other experiments cited here is open to just this effect. The partner's first action, and/or perhaps the expectancy developed on the basis of this behavior, presumably served as a similar standard with which his later message could be compared. Unexpected events, according to this analysis, are always susceptible to contrast effects. Consequently, they will be evaluated as more extreme on some relevant dimension than will anticipated occurrences.

Similar effects should be found in the judgments of frustrations generally. An expected thwarting, or one that follows on the heels of another frustration, probably will be judged as being somewhat less extreme than the unexpected or entirely novel obstruction. An anticipated rebuff from another will be seen as not too unfriendly, while an unexpected criticism will be interpreted as more severe than it really is. From the point of view of the frustrated individual, this may well mean that *unexpected frustrations are perceived as producing a greater degree of interference with his drives than are anticipated obstructions.* (It will be recalled that my earlier application of the Brown-Farber analysis to the Dollard et al. data requires just this interpretation of unexpected thwartings.) However, the present formulation does not insist that frustrations will have an ever-diminishing effect with their continued repetition. Anger may accumulate. Persistent thwartings can obstruct a wider and wider range of all the responses available to the individual, resulting in an increased degree of interference with the individual's total repertoire. For either or both of these reasons, repeated frustrations may increase the likelihood of an aggressive out-burst, even though the later obstructions may be seen as relatively mild.[6]

## SUMMARY

The present discussion of factors affecting the strength of the instiga-tion to aggression is based largely upon the analysis by Dollard and his colleagues, but some modifications have been introduced.

The first instigational principle listed in *Frustration and Aggression* maintains that the strength of the instigation to aggression is a direct function of the strength of the instigation to the thwarted response. Em-pirical data provide some support for this contention, but there also is reason to believe that the intensity of the emotional reaction may be affected by the difference in the strengths of the thwarted and opposing tendencies. A major source of ambiguity in the studies bearing on this first instigational proposition has to do with the operation of expect-ancies. People in the high-drive conditions often were more likely than those in the low-drive groups to have expected to attain satisfactions. The resulting difference in anger arousal may then be due, at least in part, to the greater frustration of activities expected to be satisfying in the high-drive conditions. The high-drive people may have been more thwarted.

The second proposition advanced by the Yale group, contending that the instigation to aggression aroused by a frustration is in direct pro-portion to the degree of thwarting, is supported by experimental data. This is perhaps the most important instigational principle, since the first and third propositions can be understood to some extent in terms of degree of frustration.

In discussing the third proposition, dealing with the number of frustrations, some modifications are suggested. It is pointed out that repeated thwartings can heighten the degree to which all of the actions available to the individual are blocked. Thus, while anger effects may summate, as the original formulation maintained, there also may be objectively more severe frustrations with continued interference with

---

[6] Davies (1962) has published an analysis of revolutions which is consistent with the present interpretation of unexpected frustrations. He reported that revolutions were most likely to occur when a prolonged period of economic and social improve-ment was followed by a short, sharp reversal. The prolonged socioeconomic im-provement, of course, could have produced rising expectations in the populace which then led to relatively intense resentment when these anticipations were not fulfilled and past gains seemed threatened. The reader will also note that Davies' observa-tions are consistent with the writer's analysis of the Hovland-Sears study. There too, indices of anger (i.e., lynchings) were associated with sudden departures from a general trend of economic improvement.

goal-directed activity. Expectancies also have to be considered in dealing with repeated frustrations; later thwartings sometimes evoke milder reactions than do the first in a series of frustrations, and this difference may be due to the later thwartings being anticipated. In general, expected frustrations produce less intense emotional reactions than do unanticipated frustrations. Two reasons are suggested: (1) Through anticipating interference with his activity, the individual may alter his actions, or even his goals, so that he actually experiences less frustration; (2) expected frustrations may be judged as less severe.

# chapter 4

# The Inhibition of Aggressive Acts

## EARLIER CONCEPTIONS

If a soldier were suddenly and unfairly severely castigated by his superior officer there is a good chance that he would become angry. The probability also is fairly great that he would show very little immediate direct aggression toward the officer in response to this treatment. Any display of temper on his part, he knows, would be decidedly unwise. Expecting punishment for any hostility he might express toward his superior, the soldier suppresses his aggression. Dollard and his colleagues have formulated a general proposition to cover this type of effect: *"The strength of inhibition of any act of aggression varies positively with the amount of punishment anticipated to be a consequence of that act"* (1939, p. 33).

This principle, as it stands, cannot be disputed. There are some additional aspects of the 1939 formulation, however, that we know to be incorrect. The Yale group thought of punishment in terms of the law of effect. Reward facilitates the learning of many behaviors, and going to the opposite side of the coin, those actions which have been followed by punishment in the past, they reasoned, will "cease to occur." Other forms of aggression may develop as substitutes, but the specific aggressive acts that led to punishment supposedly will be less likely to arise.

However, research conducted since the publication of *Frustration and Aggression* indicates punishment is not simply the reverse of reward. Punishment seems to have an inhibitory effect primarily because of the emotions it arouses. Once this emotional state (probably largely fear or anxiety) wears off, the previously punished response tendency is as strong as ever (Estes, 1944).

This newer conception obviously has some very important implications, particularly for parents who would use coercion in teaching their children not to be aggressive. Punishment, and especially physical punishment, is relatively ineffective as a disciplinary technique. The parent who relies primarily on his child's fear of punishment must be constantly on guard for violations of his rules. If his child sees that the parent is not present and believes he can get away with some transgression he is all too likely to take the chance. When a youngster is taught only that he should not fight with other children because this would lead to his being punished, he will refrain from fighting only when his parent is in a position to learn of his hostile actions. In addition, there is evidence that anticipation of punishment acts like other frustrations in increasing the strength of the instigation to aggression (Chasdi & Lawrence, 1955; R. R. Sears, 1950). More will be said about this later when the learning of hostility is discussed, but the main point to remember now is this: The expectation of punishment for an aggressive act leads to the inhibition rather than the elimination of this behavior.

Dollard and his colleagues then went on to show that the likelihood of overtly hostile behavior is governed by the strength of the tendency to aggress. Generally speaking, the probability an individual will attack someone openly varies inversely with the intensity of his fear of punishment for this behavior relative to the strength of his aggressive inclinations.

Some of the data collected in the previously cited questionnaire study by Doob and Sears (1939) can be interpreted from this point of view. Their college student subjects were asked to indicate, among other things, which reaction they actually had made to the frustrations they had experienced, how satisfying each of the possible reactions would have been to them, and how much punishment these actions would have brought. In somewhat more than one-third of the instances, overt aggression was said to be the reaction that would be most satisfying but which would also produce the most punishment. These instances were selected for further analysis. The rated intensity of the satisfaction anticipated from overt hostility can serve as a crude index of the strength of the subjects' aggressive tendencies; the angrier they were at someone and the more directly this anger led to aggression, the stronger the satisfaction they presumably would feel as the result of attacking him. Similarly, the rated anticipation of punishment probably can be regarded as a rough measure of the strength of the inhibitory tendencies. Making these assumptions, the results are consistent with the present formulation. As we would expect, overt aggression was more likely to occur when the expected satisfaction was greater than the expected punishment, i.e., when the instigation was stronger than the inhibitory tendencies (p. 35).

Dollard et al. (1939) offered a reasonable formulation regarding the combination of the opposing inhibitory and aggressive tendencies. *The strength of these antagonistic responses probably "summates negatively in some algebraic manner"* (p. 36). Thus, the final outcome is the resultant of these opposing forces, with the strength of one of the responses detracting from the strength of the other.

## RESEARCH

While a number of the more recent studies can easily be incorporated within the Yale hypotheses regarding the effects of anticipated punishment (although they also provide needed detail to this theoretical framework), several investigations also highlight a class of factors either neglected or minimized in the 1939 work, namely, internal standards defining aggressive actions as morally "wrong." Hostility is inhibited because such behavior is a violation of the individual's own rules of conduct, that is, would lead to guilt arousal, as well as because of anxiety produced by expectations of punishment. This chapter will not be concerned with the development of these internal standards. However, since their operation can be affected by situational conditions, they will be considered here.

### Anticipation of Punishment

*Inhibitory Effects.* Direct tests of the initial proposition concerning the inhibitory effects of anticipated punishment are found in two experiments, one with children, the other with rats. Chasdi and Lawrence (1955) investigated the consequences of punishment for aggression in children's doll-play behavior. Twenty-three nursery school children aged three to six years were divided approximately equally into an experimental and control group. Both groups played with a variety of dolls for four sessions, the difference being that the children in the experimental group were punished by reproofs for any aggression they exhibited in this play during the second session. Needless to say, the children receiving this treatment then showed significantly less hostility in their doll play during session 3 than did the control children. They had learned to inhibit these behaviors in order to avoid the verbal punishment.

Seward's investigations of aggressive behavior in rats also illustrate the inhibitory effects of punishment. In one experiment (Seward, 1946), he observed that the day after a fight the average loser made fewer aggressions or even advances than before not only against the winner but also against other rats. The fear of punishment in these losers apparently had generalized relatively broadly so that they now avoided fighting *any* other rats. If this generalization were to become strongly learned, with one animal's fear drive strongly conditioned to the presence of another, Seward hypothesized, a stable dominance-submission relationship would develop. The persistent loser presumably would fear and be submissive to other animals of his species. If he were to think about it, he would anticipate being defeated and severely punished in any aggressive encounters with them and therefore would attempt to avoid such conflicts.

*Social Status and Inhibitions.* Social status systems frequently involve analogous dominance-subordination relationships. Human beings learn these relationships early in life. They know that people with a favorable standing on certain (but not necessarily all) of their society's hierarchies of rank often have power to administer rewards and punishments to others with lower social status. This holds for a large variety of ranking systems, from popularity in a group to control over economic pursuits. Rewards can be obtained from meeting the high-status person's approval (gaining his goodwill itself may be a reward), while punishment may follow if he disapproves. He might withdraw his liking, which can hurt psychologically, or if he desires and has the ability, he might impose economic penalties, for example, causing the low-status individual to miss out on a promotion to a more favorable job. For any number of reasons, then, aggression directed to the high-status person can lead to punishment, and this hostility is to be avoided. We certainly see frequent examples of such hostility avoidance in the workaday world. Few adults care to antagonize their employer. Lippitt, Polansky, Redl, and Rosen (1952) observed an essentially similar process in their study of three summer camps. The children in each camp were divided into those with high or low social power (i.e., informal social status) on the basis of ratings of each child's ability to influence the others in his camp. They found, in two camps for emotionally disturbed lower-class boys and girls, as well as in a camp for "normal" middle-class boys, that the average youngster directed more deferential, approval-seeking behavior toward the high-power figures than toward those lower in status.

A variety of investigations attest to the strength and all-pervasiveness of this learning not to antagonize those high in social status. A. R. Cohen (1955) conducted a study much like the one (described earlier) by Pastore, in which college women were asked how people in general would respond to several hypothetical frustrating situations. The girls reported that less overt aggression would be exhibited when the frustrating agent was an authority figure (e.g., a professor or some executive) than when he was a peer. Graham et al. (1951) obtained similar results in their previously described survey. The adolescents in this study were to indicate how people would react to a number of instigations ranging from a physical blow to mild indications of dislike. The youngsters realistically thought that the nature of the attacker was an important determinant of the strength of the overt hostile reaction. There was a linear relationship between the intensity of the attack and the strength of the hostile response in almost all cases. However, for any degree of aggression received, siblings, friends, and peers probably would elicit a stronger reaction than would those people in authority who had the power and social right to punish aggression directed against them.

Parents constituted the major exception to the aggression-aggression relationship; they supposedly would provoke only a very minimal amount of overt hostility in response to any of their aggressive acts. As Sears et al. have noted (1957, pp. 233–239), the Mosaic injunction to honor thy father and thy mother is strongly ingrained in Western society. Not only do our norms frown on a child attacking his parents, but there also seems to be frequent and deliberate parental punishment of any aggression directed toward parents by their children. Most American parents (see Sears et al., 1957; Bandura & Walters, 1959; Bandura, 1960) apparently give their children little freedom to aggress against them. Parental frustrations undoubtedly arouse anger in children, with the strength of this emotional reaction presumably being in direct ratio to the degree of interference with drive satisfaction. However, children generally learn to inhibit their aggressive responses to this anger in order to avoid punishment.

The same pattern of findings also can be seen in studies employing more realistic frustration situations. Thibaut and Riecken (1955) had Air Force reservists listen, one at a time, to another person giving orders in a pompous and hostility-arousing manner. Depending upon the experimental condition, the reservists were led to believe that this individual was either higher or lower than they in military rank, and they were given an opportunity to communicate back to him. Not surprisingly, there was less intense aggression communicated to the instigator when the subjects believed he was higher in military rank than when they thought he had a lower rank. The level of authoritarianism in the subjects (i.e., the degree to which they were concerned with status and power), assessed at the start of the experiment, was positively related to the intensity of their aggression to the instigator, but only when he supposedly had a low rank. Highly authoritarian reservists expressed the most intense hostility toward the low-ranked instigator, perhaps because they were the ones most strongly annoyed with this individual's insulting behavior.

A low-status person's behavior toward high-status group members obviously will depend, at least in part, upon the degree to which the latter can control the former's upward mobility. A. R. Cohen (1958) experimentally established differences in status (defined in terms of the stated importance and prestige of the job) in groups of college freshmen. In addition, he told the low-status members either that they would remain in their unfavorable position throughout the experiment or that they had a chance of moving up to the high-status job. The high-status members would be the ones determining whether this upward movement would take place. As we would expect, the low-status people who thought they might gain the more desirable position if the high-status members were favorable to them were less critical of these high-status people in the communications they sent to them than were the low-status members who could not move upward. The mobile low-status subjects probably were somewhat less frustrated than the comparable nonmobile subjects, but they undoubtedly also had stronger inhibitions against hostility toward the powerful high-status people.

Inhibitions against aggression probably also account for Scott's (1948) failure to obtain increased aggression by animals following frustration. The experiment was conducted employing goats having a well-established dominance-submission order in competing for food. Pairs of goats were fed at a time, and the dominant pair member always chased the subordinate one away. The experimenter believed this situation should have provoked the subordinate goat, if the frustration-aggression hypothesis was correct. Instead, this animal did not fight. Later, when food was taken away from the entire flock, aggression did increase but only by the dominant goats. Scott argued that frustration gives rise to aggressive actions *only* [italics mine] when "the individual has a habit of being aggressive" (Scott, 1958, p. 34).

The present writer does not agree that this is the only condition under which frustration elicits aggressive responses. Hostile tendencies could have been inhibited in the subordinate animals as the result of their anticipations of punishment by the dominant goats. Scott's own data suggest this. The subordinate goats did become aggressive when they were paired with even more subordinate animals in the competition-for-food situation. Since they now were dominant over the other pair members, only relatively weak fear was aroused and their aggressive inclinations were revealed in overt behavior. *Frustration produces hostile responses, but other cues in the situation, such as the presence of a dominant or high-status person, may evoke tendencies incompatible with aggression which, if strong enough, can inhibit the hostile responses.*

*Disapproval from Others.* These cues do not have to be very prominent in order to affect the likelihood of adults' aggressive actions. In many instances all there need be is some slight sign of disapproval from others, and the adult will cut off a hostile remark he had intended to make. Most people value and seek to gain the good opinions of others, even if these others are strangers but particularly if they are attractive for one reason or another. Anticipations of disapproval from other people, therefore, are expectations of punishment and can evoke inhibitions against aggressive responses. Sometimes all that is needed to produce these inhibitions is a lack of reinforcement for hostile behaviors, such as other people demonstrating they have no interest in the person's aggressive remarks. Bandura, Lipsher, and Miller (1960) showed how relatively subtle cues of nonreinforcement can inhibit verbal hostility even in largely permissive psychotherapy situations. They analyzed the content of 110 psychotherapy interviews conducted by 12 different therapists and found that the patients tended to drop the hostility topic or change the object of their hostility when the therapists displayed an "avoidance reaction" to these comments.

The affiliation drive generally runs counter to the instigation to aggression. The person who desires pleasant social relationships with others obviously will refrain from engaging in behaviors likely to incur their disapproval. He certainly will not aggress directly against them, and he may even inhibit all overt hostility. Open aggression usually is frowned on in our middle-class society. People concerned with winning friends will therefore typically hide their aggressive inclinations to the extent that they have been successfully socialized. Gordon and Cohn (1961) found that such affiliation-engendered restraints against aggression occur even in four- and five-year-old nursery school children. In their study a group induced to become aware of social relationships (i.e., whose affiliation drive presumably was aroused experimentally) did not exhibit the rise in aggressive responses in the second session of doll-play interviews that was displayed by a nonaffiliation-concerned control group.

## Situational Conditions Weakening Inhibitions against Aggression

*Increasing the Strength of the Instigation to Aggression.* Separating out the effects of social variables upon aggressive behavior is a complicated matter. An unusually high level of hostility displayed in an interpersonal setting is not necessarily due only to the weakening of inhibitions. Aggressive tendencies can be strengthened by nonaggressive drives. Sargent (1948) had this in mind when he objected to the oversimplified contention that all aggression had its origin in frustrations. Group or cultural standards may prescribe hostile behavior as the appropriate way of acting in certain situations, he pointed out. A Sioux warrior or a youngster growing up in a city slum area may have learned that he has to attack his group's enemies, whether they are members of other tribes or rival street gangs, if he is to gain full approval from the others in his group. This hostility need not be stimulated by anger; it can be carried out in order to attain some valued goal, perhaps acceptance by the group, or even self-approval.

If anger is present in such instances, we can say the social influence has increased the strength of the individual's instigation to aggression. The drive for approval presumably adds to the impetus provided by whatever anger the young group members might feel. Floyd Allport's (1924) concept of "social facilitation" presents another way in which behavioral tendencies could be enhanced by stimulation from others. He believed crowds operate to heighten existing predispositions, as well as to lower inhibitions, through providing stimuli to which people had been conditioned to respond. Any given crowd member is set to behave in a particular fashion—in a lynch mob, for example, to attack someone. Because of the suggestible state he presumably is in, his actions and emotions supposedly are easily aroused or strengthened by the sight and sound of the people around him apparently with similar inclinations. The crowd furnishes cues automatically evoking actions from the individual members. According to Allport, social facilitation involves an increase in response strength rather than the reduction of inhibitions.

Bandura, Ross, and Ross (1961) put forth an essentially similar notion when they hypothesized that the aggressive actions of the people around an individual can provide cues evoking a relatively high level of aggressive behavior from him and also shaping the exact form of these responses. Nursery school children in this study were subjected to mild frustrations and then were given an opportunity to watch an adult play with some toys. In the *nonaggressive* condition the adult behaved in a quiet and subdued manner. By contrast, in the *aggressive* condition the adult exhibited a great deal of unusual aggressive behavior, performing novel acts of physical aggression toward a "Bobo doll," interspersed with verbally hostile remarks. The youngsters given the opportunity to observe the aggressive model later acted in a very hostile fashion when placed in a new situation (although the adult was present). They reproduced reliably more of the unusual hostile behavior than did frustrated control children, while the preschoolers in the nonaggressive group made fewer of these novel acts than did the controls. The youngsters clearly had imitated the particular actions of the adult model. Bandura et al. found, however, that this imitation was influenced by the sex roles of the children and the adult. Both male and female subjects imitated physically aggressive acts to a greater degree when the model was a male rather than a female, and boys were more imitative of physical aggression than were girls but did not differ from them in the imitation of verbal aggression. These limitations presumably arose because physical aggression was regarded as appropriate for males but not for females. Actions of other people can evoke particular responses from an individual when these responses are regarded as consistent with the individual's and the other's usual social roles, and perhaps (since the children were somewhat angered) when the person is already predisposed to make fairly similar responses.

*Reduced Fear of Being Punished Resulting from the Presence of Others.* Theoretically, social effects may lower inhibitions against aggression by reducing fear. Stimulation from others can make a person less anxious when he is faced with a potentially dangerous situation. This can come about directly and obviously; people may convince him there is little real danger in the situation. Or the stimulation may be more subtle and indirect. The mere presence of other people at times seems to provide the person with additional courage. There is an indication of this in research with children and animals. Frightened children often become less fearful when a familiar adult draws near (Arsenian, 1943), and an analogous process seems to take place with young monkeys. In one study (Mason, 1960), young monkeys showed fewer signs of emotional distress when in the presence of a peer who was similar to other monkeys with whom they had been raised than when a strange adult monkey or rabbit was nearby.

The presence of other people, therefore, might weaken the individual's fear of being punished by the target of his aggression. Consistent with such a possibility, experimental evidence does indicate that social support can increase the level of overt hostility toward some frustrater. Nevertheless, there is a question whether this is always due to greater courage in the social situation, i.e., less fear of punishment from *anyone*.

Stotland (1959) compared the reactions of subjects to a frustrating supervisor when they were either (1) working alone or (2) able to meet occasionally with other subjects working on the same task. The subjects who could talk with their peers later expressed stronger overt hostility toward the frustrater than did the subjects working entirely alone, but this difference does not seem to stem from an increased bravery in the former group of subjects. Rather, the discussion between the peers apparently heightened the subjects' confidence in their own opinions. Each individual now had another reference person, besides the supervisor, who could support his beliefs, help him solve the task's problems, and otherwise help make him independent of the threatening supervisor. The subjects in the "alone" situation may have been less hostile because they had to accept the supervisor as a reference person and thus actually were less frustrated by his attacks on their views. Strongly held opinions *of their own* were not being thwarted to any great degree.

Another experiment carried out almost two decades before this study also reports findings appearing to indicate a lessening of fear under social conditions (M. E. Wright, 1943). Pairs of nursery school children, grouped in terms of whether they were "strong" or "weak" friends, were frustrated during play activities by the adult experimenter. The pairs of strong friends were more likely to express aggression against their frustrater, even to the extent of kicking and biting him. There is little direct evidence as to just why these results were obtained, however. It is conceivable that the children assembled with strong friends dared to aggress against the adult because they assumed the friends felt as they did about attacking him. Further, the children with a great deal of liking for each other may have influenced each other more strongly so that they came to agree that hostility toward the adult was morally proper. This shared definition of the propriety of aggression reduced guilt. But in neither case is it necessary to postulate that the children grouped with a strong friend automatically had less fear of punishment from the adult.

If a person *is* less afraid when a friend is nearby, this may be the result of his believing that the friend will help him overcome the danger. Friendship implies obligations as far as most of us are concerned; friends have to aid each other. It may be only to the extent that such a perception exists that a person will be more confident of the outcome when he enters a danger situation with a close friend. The threat is not less real, but he believes he has a better chance of mastering the danger if this friend will help him.

*Acceptance of Aggressive Behavior in Cohesive Groups.* We feel free to "let down our hair" to our friends. We can say things to them we might be reluctant to admit to strangers. Our friends, we believe, will not disapprove of what we tell them and may even agree with us. This also holds for exhibitions of hostility. People assembled with others they like and who like them should be relatively unafraid of disapproval for any hostile remarks they might make. Pepitone and Reichling (1955) manipulated the degree of liking each subject (a male college student) had for the other member of his two-man group so that there were high-liking (highly cohesive) and low-liking (low cohesive) pairs. A relatively low-status instigator acted in an unjust, arbitrary, and insulting manner toward each group, after which he left the experimental room. Unknown to the subjects, an observer recorded their behavior from behind a one-way mirror. The members of the highly cohesive groups were significantly less restrained in their behavior than were the members of the low-liking pairs. They were physically more active and also expressed a greater volume of hostility toward their frustrater and the experiment. Being with a highly liked person instead of with someone less well liked apparently lowered the subjects' restraints. They may have believed the other pair member had similar feelings toward the instigator and the unpleasant experiment or would readily understand these feelings. Furthermore, as mentioned above, in thinking another person shared these feelings, the feelings were no longer "wrong." For all these reasons, the members of the high-liking pairs probably did not fear disapproval for expressing their hostility, nor did they anticipate guilt for such actions.

The lowering of inhibitions resulting from high liking among group members also can result in a high level of overt conflict within the group. People belonging to highly cohesive groups may feel relatively free to show their momentary annoyances with other members of the group. They do not have to be polite to these others all the time. French (1944), in the experiment described in the preceding chapter, studied two types of groups working under conditions in which the members were likely to see each other as frustraters. In one type of group the members had known each other for some time, while the subjects in the remaining groups did not have this history of previous contact. The observers recorded significantly more open aggression toward other members in the long-established, "organized" groups than in the newly formed, "unorganized" groups, perhaps because the higher liking produced by the greater degree of acquaintance had lowered the members' inhibitions against displaying aggression. Again, we can assume the subjects in the more cohesive groups did not anticipate as much punishment, such as disapproval, from the others for any hostility they might direct to them.

Interestingly enough, other experimental research cited in the previous chapter implies that this hostility, under some conditions, actually can cause greater discomfort in the victim the more strongly attracted he initially is to his attacker. This discomfort, however, presumably comes about primarily when the aggression is interpreted as indicating the probable disintegration of previously pleasant and important relationships. Members of long-lived groups, knowing each other well, undoubtedly are relatively slow to take every aggressive act from others in the group as a sign of this breakup. (If these acts are ambiguous enough they may not even be seen as hostile because of the perceptually distorting effect of friendliness toward the instigator.) A person may feel freer to criticize an old friend than a stranger, and this friend, in turn, probably is not as quick as the new acquaintance would be to take the criticism as a serious attack upon their relationship.

As I proposed earlier, the member of a cohesive group may have a greater willingness to exhibit aggression than the person belonging to a less attractive group because he is more likely to assume the others around him generally share his feelings and opinions. If they do have similar views he can be more certain his own feelings are correct and proper (Festinger, 1954) and need not be too afraid the other group members will disapprove of his actions. Strickland, Jones, and Smith (1960) led some of their subjects, taken singly, to believe two peers held the same opinions they had on a particular issue, while the remaining subjects were given the impression they lacked this support from these peers. Following this, each subject heard another person, whom they had rated earlier, disparage his opinion in an insulting manner. This attack produced greater overt unfriendliness toward the antagonist in the subjects believing their views on the issue were supported by their peers than in the subjects not perceiving this support. The experimenters hypothesized that this may be due in part to the greater conviction in the former subjects that their opinions were correct. The attacks upon them would be a greater thwarting in this case. However, there is an additional possibility suggested by other data from the study. The subjects made their final ratings of the antagonist under two conditions: "publicly," for the other group members to see, and "privately," supposedly for the experimenter only. Only 44 per cent of the subjects who thought their group shared their opinion on the issue under discussion were less hostile to the antagonist publicly than privately, while a reliably greater 80 per cent of the subjects who believed their fellow members did not hold similar views were less hostile in public than in private. The subjects who thought their peers agreed with them apparently generally assumed these others also would be annoyed by the attack they had received, or at least would not frown on counter aggression toward the person disparaging their opinions.

The effects just described should be differentiated from any emotional support cohesive groups might (or might not) provide for their members. The presence of familiar people at times may enable the individual to better withstand stress, as we already have noted. But this does not necessarily mean the relatively strong aggression that members of attractive groups often direct toward their frustraters stems from less intense anxiety about punishment from *any* agency supposedly automatically resulting from membership in such groups. Available evidence indicates this high level of hostility can arise from (1) influence from other group members to attack the frustrater, i.e., heightened instigation to aggression, and/or (2) the person's beliefs that the other group members can and will help him overcome the dangers of retaliatory aggression, much as he may be obliged to aid them in *their* fights, and/or (3) judgments that the other members of the attractive group would not disapprove of the individual for engaging in aggressive behavior, lessening the fear of punishment for hostility, but only with respect to punishment from the fellow group members, and/or (4) judgments that the hostile acts are socially proper because the other group members seemed to be agreed this aggressive behavior is "correct."

*Judgments of the Ethical Propriety of Aggressive Behavior.* This last effect deserves some additional comments. Social psychological research has shown that group members perceiving a high degree of consensus within their groups as to what opinions are correct or what course of behavior is desirable are more likely to adopt these opinions or carry out these actions than are people who believe their group is not in agreement on these matters (e.g., see Pelz, 1958). Thus, if a person thinks all his fellow group members would approve of his hostile actions in a particular situation, he may interpret this behavior as being morally correct. At the very least he will not see himself as committing a serious crime. Any inhibitions he might have against performing immoral acts would be nullified or weakened, and the aggressive behavior is more likely to occur. Allport's (1924) analysis of mob behavior, mentioned earlier, incorporated this type of phenomenon. Each member of a mob, he hypothesized, has an "impression of universality" arising from the projection of his own feelings onto the others around him, which causes him to believe everyone feels as he does. His own inclinations then become "morally necessary and right." He sees nothing wrong in lynching the intended victim. This action may even be regarded as necessary to the welfare of the community—everyone, he thinks, agrees this is so.

*Anonymity.* There is one aspect of crowd behavior that Allport did not stress sufficiently. Any given individual in the crowd perceives himself as just one of many. These other people do more than define his desires as socially "proper"; being many, they also help wrap the cloak of anonymity around him. He cannot be held accountable for any wrongdoings if the perpetrators of these actions cannot be identified by police or even other members of the community. As a result, inhibitions against hostile tendencies are weakened further. His actions are "right," and even if they are not, he cannot be caught and punished. Festinger, Pepitone, and Newcomb (1952) pointed out that this feeling of anonymity may help account for much of the riotous activities of American Legionnaires at their national conventions. They are away from their homes in a city where no one knows them and where they are part of a large and perceptually homogeneous mass. It therefore is safe to indulge in certain activities they normally would have to suppress. Festinger and his colleagues established a situation in which college students were encouraged to make hostile remarks about their parents to the others in their group. Active discussions were started and the students were not always able to say who had made what remarks when they were asked to make such identifications at the end of the session. The data indicate that the students' inhibitions against attacking their parents were weaker the less well they could identify the authors of the comments made during their discussion, and presumably, the more anonymous they felt in the group.

The behavior of the convention-goers in the above illustration and the subjects in the Festinger et al. experiment clearly implies that many "socially proper" actions are substantially and crucially supported by the desire to avoid disapproval from others. This seems to be particularly true for those responses controlling sexual and aggressive urges. We normally learn to limit our opportunities for satisfying these drives, but this learning apparently is somewhat ineffective in many of us. If a sufficiently "aroused" person can obtain satisfactions (getting a sexual partner if he is sexually stimulated or a suitable target for aggression if he is angry) without becoming concerned about the propriety of this behavior, and without being frowned on by people important to him, there is a good chance he will take the opportunity even though in other situations he knows such behavior is "wrong."[1] Perhaps this is due almost entirely to the strong and persistent nature of sexual and aggressive drives. However, it also may be that the control over sexual and aggressive inclinations is inadequate in many people, i.e., breaks down when they believe they are anonymous, because of the particular training methods their parents had employed in teaching them to limit their sexual and aggressive activities. As I indicated earlier, training based upon threats of punishment seems to require the almost constant supervision of the punishing agencies if the disapproved actions are to be kept inhibited. But whatever the reason for making these often socially "improper" responses, there is evidence many of us will engage in sexual and/or aggressive activities if we (1) are aroused, and (2) believe we will not be punished, and/or (3) are not concerned about whether this behavior is morally correct.

*Situational Permissiveness.* Punishment, of course, will not be forthcoming if the people who can produce pain in the individual are permissive as well as if they are not nearby. The person who thinks "anything goes," who does not anticipate punishment for his behavior from the others around him, may exert relatively little self-control over his actions if his desires become fairly strong. He may see these others as permissive because of their particular relationship to him. They can be friends who are obliged to forgive his transgressions or perhaps people

---

[1] It is important to point out that this is most likely to occur when his inhibitions are weak—for example, when he has had a few drinks—or when he has been influenced by a high degree of consensus in the actions of the others around him. In both cases, we also can say, the individual does not think of whether these actions are right or wrong. This problem does not occur to him.

who have lower social status and less power than he does. A person with extremely high status in his group often feels he is under less pressure to conform to the approved behavioral standards of the group than does someone with only moderate status (Dittes & Kelley, 1956; Harvey & Consalvi, 1960), but this may hold only when these status differences are relatively secure and permanent (Berkowitz & Macauley, 1961). Or the situation can be permissive by agreement, explicit or implicit, among the people in it.

At least two experiments demonstrate that increases in the permissiveness of social situations can be followed by heightened aggressiveness. This is seen, for example, in the famous White and Lippitt (1960) study of the effects of "authoritarian," "laissez-faire," and "democratic" leadership upon the behavior of young boys. Some of the groups placed under the authoritarian leadership developed a submissive, almost apathetic, reaction to their adult leaders in which hostility was largely inhibited. On two of the three occasions in which such groups emerged from the repressive atmosphere of autocracy into the more permissive democratic or laissez-faire climates, the investigators reported, "the first day of freedom was marked by an especially large amount of aggressive behavior" (p. 76).

The experimental children in the previously cited study by Chasdi and Lawrence (1955) were scolded for any hostile responses they made during the second of their doll-play sessions, but were not reprimanded for these actions in the remaining two sessions. The punishment for aggression in the experimental condition did not eliminate hostile responses from the children's behavior repertoire. Their overt aggressiveness increased fairly rapidly in the last two permissive sessions so that the level of this behavior rose close to the level exhibited in the nonpunished control group. The control children also tended to increase in overt hostility from the first to the last two sessions. This seems to be a fairly consistent finding in studies using doll-play measures of hostile tendencies (e.g., Bach, 1945; Levin & Turgeon, 1957; Yarrow, 1948), suggesting that the children in this type of play situation eventually learn they will not be punished for displaying aggression.

*Inhibitions against Aggression in Projective Tests.* These last results carry an important lesson for the personality tester. Psychologists frequently assume (1) that instigations such as sex or aggression are constantly operative within the individual, and if they are not revealed openly in his everyday behavior, will still be active "unconsciously," and (2) that these unconscious tendencies are readily manifested in fantasy activities, such as the Rorschach, TAT, or doll play. The above findings, and other evidence as well, indicate, however, that this last assumption at least is not entirely correct. Inhibitions learned in the home or school also can be operative to some extent in situations as far removed from "reality" as fantasy or projective tests. As we shall see in the next chapter, these restraints tend to decrease in strength the less similar the eliciting situation is to the situation in which the inhibitions were learned. Nevertheless, they can detract somewhat from the strength of the responses they oppose even in projective-test situations. In the doll-play studies inhibitions against aggression apparently were elicited in these children at first, even though somewhat weakly. It was not until their anticipations of punishment for aggression were weakened by persistent nonpunishment that the full strength of their hostile tendencies could become truly apparent.

If a person has developed extremely strong inhibitions against expressing aggression, he is not likely to display hostility readily either in fantasy tasks or in "real life." Theoretical analyses to be discussed more fully later, together with supporting research, indicate that as these restraints weaken the aggressive tendencies will be manifested in the fantasy tasks before they show up in the naturalistic setting. Bach (1945) compared the doll-play activities of two groups of nursery school children, one rated by their teachers as normally extremely aggressive in the school setting and the other rated by them as being much less aggressive characteristically. However, all is not as it appears on the surface, particularly in the case of children who seem to be especially nonaggressive. This latter group seems to have been low in overt hostility more because of strong inner restraints against aggression than because of actually weak aggressive tendencies. Their strong inhibitory habits were still operative in the first doll-play session, and the strong aggression group exhibited more doll-play aggression than they did at this time. The restraints against hostility gradually weakened, however, as the permissiveness of the play situation became clear. The children who had been regarded by their teachers as low in aggression showed a sharper increase in hostile responses over the sessions than did the other group, so that by the fourth session they actually had higher aggressive scores than did the strong aggression children. Feshbach (1956) obtained comparable results with somewhat older boys, five to eight years of age.

Although these investigators did not test the possibility, the chances are the children continued to exhibit their preexperimental differences in hostility after the termination of the play sessions. The previously highly aggressive group probably still displayed more overt hostility in their daily living than did the supposedly less aggressive group. The strong inhibitions against aggressive responses in the latter children had weakened sufficiently so these responses could be made by the end of the experiment in the fantasy situation. But the inhibitory habits presumably were still strong enough to prevent openly hostile acts from occurring in situations resembling the home environment.

This last point has another important implication for the personality tester. If inhibitions are weaker in the projective-test situation than in more naturalistic settings, the responses a person makes to the test might not be the sort of responses he would reveal in a social situation. Inhibitory tendencies are too strong in the latter situation. Thus, the personality test data would not predict actual behavior in interpersonal settings (R. R. Sears, 1951b). Bandura and Walters (1959), in a study to be reported more fully later, demonstrated just this pattern. Highly aggressive boys in their investigation apparently did not exhibit more overt hostility toward their fathers than did a matched group of relatively nonaggressive youngsters. Strong inhibitory tendencies effectively squelched aggressive behavior toward the fathers in both groups. However, when the boys were placed in a fantasy situation by asking them to respond to a thematic test, the hostile inclinations could be revealed. Inhibitions weakened, and the aggressive group expressed more fantasy aggression toward their fathers than did the control group.

This type of phenomenon probably accounts for the failure of several researchers to uncover any relationships between hostility themes on the TAT and measures of hostile behavior in social settings. Mussen and Naylor (1954) realized that the subjects employed in these studies, middle-class boys and girls, probably had learned relatively strong restraints against aggression. Lower-class culture in our society, on the other hand, supposedly does not develop such strong inhibitions against hostility. Consequently, any aggressive tendencies lower-class children show on the personality test, they hypothesized, also are likely to be exhibited in overt behavior. Consistent with this notion, the investigators obtained a significant positive association between the number of aggressive TAT themes given by twenty-four lower-class juvenile delinquents and ratings of their overt aggressiveness. Since these youngsters did not have strong, internally driven tendencies inhibiting hostility, their habitual aggressive responses were revealed in social situations almost as readily as they were evoked in the fantasy task.

Generally, the strength of the individual's overtly hostile responses should parallel the strength of the hostile responses he makes to a projective test, when the people about him who are capable of administering rewards and punishments permit or encourage aggressive behavior. The hostility he shows in real life will not "gibe" with his fantasy hostility if the important people about him punish aggressive behavior. Perhaps the best evidence for this reasoning comes from a study conducted by Lesser (1952). This psychologist obtained a significant $+.43$ product-moment correlation between fantasy aggression scores and reputation among peers for overt aggression for twenty-three elementary school boys whose mothers, when interviewed, indicated they were relatively supportive of aggression. The correlation was negative ($-.41$) in the case of twenty-one boys whose mothers said they discouraged aggression.

### *Attitudes toward Aggression as a Factor in the Inhibition of Aggression*

*Aggression as Morally "Wrong."* The previous studies deal largely with the effects of an individual's reactions to other people upon the hostility he exhibits. But these responses to others are not the only determinants of the behavior a person instigated to aggression actually will display. He also may inhibit his hostile tendencies because of his own attitudes or general reactions to such behavior. Guilt feelings would arise if he were aware that he had violated his strong internal standards of conduct condemning aggressive behavior, and he attempts to avoid this guilt arousal. Religious groups, such as Quakers, provide the most obvious illustration of this. Believing that physical violence is ethically unjustifiable, strong adherents of these groups try to "turn the other cheek" when they are provoked. Their hostile tendencies, we might conjecture, are frequently inhibited by their general attitude toward aggressive behavior. Hostility is always "bad," they feel, and must be restrained under all circumstances.

Since the present chapter is concerned mainly with situationally induced inhibitions, these fairly stable attitudes toward aggression will not be discussed here at length. It should be pointed out, however, that external cues can have an important effect on the operation of these attitudes. A person who is deeply attached to a particular group still may on occasion depart behaviorally from its norms because he does not think of the group and its norms at these times (Charters & Newcomb, 1958). A Quaker suffering a series of strong provocations conceivably can forget himself. The strain of the situation might momentarily eliminate his group membership and its ethical standards from his awareness so that he could easily strike out at his frustraters. But then, should he somehow be reminded of his beliefs regarding violence, or of his membership in a group that disapproves of aggression, the inhibitory attitude would be restored to full strength, and his hostile tendencies would be restrained. Situational cues can provide these reminders. Someone might make a remark about his group membership, or he may see something that calls his ethical beliefs to mind.

Similarly, the nature of the situation may determine whether a person's moral standards are pushed out of awareness. Crowds can have this effect. People in mobs often act as if they have been robbed of their sense of right and wrong. Some writers have suggested that critical thinking is inhibited in crowds, resulting in the crowd members being "carried away" by their desires and inclinations. What we may have here is a highly selective narrowing of consciousness. The individual crowd or mob member is almost literally bombarded with prolonged and intense stimulation from the external world. As a consequence, he responds almost exclusively to these external stimuli and is distracted from attending to opposing internal stimuli—if they are aroused at all. The participant in a lynch mob, for example, may be so intensely "focused" upon the momentary features of the mob situation—the shouting, the excitement, the talk of the "terrible crime" just committed— that his moral attitudes are not evoked in the situation, and even if they are, are not given any attention. Phenomenologically, he thinks only of the people around him and the "injustice" that must be eliminated, without stopping to consider (i.e., respond to) any other aspects of the situation.

*Judgments of Particular Aggression-arousing Situations.* Earlier, I had suggested that frustrated people may attempt to inhibit their hostile reactions when they perceive the frustration as nonarbitrary or justified (see Rothaus & Worchel, 1960). In a sense, they might regard any hostility on their part under these conditions as unreasonable if not immoral. We feel it is wrong to attack someone who *had* to be a frustrater because of the nature of the situation or the rules governing his actions.

But similarly, many people apparently also believe they should not be aggressive toward anyone who could not help being a frustrater because of his personality disturbances. This is indicated in an experiment by Jones, Hester, Farina, & Davis (1959). Pairs of college women heard another woman criticize and insult one of the pair members. Half of these pairs had been led to believe previously that this derogator was emotionally "maladjusted," while the others had been informed she was "well adjusted."

Ratings of the derogator demonstrated that the bystander and the victim of her hostility had reacted somewhat differently to her. The nature of these responses, however, varied with the information regarding her level of adjustment. The people who were not themselves attacked seemed to be able to forgive her aggression readily, at least in terms of what they said about her, when they believed she was emotionally disturbed. Perhaps they felt her maladjustment meant she was not altogether responsible for her behavior and so, in this condition, they were reluctant to rate her too unfavorably. The direct targets of this woman's aggression evidently also took her supposed illness into consideration.

Thus, while her victims expressed more open hostility toward her than did the bystanders when the woman presumably was well, they were not more hostile toward her when she was regarded as maladjusted.[2]

Aggressive acts also may be "bad" if they interfere with progress toward some goal. We usually refrain from attacking powerful, high-status people, it was pointed out earlier, because they often can seriously affect our chances of attaining certain rewards. This aggression would be costly to us, and in this sense, is punishing. Overt aggression also will be avoided in some situations, however, because it may be costly to other people toward whom we feel some sense of responsibility. Group members often make an effort to smooth over any outbursts of aggression arising during their meetings (Zander, 1958). Such hostility is literally interpersonal friction, which interferes with rapid and efficient group problem-solving. Most of the people in the group, of course, would want to eliminate such friction so that they themselves can obtain whatever goals they wanted to reach in the group situation. But there may be another factor also operating to produce this "smoothing over" in some cases. Research has indicated (e.g., Berkowitz & Daniels, 1963; Thomas, 1957) that many people in our society develop a sense of responsibility toward others who are dependent upon them (assuming these others are not disliked). For example, if Joe Smith believed another individual's likelihood of getting some valuable reward was dependent upon his (Smith's) high productivity in work, this feeling of responsibility toward the other apparently will tend to increase Smith's work output. A similar sense of responsibility toward others in the group may cause any one member to go out of his way to minimize those hostile outbursts that could be costly to the group.

*Strength of Aggressive Tendencies and Aggression Anxiety.* For one reason or another, then, whether this behavior is costly or a violation of moral standards, aggression is often defined as "bad," as something to be avoided. There actually may be two codes of conduct operating

---

[2] Some people undoubtedly would show a degree of "understanding" in this situation. Realizing that the hostile individual behaves this way to almost everyone, they might not take the aggression directed toward them as a personal affront, and thus, their self-esteem drive would suffer little thwarting. However, it seems to me that relatively few people would show such complete understanding. Few of us are trained so thoroughly in the tenets of psychological determinism that we never attribute *any* personal responsibility to an individual for his actions, or assume that the hostility directed to us has absolutely nothing to do with us. But I do believe that many people, particularly those with a college education, have absorbed enough of these deterministic notions to feel that they *should not* criticize the failings of the emotionally disturbed. It is fairly easy to regard psychotics (or other very extreme cases) as being "not responsible" for their actions, however, and the hostile behavior these people may direct to us may actually provoke little anger.

here, one for young children and one for adults. Many parents tell their children it is permissible for a boy to hit a bully. But they also are likely to believe, particularly if they are members of the middle and upper classes in our society, that they themselves, as adults, should not strike another physically. A polite snub or a cutting remark may be proper on occasion, but "civilized" adults do not punch each other on the nose.

There are important theoretical principles that can be used to account for this phenomenon (i.e., response generalization and conflicting response tendencies), but these will have to be discussed in the next chapter. In the meantime, let us note what seems to be involved here. Middle-class adults apparently anticipate stronger punishment or disapproval (from themselves or others)[3] for any strong aggressive responses they might make than for milder acts of hostility. Assuming that anxiety is the result of these expectations, this would suggest the following hypothesis: *The strength of an individual's aggressive tendencies is directly associated with the intensity of the aggression anxiety subsequently aroused in him to the extent that he anticipates punishment or disapproval for aggression.* To illustrate, suppose that Mr. Jones is angered by, say, a "nonarbitrary" frustration and there are other people watching him whose good opinion he values. He knows they will disapprove of any hostile actions he might take and wants to avoid this disapproval. According to the present hypothesis, he will become more anxious the stronger the aggression inclinations aroused in him.

There is no good evidence bearing directly on this notion, but several experiments have findings at least consistent with it. Before introducing the first of these studies, however, there is one point that should be made explicit. Aggression is inhibited because it can lead to painful consequences. If the individual anticipates that other response tendencies also will result in punishment or disapproval, they undoubtedly will suffer a similar fate. In other words, there is nothing unique about aggression here; the important thing about this behavior as far as inhibitions are concerned is the anticipated outcome. This being the case, our knowledge of the conditions affecting the inhibition of other classes of responses, such as sexual behavior, probably can also be applied to the study of conditions inhibiting aggression.

We will make this assumption in dealing with the first experiment to be reported here. In this study, R. A. Clark (1955) sought to develop

[3] If the individual is instigated to action that he knows is a serious departure from his behavioral standards, guilt would be anticipated and this could prevent the action from occurring. Both anticipation of guilt arousal and anticipation of punishment from others are here said to produce aggression anxiety for simplicity of phraseology.

TAT measures of the intensity of the instigation to sexual behavior. College men in an experimental group were sexually aroused by showing them pictures of nude women, and their responses to the projective test were compared with the stories told by a nonaroused control group. Surprisingly, analysis of these stories showed there actually were *fewer* sexual themes in the protocols of the experimental group than in the control group records. Clark hypothesized that the aroused subjects had become anxious about expressing manifestly sexual responses. Strongly instigated to actions violating their moral standards (and which also might bring disapproval from others), they apparently became so anxious they inhibited nearly all sexually tinged responses, including those sexual themes that ordinarily are expressed under low-arousal conditions. To test this explanation, the investigator established another aroused experimental condition, but this time in the context of a very permissive beer party. The alcohol and the permissiveness of the situation combined to weaken the inhibitions in this group of subjects, perhaps through decreasing the intensity of the anxiety reaction. As a result, they exhibited significantly more manifest sexual themes than either of the other groups. What seems to have happened, all in all, is that the strong arousal of socially disapproved tendencies (in this case, instigations to sexual behavior) produced a fairly intense anxiety reaction inhibiting a wide range of sexually associated responses. These responses could not become manifest until the anxiety was reduced. According to the present hypothesis, the arousal of strong hostile tendencies will evoke a similar anxiety reaction in a person anticipating punishment or disapproval (from himself or others) for aggressive behavior.

More directly relevant to our purposes, the presumed intense anxiety in Clark's first experimental group apparently led to an inhibition of aggressive as well as sexual responses to the TAT; this group had reliably fewer aggressive themes in their test protocols than did the control group. Furthermore, the hostility expressed in their stories, such as it was, seems to have been affected by inhibitions. Here Clark made use of findings obtained by some of his colleagues. Their research suggested that inhibited aggressive tendencies sometimes were revealed on the TAT by stories in which the aggressive agent was impersonal or vague. (Someone, for example, might be said to be killed or injured by an accident, animal, or illness.) Most of the hostility in the stories told by the first experimental group was attributed to such an impersonal source, while there were relatively few men in the control group who showed a high level of this inhibited aggression. The strong anxiety produced in the sexually aroused group, in other words, presumably inhibited aggressive as well as sexual themes to the TAT. It would be interesting to determine whether such extremely anxious people conform to social conventions in all respects.

Observations made by Alberta Siegel (1956) in the course of an experiment with nursery school children demonstrated a clear positive relationship between aggression and aggression anxiety. Pairs of like-sex children engaged in free play after watching a brief movie, with their behavior being scored for aggression and signs of guilt and anxiety (such as thumb-sucking, tics, and awkward and nervous movements). As we would expect, there was reliably more aggression in the boys' than in the girls' play. However, what is more relevant to our present concern, the boys also showed stronger indications of guilt and anxiety. Over all children, there was a significant positive correlation between the aggression- and guilt-anxiety scores. In general, then, the more hostile the youngster had been, the more intense and frequent were his signs of anxiety.

While there is no evidence in Siegel's study that the aggressive play had produced the aggression anxiety, findings in an experiment by Berkowitz and Holmes (1960) indicate that an aggression-anxiety reaction can follow strong anger arousal. The seventy-two subjects in this study, all female college students, were divided evenly among four experimental conditions differing in the nature and number of frustrations they received. Two frustrations were administered to the most strongly aroused group, the first by a peer and the second by the experimenter. All the subjects had several socially sanctioned opportunities to give this peer electric shocks (supposedly as a judgment of her work on each of a number of problems). As would be expected, the women who were frustrated twice administered more shocks than did the women in any other condition. The subjects then were subdivided further for analysis purposes in terms of the total number of shocks they had given the peer during the entire experiment, so that there was a comparatively highly aggressive—or strongly angered—group and one that was less aggressive and/or less strongly angered in each experimental condition.

What we are mainly concerned with here is the subjects' subsequent attitudes toward the peer following their electrical attacks upon her. Shortly after the beginning of the experiment each girl completed an attitude questionnaire in which she indicated her first impressions of the peer, and then she answered the same questions again at the end of the study. One of the items included in these questionnaires was a fairly direct measure of the subjects' level of friendliness toward the peer. It read, "Do you believe your partner was fair and right in her judgments?" A second item asked for the subjects' evaluation of the peer's work but without the implication of moral condemnation present in the former question: "How well do you think your partner did on these problems?"

Statistical analyses of the questionnaire data indicated many of the strongly aggressive subjects had experienced an aggression-anxiety-like reaction at about the time they filled out the second questionnaire. The women who were thwarted twice and then responded by giving their peer the greatest number of electric shocks were the only group whose expressed judgments of the peer's "fairness" was reliably *more favorable* at the end of the experiment than they had been at the start. They made the greatest attempt not to condemn her for unethical behavior. These subjects did not, however, undergo a "drainage" of all unfavorable feelings toward the peer; they also rated her work more unfavorably at the end of the session than did any other group.

This pattern of findings is readily interpretable from the present point of view. If these women had become greatly concerned about the hostility they had shown (and/or the anger they had felt) they probably would have attempted to mask any further displays of overt unfriendliness toward the peer, and thus, would not accuse her of being "unfair." It would have been helpful to them, however, if they could say her performance was poor. They were instructed to give electric shocks for inadequate work. An unfavorable evaluation of the peer's performance, therefore, justified the aggression they had expressed.

Other findings from the Berkowitz-Holmes (1960) study give us information about the time at which the presumed anxiety reaction took place. The subjects were to administer electric shocks on two occasions: after they were frustrated (or not frustrated) by the peer and/or the experimenter and *before* they completed the final questionnaire. The women receiving the two frustrations seemed to maintain their instigations to overt aggression with electric shocks at a more constant level during this relatively brief period than did the less angered subjects receiving fewer frustrations. The former showed a smaller decline from the first of these aggression occasions to the next in the number of shocks they administered than did the people who were thwarted by the peer but not the experimenter. Thus, *the arousal of strong aggressive tendencies in a person may delay the time at which he comes to anticipate punishment or disapproval for his aggression.* The subjects provoked twice could have been so angry with their peer they did not become fully aware of the moral and social implications of their behavior until relatively late, that is, not until they responded to the questionnaire.

Earlier research reported by Berkowitz (1960a) seems to be consistent with this reasoning. The college students in this experiment, both men and women, first exchanged written notes with a same-sexed peer. Half of the subjects received unpleasant, somewhat insulting messages from this person. Following this, the subjects evaluated the message sender on a series of rating scales, believing he was also rating them. They then were told that these evaluations would be exchanged, and the subjects were given the peer's supposed evaluations of them. Half of the people in both the provoked and unprovoked conditions received unfavorable (and unfriendly) evaluations of them from their peers, with the remaining subjects getting favorable (and friendlier) evaluations. Finally, some of the subjects in each of the four conditions resulting from these manipulations were asked to respond to four TAT cards. We will here concern ourselves only with these latter subjects. Questionnaire measures of the level of hostility toward the peer were obtained at three different times during the session: (1) at the very beginning before the notewriting, (2) immediately after this note-writing, and (3) after receiving the evaluations and responding to the TAT cards.

The psychological effects created by each condition must be understood. First, let us consider the people receiving unfavorable evaluations of themselves from their peers after getting the unfriendly messages. This group had the strongest and perhaps most justifiable aggressive inclinations. Not only had they been provoked twice (and anger effects presumably accumulate), but the peer's notes indicated he was an unpleasant person who might deserve being hurt. Thus for them, the aggression-anxiety reaction did not occur until fairly late. The magnitude of their increase in expressed unfriendliness to the peer following the insulting notes was *positively* correlated with the intensity of their subsequent hostile responses to the TAT. It was not until the time of the final questionnaire that the reaction took place in this group. The greater their TAT hostility, the reliably *friendlier* they became to the peer on the last questionnaire.

The situation is somewhat different for the group receiving the unfavorable evaluation from the peer after the friendly messages. Any anger in these subjects was relatively mild. But more than this, the poor evaluation might well have told those subjects who had increased in overt hostility to the peer after getting the friendly communications from him that this increased unfriendliness really was not justified. They could have felt that the peer rightfully objected to this sign of hostility. Not unexpectedly, these people tended to show the quickest aggression-anxiety-like reaction. The greater their increase in stated unfriendliness to the peer following the initial friendly notes, the significantly weaker was the hostility they displayed on the projective test. Their attitude turnabout, in other words, came about some time *before* taking the TAT, while this reaction did not take place until *after* the TAT in the former, more strongly aroused group. It is interesting to note that there was no indication at all of this type of attitude turnabout in the least-provoked condition, the treatment receiving friendly notes and the friendly evaluation. For them, increases in unfriendliness following these notes were reliably positively correlated with TAT hostility, and those people having the greatest level of TAT hostility then exhibited the greatest increase in unfriendliness after seeing the evaluation.

*Avoidance of the Anger Instigator.* There are a great many ways in which a person may attempt to reduce his anxiety. The women in the above-mentioned Berkowitz-Holmes experiment presumably sought to decrease aggression anxiety by making amends (i.e., saying the peer hadn't really been "unfair"), but nevertheless, still insisting that she had deserved the shocks she had received. On other occasions people might try to lower this anxiety by leaving the anxiety-producing situation. If the arousal of strong hostility ordinarily evokes fairly intense anxiety in most middle-class Americans, evoking strong anger also will impel these people to avoid both the frustrater and the instigating situation. There is a suggestion to this effect in research described by Thibaut and Coules (1952).

The subjects in this study, male undergraduates, were angered by sending them insulting notes, supposedly from a peer, in the course of an exchange of messages. Half of the subjects then were allowed to send notes back to this instigator (*communication* condition), while the remaining men were prevented from doing this by immediately giving them another task (*no communication* condition). Analysis of the written descriptions that the subjects composed of the insulting peer at the end of the experimental session showed that the men who had written back to the instigator were somewhat friendlier to him at this time than were the men in the *no communication* group. Other data obtained from a subsequent experiment also reported in this paper indicated, however, that this difference may have been caused by an increase in hostility following the blocking of communication rather than from a "cathartic" reduction of anger in the *communication* condition. This thwarting of communication back to the insulting peer seems to have increased the subjects' hostility "in spite of the fact that the instigator [was] not responsible for the interruption" (p. 773).

More important for our present purposes are the subjects' responses to a questionnaire administered at the end of the session (in the first experiment). The men were asked, among other things, whether they would like to continue with the notewriting. Ninety-five per cent of the *communication* group indicated they would like this, but only sixty per cent of the men who had been prevented from writing back to the instigator indicated a willingness to continue. This significant decrease in the proportion of people in the latter group who wished to remain in the *communication* situation apparently was not entirely due to the additional frustration they had suffered (i.e., not being able to send a message back to the peer after getting the insulting note). Thibaut and Coules found that answers to the "willingness to continue" item in the *no communication* condition were significantly and negatively related to the residual hostility scores obtained from the subjects' final description of the instigator's personality. The unfriendlier the people in this condition were to their peer, the greater was their stated desire to leave the situation. The investigators' conclusion here is consistent with the present thesis: As " . . . hostility increases, internalized tendencies to avoid aggression increase even more sharply" (p. 774).

Thibaut and Coules made an interesting extrapolation from this finding. Theodore Newcomb (1947) had formulated the concept of "autistic hostility" some years before this study, maintaining that hostile attitudes often remain unchanged because they lead to a breakdown in communication with the hated object. Such a state certainly would follow if the strength of the subjects' aggressiveness to the peer was directly related to the intensity of their desire to cease communicating with him, they pointed out. Disliking their frustrater, the subjects no longer would care to have anything to do with him and thus, would not learn more favorable things about him. As further support for the autistic hostility notion, they reported that the subjects' initial level of hostility toward their peer, as indicated by written "first impressions" of him composed at the start of the study, was negatively correlated with the volume of communications sent to the peer throughout the experiment. There are, of course, many possible explanations for these findings, but the present aggression-anxiety-avoidance hypothesis seems as reasonable as any. According to this contention, the subjects sought to cut off communications with a person who, they believed, might heighten their aggressive inclinations and therefore, would also increase their anxiety about this hostility.

Other means of aggression-anxiety reduction also are possible. To list only two, the individual may attempt to justify his hostile tendencies by insisting his frustrater deserved the injury done to him, or he may exhibit a "reaction formation" in which he "leans over backward," so to speak, in avoiding all semblances of aggression. As a result, an extremely wide range of aggressive responses is inhibited. Little is known about the factors determining which of these (or other) modes of lessening anxiety will occur. One reasonable guess is that the reaction-formation process arises because of extremely strong moral standards condemning practically all forms of hostility. But whatever the explanation, there seems to be little doubt that most adult members of the middle class seek to avoid anticipated punishment or disapproval for their aggression (i.e., they attempt to decrease aggression anxiety) by withdrawing from the anger-instigating person. The magnitude of this withdrawal tendency appears to be directly proportional to the strength of the aggressive responses evoked in the individual, and probably also to the extent that high "costs" are expected to be the consequence of any hostile behavior.

*Social Definition of the Propriety of Aggression.* Situational factors probably affect the extent to which an individual's aggressive behaviors provoke aggression anxiety within him. Under certain conditions a person can feel entirely unconcerned about his hostile actions. Some of these conditions were discussed earlier in this chapter. It was pointed out, for example, that our reaction to our own behavior frequently depends upon the degree to which other people about us define this behavior as appropriate or morally correct. A member of a lynch or riot mob believes aggression is justified and even morally necessary because "everyone" around him seems to share his hostile inclinations. Such socially mediated favorable evaluations of aggression reduce guilt reactions. This type of process probably was responsible for the earlier-mentioned increase in doll-play aggression as the permissiveness of the fantasy situation became clear to the children (e.g., Chasdi & Lawrence, 1955; P. Sears, 1951). The situational permissiveness defined aggression as ethically justified.

But we must be clear as to what this "permissiveness" entails. Alberta Siegel has emphasized that adult permissiveness frequently involves more than the lack of punishment. Children may regard an adult's failure to punish their aggressive behavior as, in fact, adult approval of such behavior. Thus, if a grown-up does nothing upon seeing them engage in actions whose propriety is somewhat dubious, it must mean, the children could well believe, that there really is nothing wrong with these actions. They previously had been punished for expressing hostility, but since punishment was not forthcoming now, aggression could not be so bad in this situation. The youngsters, in essence, have given the adult the role of "moral evaluator." He is their "superego," and they themselves presumably need not bother about the correctness of their behavior.

Siegel employed this reasoning to explain findings that, at first glance, appeared to contradict the Iowa doll-play results. In her first investigation (1957), the social play of like-sex pairs of nursery school children was observed in two sessions a week apart, with the observers stationed behind a one-way vision screen so the children were unaware they were being watched. Unlike the earlier doll-play studies, this research showed a *decrease* in overt aggression from the first session to the next. What must have happened, Siegel maintained, was that the children in this situation had come to feel somewhat anxious about their aggressive behavior and consequently inhibited their later aggressive inclinations. The Iowa preschoolers, on the other hand, supposedly had "abdicated superego and ego control functions" to the watching adult experimenter. His persistently nonpunitive behavior had defined aggressions as "not wrong." In this more recent case, however, there was nothing in the situation to tell the nursery school children that certain specific hostile responses were permissible.

A second experiment (Siegel & Kohn, 1959), conducted to test this interpretation, yielded supporting evidence. Pairs of young children were observed playing with various toys for two sessions (although only one child in each pair was of concern to the experimenters). But this time half of the pairs played in the presence of a permissive adult, while there was no one else in the room with the remaining pairs. Consistent with Siegel's analysis, most of the preschoolers in the *adult-present* setting showed more aggression in the second session than in the first, but all of the subjects in the *adult-absent* condition exhibited a session 2 decrease in aggressive play with the toys. Levin and Turgeon (1957) have obtained essentially similar results with preschoolers in a two-session doll-play study. The first period involved only the child and the experimenter. However, the second session was watched either by the child's mother or by a strange adult. The presence of the mother produced a rise in aggressive play, while most of the youngsters showed less aggressive play if the strange adult was present. Levin and Turgeon, like Siegel, hypothesized that the child had transferred his "superego functions" to a familiar adult (the mother in their study) present in the situation. By being nonpunitive, this permissive adult had implicitly put her stamp of approval upon the morally ambiguous behavior, and conscience-driven inhibitions against hostile responses were weakened.

The children in this research may have used the watching adults as the reference for defining the propriety of hostile behavior because they themselves were too young to have firm, well-established standards of conduct. Nevertheless, many actions performed by adults are also susceptible to the same type of social influence. Adults often are not morally anxious about a particular act when they can believe *this* act was not wrong. Other people often aid the individual in making such a judgment; they may tell him, explicitly or implicitly, particular hostile acts of his are socially proper.

A person also may develop guilt reactions when he becomes concerned about the moral correctness of his aggressive behavior, i.e., when he applies his own evaluative standards to his actions. This self-evaluation of one's own behavior does not automatically come about in response to the behavior. The person can be so affected by the excitement around him he does not stop to think whether his acts are right or wrong. Such a phenomenon, of course, occurs in aggressive mobs.

Sometimes an individual's hostility may be so indirect he himself is not aware of what he has done. He does not feel guilty about his aggression because he does not consciously recognize it as hostility. This may be one reason why, as was proposed earlier, the intensity of anxiety-guilt reactions tends to be directly associated with the intensity and directness of aggressive acts; direct, intense hostility is more readily recognizable as *hostility*. Moreover, responses from other people may aid in the recognition of such actions. The individual hurt by the aggressive behavior, or the reactions of other observers, can provide feedback, telling the unknowing aggressor what it is he has done, and again, this feedback probably will be stronger and more informative the more direct and intense the aggression.

## SUMMARY

Aggressive actions are inhibited when the individual anticipates punishment for such behavior and/or believes that these hostile acts will violate the standards of conduct he wants to uphold. These two sources of inhibitions yield somewhat different reactions. Punishment generally is effective only when the punishing agent is in a position to learn of and punish deviations from his rules.

The strength of the inhibitions against aggression is a direct function of the amount of punishment anticipated for aggressive behavior so that with instigation to aggression held constant, overtly hostile behavior is less likely the stronger the expected punishment and the more probable the occurrence of this punishment. This principle affects the social relationships involved in the dominance hierarchies established in both animal and human groups. Just as animals learn to avoid attacking others of their own species who can punish their hostile actions, human beings learn that high status members of their groups often have the power to administer rewards and punishments to others lower in status. In both cases there is a strong tendency to avoid aggressing against other, more dominant (or higher status) species or group members. Human beings usually also avoid antagonizing those high status people who control the means to the goals they are pursuing.

Human beings fear more than physical punishment. They also seek to avoid the punishment arising from disapproval by others. Aggressive behavior is often inhibited when the individual believes such behavior will incur disapproval, particularly if the others who would disapprove are highly attractive to him.

Social influences can affect the likelihood of aggressive behavior in a number of different ways. Cues provided by other people may increase the strength of the individual's instigation and also weaken his inhibitions against displaying hostility. Research has shown that young children and monkeys have less fear when in strange surroundings if a member of the same species is present, but it is doubtful whether such an automatic fear-reduction process is responsible for every apparent heightening of overt hostility in social settings. Individuals assembled with attractive peers sometimes exhibit stronger overt aggression than people who are alone or who are grouped with less attractive peers. This difference can arise from (1) influence from the attractive group members to attack a given object, (2) expectations that the attractive group members will help the attacker overcome any retaliatory aggression, (3) judgments that the other members of the attractive group would not disapprove of the individual for engaging in aggressive behavior, and (4) socially induced judgments that hostile actions are morally proper.

In addition to these determinants, anonymity also leads to hostile behavior by people already instigated to aggression.

Inhibitions against displaying aggression generally are weaker in projective-test situations than in more "lifelike" circumstances. Any aggressive inclinations the individual possesses may then be revealed in projective tests, but projective-test performance may not predict the individual's behavior in actual social settings because of his internal restraints against aggression in such situations.

Attitudes regarding the moral propriety of hostile behavior also govern the likelihood that a person will act aggressively. The operation of such attitudes can be affected by situational factors. The nature of any given situation may determine whether the individual is aware of his moral standards regarding aggression or applies these standards to a particular hostile act.

Assuming that a person would feel anxious or guilty about any aggressive action of his in a certain situation, the stronger the aggressive inclinations aroused in him, the stronger is his resulting anxiety and/or guilt. However, strong anger arousal may delay the onset of this anxiety-guilt reaction. As one possible manifestation of such an aggression-anxiety response, there is a fairly common tendency in our society to avoid further contacts with someone who angers us.

The people about us may lessen or eliminate such aggression anxiety if they define hostile behavior as being socially proper in a given situation. Adult permissiveness toward aggression may result in such a social definition of aggression for children, the children transferring their "superego functions" to the watching adult.

# chapter 5

# The Nature and Target
## of the Aggressive Response

Little Willy Brown was a problem—a heartache and a disappointment to his mother, a nuisance to his teacher and playmates. His parents, afraid he might "run wild" or get into fights with the other children in the neighborhood, had tried very hard to mold him into their image of a well-behaved, good-mannered boy. They could not understand why his teacher insisted he was nasty to the other children in his class and to her as well. It wasn't that he bullied these children outright or picked fights with them, she said. He was just plain mean, constantly teasing smaller children, often deliberately disrupting the games or even the schoolwork of other youngsters, pinching and scratching those who objected, and frequently even harassing her. But that wasn't like Willy, his mother would reply. He was so quiet and polite at home. His father and she had trained him to be a perfect gentleman.

This brief anecdote has not been introduced to demonstrate the shortcomings of particular methods of child rearing. Our discussion of child-training practices is reserved for a later chapter. Rather, this case can illustrate how inhibitions against aggressive behavior may affect both the nature of a person's hostile behavior and the situations in which such actions will occur. Willy's parents had rarely seen their son display any overt hostility, and no wonder. They had been quick to punish him any time he showed a burst of temper. Since this was a regular consequence of his aggressive actions, the boy soon learned to inhibit his hostile tendencies when he was at home. He was polite and obedient to his parents—they left him no other choice. But what Mr. and Mrs. Brown did not realize was that Willy was an angry boy. Often frustrated at home by their stringent, unrealistic demands, he frequently went off to school with his anger aroused. There, in a situation that to him was

104

entirely dissimilar to his punitive home environment, his inhibitions against aggression weakened sufficiently so that hostility could become manifest if appropriate aggression-evoking cues were present.

The reader undoubtedly is familiar with this general phenomenon and probably also recognizes it as an instance of *displacement*. This concept has become well known through the writings of Freud and others, and its general applicability is understood widely. Storytellers and cartoonists often remind us of the man who, severely frustrated by his employer, comes home to berate his wife, who then scolds her child. The boy, in turn, takes it out on his dog, and this animal has no one to pick on but a nearby cat. Dollard et al. (1939) tell of an unusually mild-mannered young woman who exhibited "a sudden, violent and seemingly irrational outburst of temper" upon suffering a minor frustration after having had a severely annoying experience with her landlord (pp. 41–42).

In each of these incidents, according to the original psychoanalytic formulation of displacement, energy is transferred from one object to another. The aggressive energy cannot be released in actions against a potentially dangerous object. The man did not dare attack his employer, the wife was reluctant to talk back to her husband, and the boy was afraid to act aggressively toward his mother. Similarly, the "mild-mannered" girl, for one reason or another, was afraid to be hostile toward her landlord. All these people presumably found an "outlet" in aggression against a safer object.

The shortcomings of this energy interpretation of aggression have already been discussed and will not be repeated here. These difficulties, however, do not invalidate the clinical observations regarding the existence of displacement, particularly hostility displacement. There certainly cannot be any doubt such phenomena occur. The important task for the psychologist interested in this concept is not the mere demonstration of displacement, but, rather, the explication of the conditions under which it takes place. We can make at least a beginning in this direction. Where *Frustration and Aggression* represented one of the first, almost exploratory, products of the union of clinic and experimental laboratory, subsequent empirical and theoretical developments have clearly demonstrated the fruitfulness of this union. This can be seen most readily in the analysis of psychoanalytic displacement. Neal Miller, one of the coauthors of the 1939 monograph, and following in its tradition, has since shown how this concept can be understood in terms of the laboratory concept of stimulus-response generalization (1948; 1951; 1959). By relating the clinical and naturalistic observations to experimental analyses of conflict and learning, he has presented a model accounting for both the target and form of the displaced aggression. Before going any further, then, this important formulation should be described.

## THEORY

### Displacement and S-R Generalization

The fundamental assumption in Miller's system, the concept of generalization, grew out of Pavlov's research on conditioning. The typical experiment carried out in those investigations is well known. First, a bell was sounded just before food was given to a restrained but hungry dog harnessed to a device recording the dripping of his saliva. After several repetitions the sound of the bell alone would elicit salivation. This response, previously made to the sight of food, was now conditioned to the tone. Next, other tones were sounded, varying in pitch from that of the original bell. The dog also salivated to these new tones; the salivary response transferred or *generalized* from the original to the new tones. There are orderly relationships between the magnitude of the salivary response and the similarity between the new and original tones. The greater this similarity, i.e., the closer the pitch of the new tone was to that of the first sound, the greater the salivation. This relationship between response magnitude and similarity of the new stimulus to the original conditioned stimulus is called the *gradient of generalization.*

In his first major translation of displacement into learning theory terms (1948), Miller jumped imaginatively from Pavlov's laboratory to the clinical observations in six basic assumptions. Five of them were introduced to account for the occurrence of displacement in those situations in which the direct response to the instigating stimulus is prevented by internal conflict. These are:

(1) That the direct response to the original stimulus generalizes to other similar stimuli, with the amount of generalization becoming smaller the less similar the stimuli; (2) that the response which conflicts with the occurrence of the direct response to the original stimulus also generalizes to other similar stimuli, becoming weaker the less similar the stimuli; (3) that the gradient of generalization of the conflicting response falls off more steeply with dissimilarity than does that of the original response which it inhibits; (4) that when two or more incompatible responses are simultaneously excited, the one with the greatest net strength will be the one which will occur; and (5) that the net strength of a response will be its strength minus that of any response incompatible with it which is excited at the same time (pp. 167–168).

In addition, one other assumption is useful for dealing with differences in drive strength:

(6) that an increase in the drive involved in either type of gradient will raise the overall height of that gradient (p. 168).

*Hostility Displacement.* To illustrate how this model would work in the case of aggression, let us imagine a man who is frustrated by another person. This frustrating person is the instigating stimulus object. Suppose further that there are no inhibitions against aggression within the angered man, but that he cannot attack his frustrater, who is absent from the scene. Should he then encounter other people with varying degrees of similarity to the instigator (assuming he remains angry and uninhibited), the person most resembling the instigator on the relevant

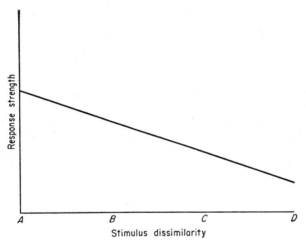

Fig. 5.1. The stimulus generalization gradient. If stimulus object *A* evokes the strongest response from a person, other objects (*B*, *C*, and *D*) increasing in dissimilarity to *A* will evoke increasingly weaker responses from the person.

similarity dimension will elicit hostile responses which, although not as strong as those the original instigator would have aroused, are still stronger than the responses evoked by people less similar to the frustrater. This situation is diagrammed in Figure 1. The anger instigator is at position *A*, while the other people are at *B*, *C*, and *D*. Of these three, the individual at *B* is the one most similar to the original frustrater and thus would receive the strongest displaced aggression.

The first hypothesis advanced by Dollard and his colleagues in their 1939 analysis of factors affecting the direction of aggression clearly is a special case of this more general principle. They had suggested then that *the strongest aggressive tendencies aroused by a frustration would be directed against the frustrating object* (p. 39). *The later formulation* makes the same prediction, and in addition, *proposes a generalization of hostile responses to other objects, with the strength of these responses declining with increased dissimilarity to the instigator.*[1]

The direct aggression to the initial instigator could not take place in the above case because of the instigator's absence. There is a somewhat different situation existing, however, if this direct response is inhibited by internal restraints. As Figure 2 illustrates, the strongest displaced aggression would be toward objects of intermediate rather than greatest similarity to the instigator. Again, let us say we have a person thwarted by individual A who then encounters people located at

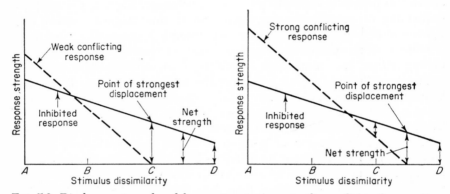

Fig. 5.2. Displacement produced by greater steepness in the gradient of generalization of the conflicting response (assuming linearity). It can be seen that displaced responses can occur and that the strongest displaced response will be expected at an intermediate point, C in the diagram on the left. Increasing the strength of the conflicting response weakens the strongest displaced response and causes it to be elicited by less similar stimuli, those between C and D in the diagram to the right. Although straight lines were used to simplify these diagrams, the deductions are not dependent upon the assumption of linearity. (*Reproduced from N. E. Miller, 1948, p. 169, with permission.*)

B, C, and D on the stimulus dissimilarity dimension. He is somewhat afraid of A, and consequently his aggressive inclinations are inhibited by anticipations of punishment conflicting with and restraining the hostile responses. If these inhibitory tendencies are relatively weak, we would have the situation shown in the left-hand diagram. Empirical evidence supports the assumption that the slope of the inhibitory (or avoidance) gradient under these conditions is steeper than that of the tendency to make the instigated response (see N. E. Miller, 1959), and so there

[1] This proposition certainly is consistent with the present formulation concerning the "activation" of "aroused" tendencies by relevant cues. The frustration creates an arousal, but cues are necessary if responses are to be performed. The substitute objects having some degree of association with the instigator evoke aggressive responses, activating the frustration-engendered predisposition.

might be fairly strong restraints against attacking the person at *B*, but not against injuring the man at *C*. Making use of Miller's (1948) fifth assumption, given above, we regard the strengths of the two opposing tendencies as detracting from each other. The net strength, therefore, is the outcome of this conflict, i.e., the strength of the resultant tendency to aggression. In this particular situation the net strength is very low at position *B*. The person at this location on the generalization gradient resembles *A* too closely, we might say, evoking inhibitory responses almost perfectly countering the hostile responses he also elicits. The net strength may be so weak that the tendency to attack this person is not revealed in overt behavior. There is the greatest probability of open aggression, according to this diagram, against the individual at position *C*, where the net strength is greatest.

Miller's sixth assumption maintains that increases in the drive impelling either the conflicting (inhibitory) or inhibited (aggressive) responses raise the over-all height of the relevant gradient. The right-hand diagram in Figure 2 schematically represents the situation existing when relatively strong inhibitions are elicited. The restraints opposing hostility are stronger than the aggressive tendencies toward both the instigator and the person at position *B* in this case, and there also is only a fairly weak resultant tendency to injure the person located at *C*. Furthermore, there now is a somewhat greater probability that the man at position *D* will be attacked than that the individual *C* will be aggressed against; the resultant hostile responses finally evoked by the former will tend to be stronger than those directed to the latter. As we can see, heightening the strength of the responses opposing aggression toward the frustrater shifts the likeliest (or strongest) displaced responses toward objects of increasing dissimilarity to the instigator, providing that the intensity of the aggressive inclinations is not altered. Raising the strength of the tendency to aggression without changing the height of the inhibitory gradient, on the other hand, would result in objects of greater similarity to the frustrater receiving the strongest displaced aggression. Thus, if two people were equally afraid of someone who had insulted them, the individual with the stronger instigation to aggression would be the one more likely to vent his hostility upon another person closely resembling the initial instigator.

Some of the assumptions involved in this model may seem rather arbitrary. The diagrams employed in describing the Miller formulation, for example, are based on linear gradients of generalization, and the reader might quarrel with this assumption. However, in actuality, this is a minor matter; the above deductions are not seriously affected whether linear gradients or negative growth curves are postulated (N. E. Miller, 1948).

*The Slopes of the Opposing Gradients.* We cannot dismiss another objection this quickly, unfortunately. One of the most important features in Miller's analysis concerns the relative steepness of the opposing gradients. Is the generalization gradient for the conflicting response necessarily always steeper than that of the inhibited tendency? The experiments conducted by Miller and his colleagues generally require this notion. Otherwise, it would be difficult to explain why their animals ever approached a desired but still feared goal. (Stimulus dissimilarity and distance are equated in this case.) When the animals were some distance from the goal, the responses elicited by anticipation of its desired aspects apparently were stronger than the opposing tendencies evoked by anticipation of the noxious consequences. These latter conflicting responses then seemed to increase more rapidly in strength as the organisms drew near the food or water; if the inhibitions were strong enough, the animals came to a stop some distance before the goal, with this distance being greater the stronger the noxious stimulation.

Nevertheless, Miller believed this difference in slope need not always hold (1948, pp. 172–173; 1959, pp. 212–213, 222). The animals employed in these studies typically attempted to attain their goals because of persistent internal physiological factors, such as hunger motivation. These factors were constantly active under the experimental conditions, although the closer the organism was to the point of reinforcement, the greater was their motivational impact (i.e., the greater their effect on the tendency to respond). The avoidance or inhibitory tendencies, on the other hand, usually were motivated by fear arousal, and fear, as a learned drive, presumably is "elicited primarily by situational cues" (1959, p. 213). Putting it simply, the approach tendencies in these particular animals were largely affected by internal cues, while the opposing inhibitory tendencies were more dependent upon situational cues. These latter responses, then, declined more rapidly in strength with distance from the feared point.

It is possible to think of situations in which the gradient of the aggressive tendency would be steeper in slope than that of the inhibitory tendency. A person with the strong attitudinal prohibitions against hostile acts of any sort, for example, would have relatively constant restraints against aggression in almost all situations (assuming he always was conscious of his moral standards). If he has been angered by someone and then encounters people of varying similarity to the instigator, there should not be too much difference in the strength of the inhibitions against aggression that are aroused as he goes from one of these people to the next; there is a relatively flat slope to the inhibitory gradient with increasing dissimilarity to the instigator. But then suppose he meets the instigator again and hears this individual taunt him. His anger might flare up to the point where he would even lash out at his frustrater. Near the instigator his aggressive tendencies are strong; far from him they are weak as he disregards the insults. Thus, in this case, the aggressive response gradient has a steep slope. This person with strong attitudinal restraints against aggression would be less likely to express overt hostility against his frustrater the further away he was from him.

This type of situation may be relatively infrequent, however. Although supporting evidence is lacking, the original displacement model assuming somewhat steeper inhibitory gradients seems to fit more aggressive occurrences than does the alternative conception postulating steeper hostile tendencies. We all know of incidents in which some person far from the scene of his frustration angrily boasted how he was going to aggress against some relatively powerful frustrater, only to "think better of it" when he finally approached the instigator. Thus, a man might tell his wife while they are at breakfast in their home that he is going to talk to his frustrating supervisor that day. Thinking of what he will say or the "injuries" done to him, he may even insult the frustrater either to himself or to his wife. The aggressive tendency is stronger than the inhibitory one at this distance. But then, later, when he does confront the supervisor at work, his anticipation of punishment becomes paramount and the aggressive responses are inhibited.

If the situations presented here are representative of the conditions under which the slopes of the opposing gradients are altered, two factors appear to be particularly important in affecting these slopes: (1) *The inhibitory gradient probably is relatively steep when these restraining responses are elicited largely by fear*—that is, by anticipation of punishment for aggression—*rather than by persistent attitudes defining hostile actions as "wrong"; (2) persistent aggressive inclinations,* which would result from frequent recall of the frustration suffered at the hand of the instigator, *produce relatively flat hostility gradients.* Either or both of these conditions seem to be operative in most anger-arousing situations.

The transfer process considered until now is termed *stimulus generalization* since it deals with the range of stimuli eliciting a given response. Factors affecting the target of aggressive behavior, therefore, can be interpreted employing notions involving variations in stimulus conditions and the generalization of responses from one stimulus object to another. These would be the concepts to apply (among others) in explaining why Willy aggressed against his teacher and his schoolmates instead of his frustrating parents.

*Response Generalization.* There is another aspect of the boy's behavior, however, that can also be accounted for by the generalization concept. Note that Willy harassed his teacher instead of striking her directly. Nor was his aggression against his peers too direct; he teased the younger children much more often than he punched them. A somewhat similar phenomenon was described in the previous chapter. Most middle-class adults in our society seem to display verbal aggression much more readily than open physical attacks. In all of these cases there apparently are relatively strong inhibitions against the most direct aggressive responses, while the strength of the more indirect aggressive responses seems to be stronger than the restraints against them.

The generalization gradients shown in Figure 2 can clarify this situation, if some modifications are made. Instead of labeling the horizontal axis "stimulus dissimilarity," consider this as referring to a response dimension. Point A, then, is an act of direct aggression, perhaps involving strong physical blows; "bawling out" the frustrater or insulting him to his face might be at B; derogating him behind his back or carrying tales about him at C; and giving him a "nasty look" at D (see Graham et al., 1951, p. 513).

With this difference the interpretations are the same as before. As Dollard and his colleagues had proposed in 1939, the strongest instigation aroused by a frustration is to acts of direct aggression (pp. 39–40). But there also are the strongest inhibitions at this location on the response generalization dimension, usually stronger in most of us than the tendency to make the act. Consequently, these direct aggression responses typically do not occur in overt behavior until the height of the response gradient is raised. This comes about when the individual is strongly angered and/or has a habit of making violent attacks upon the frustrater activated by intense anger arousal. The inhibitory responses decline in strength fairly rapidly as the aggressive acts become less direct, so that the net strength of these indirect acts actually may be greater than the net strength of more direct aggressive responses. Indirect aggression, therefore, becomes a more probable occurrence than direct hostility.

A combination of stimulus- and response-generalization gradients obviously is needed to account for Willy Brown's behavior. Suppose he goes off to school one morning in a rage. He sees his teacher, and aggressive responses generalize from his parents to her. However, since she resembles his parents in being an adult (and perhaps in other stimulus characteristics as well), the sight of her also evokes strong inhibitory tendencies. These conflicting responses are strong enough to inhibit all but the most indirect acts of hostility, and the most Willy can do to her, say, is to be mischievous. Willy's playmates, on the other hand, being further along on the stimulus generalization dimension (greater dissimilarity to the instigator-parents), elicit weaker aggressive responses than does the teacher, but also arouse only very weak inhibitory responses. In this case there is a greater net strength for the aggressive responses at the playmates' position on the stimulus dissimilarity dimension than at the teacher's position. As a result, it is possible for Willy to express more direct hostility to his playmates than to his teacher. He can tease them, but cannot do this to her.

*Psychological Distance.* Some additional comments should be made concerning the dimensions involved in the stimulus generalization. Most of the above discussion of this process had to do with *stimulus dissimilarity*. This need not be similarity along physical dimensions, even though Pavlov's generalization continua (e.g., the pitch of tones) did deal with this type of variable. The similarity can be qualitative, created by the perceiving individual in his subjective reactions to the people around him. He may, for example, respond to them in terms of their social statuses—how rich, powerful, or popular he thinks they are —or how different they seem to be from the people to whom he is accustomed, or, and this will be discussed more fully later, he may differentiate people in terms of how much he likes them, for one reason or another. These qualitative dimensions along which people are distinguished, whatever they may be, theoretically can comprise the dimensions along which stimulus generalizations take place (N. E. Miller, 1951, 1959). A great many writers have made this type of assumption. Some have maintained, to cite but one illustration, that highly ethnocentric people respond to social authorities generally as they had learned to respond to their fathers, the initial authority figure in their lives (Adorno, Frenkel-Brunswik, Levinson, & Sanford, 1950). The affective reactions evoked by their fathers presumably are generalized to other authority figures.

Considered from the perceiver's viewpoint, these similarity dimensions can be thought of in terms of some construct such as "psychological distance." Thus, there is a relatively great "distance" psychologically between person A and person B for the individual who sees the former as extremely wealthy and the latter as being very poor. For Willy Brown the "distance" between his parents and his teacher was less than that between his parents and his playmates. Employing this construct makes it easy for us to see why Miller (1959) and others (e.g., J. S. Brown, 1957) have suggested that the stimulus gradients underlying the opposing response tendencies can involve spatial and temporal as well as similarity variables. Reference has already been made to the conceptual equation of spatial distance with stimulus dissimilarity. It is possible to define spatial and temporal distance from a goal in stimulus terms so that the reasoning regarding generalization along physical similarity dimensions can also be applied to variations in physical distance or time. Since going into this any further is beyond the intended scope of this book, these definitions will not be attempted here. The major points to be made, however, can be spelled out simply: As the organism moves nearer to a goal having both positive and negative aspects, the tendency to approach this goal and the tendency to avoid it both increase in strength, with the latter tendency generally increasing at a faster rate. "Moving near" can be thought of as coming closer to the instigating stimulus object phenomenologically, closer to it either spatially, temporally, or in terms of other objects resembling it. If this object is a frustrater evoking both aggressive responses and aggression anxiety, the closer the angered individual comes to his instigator, whether in physical space, the time at which he might encounter him, or through meeting other people similar to him, the stronger are the tendencies to aggress against him and to avoid these acts of hostility. Except under certain conditions specified earlier, these inhibiting responses probably will demonstrate a more rapid increase in strength.

## Extensions of the Theoretical Analysis

*Evidence for Displacement.* Dollard et al. could offer at best only tentative evidence in support of their formulations. Since their book was written prior to the full development of the stimulus-response generalization analysis of displacement, their main concern in 1939 was merely to demonstrate the existence of this phenomenon. The Yale writers cited findings from four different investigations as being consistent with their hypotheses. In the first of these, Miller and Davis (reported in N. E. Miller, 1948) trained rats to strike one another upon receiving electric shocks. After a while, these signals alone came to elicit the fighting behaviors, causing rats to attack each other instead of a small celluloid doll placed in the cage with them. However, if rats were individually placed in the cage with the doll and then shocked, they tended to strike the doll. In other words, when aggressive responses were elicited by the appropriate cue (the shocks), a rat would attack a previously neutral object if aggression against the other rats was prevented by their absence.

While it may be argued that the hostile behaviors in this last study represented instrumental aggression (i.e., learned ways of achieving other nonaggressive goals—escaping shocks in this case) and thus might not fit the frustration-aggression displacement paradigm, this objection cannot be raised against the other studies. Miller and Bugelski (cited in Dollard et al., 1939, pp. 42–43) came closer to the usual interpretation of displacement as a frustration reaction by demonstrating that frustrated subjects evaluated their friends (who were not at all responsible for their unpleasant experiences) more unfavorably than did nonthwarted control subjects.

Another experiment by the same investigators is now one of the classic studies in social psychology (Miller & Bugelski, 1948). Boys in a CCC camp were prevented from attending the very attractive bank night at the local movie house by giving them a series of long, dull, difficult tests. Attitude questionnaires administered before and after this frustration indicated that Mexicans and Japanese were regarded more unfavorably following the blocking than they had been prior to it. (There was a reliable drop in favorable attitudes and some increase in negative attitudes toward these groups.) Proponents of the "scapegoat theory" of prejudice frequently point to this finding as confirmation of the theory. These particular minority groups presumably were the innocent scapegoat outlets for the boys' frustration-produced hostility. However, as we shall see later, this over-simplified formulation has to be specified in more detail; many frustrated people do not generalize their aggression to minority groups, and certainly not every minority group in the United States becomes a target for displaced aggression. Any adequate explanation of "scapegoating" must account for these exceptions.

For their final demonstration of displacement, the Yale psychologists referred to the findings in the previously mentioned investigation by Hovland and Sears (1940). Negroes were not to blame for the frustrations created by poor economic conditions, but yet, as indicated by the relatively high number of Negroes lynched when cotton values were low prior to the 1930s, they apparently were the recipients of much of the hostility engendered by these economic privations.

*Inhibited Aggression.* Some of the hypotheses regarding hostility generalization spelled out in the 1939 work are extensions of the theoretical line described above, but deal with matters left largely untouched until now. There is, for example, the question of the effects of inhibited aggression. A *frustration* is defined as any interference with an instigated response sequence. This definition also applies to the blocking of aggressive responses. Since one result of such a thwarting is an increase in the instigation to aggression, inhibiting hostile responses must lead, logically, to a heightening of the individual's aggressive inclinations. With direct aggression blocked by restraints, however, it is only the tendencies to the less direct aggressive acts that can be strengthened by this increased anger. Thus, Dollard and his colleagues hypothesized (1939, p. 40) that *interference with acts of direct aggression is an additional frustration increasing the instigation to other aggressive responses and making these less direct hostile acts more probable occurrences.*

*Self-aggression.* Another problem concerns the target of the aggressive tendencies evoked by these internal inhibitions against aggression. If the individual sees himself as the cause of these inhibitions, the aggressive responses they produce theoretically should be directed against himself. Dollard et al. suggested that *self-aggression may result when direct hostility toward others is "inhibited by anticipation of punishment"* (pp. 46–47), but they indicated that *ultimately in this case it is the self rather than some external agent that is perceived to be the source of the frustration* (p. 48). The Yale group did not do more than present the gross outline of their analysis of self-aggression. As a consequence, they did not delve sufficiently into the implications of this notion regarding the perceived source of the blocks against aggression. After simply stating that aggression is turned against the self when direct aggression is inhibited by the self (p. 48), they concentrated their attention upon the extent of the restraints against aggression rather than on the causal locus of these inhibitions. Self-aggression produces unpleasant, punishing consequences for the individual, they pointed out, and therefore "should be a relatively nonpreferred type of expression" (p. 48). *It occurs as a displacement reaction,* they argued, *only when other aggressive responses are even more strongly inhibited by anticipations of punishment.*

Dollard et al. illustrated their conception with the case of a small boy who, under the extreme discipline of the institution in which he lived, had to inhibit his strong aggressive tendencies. He ceased to attack others, presumably having learned he would be punished for doing so, only to direct his aggression onto himself. The boy began to beat himself physically, and this did not stop until his frustrations were lessened. Aggression against adults became possible in the course of therapy, and self-aggression finally disappeared (1939, pp. 49–50).

There is some similarity between this view and Freud's concept of "moral masochism" mentioned in the first chapter of this book. Freud had suggested, it will be recalled, that self-aggression in the form of an overly strict conscience results from the inhibition of aggressiveness toward others (S. Freud, 1959a, p. 267).[2] But instead of arguing that self-aggression is the consequence of a flow of the death instinct back onto the self, as Freud did, the Yale psychologists hypothesized that the self-aggression is produced by the self-imposed restraints against hostility toward others arising from expectations of punishment for *any* such actions.

I have some doubts as to the adequacy of this explanation of self-aggression. For one thing, the 1939 formulation does not seem to give

---

[2] Hartmann et al. (1949) had a similar thesis. They believed that if aggressive "energy" is not discharged in fights it may be internalized and become the source of guilt feelings.

sufficient consideration to the individual's interpretation of the hostility-restraining situation. According to the Yale thesis, aggression against the self is primarily the result of the blocking of all alternative modes of hostile expression due to anticipations of punishment. Nevertheless, we might ask, would the self necessarily be seen as the source of this blocking when others will inflict the punishment? If I restrain myself from attacking another person because I know this individual will punish me severely for any such actions, the ultimate frustrating agent in this situation is this person rather than myself. His anticipated reaction to the hostility leads to the inhibitions. As we can see, there is some confusion in the Dollard et al. conception. If the blocking of all alternative aggressive responses is the important determinant of self-aggression, it is entirely unnecessary to postulate that self-aggression arises when the self is perceived as the source of the frustration. On the other hand, if the self as the source of the thwarting is the important determinant, the degree of interference with aggression is a secondary consideration, possibly affecting only the intensity of the self-hostility. My own inclinations are toward this latter view. As I will attempt to show later, hostility toward the self generally seems to follow when the individual regards himself as the cause of his frustration.

## RESEARCH

### Tests of the S-R Generalization Analysis

*Attacks on the Frustration Source.* Empirical evidence generally supports the stimulus generalization analysis of target selection, but also indicates the desirability of including other factors, particularly interpretations, in accounting for such phenomena. This becomes apparent even when dealing with the first Yale hypothesis in this area. As Dollard and his colleagues had proposed in 1939, and as Miller's later elaboration requires, uninhibited frustration-produced aggressive responses tend to be directed toward the source of the frustration. But the individual's interpretation of the situation often determines what agent will be seen as the source of the thwarting.

Perhaps the clearest support for the initial hypothesis can be found in the previously cited experiment by Pepitone and Reichling (1955). The subjects, organized in pairs, were insulted by the experimenter, who then left the room. Since this instigator was now absent from the scene, the subjects in both experimental conditions knew they would have little to fear from him for the next few minutes. In one of these conditions, the reader will remember, the pairs were composed of men with relatively high liking for each other, while this liking was much lower in the other condition. As reported earlier, the people in the high-liking condition displayed more aggression during the supposed intermission. The total restraints against aggression apparently were weaker in this condition. Thus, while the subjects in both conditions directed most of their verbal hostility toward the instigator (followed in descending order of frequency by attacks upon psychology and the physical setting), the less inhibited people in the high-liking groups expressed a far greater proportion of their total hostility in remarks against the instigator. According to the experimenters, 83 per cent of the verbal aggression exhibited in the low-inhibitions condition was directed toward the absent frustrater. The more restrained low-liking pairs, on the other hand, did not concentrate whatever hostility they did display so exclusively upon the instigator. Their aggressive remarks were directed more evenly against all available targets. Reduction of inner restraints against aggression increased the total volume of hostility exhibited in overt behavior and also increased the tendency for this aggression to be directed primarily against the source of the frustration.

It would be a mistake, however, to assume that the individual most closely associated with the onset of the frustration through contiguity automatically becomes the recipient of the uninhibited hostile responses elicited by this thwarting in some blind conditioning process. Frustrated people often aggress against those they blame for their unpleasant experiences, *but they do not always blame those who actually are most contiguous with these events.* Reference was made to this fact in Chapter 2, where it was pointed out that World War II air-raid victims frequently did not show any sharp rises in hostility against the nation directly responsible for these raids. Public-opinion surveys taken in England during the first years of the war provide some of the indications of this failure to direct war-induced aggression primarily toward the enemy (Janis, 1951, pp. 127–128). The British civilians who had suffered the most from the German air attacks were not as ardently in favor of the aggressive "Bomb Berlin" policy as the civilians who had escaped these heavy bombings. There is no indication the former people were inhibiting their hostility toward the Germans. They apparently did express aggression. Civilians from heavily bombed areas of England, for example, were more critical of their own government than were people from unbombed communities, and they certainly would have been more likely to inhibit the hostility toward other Englishmen than the hostility toward the Germans if such restraints were in operation. The air attacks did heighten anger and resentment toward the enemy. From available evidence, however, it seems the serious frustrations produced by the air warfare did not yield as much hostility toward the attacking nation as we might have expected, and also produced a substantial degree of resentment toward other groups in the populace's own country, particularly the government.

Janis has offered a number of explanations for these findings in his survey of the effects of air warfare (1951, pp. 133–138). One plausible possibility (and undoubtedly many factors were involved) is that the air-raid victims felt their governments had not provided them with sufficient protection and nurturance. These people may have transferred early learned attitudes from their parents to the parent-surrogates that are government authorities. As children (and perhaps unconsciously as adults), we expect and want our parents to protect us when dangers arise. But similarly, we also want the government to protect us when grave emergencies confront us as a community or nation. The hostility the air raid victims directed toward their government, then, may be an outgrowth of their belief the authorities had "let them down." The government had not shielded them from danger and therefore was responsible for the frustrations they had suffered.

Instrumentality in causing a frustration, as defined by an independent observer, does not automatically bring blame. Other illustrations of this also can be found. Several years ago a polling agency surveyed opinions in Elizabeth, New Jersey, after three transport planes had crashed into the community (Bucher, 1957). The people in this city generally did not blame or direct hostility to the airplane pilots, the individuals most immediately associated with the cause of the disasters, or even the mechanics and control-tower operators. By and large, their grievances were aimed chiefly at the higher authorities whom they thought had the power to prevent the recurrence of the conditions producing the crashes.

These analyses clearly do not invalidate the Yale hypothesis. They do indicate, nevertheless, that the people actually exposed to a frustrating situation may interpret this situation in a somewhat different manner from the way it would be seen by an outside observer. Aggressive tendencies are directed toward the perceived source of the thwarting, but people may differ in whom they regard as the frustrating agent. If we are to predict the target of an individual's aggression, in other words, we must know who (or what) he will see as the cause of his frustration, and this is not always easy to determine beforehand. Blame may be attributed in an "irrational" manner. According to Durbin and Bowlby (1939), human beings have a "universal tendency" to attribute events "to the deliberate activity of human . . . will." The person frustrated by some happenstance supposedly will tend to think somebody deliberately produced this thwarting unless the evidence to the contrary is fairly clear. Whether this is the case or not, cognitive processes following principles other than the laws of logic can influence the individual's interpretation of the frustrating situation. For example, he may project his own emotional state onto certain other people (Feshbach & Singer, 1957b), particularly if they are somewhat similar to him, or perhaps attribute the opposite emotion to them if they are regarded as being very different from the self (Berkowitz, 1960d), thus blaming particular others for the frustration because he unrealistically thinks they are angry with him. Certainly, much more has to be known about the factors affecting our perception and understanding of emotion-arousing situations before the a priori determination of the perceived frustration source can be made with any accuracy.

*Generalization along Similarity Dimensions.* There obviously are other difficulties also confronting the application of the stimulus generalization model to aggressive behavior. It is not always possible to ascertain beforehand (1) what particular stimulus dimension will be involved in the generalization process, (2) the ordering of the available stimulus objects on this dimension, and (3) the exact slopes of the generalization gradients. The most that can be done in some situations, since this information is lacking, is to reconstruct the stimulus conditions from knowledge of the outcomes. In other cases, however, much of this necessary information is available in a relatively unequivocal manner. The findings in these latter studies generally support the model.

This can be seen in two correlational investigations. In one of these, Murney (1955) asked judges to rank twenty cardboard figures on the basis of a "global impression" of their similarity to the figure of an Army officer. The judges showed respectable agreement in the ordering of ten of the figures. These were used to define a continuum of similarity to the officer in the second part of the study conducted with ninety male patients at a VA center. The experimenter first related a story to each of these subjects in which an Army officer arbitrarily frustrated a private, after which he asked each subject to describe what the private would do upon encountering the other figures. They were encouraged to give aggressive responses. If these men placed themselves in the private's boots, the primary target selected for their aggressive response would be determined by the absolute and relative strengths of their aggressive and inhibitory tendencies. The experimenter employed TAT responses obtained on another occasion to assess the strength of these tendencies and found evidence consistent with the stimulus generalization model. As Miller would have predicted, the stronger the aggressive inclinations, with the inhibitory tendencies held constant, the more similar the figure chosen as the aggressive target was to the actual instigator. Furthermore, the object for the target of the displaced hostility was less similar to the instigator the stronger the aggression anxiety with the aggressive-tendency measure held constant.

In a second correlational study, G. O. Wright (1954) assumed, as a number of investigators had done before him, that the folktales related by the members of a particular society generally reflected the dominant values and motives of that society. He analyzed twelve folktales from each of thirty-three societies to test the hypothesis that the objects chosen for displaced aggression in these stories would be further out on the generalization continuum, the greater the aggression anxiety in the society. Wright believed the hero of each tale could be regarded as "the point of original response" on a similarity dimension beginning at the hero and continuing through friends, relatives, and acquaintances to the least similar objects, strangers. (Another way of looking at this is to say these stimulus people were arranged in order of increasing "psychological distance" from the hero.) Each of the societies was rated as to the extent to which its children typically were punished for aggression on the basis of anthropological reports. Wright assumed aggression anxiety would be strongest in those groups having the severest punishment for aggression. Again, the results tended to confirm the theoretical expectations. The greater the inferred level of aggression anxiety in the society, the less similar were both the object and agent of the aggression to the hero of the story. People with strong aggression anxiety apparently cannot tolerate the idea that folktale heroes, or people similar to them, can aggress against others or be the target of aggression from others. The inhibitory tendencies seem to have displaced the idea of aggression as far from the self as possible.

*Relatively Weak Inhibitions in Fantasy Situations.* Folktales can probably be regarded as the projective-test protocols of a society (providing the society is relatively homogeneous). The themes revealed in these fantasy stories yield information about many of the people living in the society, much as the imaginative stories an individual might construct in response to the TAT tell something about him. But exactly what these fantasy productions tell us depends greatly upon our theories. The S-R generalization model is helpful in obtaining maximum understanding of the thematic data. If inhibitory tendencies do decline more rapidly in strength than do the tendencies to approach particular goals with increasing "distance" from the instigating environment, for example, response tendencies could well be revealed in fantasy which normally are inhibited. Wright made this assumption in testing one other hypothesis. Administering punishment for aggressive behavior should be a frustration and, therefore, actually should increase the punished individual's anger. Inhibitions will prevent aggressive responses from occurring in situations similar or "close" to the punishing environment, but the hostility can be exhibited in other situations, such as in fantasy tasks, that are fairly different from this environment. Hostility themes certainly would be expected in the fantasy production if, as was discussed earlier, the restraints are based upon fear avoidance. Consistent with this reasoning, Wright found that folktales from societies practicing severe punishment for childhood aggression contained reliably more intense aggression than did folktales from less punitive societies.[3]

Research conducted earlier at the Iowa Child Welfare Station (Chasdi & Lawrence, 1955; R. R. Sears, 1950, 1951a, 1951b) had obtained essentially similar results with children's doll-play behavior. Nursery school children were divided into three groups, depending upon the amount of punishment for aggression they had suffered in their homes. Observing the interactions among the children in the nursery, the investigators found that the moderately punished children had a higher frequency of overt aggression than the less punished preschoolers, but that the highly punished youngsters were no more hostile than this low-punished group. This relative absence of overt aggression of course does not mean the highly punished children had only weak aggressive tendencies. Their fantasy behaviors during several sessions of doll play demonstrated they had stronger aggressive tendencies than any of the other children. Punishment for aggression in the home was directly related to the frequency of aggressive acts in this fantasy situation. The aggressive tendencies elicited in the highly punished children in the nursery environment had been inhibited presumably because of the similarity of this situation to their homes. However, when they were placed in the fantasy situation, which was distinctly dissimilar to their homes, their strong hostile tendencies were revealed.

The relatively sharp decline in the strength of the inhibitory tendencies with increasing "distance" from the feared anger instigator has particular relevance for the scapegoat theory of prejudice. According to this familiar social science doctrine, it will be recalled, thwarted individuals who are afraid to attack the real source of their frustration will tend to vent their hostility upon some innocent victim. Such an occurrence would come about, theoretically, if this victim were associated with the instigator closely enough so that he would arouse fairly strong aggressive responses, but still were sufficiently removed from the instigator psychologically so that the restraints against aggression would be weaker than the tendencies to attack.

*Self-aggression.* Appropriately, self-aggression is the last topic to be discussed in this general consideration of targets for aggression. Dollard and his collaborators essentially saw self-aggression as the final possible reaction to extreme frustrations. It supposedly arose as a displacement of aggressive responses to the self when all alternative hostile actions had been blocked by anticipations of punishment.

---

[3] M. Brewster Smith (personal communication) has pointed out that there is uncertainty about the exact nature of the causal relationships involved in this finding. It is possible, for example, that the harsh socialization practices did not give rise to the particular folktales. Both the socialization practices and the folktales may have been the outgrowth of beliefs about the nature of the world.

Reasoning from this formulation, R. R. Sears (1961) hypothesized that high self-aggression in children would result from their being severely frustrated in their home environments and also prevented from openly attacking their frustrater. He assessed the self-aggression tendencies in a sample of twelve-year-old children by means of questionnaire items asking about such things as impulses toward suicide. The mothers of these children had been interviewed approximately seven years earlier (Sears et al., 1957), and information about some of the possible antecedent conditions of these self-aggression responses obtained from these interviews was then related to the questionnaire scores. Some evidence consistent with the Yale interpretation was obtained for boys but not for girls. The boys, Sears reported, who had been subjected to the earlier frustrating condition of severe toilet training and who also had been blocked from expressing aggression by the combination of low parental permissiveness for aggression and high parental punishment of the child's aggression had significantly higher self-aggression scores than the boys exposed to less severe toilet training and who had been permitted to express hostility in the home.

Nevertheless, there are other possible explanations for Sears's findings. It is conceivable, for example, that the parents imposing harsh discipline upon their sons (unrealistic toilet-training demands and severe prohibitions against aggression) generally established extreme performance standards for their sons. If so, these boys may not have been able to live up to these ideals and consequently may have developed the notion they were "no good." The result was self-aggression. Clearly, if this interpretation is correct, the determinant of the type of self-aggression studied by Sears is the nature of the perceived self. These youngsters may have derogated or even hated themselves because they saw themselves as generally incompetent; they blamed themselves for their failures.

As I indicated earlier, there is ample reason to doubt the adequacy of the Yale thesis attributing self-aggression to the inhibition of alternative hostile responses. This line of thought cannot account for masochism, for example, in which people supposedly obtain erotic pleasure from hurting themselves. Nor can this particular formulation satisfactorily explain other forms of self-aggression such as suicides. Durkheim (1951) demonstrated before the beginning of the twentieth century that these extreme cases of self-aggression were associated with a variety of social conditions producing isolation, estrangement from the values and fellowship of social groups, and anonymity. These situations, in which the individual is apart from others, are not likely to give rise to strong anticipations of punishment from others. They may, however, cause the individual to undervalue and dislike himself. ("I am all alone. I am not important to anyone. I am worthless and no good.")

Findings in a recent investigation by Schramm, Lyle, and Parker (1961) provide further evidence against the inhibited-aggression explanation of self-aggression. The researchers administered Sears's aggression scales to a sample of adolescents in the Rocky Mountain area in the course of a survey of television viewing by children. (Additional results of this survey are reported in Chapter 9.) Among other things, Schramm et al. noted that the teen agers' degree of conflict with their parents over their educational and occupational plans was significantly related to the youngsters' descriptions of themselves on several of these scales. The greater the parent-child conflict, the stronger were the adolescents' antisocial aggression *and* self-aggression tendencies (pp. 126–129). In this case at least, then, self-aggression did not seem to stem from restraints against all other forms of hostility.

This topic will be set aside for now, but it will be brought up again in the chapter on suicides and homicides. Aggression against the self is a complex matter and cannot be disposed of in only a few words.

*Response Generalization.* The above discussion, by and large, deals with stimulus generalization, that is, continua composed of the stimuli evoking aggressive and inhibiting responses. Variations in the *form* of the aggression, from direct physical attacks to indirect expressions of dislike, on the other hand, involve response generalization. There seems to be little doubt that inhibitions against direct aggressive acts generally produce more indirect forms of hostility. French (1944) observed this type of phenomenon in his previously mentioned study of "organized" and "unorganized" groups. The members of the former groups exhibited less restraint in their dealings with other group members, apparently because of their greater degree of intragroup acquaintance and liking. As a result, the hostility expressed in these groups was more likely to be direct aggression than was the case within the more inhibited "unorganized" groups. Where there were sixty-one instances of direct aggression, such as physical or verbal attacks upon other members, in the less inhibited condition, the relatively strong restraints existing in the other condition gave rise to only indirect acts of hostility, such as arguments and hostile jokes.

Dinwiddie (1955) made explicit use of the response generalization concept in a study using personality-test scores. On the basis of Miller's theoretical analysis, he hypothesized that the degree of similarity between the most aggressive response possible in a situation and the response the subject does make will vary (1) inversely with the strength of the inhibitory tendencies, and (2) directly with the strength of the aggressive tendencies. With each of these tendencies assessed by self-report questionnaire scales, he reported that subjects with high scores on a measure of "social anxiety" (assumed to be the instigation for the inhibitory responses) displayed more indirect aggression in responding to the Rosenzweig P-F Study than the subjects who were low on this anxiety measure, with the strength of the hostile tendencies statistically held constant.

*Increased Instigation to Indirect Aggression Following Inhibition of Direct Aggression.* We now come to the hypothesis presented in the 1939 work that is not derivable from Miller's (1948) analysis of displacement. The later paradigm predicts that individuals with strong internal restraints against aggression would show less intense manifesta- tions of all forms of aggression than would people having weaker in- hibitions against hostility. According to the earlier analysis, however, this need not be the case. Dollard and his collaborators had proposed, it will be recalled, that interference with direct acts of aggression ac- tually heightens the instigation to more indirect forms of hostility (p. 40). Two assumptions are involved here: (1) The blocking of an ag- gressive response sequence, like any other frustration, increases the impetus to aggression; and (2) this increased instigation adds to the strength of the tendencies to more indirect hostile responses.

The previously cited experiment by Thibaut and Coules (1952) seems to support the first assumption. Two conditions were established in one part of this investigation after all the subjects had been angered by notes supposedly written by a fellow college student. In one of these conditions the subjects were interrupted by the experimenter for three minutes immediately after they had received and read the insulting message and before they could reply, while the remaining subjects were allowed to write one note to the instigator before this informal interruption occurred. Then, after the interruption, the subjects in both treatments continued communicating with the instigator. There was a significantly greater volume of aggression communicated to their insulting fellow student by the former subjects, even though the experi- menter rather than this person was responsible for the interruption. Assuming there was little cathartic reduction of hostility in the writing of the single note, it would appear that the interference with the aggres- sive response brought about by the experimenter's interruption was in itself frustrating and that the hostility produced by this thwarting added to the instigation to aggression created by the insulting notes. As we saw earlier in this book, anger effects apparently accumulate with repeated frustrations if these frustrations are relatively close together in time.

Findings from several investigations point to a heightened instigation to indirect forms of hostility after direct aggression is blocked. Some of this evidence can be found in Sears's (1961) follow-up study of the children employed in the earlier investigation by Sears et al. (1957).

Sears attempted a direct test of the present Yale hypothesis (as one part of this later study) by comparing the self-report questionnaire responses given by two groups of children. Both groups had been highly aggressive when they were about five years of age, according to interviews with the mothers obtained at that time, but now, seven years later, only one of these groups was composed of children who described themselves as high in antisocial aggression (i.e., they indicated that aggressive responses normally unacceptable socially were acceptable or desirable to them). The children in the other group reported themselves as low in this antisocial aggression. As Sears has remarked, all these children had been control problems to their parents when they were five, but for unknown reasons some of them (those low in antisocial aggression) seem to have been socialized more successfully than the others. There were no substantial and important differences between the two groups on the measures obtained when the children were five, although there were some (statistically nonsignificant) indications the mothers of the presently low antisocial children had been initially more controlling and less inciting of aggression. The investigator assumed the two groups differed primarily in the extent to which their previously strong aggressive tendencies had been restrained by the subsequent development of inhibitions. Support for this belief is provided by the reliably higher level of aggression anxiety in the low antisocial group, as indicated by their self-descriptions at twelve years. Now, the question is, how did the two groups differ in other forms of aggression at this age? According to the present hypothesis, youngsters low in antisocial aggression should have a higher level of indirect or otherwise controlled aggression. This expectation is confirmed by Sears's findings with measure of "prosocial aggression." The low antisocial children voiced a stronger desire to employ hostility in socially approved ways— for example, in law enforcement and in inflicting punishment for rule breaking. (The difference between the high and low antisocial aggression groups was statistically significant for the boys and was nearly significant in the girls.) Apparently, the restraints the "low" children had developed against their previously strong aggressive tendencies effectively inhibited the direct and antisocial forms of hostility, but also presumably increased the strength of the less direct, socially acceptable modes of expressing aggression.

General evidence for the entire line of reasoning summarized in this chapter can be found in the study of fifty-two adolescent boys published by Bandura and Walters (1959). Half the boys had histories of difficulty with the law or school authorities due to their aggressive antisocial behavior. They were matched with an appropriate control group of boys who "were neither markedly aggressive nor markedly withdrawn." Comparisons of these two groups on data obtained from interviews with each of the parents and the boys themselves, and from projective tests given to the boys, indicated the highly aggressive youngsters had much stronger aggressive inclinations toward their fathers. Since few of the fathers in either group were permissive of aggression to them, it seems fair to say the two groups were fairly close together in the strength of their restraints against attacking their fathers, while the strength of the aggressive tendencies was much greater in the aggressive boys. There also is some suggestion (p. 138) that the inhibitions against aggression in the control boys arose to some extent from their beliefs that hostility was socially improper. The inhibitory gradient, therefore, would be relatively flat in these boys, probably covering a fairly wide range of situations. In the aggressive boys, on the other hand, these restraints appear to have been impelled largely by fear arising from expectations of punishment of aggression. As a result, they would have a steeper inhibitory gradient than would the controls. Arranging the stimulus people for whom data are available along an appropriate continuum in order of dissimilarity to the instigator, we have the dimension, father-teacher-peers. Similarly, a response continuum can be constructed from the following arrangement of actions: physical aggression, verbal aggression, and, finally, other more indirect forms of aggression. Inhibitions theoretically should weaken as the object is further from the father and as the hostility becomes increasingly indirect.

Both groups of youngsters had strong inhibitions against attacking their fathers, and very few of the fathers reported acts of physical aggression against them. Thus, if the boys became angry with their fathers, they would not attack them too directly, but would instead resort to indirect forms of hostility. According to data obtained from the interviews with the fathers (p. 99), indirect hostile actions were somewhat more common in both groups of boys than were the more direct forms of aggression. Also consistent with Miller's theoretical formulation, the highly aggressive boys exceeded the other youngsters reliably in hostility toward the father only in the case of the most indirect forms of aggression.

Turning to the results with the youngsters' interviews, Bandura and Walters presented data concerning aggression toward the teachers. The findings again were as expected (1959, p. 117). For both the aggressive and more "normal" boys indirect forms of aggression were more common than the more directly hostile actions. However, since the inhibitory tendencies elicited by these particular stimulus people—somewhat dissimilar to the fathers—undoubtedly had declined fairly sharply in strength in the aggressive boys (as contrasted with the restraints evoked by the fathers), it is not surprising that these adolescents were reliably more hostile to their teachers than were the controls in all categories of aggressive behavior.

The measures obtained from the interviews with the boys pertaining to their aggression toward peers also yielded findings supporting the present hypotheses. In order to understand these data it is necessary to assume that the restraints against aggression to the peers within the extremely hostile boys were very weak or virtually nonexistent, but that they were still fairly strong in the control group. (This is reasonable if, as mentioned earlier, the inhibitions against aggression in the former boys were instigated largely by fear, while the restraints in the more "normal" boys were based to a greater extent on guilt feelings.) In line with the Yale notion that the strongest instigation in the absence of inhibitions is to direct acts of aggression, the aggressive youngsters reported more direct than indirect hostility responses to their peers. The control boys, however, still exhibited a greater tendency toward the indirect rather than direct forms of aggression.

The difference between the aggressive and control youngsters on the measure of indirect aggression toward the peers provides a test of the 1939 hypothesis concerning the instigational effect of inhibitions. Where Miller's 1948 formulation would maintain that the present group of aggressive boys would never exhibit *less* intense forms of *any* hostile responses than the control boys, the Dollard et al. proposition could predict this occurrence with indirect modes of aggression. Bandura and Walters described just such an outcome (1959, p. 121); the control group showed considerably more indirect hostility to their peers than did the aggressive boys.

Of course, we cannot say unequivocally why these particular results were obtained. It is conceivable that the highly aggressive boys had been so busy performing acts of direct aggression they had little time or energy left for the indirect forms. Whether they actually could have been *this* busy, however, seems doubtful. There is a good possibility the blocking of the directly hostile acts in the control youngsters increased the strength of their instigations to indirect aggression.

In a later investigation, Bandura (1960) compared thirty highly aggressive elementary school boys, selected on the basis of behavioral observations rather than because of any trouble with authorities, and thirty inhibited but demographically comparable boys. To summarize the general pattern of findings, the aggressive youngsters seemed to have both stronger tendencies toward aggression and considerably weaker restraints against this behavior. Thus, while parents of both groups generally punished attacks upon them, the mothers and fathers of the extremely hostile children often rewarded and encouraged their boys' aggression outside the home, and the parents of the inhibited children consistently discouraged these actions.

As in the earlier Bandura-Walters study, both groups of children were described by their parents as displaying more indirect than direct aggression to them. In this case, however, as we move outward on the continuum of targets for aggression, from the parents, through siblings, teachers, and finally peers, it was not until the boys' aggression toward siblings was contrasted that the difference between the groups became statistically significant. The inhibitory gradient clearly had declined sharply in strength in the aggressive youngsters with increased "psychological distance" from the parents, and these hostility differences remained significant for all of the nonparental stimulus people.

Most relevant for our present purposes are the comparisons in the aggressive responses to a thematic test administered to the children. Some of the cards shown to the boys elicited stories of aggression toward peers. Analyses were made of the intensity of three different modes of hostile fantasy behavior varying in their position on the response generalization continuum: physical aggression, verbal aggression, and an indicator of more indirect aggression, statements about hostile "feelings." Since there are the strongest restraints against physical aggression, we can readily understand why the inhibited boys, having considerably stronger internal restraints, expressed significantly less physical aggression toward peers in these stories. There was no difference between the two groups in verbal aggression. When the most indirect form of aggression was considered, however, a clear-cut difference again emerged, but this time the inhibited boys were found to exhibit the strongest aggressive responses. As Bandura concluded (1960):

Apparently, it is only in the case of the most indirect fantasy forms of aggression against objects that are highly dissimilar to the parents on the generalization continuum that the inhibited boys' aggression anxiety is sufficiently reduced to permit the occurrence of a displaced response that exceeds that of the aggressive group (p. 17).

Assuming the inhibited children had generally weaker aggressive tendencies than the other youngsters, their higher level of hostile feelings revealed on the projective test could have been the result of an added instigation to these indirect aggressive responses produced by their restraints blocking the more direct hostile acts. However, we cannot be certain the inhibited children did have characteristically weaker aggressive inclinations. While the available evidence pertaining to the present hypothesis is encouraging, the ultimate test of this notion must come from experimental investigations in which the strength of the initial instigation to aggression is brought under control.

SUMMARY

Neal Miller's (1948) theoretical analysis of the psychoanalytic concept of displacement serves as the foundation of the present discussion of factors affecting the nature and target of aggressive reactions to frustration. Employing this analysis, which is based on the laboratory phenomena of stimulus and response generalization, the following hypotheses can be derived regarding the *target* for the aggressive response:

1. The strongest aggressive response evoked by a frustration is directed against the perceived source of the frustration.

2. Aggressive responses also generalize to objects regarded as being similar to the frustrating agent (or which are psychologically "close" to this agent), with the amount of generalization becoming smaller the less similar the object is to the agent (or the greater the psychological "distance" between the two).

3. Responses inhibiting aggression also generalize to objects similar to the instigator, with the strength of these inhibitory responses declining the less similar the object is to the instigator (or the greater the psychological "distance" between the two).

4. The strength of these incompatible responses causes them to detract from each other.

5. An increase in the drive involved in either the aggression or inhibitory gradient will raise the over-all height of that gradient.

6. The gradient of generalization of the inhibitory responses falls off more steeply with dissimilarity (or "distance") if the inhibitions are based upon fear of punishment for aggression rather than on interiorized moral prohibitions against aggression.

There are several predictions that can be made from these hypotheses. For one, if the angered individual is prevented from attacking his frustrater solely because of the frustrater's absence, his strongest hostile tendencies will be directed against those available people who are "closest" or most similar to the instigator. However, if the angered person cannot attack the frustrater because he is afraid of punishment, he will be most likely to display overt hostility against some object of intermediate similarity to the instigator. The stronger the aggressive tendency relative to the restraints against aggression, the more similar this object will be to the frustrater, while the substitute target will be less similar to the instigator the stronger the inhibitions relative to the aggressive tendencies.

What empirical data there are seem to support this analysis. However, most of the quantitative investigations of this problem have employed fantasy (e.g., projective-test) productions, and further research is needed in more realistic situations. Laboratory findings also indicate that people having relatively strong restraints against aggression do not concentrate what hostility they do display as heavily against the frustrater as do less inhibited people. Instead, the former's attacks (such as they are) seem to be distributed over a broader range of objects. There also are suggestions that people do not automatically direct their aggression against the agent actually most contiguous with the onset of the frustration. They tend to attack the perceived source of the frustration to the extent they are not restrained, but do not automatically blame the person physically most closely associated with the onset of the thwarting for their unpleasant experiences. Thus, a good deal of the hostility aroused by the German air attacks upon England during World War II was directed against the British government rather than the Germans.

The generalization model also proposes a number of hypotheses regarding the *form* of the aggressive response to frustrations. The strongest aggressive instigation arising from a frustration is to acts of direct hostility, and there are increasingly weaker instigations to increasingly more indirect aggressive responses. Inhibitions against aggression give rise to indirect modes of response, but these overt hostile acts tend to be more direct, the stronger the aggressive tendency relative to the restraining tendency.

There is much less research bearing upon the form of the hostile reactions to frustration, but the available evidence tends to support the theoretical analysis.

The hypotheses concerning the nature and form of aggressive responses listed in the 1939 *Frustration and Aggression* monograph can be considered as special cases of this S-R generalization model. However, there are two places where the 1939 work does not fit into Miller's later theoretical analysis. The first of these deals with self-aggression. The Yale group proposed that self-aggression would arise when all alternative modes of aggressive response were blocked by fear of punishment for aggression. The present writer has objected to this hypothesis and, instead, prefers a hypothesis mentioned—but apparently neglected—in the book. Self-aggression results when the *self* is perceived as the source of the frustration.

The other 1939 hypothesis seems to be consistent with empirical data. The blocking of aggressive responses is a frustration that, like other frustrations, increases the instigation to aggression. This means that there should be an increased instigation to indirect modes of hostility when direct hostile acts are inhibited.

# chapter 6

# Intergroup Hostility: I.
# Displacement Reactions

*Introduction*

When the Civil War broke out, President Lincoln offered Robert E. Lee the command of the Federal armies. Lee could not turn against his home state, and resigning his commission in the United States Army, went on to lead the Southern military forces in Virginia. He did not believe in the dismemberment of the Union, but did his best to tear it apart violently. Lee fought, not out of adherence to the ideological principles of the Confederacy, but because of his loyalty to a region. He was responsible for the death and injury of hundreds of thousands of Northern soldiers, not because he hated them and what they symbolized, but for love of the state in which he had grown to manhood. In a very real sense, he initiated countless acts of aggression (as such behavior is defined in this book) solely because of his membership in a group.

Unless some psychoanalyst-historian can uncover additional as yet unsuspected information about Robert E. Lee, it is virtually impossible to explain his behavior in terms of the frustration-aggression hypothesis. He had met with relatively little frustration in his successful career in the United States Army. There also is relatively little to be gained from the application of the frustration-aggression formula to the problem of the origin of the Civil War. This proposition can perhaps account for much of the violent hatred expressed during the war, but does not say why the thwarting conditions had arisen. Any complete description of the Civil War, or any other conflict for that matter, obviously must involve the full range of the social sciences: political, historical, sociological, and economic considerations, as well as those taken from psychology. It simply is not possible to discuss the origins of the Civil War adequately without mentioning the political structure of the Federal system, or the historic-sociological factors in the cultures of the North and South, or the economic foundations of these cultures. The study of intergroup conflict, of necessity, is a multidisciplinary matter.[1]

*The Need for a Multidisciplinary Approach.* Nevertheless, most of the writings dealing with intergroup relationships have been, and will continue to be, somewhat one-sided, emphasizing one approach to the minimization of others. The present work is no exception; most of our attention is given to individualistic considerations. But this type of bias reflects the interests of the writer and the necessity of impressing some limitations upon the scope of the book, more than a belief that group and systems variables are relatively unimportant.

The importance of a multidisciplinary approach to intergroup hostility can easily be documented. Historians have insisted, for example, that present-day ethnic relations can be understood fully only by considering the historical background of these relationships. According to one such writer (cited in Klineberg, 1950, p. 192), there is much less race prejudice in Brazil than in the United States because the original Portuguese settlers in that country had previously known another "colored" group, the Moors. This earlier contact presumably had "predisposed them to a friendly and even respectful attitude" toward colored peoples. Other more contemporaneous factors also can affect intergroup relations; groups sharing a common history may develop along different lines. Thus, Klineberg (1950) has indicated that Argentine Negroes are not treated in the same manner as are Negroes in Brazil, even though the Spaniards settling Argentina had also previously lived in contact with the Moors (p. 193). Traditional attitudes regarding colored people, for one reason or another, apparently differ in these two countries, giving rise to different patterns of behavior toward Negroes.

One way of dealing with such a complex pattern of interacting variables is to establish categories of intergroup conflict. Some classes of causal factors might be important in one conflict type, but yet be relatively unimportant in other cases. Rose (1956), for example, proposed the following classifications: (1) "political" struggles, involving conflict over scarce political and economic values, properties, and positions; (2) "ideological" conflicts over different ways of life; and (3) "racist" struggles over biological dominance (pp. 506–507). Other analytic schemes have also been devised (*cf.* Mack & Snyder, 1957).

*Difficulties in Integrating the Various Approaches.* Nevertheless, any one classification system or analytic scheme probably cannot completely reconcile the different approaches to the study of intergroup conflict. Two major obstacles bar the road to a complete integration. There is a

---

[1] The political, sociological, historical, and psychological explanations obviously overlap, however. Thus, economic and ideological conflicts can be interpreted in frustration-aggression terms.

relatively minor problem in the language and constructs employed by the various scholars in the field. They may employ different levels of analysis, some preferring to deal with the behavior of individuals, while others isolate regularities common to collections of individuals. A somewhat more important difficulty confronting the integration of the various approaches stems from differences in what are regarded as the important aspects of the struggle situation.

Both types of problems can be found in the contrast Jessie Bernard (1957) drew between *sociological* and *social-psychological* conceptualizations of intergroup conflict. For one thing, these two types of formulations operate at different levels of analysis; the sociological approach generally deals with relations between or among systems, while the social-psychological view emphasizes processes within the individuals. But there also are differences here in the phenomena singled out for particular attention. For the typical adherent to the former approach, according to Bernard, intergroup conflict arises from "incompatible or mutually exclusive goals or aims or values" (p. 38). (Rose's above-mentioned classification system is readily seen as an example of this type of view.) Thus, for Bernard, hostility toward minority groups essentially arises from mutually exclusive values, and violence is just one kind of strategy a system may adopt in its relations with other systems (p. 38). Those taking the social-psychological approach, on the other hand, place particular stress upon the "nonrational" components of conflict, frequently regarding aggression as a reaction to inner tensions resulting from the frustrations of life.[2]

*Emotional Tensions and Intergroup Conflict.* The present writer believes the utilization of either of these two orientations alone would result in a serious neglect of important phenomena in the field. Social psychologists engaged in studies of intergroup relations generally *have* neglected considerations of struggle over scarce values and the strategic aspects of aggression. This is not to say, however, that emotional tensions play an insignificant role in all forms of social conflict (*cf.* Mack & Snyder, 1957, p. 222), even though, as Bernard claimed, such tensions are relatively unimportant determinants of modern wars. To support this point, she cited an investigation of twenty-five major wars, reporting that "in no case is the decision [to go to war] precipitated by emotional tensions, sentimentality, . . . or other irrational motivations" (Bernard, 1957, p. 40). Emotions, nevertheless, can play a vital part in some

[2] It would be a serious mistake, however, to contend—as Bernard implies—that this is the only view of intergroup conflict taken by social psychologists. Several, for example, have pointed up the important role played by shared group attitudes in the development of racial prejudice (e.g., Horowitz & Horowitz, 1937). Nevertheless, the tension-reaction interpretation of group conflict does appear to be the dominant view taken by social psychologists.

aspects of international strife. Government leaders interested in starting a war still find it convenient to arouse hatred toward the prospective enemy. Anger arousal makes their people more willing to fight. Emotional tensions have some significance in most instances of group conflict, whether they are the primary cause of the groups' coming to blows or not. This being the case, *the present chapter will discuss the role of such tension effects as displaced aggression in social conflicts and particularly in social prejudice.* The following chapter will consider group and social factors involved in these struggle relations.

## Displaced Aggression in Social Conflicts

It has become commonplace to explain much of the hostility shown toward minorities in terms of some displaced aggression or "scapegoat theory" of intergroup relations. Such notions are practically as old as social science. In his scholarly and important work, *The Nature of Prejudice,* Gordon Allport (1954) recorded one version of this theory, written well before the onset of the twentieth century, attributing anti-Semitism to a psychological need for some target to be attacked (p. 343). Allport also pointed out that scapegoating has long been recognized in everyday life. More than one person has complained to a frustrated friend after receiving an unwarranted attack from him, "Don't take it out on me." The recipient of the aggression in these cases, knowing he was just the happenstance victim of anger generated by some thwarting the other person had experienced, usually excuses the outburst. The anger "just had to come out," he would say. As mentioned in the previous chapter, psychoanalytically influenced writers tend to have a somewhat similar view. They often interpret the hostile attack upon the innocent victim as providing a "safety valve" or "outlet" for pent-up aggressive "energy."

But whatever the details of the particular interpretation, there are certain features common to all analyses of scapegoating: (1) that interferences with goal-directed activities have given rise to aggressive tendencies; (2) that the thwarted individual was unable to direct his hostility toward the actual frustrater (either because the instigator was not apparent or was too powerful to attack); and (3) the frustrated person therefore found a scapegoat in an innocent victim who could be attacked without fear of retaliation.

Before reporting some of the research findings supporting the scapegoat theory, one important point should be made: Along with most social scientists, the present writer does not claim that all ethnic prejudice is an outgrowth of emotional tensions. Many people are unfriendly, if not downright hostile, to particular groups because such negative attitudes are prescribed by the culture to which they belong. In exhibiting prejudice against these groups, then, these people may be revealing beliefs they had learned in their culture independently of any frustrations they had experienced. The prejudiced behavior may also be carried out in conformity to the cultural norms. That is, people may display hostility to Negroes, Jews, or any other group in order to maintain or enhance their acceptance by others in their society; friendly behavior to these groups may mean social rejection.

We all know of instances in which individual Southern whites have been made to suffer some penalty, such as ostracism, for treating Negroes as if they were their equals. The cultural norm in most Southern white communities maintains that Negroes must be regarded as inferior and potentially dangerous beings. Conformity to such a norm means prejudiced behavior. In the North, however, where community norms regarding the status of the Negro are not as clear-cut or strong, people who are prone to submit to the beliefs of the others about them are less likely to be unfriendly to Negroes in their actions. Pettigrew (1959) found that those Southern whites with the strongest conformist tendencies (i.e., females and church attenders) were much more anti-Negro than their less conformist counterparts. The former seem to have submitted to the anti-Negro social pressures in their communities because similar people with conformist tendencies in the North were not generally more anti-Negro than their neighbors.

But, acknowledging the importance of social factors in ethnic relations, emotional tensions may still affect the relative intensity of the hostility displayed against a particular group. Pettigrew has also observed that those personality characteristics related to antiminority attitudes in Northern samples (i.e., authoritarianism) also predict the relative strengths of anti-Negro attitudes in the South. Even though prejudice is socially prescribed in the South, highly authoritarian Southerners tend to be more aggressive toward Negroes than are their less authoritarian peers.

*Empirical Evidence for the Scapegoat Theory of Prejudice.* Several investigations have provided evidence consistent with the scapegoat theory, although some of the findings are equivocal. Reference has already been made (in Chapters 3 and 5) to studies showing that economic hardships in the South prior to the 1930s were associated with the number of Negroes lynched in that area. The magnitude of this correlation may perhaps be questioned, but there seems to be little doubt that some such relationship existed in the period covered by the investigations. Furthermore, there are other indications that aggression toward the Negro is correlated with economic frustrations. For example, there were twenty-one lynchings in 1930. The Southern counties in which these acts of violence occurred generally were more deprived economically than the counties having no lynchings. Relative to the average level in their states, the counties with lynchings were lower in per capita bank deposits, per capita farm and factory income, and automobile and farm ownership (Raper, 1933). More recently, Pettigrew and Cramer (1959) have reported that economically backward Southern areas often vote more heavily for politicians advocating hostility toward Negroes (i.e., who are racists and strongly prosegregation) than do more prosperous Southern areas. Thus, in Virginia in 1956 prosegregationist voting was correlated negatively with white family income (—.45). Poor economic conditions, of course, probably exist in those Southern regions having the strongest anti-Negro traditions, but these traditions may be maintained and enforced because they provide an outlet for frustration-engendered aggression.

Frustrations may foster hostility against a number of minorities. Bettelheim and Janowitz (1950) interviewed 150 World War II veterans, categorizing them on the basis of their answers into groups having different levels of hostility toward Jews and Negroes. These ethnic attitudes were related to changes in the veterans' social status. Some of the men were now in jobs having a lower social status than their prewar occupations, others were in jobs of equal status, and the remainder in jobs having a higher status level. The majority of the "downward mobile" men were strongly hostile toward Jews and/or Negroes, while most of the "upward mobile" veterans were tolerant toward one or both of these minority groups. Although there are a number of ways these findings may be explained, Bettelheim and Janowitz hypothesized that the shifts in social status were responsible for the attitudes toward the minority groups. If so, we can assume the downward movement in the social ladder was frustrating to the men having this experience and that this thwarting produced the hostility displaced upon the Jews and Negroes.

Similar assumptions can be applied to the results of a survey conducted by Campbell (summarized in G. W. Allport, 1954, p. 224). Anti-Semitism was found to be far stronger in people who were dissatisfied with their jobs than in people expressing contentment with their employment. The occupationally dissatisfied individuals probably were suffering from at least some economic frustrations. These experiences, in turn, could well have given rise to resentment, contributing to their unfavorable attitudes toward Jews.

Correlational findings such as these, however, permit relatively many alternative explanations. The direction of causation is always uncertain in these relationships. Definitive tests of the scapegoat theory will have to be obtained from experimental investigations such as the one conducted by Miller and Bugelski (1948). As reported in the preceding chapter, the results in this experiment support the interpretation of prejudice as displaced aggression. The frustrated boys in the sample observed by the Yale psychologists demonstrated increased unfriendliness toward Mexicans and Japanese.

*Conditions under Which Scapegoating Occurs.* However, despite the findings cited here, there are good reasons to doubt whether thwartings necessarily always heighten hostility toward minority groups. Allport (1954, pp. 350–351) has listed a number of important qualifications facing the scapegoat theory which, in effect, seriously restrict the generality of this doctrine. Three of the limitations mentioned by Allport are particularly relevant here (but they will be discussed within the framework of the present book).

1. *Aggression is not always the dominant response to frustration.* This argument is consistent with the position taken in this book; with Dollard and his collaborators, I have suggested that interference with some goal-directed activity increases the instigation to aggression, or what is here termed anger. Aggressive responses are usually evoked by this emotional state (if suitable cues are present), but other frustration-induced response tendencies capable of inhibiting these hostile responses may be stronger in many people, at least in certain situations. Consequently, a person can show nonaggressive reactions to frustrations.

2. *Aggression is not always displaced onto some innocent victim.* This is an important point frequently neglected in many discussions of hostility displacement. The 1939 *Frustration and Aggression* monograph and Miller's later papers on S-R generalization processes, still the most cogent presentations of the displacement thesis, indicate that the strongest aggressive tendencies resulting from a frustration are directed toward the perceived source of the interference. If the frustrater is available as a target for aggression and there are no restraints against attacking him, hostility will not be displaced onto someone else. Furthermore, the aggression may be directed toward the self, i.e., there is an intropunitive reaction, when the self is regarded as the source of the frustration.

3. *A defenseless minority or the safest available target is not always the recipient of displaced aggression.* Perhaps the most serious mistake made by both exponents and critics of the scapegoat theory has to do with their oversimplified contention regarding the target for the displaced hostility. Many have assumed, almost as a matter of course, that the frustrated individual who is afraid to attack the actual anger instigator will aggress against the person least likely to harm him by retaliatory aggression (e.g., Williams, 1947, p. 52). This assumption is not warranted either empirically or theoretically. Allport has reminded us (1954, p. 351) that the dominant majority group also may serve as a

scapegoat; Negroes can hate whites, and Jews may discriminate against gentiles. The S-R generalization analysis of displacement described in the previous chapter clearly does not maintain that hostility will be displaced only to the safest targets available. Safety is not the most important determinant of target choice; rather, this is also a matter of the similarity (or "psychological distance") between the instigator and the available targets. It was shown earlier that the chosen scapegoat is more similar to the actual instigator, the stronger the thwarted individual's aggressive tendencies are, relative to his inhibitory tendencies. Thus, if a person cannot attack his frustrater only because this latter individual is absent, his hostile responses will tend to generalize to other people, and the individual psychologically "closest" to the instigator of all of these available others will be the one most likely to receive the displaced aggression. On the other hand, when the direct attack upon the frustrater is prevented by internal restraints against aggression stemming largely from fear of punishment, the likeliest target for the displaced aggression will be an individual of *intermediate* similarity to the instigator. The stronger the aggressive reaction relative to the strength of the inhibitory responses, the greater the similarity between the instigator and the object aggressed against.

An individual's power to inflict injury to others may be one of the dimensions along which hostility generalization takes place, or at least may be correlated with such a generalization dimension. The person seen as being unlikely to hit back if attacked probably will be regarded as entirely different from the thwarting agent; many frustraters are socially powerful and have little timidity. According to this analysis, therefore, the recipient of displaced hostility is more likely to be at least moderately capable of punishing his attacker than to be completely lacking in this ability.

White and Lippitt (1960), among others, have not interpreted hostility displacement in the manner proposed by Miller's S-R generalization model. They observed a number of instances of scapegoating under the autocratic "climates" in their previously mentioned leadership study. The boys in these autocratic groups presumably were frustrated by their dictatorial adult leader, but being afraid to aggress against him, "took out" their resentment upon other club members (pp. 69–70). Aggression, for White and Lippitt, was almost always oriented toward restoring the self-esteem supposedly weakened by the frustration. (Thwartings, they maintained, elicit hostility only when they lower self-esteem.)

In defense of their thesis, the investigators reported that the scapegoats were never the weakest or most passive boys in the club (p. 166). The boys singled out for aggression in one autocratic group "were both boys who could hold their own against any of the others taken singly," while in another club the scapegoat was the largest and heaviest boy. These youngsters would not have been attacked, White and Lippitt argued, if the sole aim of the aggression were to blow off steam safely; easier and safer targets supposedly would have been chosen for this purpose. The writers suggested these particular boys were aggressed against in an attempt to recover status or self-esteem. They were fairly strong and dangerous, although without being excessively formidable, so that the individual directing hostility against them could regard himself as potent and strong in his own right (p. 166).

Many hostile actions undoubtedly are carried out in order to gain or enhance self-esteem. Bullies frequently are motivated by this type of desire. They have learned to attack others as a way of increasing their status in their own eyes and to others. The present book contends, nevertheless, that not all aggression is instrumental aggression in this sense. Hostility can arise solely as a reaction to frustration. If a husband is angry with his wife because she placed some minor dents in their car, requiring, say, fifty dollars' worth of repairs, the anger need not have been produced by loss of self-esteem. The husband is more likely to resent the loss of the fifty dollars. Similarly, the attacks upon the scapegoats observed by White and Lippitt need not have arisen in an attempt to restore self-esteem. They may have been direct reactions to frustrations. These particular boys, being moderately assertive (according to the observers), may have interfered with activities carried out by the other group members which, since the others were already fairly angry, readily evoked overt hostility from them. On the other hand, if the youngsters were the recipients of displaced aggression, without instigating hostility through their own behavior, they could have been aggressed against because they were somewhat similar to the frustrating adult either physically or behaviorally. Miller's displacement analysis applied to this situation does not maintain that the displaced aggression would be directed against only those boys unlikely to retaliate. Such "safe" targets probably would be much too dissimilar to the autocratic adult leader for aggression to generalize to them.

But even with the most sophisticated versions of the scapegoat theory, there is no reason to believe hostility always will be displaced upon an innocent victim. Putting it simply, the thwarted individual may not associate an available object with his frustrater. The present theoretical formulation insists aggression is generalized to the available object only to the extent that such an association can be made. It is not surprising, therefore, that other investigators have not always replicated the Miller-Bugelski findings. Stagner and Congdon (1955) repeated the essentials of the earlier investigation in an experiment with college students. The subjects, males and females, first completed a series of attitude scales and then were given four performance tasks. Some subjects were severely frustrated by failing them on all four tasks, others were moderately frustrated by failing them on two of the tasks, and the control subjects were passed on all four tests. Following this test performance, the subjects again responded to the attitude scales. In contrast to Miller and Bugelski, however, Stagner and Congdon did not obtain any heightened attribution of undesirable characteristics to minority groups in the experimental subjects. Then, to add to the confusion, Cowen, Landes, and Schaet (1959) more recently reported evidence consistent with the Miller-Bugelski thesis. Their college student subjects tended to increase in unfriendliness toward Negroes following the experimental frustration (with the males in this study showing a somewhat greater increase in overt prejudice than the females).

## Personality Differences in Scapegoating

We cannot say, with any certainty, just why the displacement studies have not yielded consistent results. The "now-you-see-it, now-you-don't" findings do indicate, however, that the scapegoat theory, as usually formulated, is incomplete. Additional details have to be specified in order to handle the apparent exceptions. Some versions of this theory attempt to provide this needed detail by maintaining that there are reliable individual differences in readiness to exhibit scapegoating behavior. Highly prejudiced individuals, it is sometimes suggested (e.g., Fenichel, 1946), for one reason or another presumably have learned to blame other people for their frustrations. Where the tolerant person might attribute the thwartings he encounters to his own shortcomings (assuming it is difficult to determine the actual source of the frustration), the individual who is characteristically unfriendly to minority groups supposedly denies such self-responsibility. But further, he also is unwilling or unable to attribute blame to the dominant sources of power in his society; according to the conceptions of the authoritarian personality (Adorno et al., 1950), highly prejudiced people typically perceive themselves as too weak to attack these power sources and also try to compensate for this weakness by associating themselves with these dominant authorities. Therefore, since they usually do not criticize themselves or the dominant majority groups, they supposedly can only attribute their frustrations to the weaker minority groups.

The line of thought just outlined obviously is a highly complex affair based on a number of important assumptions. We already have seen the difficulties encountered by the notion that displaced aggression is automatically directed to the safest and weakest target available. Another and more valid assumption in this reasoning should be made explicit. Much of the following discussion, although not all of it, deals with the individual who is intolerant toward minority groups primarily because of the nature of his personality.

Evidence accumulated with the growth of social science clearly documents the existence of such a "prejudiced personality" (Adorno et al., 1950; G. W. Allport, 1954; Harding, Kutner, Proshansky, & Chein, 1954). Group norms transmitted by family and friends can prescribe nonequalitarian behavior toward particular groups. Southern whites learn to regard Negroes as inferior and potentially dangerous beings without necessarily being taught the same thing about other minorities, such as Jews. But many people develop a fairly uniform negative attitude toward a surprisingly wide range of groups. Adorno and his collaborators (1950) found, as others had, that hostility and intolerant attitudes toward one outgroup (i.e., a group to which the individual does not belong) generally are associated with similar sentiments toward other outgroups. The white Protestant individual who is prejudiced against Jews often is also somewhat prejudiced against Catholics and "foreigners." Since this type of person also tends to glorify those groups to which he belongs, Adorno et al. refer to him as an *ethnocentric* individual. The personality characteristics of this individual figure prominently in much of the material to be presented below. Thus, highly ethnocentric people may have a strong tendency to displace hostility onto innocent objects.

*Individual Differences in Scapegoating.* The first experimental test of this personality hypothesis was conducted by Lindzey (1950). Twenty college students, half previously determined to be very high in minority group prejudice and the others very low in prejudice, were individually subjected to severe frustration in a small-group situation. (The other group members, unknown to each subject, were the experimenter's confederates.) Comparisons with a control group, matched in terms of prejudice scores and age, showed that the frustrated subjects had a significantly greater increase in hostility scores on two projective tests; the thwartings they had experienced had heightened the strength of their aggressive tendencies.

There were no differences between the high and low prejudiced subjects, however, in the degree of displaced aggression expressed on the projective tests following the thwarting, even though observers' ratings of the subjects' reactions as well as postexperimental interviews with the students indicated the frustration was more upsetting to the prejudiced men. Lindzey (p. 305) and G. W. Allport (1954, p. 348) suggested that people high in prejudice against minority groups are more susceptible to frustrations than are those with a lower level of prejudice. That is, they are more likely to display a strong emotional reaction when thwarted, but—these writers believed—this is not necessarily channeled into aggression against other people.

Other explanations are also available. At least some of this failure to obtain displacement can perhaps be traced to Lindzey's procedures. For example, in one of his projective tests, the TAT, he assumed hostility displacement would be manifested in the tendency for "self" figures to direct aggression against "nonself" figures. However, these latter figures (drawings) may have been so dissimilar to the actual source of the frustration, hostility could not generalize to them.

Berkowitz (1959) employed an actual person as the target available for hostility in his study and obtained findings consistent with the scapegoat theory. In this experiment female college students, scoring either very high or very low on a scale of anti-Semitism, were individually subjected either to an annoying, frustrating treatment administered by the experimenter or to a more neutral experience with him. After this treatment, the subjects were given a topic to discuss with another girl, actually the experimenter's confederate, but introduced to them as another subject who had been working in an adjoining room. Questionnaire ratings of this other girl, made immediately after the conclusion of the discussion, constituted the hostility index. This procedure did yield indications of hostility generalization. In comparison with the similar nonfrustrated subjects, the thwarted, highly anti-Semitic girls apparently had increased in unfriendliness toward their peer. The more tolerant co-eds receiving this harsh treatment, on the other hand, seemed to have become friendlier to the other girl. For the former subjects, then, the hostility engendered by the frustrating experimenter presumably generalized to the neutral bystander, while this generalization did not take place in the less prejudiced group.

Other findings in this study also have some relevance for the scapegoat theory. For one thing, in half the cases the confederate was given a Jewish name when she was introduced to the subject and a gentile name in the remaining cases. The name assigned to the bystander did not seem to have any effect on the extent to which hostility generalized to her, perhaps because the name did not "register" with many of the subjects. Nevertheless, the evidence of a displacement reaction in the frustrated anti-Semitic girls suggests this may be a fairly reliable tendency, occurring whether the available target is a minority-group member or not.[3] In other words, highly prejudiced people such as these may have a tendency to become more unfriendly to almost any other

[3] It is not certain that the frustrated anti-Semitic girls did not suspect the confederate was Jewish regardless of the name assigned to her. Elliott and Wittenberg (1955) demonstrated that anti-Semitic people are likely to guess that an ambiguous person is Jewish, and this conceivably could have happened here.

stranger, regardless of the stranger's group membership, when they are frustrated.

There is no good evidence in this experiment as to why this generalization took place. The usual conception of the prejudiced personality summarized earlier suggests displacement arises because the individual supposedly cannot blame himself for the unpleasant experience he has suffered and thus has to blame others. Consistent with this hypothesis, Lesser (1958) showed that highly anti-Semitic people characteristically exhibit extrapunitive reactions to frustrations. Some of the questionnaire results obtained in the Berkowitz experiment do indicate the aroused anti-Semitic girls had a tendency to deny self-responsibility for the frustration, but my present inclination is to attribute the hostility generalization in these subjects to the nature of their perceptions of the neutral bystander. In essence, I believe the thwarted prejudiced women perceived relatively little difference between the bystander and the frustrating experimenter. Both presumably were regarded as the same kind of person.

This conception does not insist aggressive responses will never be generalized to figures in fantasy situations. Studies reported in the previous chapter have indicated such generalizations can take place. The point made here, rather, is that many fantasy figures are so dissimilar to the instigator they can elicit only very weak (if any) generalized aggression. Furthermore, the fantasy objects themselves can vary in their similarity to the frustrater. Some fantasy objects may be psychologically "closer" to the instigator than are, say, the nonself TAT figures Lindzey used in his measure of hostility displacement. This reasoning can account for the positive results Weatherley (1961) obtained in his test of the scapegoat theory. As in the other studies, college students (this time males), selected on the basis of extreme scores on a measure of anti-Semitism, were assigned to either an experimental or a control group. The experimental subjects were deliberately angered and then were asked to respond to a specially designed fantasy test containing both Jewish and non-Jewish figures. The control subjects, of course, took the fantasy test without the prior provocation.

Analyses of protocols revealed significant differences in the number of aggressive acts directed toward the fantasy characters, which varied with the level of anti-Semitism in the subjects and with the name (Jewish or gentile) assigned to the story character. Thus, when compared with the nonthwarted but matched group, the frustrated prejudiced subjects directed more aggression to characters with Jewish names and fewer hostile acts to the non-Jewish figures. This is what some versions of the scapegoat theory would predict; prejudiced subjects have a tendency to become hostile toward Jews when they are frustrated. To anticipate the theoretical position elaborated in greater detail below, this displacement may occur because *prejudiced people usually associate Jews with the more immediate frustraters.*

In line with the results in the Berkowitz (1959) experiment, the tolerant group generally exhibited a decrease in hostility toward the fantasy characters when frustrated. If we assume the level of hostility in the matched control subjects represents the type of behavior the thwarted people would display in a neutral situation, it appears that over all targets the less prejudiced subjects showed a greater change toward fantasy expressions of friendliness after they were provoked by the instigator than did the highly anti-Semitic subjects. Interestingly enough, this *decrease* in aggressive acts directed toward the story characters by the tolerant group was reliably greater for the Jewish than non-Jewish figures; these people seemingly had become somewhat friendlier to Jews than toward gentiles when frustrated. Weatherley interpreted this heightened friendliness toward Jews as an anxiety reaction. Aggressive inclinations supposedly had generalized to the Jewish characters. But the subjects then presumably became anxious about these hostile tendencies, perhaps after becoming aware of the nature of their responses to the Jewish figures. As a result, they leaned over backward to avoid displaying hostility to the Jewish characters.

This interesting hypothesis is potentially an important contribution to the study of ethnic relations. It suggests that people admitting to relatively little anti-Semitism are not really unprejudiced if we define prejudice as involving a failure to differentiate among the members of a group. They actually may have learned to react to Jews as a class. But what they have learned, according to this notion, is to avoid showing hostility and prejudice in response to Jews.

*Judgment and Perception in Hostility Generalization.* Weatherley's aggression-anxiety interpretation of the tolerant group's behavior toward Jews can be neither proven nor disproven at this time. It is, nevertheless, a fairly limited hypothesis, unable to deal with several important problems. For example, it does not tell why the less prejudiced girls in the Berkowitz experiment tended to become somewhat friendlier toward their peer following the frustration. There is no reason to believe these co-eds perceived this bystander as being Jewish. Further, although the difference is not statistically significant, this interpretation cannot say why the thwarted tolerant subjects in the Weatherley study seemed to have a greater increase in friendliness toward the gentile character than did the similarly treated highly anti-Semitic men. Both of these questions can be answered, however, by employing the type of judgmental analysis used in Chapter 3 to explain some of the effects of repeated frustration.

To recapitulate some of the points made earlier, psychophysical investigations have demonstrated that the judgmental process essentially involves a comparison between some standard and the stimulus object or event being judged. A relatively slight discrepancy between the standard and the given object (or event) on some appropriate dimension usually produces an *assimilation effect* in which this discrepancy is further minimized. Thus, if a person has seen many cases of bizarre behavior, these events will tend to become the judgmental standard used in evaluating any later instances of such behavior. Should he then witness a moderately abnormal act fairly similar to the average bizarre experience composing his standard, there will be an assimilation effect bringing the judgment closer to the standard. As a result, the act will be seen as more bizarre than it "really" is. On the other hand, great discrepancies between the standard and the object generally give rise to a contrast effect, exaggerating the difference. Suppose another individual, who has never observed anything but the most "normal" behavior, and a third person, who has had a great deal of acquaintance with mildly bizarre behavior, also saw this moderately abnormal act. There is a relatively sizeable discrepancy between the standard and stimulus event in the former but not in the latter case. The resulting contrast effect in the former person would mean he probably would judge the moderately strange act as being quite bizarre—the strangeness of the behavior is exaggerated by contrast. The latter individual, however, probably would interpret this act (through assimilation) as being only mildly abnormal.

The present writer has suggested elsewhere that these judgmental phenomena may have their counterparts in some instances of hostility displacement (Berkowitz, 1960d, 1961). But before this analysis is described, its relation to S-R generalization should be made clear. Miller's generalization model can account for the differences between the high- and low-prejudice frustrated groups in the Berkowitz anti-Semitism experiment in two different ways: by postulating differences in the strength of the aggressive tendencies aroused by the frustration, or by proposing differences in the generalization continua. As for the first of these possibilities, the highly anti-Semitic girls could have generalized their aggression to the neutral bystander, while the more tolerant girls did not do this, because stronger aggressive inclinations were aroused in the former, extending the generalization gradient over a wider range of objects. This hypothesis seems to be ruled out, however, by the nonreliable questionnaire differences between the two groups in the extent to which they felt provoked by the experimenter's treatment of them.

The possibility of differences in generalization continua therefore appears to offer greater promise. But again, there are two ways in which this occurrence can operate:

1. The frustrated anti-Semitic subjects could have seen little difference between the instigator and the bystander on some appropriate judgmental dimension because they characteristically tend to make only gross discriminations among stimuli when they are emotionally aroused. The tolerant women, on the other hand, could have reacted to their thwarting by more sharply differentiating between the frustrater and the bystander, and this too can be a reflection of a general stress-induced tendency to make finer discriminations among stimuli.

2. Attitudes aroused in the prejudiced women may have created a generalization gradient associating the peer bystander with the frustrating experimenter. Research evidence indicates both processes could have been involved in the above-mentioned experiments.

Frustration-produced differences in the sharpness of the discriminations made between instigator and peer may explain why the less ethnocentric people tended to become friendlier to the bystander while the intolerant group exhibited an increase in unfriendliness. To illustrate how this may have occurred, let us assume the experimenter (in the Berkowitz study) served as the judgmental standard with whom the subject's peer was compared. The fact that the tolerant girls increased in friendliness toward their peer following their experience with the unpleasant experimenter suggests they reacted to the stress by drawing a finer distinction between the instigator and the bystander. In comparison to that unpleasant person she seemed very nice, and the resulting contrast effect heightened the favorability of this impression. A different judgmental phenomenon presumably occurred in the ethnocentrics. The highly prejudiced co-eds appear to have exhibited an assimilation effect in their judgments following the frustration. Instead of contrasting the peer with the unpleasant experimenter, they apparently decreased the difference between these two stimulus people. One stimulus person was relatively similar to the other in certain important ways for them, and consequently the hostility evoked by the experimenter could easily generalize to the peer.

Confirmation of this reasoning requires a demonstration of individual differences in judgments made under stress. Highly prejudiced individuals should make grosser discriminations when they are frustrated or otherwise under stress than they would normally, while extremely unprejudiced people should react to such emotion-arousing situations by making finer differentiations among the stimuli confronting them. Two earlier papers by the present writer (1960d, 1961) have presented such a demonstration. In these studies, highly anti-Semitic[4] college students apparently made sharp differentiations between the two sets of stimuli presented to them when they were under a low stress condition, but did not draw such fine distinctions under mild stress. The reverse was true for the less prejudiced subjects; they seemed to place the two sets of stimuli further apart on the relevant judgmental dimension under the stress condition than under the more neutral treatment.[5]

These findings conceivably can account for the results in the above hostility displacement studies. Highly ethnocentric individuals in our society, who characteristically discriminate (socially) against minority groups such as Jews and Negroes, actually may be relatively poor at making discriminations (perceptual) when they are in a stressful, emotion-arousing situation. People they do not know too well can be regarded as fairly similar. If any one of these strangers treats them harshly, they might think, the others probably also would do this.

Those individuals expressing extremely little intolerance, on the other hand, seemed to respond to frustrating situations by drawing finer distinctions between the source of the thwarting and the other people about them. The increased friendliness the less prejudiced subjects displayed toward the female bystander in the Berkowitz experiment and toward the fantasy characters in Weatherley's study could then be the result of a judgmental contrast effect. It is possible, furthermore, to order the fantasy figures used in the Weatherley investigation in terms of their probable dissimilarity to the experimenter; the gentile characters undoubtedly were "closer" to him psychologically than were the Jewish characters. Since the magnitude of the contrast effect is a direct function of the discrepancy between the judgmental standard (assumed to be the experimenter) and the objects being judged (the fantasy figures), there should be a stronger contrast effect with regard to the Jewish than the non-Jewish characters. This, of course, is what Weatherley found; there was a greater increase in friendliness toward the Jewish

[4] The manner in which the students in the 1961 study were selected indicates the anti-Semitism is but one component of the general ethnocentrism discussed earlier.

[5] Easterbrook (1959) has hypothesized that the "range of cue utilization" shrinks under emotion-arousing conditions, resulting in a broader generalization gradient or, to put it in another way, a decreased use of peripheral, partially relevant cues. According to this thesis, then, the grosser discriminations made by the prejudiced subjects are the usual perceptual concomitants of emotion arousal, and it is the behavior of the extremely unprejudiced subjects that is unexpected. Berkowitz (1959) found that emotion was elicited in these more tolerant people under his frustrating conditions. Thus, if the increased friendliness these people displayed toward their peer is a reliable phenomenon, it may be that individuals of this personality type have learned to respond to emotion-provoking conditions by making relatively fine differentiations.

story figures, presumably because they were the least similar to the unpleasant experimenter.

## Stimulus Characteristics of Minority Groups

*Why Are Particular Groups Selected as Scapegoats?* The reasoning spelled out so far can explain why aggressive responses generalized to the stimulus objects *that happened to be available* for displaced hostility in the above studies. Judgmental processes resulting in the placing of one object close to another on some relevant dimension facilitated the generalization of responses from one of these objects to the other. However, this line of thought still does not satisfactorily account for the selection of *particular* targets when there are many potential targets available. Several writers have criticized the scapegoat theory on just these grounds (e.g., G. W. Allport, 1954, p. 351; Zawadski, 1948). Zawadski, for example, has characterized this theory of prejudice as a "pure drive" notion, maintaining that it explains the behavior of the intolerant individual "out of the inner workings of his emotional life" but disregards "the characteristics of the stimulus" (1948, p. 132).

This is a valid point. Most descriptions of the scapegoating process do not say why a particular minority is selected for hostility displacement when there are several presumably "safe" groups to choose from. If all that is required for displacement is a nonfeared victim, why are Jews attacked rather than, say, people of Scottish descent? The solution to this problem of target selection can only come from a consideration of the stimulus qualities of the various groups in our society—how they are perceived by the prejudiced and unprejudiced.

*Visibility.* Williams (1947) advanced a formula to account for the choice of victim that is only partially satisfactory. Groups become substitute objects of aggression, he proposed, not only when they are "safe" (i.e., not in a position to retaliate), but also to the extent they are "highly visible" (p. 52). Jews are attacked more frequently than Scots supposedly because they are more strikingly apparent. They do not necessarily have to be more numerous, according to this argument; the important thing is that they stand out from other groups by possessing many unique, differentiating features, such as different physical appearances and/or different values and customs. Increased numbers can make this factor of a group's uniqueness more salient to other people as well as multiply the instances of intergroup competition for scarce economic properties (e.g., housing and jobs), but it is not the density of minority group members in a given area that is the crucial factor in itself. Several authorities insist the *visibility* of the minority group is an important determinant of the degree to which the competition will engender group antagonisms (Williams, 1947, pp. 54–55). An influx of foreigners in a city may increase the competition for jobs, but the older residents are unlikely to think it is the foreigners *as a group* who are depriving them of the things they want unless these newcomers stand out as a group. They must possess certain characteristics in common, innate or culturally acquired, which differentiate them from other groups. It is these differentiating characteristics that make them visible as a frustrating group.

Perceptual prominence certainly is an important factor affecting the degree to which a group will be singled out for attack. Nevertheless, the writer believes visibility (i.e., awareness of the group) is a necessary rather than sufficient determinant of the group's becoming an object of hostility displacement, assuming the group is not seen as the direct cause of the frustration. If the theoretical scheme presented here is to be taken seriously, we would have to say the substitute object *elicits* (i.e., draws) hostile responses from the frustrated individual. Some particular stimulus quality of the visible object, as well as its availability, is needed to make it capable of eliciting these aggressive actions from the angered person.

*Strangeness.* The nature of this quality is implicit in the above discussion: The scapegoats are visible because they are different and strange. The *strange* object, then, sometimes evokes hostility. Indeed, a number of students of intergroup relations maintain that strangeness or difference itself is disturbing.[6]

Allport (1954, Ch. 8) has suggested that whatever instinctive basis there may be for group prejudice can perhaps be found in the "hesitant response . . . human beings have to strangeness" (p. 130). Babies about six months of age or older frequently cry, or otherwise indicate they are emotionally upset, when a stranger draws near, he pointed out, and many people continue to be shy toward strangers through the pubertal years and even sometimes into maturity. One reason for this hesitancy and shyness, of course, is that we may not know how to behave toward the stranger unless we can place him in some familiar category of people. But even if the particular groups he belonged to were known, the very fact he was a member of a different group, such as a different ethnic group, often strongly implies differences in behavior, beliefs, and values. For many people these differences are bad, indicating there is something "wrong" with the person.

Research conducted at Carmel College, a famous Jewish boarding school in England, seems to support the view that group differences

---

[6] As an illustration of this contention, Lundberg and Dickson (1952) argued that "it is hopelessly contradictory" for a group to want to maintain a distinctive group identity but to expect not to be discriminated against on the basis of this exclusive identity.

themselves can be the source of group antagonisms. The Jewish boys in this school were found to express anti-Christian attitudes even though the school authorities believed nothing in the Carmel environment explicitly fostered such sentiments. The only explanation they could advance was that "the growth of group consciousness itself produced negative social attitudes toward close rival groups." An experiment then was carried out with two neighboring dormitories in the same school to test this hypothesis. Bedtime stories were told once a week to the nine-year-old boys in each dormitory, but the stories in one of the groups were designed to create a "consciousness of kind," heightening the solidarity among these particular youngsters and setting them apart from the other dormitory. The other group heard only the usual type of bedtime story. According to one report of this research (Schmidt, 1960), as group consciousness developed in the former group, its members became increasingly aggressive toward the other dormitory. Hostility toward other groups presumably is the "by-product of positive group formation."

However, there are other factors that also could have given rise to the antagonism toward the outgroup described above. The Carmel boys, for example, undoubtedly had many opportunities to develop anti-Christian attitudes outside the formal school environment. They might have absorbed much of this sentiment from their parents, relatives, and friends at home. Probably more important, as the youngsters learned they were Jewish and thus different from non-Jews, they probably also learned that Jews were often discriminated against in English society. Being Jewish meant they had a somewhat insecure status in this society. Gentiles were not only different, they also symbolized the frustrations suffered by the Jews and, as a group, probably were seen as the source of these frustrations. As for the dormitory experiment, the investigators may have created a spirit of competition and rivalry between the two groups, with this feeling being the prime cause of the interdormitory hostility.

Encountering people who are different or strange is not necessarily threatening to most adults. An alien group does not disturb everyone. As a matter of fact, novelty and uniqueness often are enticing. Animals may go out of their way to investigate strange surroundings, apparently only to satisfy curiosity or exploratory drives (R. W. White, 1959), and tourists flock to foreign countries. Fear of a stranger largely arises when the individual expects the unknown person to be potentially dangerous. The stranger in this case functions as a projective test since the individual does not have much information about him. He is responded to generally as the individual has learned to respond to and perceive other people. If a person is afraid of strangers, he probably views most people as being dangerous. As some writers have said (*cf.* G. W. Allport, 1954, p. 396), the ethnocentric personality possesses a "threat orientation." He supposedly is uncertain of himself, the world about him, and his place in this world. He expects bad things to happen because for him people are not to be trusted. In a study by Allport and Kramer (1946), highly prejudiced adults were much more likely than their more tolerant peers to agree that "the world is a hazardous place in which men are basically evil and dangerous." Having these feelings, it is not surprising that the ethnocentric individual is unfriendly toward people who are different. His perception of aliens is a reflection of his general outlook upon life. Since the world is a dangerous place, he feels, an unknown person from this world also is dangerous.

Strange and unfamiliar surroundings can also be threatening to the prejudiced personality. Ambiguous situations are looked on as possibly dangerous, much as strangers are to be feared and guarded against. The only way these uncertain, ambiguous conditions can be made safe is to construct an order out of the chaos, a structure possessing rules and regulations. (Then, by following these rules, one can be secure.) Consistent with this analysis, two investigators (Block & Block, 1951) demonstrated that highly ethnocentric subjects established order in a highly ambiguous situation sooner than did tolerant people. This rapid structuring of an ambiguous environment probably is the result of the high level of anxiety such uncertain conditions often arouse in ethnocentric individuals (Smock, 1955).

*Prior Dislike for the Group.* The alien group obviously cannot be feared too much or else the prejudiced person would never attack it. It nevertheless is somewhat threatening and, because it is threatening, is disliked. This dislike for the strange, dislike created by fear, may be the main reason why a highly visible alien group is so often the object of displaced aggression. The determinant is not the visibility or strangeness in themselves but, rather, the meaning these factors have for the frustrated person. In general, *the strange group receives displaced hostility* (assuming there are no strong anticipations of being punished for this aggression) *to the extent it is disliked for its differences.* Highly ethnocentric people, being usually suspicious and fearful of the different, tend to dislike strangers or others who are different from them, and therefore are prone to take out any resentment they might feel on available strange groups. This displacement tendency is not necessarily limited to the highly prejudiced, however. Anyone who dislikes alien or strange groups for any reason also is likely to employ these groups as scapegoats.

This is not to say that particular characteristics of the minority group have no part in determining its likelihood of becoming a scapegoat.

While investigators of the authoritarian personality usually maintain only that a group is attacked merely because it is an outgroup (*cf.* Adorno et al., 1950, p. 233), they sometimes, in company with other psychoanalytically oriented writers, also emphasize the importance of the group's perceived qualities. The prejudiced individual, for example, supposedly projects his own disapproved sexual wishes onto Negroes because the stereotype of this group easily accommodates such a projection, and then hates Negroes because of their perceived sexuality. Similarly, Jews are said to symbolize other properties the authoritarian personality unconsciously sees and detests in himself.

But what is the significance of the characteristics attributed to (or actually possessed by) the outgroups? Jews share few, if any, specific features with Negroes. In the United States at least, sexual qualities typically are not assigned to the former (G. W. Allport, 1954), but both groups are likely targets for the same prejudiced individual's hostility. Just what do Jews, Negroes, and other outgroups have in common that results in their all being victimized? Most investigators of authoritarianism have been too concerned with the detailed depths of the prejudiced personality to look for the abstract principle that effectively integrates the various instances of scapegoating.

The specific characteristics perceived in a group do four things from the present point of view.

1. Most important, they determine whether the minority is disliked and, if so, how strongly. This is the quality shared by the victims of displaced hostility. They are disliked for different reasons, but all are disliked. As a result of being the object of negative attitudes, then, hostility engendered by some frustration will generalize fairly readily to these outgroups.

2. The extent of hostility generalization is a function of the total degree of association between the immediate frustrater and the objects available for scapegoating. The perceived properties of these latter objects, as well as the dislike for them, contribute to the psychological ties the thwarted person can draw between his frustrater and the available targets. The generalized aggressive tendencies of course will not lead to overt attacks if the intolerant person fears he will be punished for displaying aggression and/or believes such hostility is morally improper. The outgroup characteristics also may affect these factors.

3. They can determine whether the prejudiced individual believes it is safe to attack a given outgroup.

4. They can determine whether he is ethically justified in doing this.

*Evidence for the "Dislike" Hypothesis.* The above discussion argues for a fairly basic proposition. *Hostility will generalize from the anger instigator to another individual in direct ratio to the degree of dislike for this person.* Three experiments conducted in the writer's laboratory provide supporting evidence.

The first of these investigations indicates this presumed transfer of aggressive tendencies from the frustrater to the disliked individual is indeed a generalization process (Berkowitz & Holmes, 1959). The basic design in this experiment has been described in earlier chapters. Pairs of same-sexed college students, either males or females, were assigned to work on individual problem-solving tasks. Each subject was told his partner would serve as the judge of his work and would evaluate him by giving him electric shocks. Half the sixty-eight subjects were made to have an initial dislike for their partner by giving them a relatively great number of shocks under the pretext it was the partner administering them. The remaining students received no shocks and consequently developed stronger liking for the partner. Then, in the second phase of the study, half the subjects in each of the above two conditions were insulted by the experimenter while working alone on another task and the other subjects were given a friendlier treatment by him. The two subjects were brought together again in the final phase and instructed to work together in assembling a footbridge out of the materials provided in the room. Questionnaire ratings made just after the interaction with the experimenter during the second part of the study, and then again immediately after the joint task, constituted the major dependent variables in the experiment.

As the result of the experimental manipulations, then, the subjects in one of the conditions were made to have some dislike for their peer partners and also were frustrated by the experimenter. If the hostility engendered by the latter instigator generalized to the disliked peer, those people in this condition expressing the strongest hostility to the experimenter should display stronger aggressive inclinations toward the partner than (1) the people also in this frustration condition having weaker hostile tendencies toward the experimenter, or (2) the subjects in other conditions who were not provoked by the experimenter and/or who had not learned to dislike their peer. These expectations were fulfilled.

The students within each of the four experimental conditions were divided into two groups in terms of the favorability of their questionnaire ratings of the experimenter immediately after the second phase of the study. (The subjects would have no further connection with the experimenter and had no reason to expect punishment for anything they said about him. But they also knew he probably would see their questionnaires so that unfavorable ratings can be regarded as direct acts of hostility.) Table 6.1 summarizes the findings obtained in this analysis. The subjects exhibiting the strongest aggressiveness toward the frustrating experimenter generally showed the greatest increase in hostility toward the disliked partner—from their first impression of him at the start of the study to the final attitude statement after the bridge-building task. Thus, in the case of the people who were trained to have an initial dislike for the partner, those who had been ill-treated by the experimenter and who then responded with relatively strong hostility to him exhibited a significantly stronger total increase in hostility to the partner than any of the subjects not receiving such harsh treatment from the experimenter. The strong aggressive tendencies produced by the frustrating experimenter apparently had generalized and increased the strength of the unfriendliness to the disliked partner.

Table 6.1. *Mean Change in Unfriendliness-toward-partner Scores from First Impression to Final Attitude Assessment*

|  | Initial dislike for partner | | Initial liking for partner | |
|---|---|---|---|---|
|  | Frustrated by experimenter | Not frustrated by experimenter | Frustrated by experimenter | Not frustrated by experimenter |
| Expressed hostility to experimenter on preceding questionnaire: | | | | |
| High | $1.62_a$ | $0.25_{bc}$ | $-0.35_{bcd}$ | $-0.22_{bcd}$ |
| Low | $0.37_{bc}$ | $0.34_{bc}$ | $-0.88_{cd}$ | $-1.33_d$ |

NOTE: A positive score indicates an increase in unfriendliness from the first impression. Cells containing the same subscript are not significantly different from one another by Duncan Multiple Range Test.

A subsequent experiment (Berkowitz & Holmes, 1960) demonstrated that this generalization process also affects stronger and more direct acts of hostility than questionnaire ratings. Essentially the same procedure was employed as before with a sample of female college students, but this time, after the second-phase interaction with the experimenter ($E$), the subjects had two socially sanctioned opportunities to give their partners electric shocks. Each subject received what ostensibly was her partner's work on an assigned problem and again was told to evaluate this work by administering electric shocks: one if the work was very good and more than this if it was a poor performance. After she had "evaluated" the partner's product, it supposedly was this other girl's turn, and each subject was given one shock as her evaluation. Finally, another problem was assigned with the partner supposedly providing the first evaluation. Each girl was given three shocks, after which she "rated" the partner with the shocks. The results are presented in Table

6.2. Three sets of scores are entered in this table: the mean number of shocks each subject in the condition had administered during the first phase of the experiment before the interaction with $E$ (the base-line period), and the mean changes from this base line on each of the two subsequent occasions.

*Table 6.2. Differences from the Base-line Period in the Mean Number of Electric Shocks Given to Partner*

| Period | Initial dislike for partner | | Initial liking for partner | |
|---|---|---|---|---|
| | Frustrated by experimenter | Not frustrated by experimenter | Frustrated by experimenter | Not frustrated by experimenter |
| Base line*.... | 2.78 | 2.50 | 1.28 | 1.44 |
| Time 2†...... | $2.11_a$ | $1.61_{ab}$ | $0.22_c$ | $-0.22_c$ |
| Time 3....... | $1.11_b$ | $0.22_c$ | $0.39_c$ | $0.11_c$ |

* The base-line-period scores are the absolute number of shocks administered to $P$. The only significant effect at this time was the main effect for the differences in initial dislike for $P$ ($p < .001$).

† The time 2 and time 3 scores (differences from the base-line period) were combined in one "repeated measures" analysis of variance. Cells having the same subscript are not significantly different from one another (at the .05 level) by Duncan Multiple Range Test.

As can be seen in the table, the girls who had been frustrated by the experimenter and who then had an opportunity to shock a disliked peer administered more shocks to their peer than did the subjects in any other condition, with this difference becoming statistically significant by time 3. Again, it seems as if the aggressive tendencies evoked by the experimenter's harsh treatment had generalized and increased the strength of the hostile inclinations to the disliked partner.

Additional evidence obtained in a more recent investigation (Berkowitz & Green, 1962) appears to rule out one alternative explanation for the above-mentioned findings. It might be objected that the relatively great increase in hostility toward the partner by the end of the experimental session simply results from the accumulation of frustration effects. The subjects who had been insulted twice, by their peer and by the experimenter, could have been extremely angry *toward practically everyone.* Since the partner happened to be the only available target, this view would maintain, he felt the force of these strong aggressive tendencies.

The experiment by Berkowitz and Green provides data contrary to this alternative hypothesis. In this study, after the subjects in the crucial condition were frustrated by the experimenter, they were presented with two potential targets for their hostility: a person they had been trained to dislike (as in the preceding investigations) and a neutral individual. If the earlier findings arose from a generalization of aggression to disliked objects, this neutral person should not receive attacks as intense as those directed to the disliked peer. Results consistent with this reasoning were obtained.

Essentially the same procedure carried out in the Berkowitz and Holmes experiments was employed, but in this investigation each subject (male college students only) believed there were two other subjects also present. One of these others was a naïve student, but the third "subject" actually was a paid confederate. At the start of the experiment the subjects rated each of the other two men on one form of an adjective checklist, thinking they were describing the others' personalities but in reality indicating the favorableness of their attitudes toward these others. After this, the earlier experimental manipulations were repeated with the two "real" subjects. Half the seventy-two men were induced to dislike their partners, and the others were led to have a stronger liking for them. Then, half of those in each of these two conditions were individually frustrated by the experimenter ($E$), and the others received a kindlier treatment from him. Finally, in the last part of the experiment, the three men were brought together and instructed to work together in assembling the footbridge employed in the first study. (This was the only time the subjects had interacted with the confederate.) An alternative form of the adjective checklist was administered upon conclusion of this phase. Table 6.3 reports the mean level of unfriendliness to the partner and to the experimenter's confederate in each condition at the start and end of the study.

The table indicates the subjects began the experiment feeling much more friendly to the other "real" subject assembled with them (i.e., those slated to be their partners) than to the confederate. However, the negative attitudes toward the confederate apparently were only weakly held, and there was a significant decrease in unfriendliness to the confederate in all conditions by the time of the final questionnaire; increased acquaintance under the present conditions had lessened the negative inclinations toward him. A similar reliable decline in level of unfriendliness to the partner occurred in three of the four conditions. The only subjects not becoming decidedly friendlier to their partners were those who had been taught to dislike them and then were insulted by the experimenter. As a result, these subjects had a significantly higher level of hostility to the partner at the end of the experiment than did the subjects in any other condition. Increased contact presumably did not lower the level of unfriendliness to the partner in this case because of their strong hostile inclinations toward him—hostile tendencies first produced by his earlier harsh treatment of them and then augmented by a generalization of the aggressive tendencies elicited by the frustrating experimenter. The above findings suggest, then, that the hostile responses aroused by the anger-instigating experimenter had generalized to the previously disliked person to a significantly greater degree than to the somewhat "neutral" confederate.

*Table 6.3. Mean Adjective Checklist of Unfriendliness to the Partner and to the Experimenter's Confederate (a "Neutral" Person)*

| | Initial dislike for partner | | | | Initial liking for partner | | | |
|---|---|---|---|---|---|---|---|---|
| | Frustrated by experimenter | | Not frustrated by experimenter | | Frustrated by experimenter | | Not frustrated by experimenter | |
| | Part-ner | Confed-erate | Part-ner | Confed-erate | Part-ner | Confed-erate | Part-ner | Confed-erate |
| "First impression"... | $9.0_{cd}$ | $11.1_e*$ | $9.5_d$ | $11.0_e$ | $8.9_{bcd}$ | $12.2_f$ | $8.4_{bc}$ | $10.9_e$ |
| End of study ... | $8.4_{bc}$ | $8.2_b$ | $6.4_a$ | $8.5_{bc}$ | $6.2_a$ | $8.7_{bc}$ | $5.8_a$ | $6.5_a$ |
| Change scores.. | $-0.6$ | $-2.9$ | $-3.1$ | $-2.5$ | $-2.7$ | $-3.5$ | $-2.6$ | $-4.4$ |

NOTE: The absolute scores obtained at the start and conclusion of the study were subjected to one analysis of variance. In the above table the higher the mean, the more unfriendly the attitude toward the given stimulus person. Cells having the same subscript are not significantly different from one another by Duncan Multiple Range Test.

\* Since there apparently was some feeling of unfriendliness to the confederate at the beginning of the experiment, it might be expected that hostility would generalize to him. However, the writer's experience suggests that initial attitudes function as an "adaptation level," or base line, for the experimental effects, possibly because the initial attitudes are not held with any strong conviction. Changes from this base line generally seem to be more sensitive indicators of these experimental effects than the final absolute scores.

There are indications in Table 6.3, nevertheless, of a relatively slight but still significant amount of hostility generalization to the confederate. Those subjects undergoing at least one of the thwartings exhibited a reliably smaller decline in unfriendliness to this person than the men who had not been provoked by either their peer or the experimenter. The unpleasant experiences the former people had been subjected to apparently produced some resentment, interfering with the full friendship-developing benefits of the increased contact.

All in all, however, the results in these last three studies support the hypothesis of a hostility generalization to disliked objects. There are no clear-cut data available to help explain why this presumed transfer process took place, but Berkowitz (Berkowitz & Holmes, 1959, 1960) has suggested that a generalization gradient developed based on feelings of dislike. In essence, this notion maintains that the aggressive responses were generalized from the actual frustrater (i.e., the experimenter) to the negatively valued peer because these people had an important stimulus quality in common: Both had provoked unpleasant emotions. There are at least two ways in which a stimulus dimension uniting the two anger instigators could have arisen:

1. The unpleasant affect (including anger) in itself could have produced the generalization gradient, associating the two men with each other because both had evoked somewhat similar emotional responses in the subjects.

2. The subjects may have made the same thought responses to each of the two men since both had been unpleasant to them. The same implicit label could have been applied to both, placing them in the same negatively evaluated category.[7] This labeling, then, could have produced the association between the two instigators.

But regardless of the exact manner in which this generalization occurs, the net effect is that one frustrating agent can be equated subjectively with other frustrating people. A disliked minority (or a majority group for that matter) can be associated with an immediate frustrater, permitting the transfer of hostility aroused by the latter to the former. Some such process could have produced the hostility generalization to the neutral bystander within the frustrated anti-Semitic women in the Berkowitz (1959) study. Ethnocentric people apparently are generally hostile toward others (S. Siegel, 1956). They have a strong predisposition to dislike many of the people they encounter. The highly prejudiced women, therefore, being strongly inclined to dislike the bystander even though she may not have been Jewish, could have easily associated this person with the other disliked individual, the frustrating experimenter. Aggressive tendencies then transferred from one unpleasant person to the other.

If this reasoning can be substantiated by additional research, we would have a relatively simple solution to the problem of target choice in scapegoating; at least some of the displacement of hostility upon certain minority groups can be accounted for by the thwarted individual's prior dislike for these groups. Feeling this way about them, he presumably associates these people with his most recent frustraters. An industrial worker may become more hostile to the Jews in his

---

[7] Dollard and Miller (1950) have advanced a somewhat similar concept, "acquired equivalence of cues," contending that a previously neutral stimulus will produce the responses elicited by a particular category of stimuli after the subject has learned to apply the category name to this stimulus.

community after receiving a cut in pay because he associates the disliked Jews with the factory owners and managers.

*Other Associative Factors.* Other variables, however, also can intervene to affect the total strength of the association between ethnic group and immediate frustrater. This linkage may be weakened somewhat by knowledge forcing a discrimination between the particular minority and the frustrating source. For example, the disgruntled factory worker may know Turks have nothing to do with his economic situation. Therefore, even though he might hate Turks as much as Jews, the information that the former people are irrelevant to the job he has weakens the associative bond between this ethnic group and factory owners, and Jews become a likelier target for his displaced hostility than Turks.

The total association between ethnic group and frustrater also can be strengthened by characteristics they have in common.[8] In the present illustration, the factory worker may regard both the factory owners and Jews as rich and unscrupulous; these shared attributes also would heighten the bond between the two disliked groups. Several stimulus generalization gradients tie the ethnic group together with the immediate frustrater in this case, facilitating the degree to which the aggression elicited by the latter can be generalized to the minority group.

Somewhat similar generalization gradients, of course, may exist within any particular Jew or Negro, linking various frustrating groups together for them. As a consequence, they too can exhibit scapegoating behavior. The hostile tendencies aroused in them by a thwarting agent can be displaced upon the groups *they* dislike strongly, particularly if there are a number of prominent qualities shared by the frustrater and disliked groups.

This type of formulation provides a convergence between the "pure drive" notions of the classical scapegoat theory and those "pure stimulus" theories of prejudice (*cf.* Zawadski, 1948) attributing intergroup hostility solely to the characteristics of the minority group. Certain groups can become the innocent victims of hostility engendered in the frustrations of living, but they are the recipients of this displaced hostility because of the stimulus qualities they have for the frustrated people.

*Perceived Group Attributes.* There is a strong element of circularity in this process. A group is disliked because of its characteristics, becomes the target for displaced hostility, is disliked still more—or probably better, the dislike for this group is maintained—as a consequence of this displacement, and again is the victim of scapegoating. Such a "circular-causal" process can help account for the persistence of intolerant attitudes toward particular groups, but other factors un-

---

[8] See Hull (1943, pp. 209–10) for evidence consistent with this hypothesis of a summation of conditioning effects.

doubtedly also contribute. The distaste for some ethnic groups can be enhanced by "realistic" considerations. A person may be in competition with minority group members for jobs and/or status, and many people in the disliked group actually may possess the qualities attributed to the group as a whole—there *is* a high crime rate among Negroes, for example. These actual occurrences fanning the fires of prejudice can be buttressed further by cultural norms and social reinforcements.

Attitudes toward the different ethnic groups composing our society are widely shared in the United States. In some studies, college students at a variety of institutions, including a highly liberal private college for women, a Negro university, an eminent Ivy League university, and a free, public-supported municipal college, were asked to indicate their relative preferences among a variety of ethnic groups. Despite the students' differences in cultural background and economic circumstance, they tended to agree in their liking for the various groups (Hartley, 1946). Other investigators have obtained similar findings with samples of college students differing greatly in geographical location and the year in which the data were collected. Interestingly enough, children coming from a variety of social, economic, and religious backgrounds have been found to rank ethnic groups in pretty much the same order of preference they were ranked by the older college students. By and large, the English, Canadians, Irish, Scots, and French were the most preferred groups, and Jews, Greeks, Mexicans, Japanese, and Negroes were the least preferred (Harding et al., 1954, p. 1026). There apparently even is considerable agreement within our culture as to the traits supposedly possessed by the various ethnic groups (pp. 1023–1025). The stereotyped conception of a German typically is that he is "scientifically minded, industrious, and stolid," while Jews are often seen as "shrewd, mercenary, and industrious" (Katz & Braly, 1933).

Any given person growing up in the United States is likely to encounter these ethnic attitudes in the remarks and behavior of the people around him as a result of this consensus of opinion. If his parents and friends share these views regarding the different minority groups, they will seem right and proper. The opinions are validated by agreement among the people important to him. Anglo-Saxons, he will come to believe, *are* "nicer" than Mexicans, "everybody" (i.e., his relatives, neighbors, and friends) says so (*cf.* Horowitz, 1936; Harding et al., 1954, pp. 1038–1041). For him, therefore, it is true that some ethnic groups are to be preferred as social or business companions and others are to be avoided. Further, his image of these groups also will be shaped by the consensus within his primary groups (and also by the stereotypes spread by the mass media). Social reality, then, defines particular ethnic groups as being unpleasant if not detestable.

These stereotyped conceptions of the various minorities also contribute to the scapegoating process through affecting the particular traits assigned to these groups. When a frustrated person vents his hostility upon a certain minority, he frequently feels this group deserved the attack (and also, that the group cannot punish him for his aggression). The perceived characteristics of the group both justify and permit the scapegoating. Knowing the group's traits, he may believe the group is relatively safe to attack. The qualities seen in the group also make it possible for the thwarted individual to believe he in one way or another has attacked the source of his frustration and, to some extent, may prevent him from aggressing against the group in response to altogether different frustrations. A small businessman in the North faced with financial problems arising from competition by other firms is more likely to become aggressive toward Jews than toward, say, Negroes. He can associate Jews with his frustraters because of the qualities he perceives them as having; he has learned in his culture that Jews are shrewd, mercenary, and conniving businessmen. These characteristics certainly excuse the hostility he may express toward Jews, but they probably also define Jews as being the appropriate target for this particular set of frustrations. Jews can reasonably be connected with the troubles confronting him. Negroes, on the other hand, are not seen as businessmen, or if he knows Negroes are among his competitors, he is not as likely to believe they are shrewd and unscrupulous. The perceived qualities of the Negro group make it more difficult for him to associate Negroes with his frustrations, and therefore, make them less probable victims of the aggressiveness provoked by his economic difficulties. Should he have labor problems with his Negro employees, however, there would be a different story. Other colored people could readily be linked with his employees (the perceived source of his frustration) in this case and thus become objects for displaced hostility.

## SUMMARY

No one set of considerations, whether from psychology or any of the other social sciences, can satisfactorily explain all manifestations of intergroup conflict. Many instances of fighting between groups have been precipitated by competition for scarce values or properties. Other cases of intergroup aggression originate in emotional tensions. Some people are the more or less innocent victims of hostility engendered by the frustrations of living. As scapegoats, they are the victims of prejudiced (i.e., hostile) attitudes for which they, to some extent at least, are blameless.

This scapegoat theory of prejudice is not a complete account of ethnic relations. Aggressive attitudes and behavior toward particular groups are not necessarily always the result of frustrations. Prejudiced behavior may be prescribed by cultural norms. But even then, personality characteristics can contribute to the relative intensity of the individaul's hostility toward an outgroup. After citing correlational evidence indicating that economically thwarted people are often aggressive toward Negroes and Jews, it also was pointed out that frustrations do not always lead to stronger resentment against minority groups. Three important restrictions to the scapegoat theory, first listed by Allport, were discussed: (1) Aggression is not always the dominant response to frustration; (2) aggression is not always displaced onto some innocent victim; (3) the safest available target is not always the recipient of displaced aggression.

This last-mentioned restriction refers to a common misconception. Many authorities have automatically assumed the scapegoat is selected primarily because it is a safe object to attack. Empirical observations and the theoretical analysis described in the preceding chapter rule against this assumption. We here argue that the available object must have some degree of association with the frustrater if it is to be attacked.

Laboratory investigations of the scapegoat hypothesis have not always yielded consistent findings. The theory obviously is incomplete as it usually stands. There are two ways in which the needed additional detail can be provided: (1) by proposing reliable individual differences in readiness to displace hostility onto others; (2) by maintaining that certain objects are likelier targets for displaced hostility than are other objects. Both of these refinements can be supported by experimental research.

Although the first experiment in this area obtained negative results, two more recent studies indicate that highly anti-Semitic college students may be more prone to aggress against (1) a presumably neutral bystander and/or (2) Jewish figures than are less prejudiced students, but only after experiencing frustrations. Two reasons can be advanced for these findings, both with some empirical support.

First, the highly prejudiced person under stress may tend to make only relatively gross discriminations among the people around him. This would mean that the intolerant individual regards many people he does not know too well as being essentially "all alike." As a consequence, the aggressive responses evoked by one of these people can generalize fairly readily to others perceived as being quite similar to these instigators. The second reason suggests a basis for this similarity. The prejudiced person, it is proposed, is relatively quick to dislike others, particularly strangers. (Thus, strangers are basically similar in that they are all seen as being unpleasant.) In this connection, then, the writer has hypothesized that hostility generalizes from one frustrater to other disliked people.

This reasoning can be extended to explain the selection of particular groups for scapegoating. According to the present argument, the groups receiving displaced hostility are groups the individual has learned to dislike for whatever reason. Particular characteristics attributed to (or actually possessed by) the victimized group are important in that they (1) determine whether it is disliked and, if so, how strongly; (2) may strengthen or weaken the total degree of association between the group and the individual's more immediate frustraters; (3) affect whether the thwarted individual believes it is safe to attack this group; (4) determine whether he feels it is ethically proper to attack the group.

# chapter 7

# Intergroup Hostility: II.
## Situational Conditions
# Enhancing or Reducing Conflict

The previous chapter is in many ways typical of the dominant approach taken by American social psychologists interested in the cause and cure of intergroup conflict. In focusing on the generalization (or displacement) of aggressive tendencies to particular ethnic groups, I have implicitly attributed the hostility to "irrational" processes within the individual. Frustrations, obstacles to the pursuit of happiness, tensions arising from life in a complex society, all supposedly breed aggressive tendencies directed toward innocent victims. For many social scientists this is an essentially optimistic interpretation. They believe the target for the displaced hostility is attacked largely because of the frustrated individual's misperceptions. Their formula for minimizing conflict, then, is basically fairly simple (in conception although not in achievement). Provide information about the disliked group, clear up the misunderstandings, and much—but unfortunately not everything, they admit—will be done toward the reduction of scapegoating.

Social scientists working under the auspices of the United Nations Educational, Scientific, and Cultural Organization (UNESCO) have devoted a great deal of time and effort to the study of intergroup "tensions" from this point of view. Their difficulties were great. The very concept of *tension* itself is unsatisfactory, scientifically, since it is burdened with altogether too many connotations. But even if the term were confined to the emotional effects of frustrations, it obviously would be unrealistic to hope for the elimination of frustrations. Tensions, like the poor, will always be with us. The most science can do, these writers felt, was not to reduce emotional tensions, but "to direct them into useful channels and to turn them into constructive social ends" (International Sociological Association, 1957, p. 11). Peace could perhaps be preserved by removing the sources of misunderstanding between nations. The UNESCO-sponsored social scientists therefore largely concentrated their efforts on the investigation and elimination of the misleading attitudes and stereotypes people had concerning other national groups.[1]

Few would quarrel with the potential significance of such research in eliminating *some* causes of interpersonal friction. As we saw in the previous chapter, the perceived characteristics of a group affect the likelihood of its becoming the recipient of displaced aggression. Jews frequently are disliked, for example, because of the qualities they supposedly possess. Believing they are "unscrupulous" (one of the components of the stereotyped image of this group) makes it easier to generalize hostility to them. Reality considerations as well as optimistic beliefs about the fundamental goodness of man justify attempting to dispel intergroup misconceptions in order to preserve peace; providing information making a group appear less strange or enhancing the degree of liking for these people could do much to lessen the possibility of conflict with them.

Most differences of opinion on this matter involve not *whether* such information campaigns are useful but rather their *degree* of utility. Jessie Bernard (1957), as was reported in the preceding chapter, reflected the views of many scholars when she strongly criticized the tension approach to conflict. Many clashes between groups, she insisted, derive from "incompatible or mutually exclusive goals or aims or values." Further, the aggression revealed in this conflict can be part of a strategy for winning rather than the irrational product of frustration-engendered emotions. Clearing up misunderstandings does not necessarily eliminate conflict and may even intensify the hostility by sharpening the issue (pp. 40–44).

A number of writers also have questioned the usefulness of the frustration-aggression or tension formulation in the study of intergroup hostility by maintaining that concepts drawn from the level of individual behavior cannot be applied directly to groups.[2] For one thing, these critics have pointed out, the activities of most functioning groups are not determined by the motivations of each member in equal proportion to the others in his group. A group cannot always be regarded as the

[1] Much of the relevant literature is reported in a volume growing out of the UNESCO "tensions project," *The Nature of Conflict* (International Sociological Association, 1957). Some of the titles of publications stemming from the "tensions" approach can throw additional light on the implications of this view. Thus we have: "Tensions affecting international understanding," "National stereotypes and international understanding," etc.

[2] *The Nature of Conflict* (International Sociological Association, 1957) presents several discussions of problems in the conceptualization of intergroup conflicts which should be consulted by serious students of this topic.

simple additive sum of its members; power is not distributed equally among the members. Many of the people in the group (or nation) may be frustrated without these frustrations necessarily affecting the likelihood of conflict with other collectivities. What the group does in any given situation often is a function of its leaders and not the rank and file. Because of these power differences, furthermore, a nation's images of other people at times are the *result,* not the cause, of decisions taken by the policy makers (cf. Aron, 1957).

Granting all this, the present writer is still inclined to emphasize the importance of individualistic considerations in the field of group relations. Dealings between groups ultimately become problems for the psychology of the individual. Individuals decide to go to war; battles are fought by individuals; and peace is established by individuals. It is the individual who adopts the beliefs prevailing in his society, even though the extent to which these opinions are shared by many people is a factor governing his readiness to adopt them, and he then transmits these views to other individuals. Ultimately, it is the single person who attacks the feared and disliked ethnic minority group, even though many other people around him share his feelings and are very important in determining his willingness to aggress against this minority. Theoretical principles can be formulated referring to the group as a unit and these can be very helpful in understanding hostility between groups. But such abstractions refer to collections of people and are made possible by interindividual uniformities in behavior.

The present chapter, therefore, will discuss situational conditions inciting or augmenting intergroup conflict from the point of view of the individual group member. We will deal with such phenomena as group differences in beliefs and intergroup competition for scarce values as they affect the individual. This type of analysis will demonstrate that there is no real incompatibility between group-level considerations of social conflict and individualistically oriented discussions; differences of opinion and competition can incite anger because of the frustrations they create. Following this, there will be a brief discussion of strategies producing intergroup conflict and finally a consideration of factors that may reduce such hostility.

## INCREASING HOSTILITY

### Requirements for Intergroup Hostility

The present and preceding chapters deal with conflict between groups *as groups.* A person may aggress against a particular foreigner, I pointed out earlier, without generalizing his hostility to all foreigners. The target for his aggression depends upon whom he perceives as the source of his frustration. Is he being thwarted by a single individual or a group of people? In his survey of research on intergroup tensions, Williams (1947) listed four minimum conditions for group conflict: (1) visibility of the groups; (2) contact between the groups; (3) competition between the groups; and (4) differences between the groups in values and behavior patterns. These surely are important factors and will be considered more fully below. However, Williams did not give sufficient attention to the basic requirement: People must be categorized together as a unit and collectively regarded as the frustrating agent if there is to be aggression toward a group.

*Categorization as a Group.* The necessity of such a categorization is obvious but should not always be taken for granted. There may well be reliable individual differences in the extent to which a person sees other people as more or less equivalent. Evidence was cited in the previous chapter (Berkowitz, 1961) suggesting that highly ethnocentric individuals under stress often make only relatively gross differentiations among people they do not know too well. An emotionally aroused, highly prejudiced person may be more inclined to categorize other people together indiscriminately than someone who is characteristically less prejudiced and perhaps even more than the nonaroused ethnocentric. Not everyone is likely to regard foreigners, or even ethnic minority group members such as Negroes and Jews, as being "all alike." Differentiations can be made among the members of these groups; the extent of such discriminations apparently varies with the personality characteristics of the individual and the state of his emotions.

*Visibility and Contact.* Assuming a group is in competition with other people, the probability it will be seen as a source of frustrations is a direct function of (1) its *visibility* to these others and (2) their frequency and intensity of *contact* with the group. To use the illustration employed in the preceding chapter, suppose the influx of foreigners into a city were to seriously deplete the number of jobs available in the area. Foreigners would become the object of hostility only to the degree they were clearly apparent as the source of the economic frustrations. The greater the difference between these foreigners and the older residents in physical appearance and/or customs, the more salient (i.e., visible) they will be to the others in the city, if these others have at least a minimal awareness of their presence. Contact with the foreigners also would enhance this awareness, but since the older residents and the newcomers are somewhat in competition, many of the encounters between these groups are bound to be frustrating to the townspeople.

Greater contact between groups does not necessarily promote friendship. Contrary to the oversimplified formulations of many men of good will, bringing people together who have mutually exclusive aims or values usually heightens the chances of conflict. Their coming together produces friction. *For groups in competition or with opposing beliefs, in other words, the amount of contact between them is directly related to both the frequency and degree of frustration one group imposes upon the other.*

There seems to be ample evidence for such a proposition. For one thing, hostility toward Negroes generally is greatest in those Southern states having the highest ratio of Negroes to whites (G. W. Allport, 1954, p. 227; Pettigrew & Campbell, 1960, pp. 446–447). The Southern white, encountering many members of a group whose aims and values for itself are opposed to his aims and values for it and often aware of this group (i.e., it is highly visible to him), has stronger anti-Negro feelings than, say, the white man who has never seen a Negro.

It would be a grave mistake to assume the above relationship holds only for contacts between the white and colored races in our South (and in South Africa). Williams has offered a general formulation regarding contact and intergroup conflict that apparently fits all too many cases. He stated: *The movement of a "visibly different" group into an area heightens the probability of conflict, with the likelihood of intergroup hostility being in direct proportion to* (*a*) *"the ratio of the incoming majority to the resident population," and* (*b*) *the speed of influx* (1947, pp. 57–58). Allport cited a number of observations supporting the essential validity of this "sociocultural law." For example, prejudice against colored people increased greatly in English industrial cities with the rapid migration of Negroes into these areas following World War II, while the occurrence of riots in American cities frequently "coincided with the immigration of large numbers of unfavored groups," such as the Irish in 1832 and Mexicans and Negroes in 1943, into these communities (1954, p. 228).

*Insecurities and Potential Dangers.* The hostilities arising from such sudden and frequent contact between greatly different groups usually are the product of competition and/or incompatible values and beliefs. But other factors also can contribute to the conflict. Different or strange people often are threatening to the insecure—whether this insecurity is a personality characteristic or is situationally induced, for example, by economic depression. Great numbers of aliens migrating into an area would then be highly discomforting to those who are already anxious. In other cases, however, these visibly different people could pose a threat (and hence be frustrating) even to more secure individuals; they might be competitors for scarce houses or perhaps are seen as lowering property values.

Being highly visible, the newcomers are less apt to be forgotten by the older residents. Rapid migration into the area, of course, means there is little opportunity for assimilation or the development of friendships based upon mutual interests and equal status. There is little time for the immigrants to lose their strangeness to the others and little chance for mutual accommodations or adjustments between the groups.

All these factors may explain the hostility and prejudice the established Yankee residents of New England mill towns directed against new Italian and Greek settlers in their area (G. W. Allport, 1954, p. 229). The newcomers, speaking a foreign language and having strange customs and values, were visibly different. But more than this, they also decreased the number of jobs available in the town, sometimes reducing income and increasing unemployment. Frequent contact with these foreigners arising from the fairly rapid influx of Italians and Greeks almost inevitably produced resentment in the old Yankees with whom they were in competition. According to Allport, intergroup hostility finally lessened when "each ethnic group [found] a distinctive level in the division of labor," reducing the competition somewhat, and when the newcomers lost their strangeness.

## Opposing Beliefs

One of the paradoxes in the history of many religions is the frequent disparity between their emphasis upon peace and love on one hand, and their aggressiveness toward nonbelievers on the other. Christianity has been divided by schisms, but its branches have not always lived together in peace and brotherhood. Heretics have been burned at the stake, followers of dissident sects have been slaughtered, Protestants and Catholics have murdered each other—all in the name of the Prince of Peace. If the stones of Constantinople could speak, what a horrible story they would relate of the thousands and thousands killed in the city streets because of doctrinal differences among people all calling themselves Christian—to say nothing of the additional thousands killed in the clashes between Muslim and Christian. Why did these conflicts arise?

*Direct Gains.* In many cases, of course, the combatants thought there were direct gains to be achieved through attacking the opposing religion. To die in defense of their own faith supposedly was a means of attaining eternal salvation. In other instances the aggression against the rival group was regarded as destroying or warding off a danger, either present or imminent, to their own religious activities. This sentiment persists today. There are quite a few people in this country, for example, who believe the Roman Catholic Church, by its very nature, represents a grave threat to Protestantism. They argue that Catholicism would destroy religious liberty if it were to achieve dominant political power in the United States and, thus, their anti-Catholicism, they maintain, is in defense of their own beliefs.

Generally speaking, ideological conflict frequently results from essentially similar conditions, that is, perceiving aggression as a means of gaining ends dictated by one's beliefs. Ideologies, being extremely broad and far-reaching belief systems, usually advocate particular forms of social organization or definite modes of social conduct. People having these beliefs often attempt to influence others to behave in conformity with their standards and sometimes even try to impose these standards by legal means or even force. This is true of such different ideological movements as puritanism, prohibitionism, and communism. But whether or not there is any active proselytizing on the part of the ideology, or any desire to press the beliefs onto others, people maintaining opposing beliefs frequently are threatened by the very existence of the rival system. The chieftains of the competing ideological movement *may* attempt to widen their sphere of influence in the future. Although American Communists probably offer little real danger today, police agencies still keep them under surveillance because of their potential threat. Similarly, for some people the Catholic Church represents a potential danger.

Hostility between rival ideological systems clearly arises from the frustrations each system imposes upon the other. The followers of one ideology may prevent adherents of the competing movement from satisfying their needs or may severely restrict opportunities for need satisfaction. Furthermore, even if these thwartings do not actually occur, they can be anticipated and thus produce anger.

*Dissonance.* There is another source of danger in the rival belief system that also can produce intergroup aggression. For the devotee of any one ideological movement the existence of an opposing set of beliefs may make him less certain his own beliefs are correct. This lack of certainty also can be frustrating, particularly if the individual is strongly committed to his beliefs. We are not always consciously aware of this type of threat; the follower of a religious group rarely cares to admit his doubts. Nonetheless, these doubts often are very upsetting. Is it not possible, for example, that some Catholics watching the spread of Lutheranism during the period of the Reformation wondered if their church was right after all? Their faith conceivably could have been weakened by the opposing Lutheran doctrines and the apparent success of this "heresy" in gaining followers. But similarly, Catholicism may have caused uncertainties within the newly formed Protestant churches. Some Protestants could have asked themselves if maybe they were not committing a heresy. In both cases, those people giving their all for their religion, whether Catholicism or Protestantism, and who nevertheless still felt unsure about the validity of their beliefs, might well have become extremely antagonistic to the opposing religion for shaking their faith. The other religion produced "dissonance" (Festinger, 1957) within the individual strongly committed to his church, and hence was frustrating.[3] As a result, the early wars between Catholics and Protestants were among the bloodiest in European history.

It is true, of course, that there were many reasons for these conflicts. The Protestant princes were motivated by a number of desires: for the property formerly belonging to the Catholic Church; for the right to be their own masters in their own spiritual and temporal households; etc. Similarly, the Catholic hierarchy was prompted by the advantages they would gain if the Protestants could be vanquished; they might regain material as well as spiritual supremacy. Nevertheless, most of these motives were not relevant for the very great majority of the people involved in the hostilities between the opposing religions. Why were they angry? Their leaders could not have stirred them to such fury unless the opposing camp represented a very real danger to them. It is at least conceivable that part of this danger was the threat to the solidity of their religious convictions; each side hated the other for undermining its own certainty.

*Attitudinal Similarity and Friendship.* If the above analysis is correct, we would expect to find that people generally should have a greater liking for others whom they believe hold views similar to their own than for those whose opinions they think differ greatly from theirs. Such seems to be the case. Investigations have shown again and again that there is a direct relationship between attitudinal similarity and friendship. We do often assume people we like have beliefs resembling our own (Fiedler, Warrington, & Blaisdell, 1952; Lundy, Katkovsky, Cromwell, & Shoemaker, 1955), and these similarities frequently actually exist (Lindzey & Borgatta, 1954). The problem a number of psychologists have addressed themselves to, and the issue of immediate concern to us here, is why these relationships occur. Why is there generally greater attraction toward others holding, or believed to hold, similar attitudes and values? Taking the other side of the coin, why do differences of opinion sometimes promote rejection and antagonism?

Newcomb (1959) hypothesized that attitudinal similarity (or what he termed similarity in systems of orientation) generally comes to be valued for its own sake because the adult has learned pleasant consequences usually follow such similarity. Communication is facilitated and people are not likely to "rub each other the wrong way" if they do

[3] The aggressive action taken against the opposing church could further heighten the anger against the "heretical" religion. According to dissonance theory, a person who is induced to carry out behavior (such as attacks upon the other religious group) somewhat in opposition to other beliefs of his (e.g., believing these religions may be "correct") may attempt to reduce his discomfort by justifying the behavior and disparaging the opposing religion. As a result, he will intensify his dislike for the dissonance-producing group.

not have opposing values. For Newcomb, then, differences in opinions and values are unpleasant in their own right, although differences on important issues and/or on matters of relevance to both the perceiver and perceived supposedly arouse the greatest discomfort.

Rokeach (1960) is another writer postulating a direct relationship between attitudinal similarity and friendship. Indeed, he went somewhat further than Newcomb by making interpersonal congruence in belief systems "more important than other kinds of categorizations, such as race or ethnic grouping, in determining our relations with others" (p. 391). Several of his studies are relevant to the problem of interdenominational conflict. College students in one of these investigations were asked to rank different religions in terms of their over-all similarity to their own religion. "Social distance" measures also were obtained for each of the other religious groups, i.e., indicators of the extent to which the subject was willing to enter into psychologically close relationships with members of these groups. Over all groups, the religious systems seen as most resembling the individual's own religion were the ones most accepted, while the dissimilar groups usually were most strongly rejected. Socioeconomic class was unlikely to have entered into these results. Since the students generally agreed with each other and with clergymen as to the similarity between the various denominations, the similarity judgments presumably were realistic and unaffected by attitudes toward the religious groups. Congruence in belief systems then can be said to have produced the liking for the religion (pp. 295–300).

Other data collected by Rokeach and his colleagues further attest to the attraction-belief similarity relationship. For example, married couples, one of whom was always a Methodist, filled out a questionnaire dealing with instances of premarital and marital conflict between the man and wife. For both the premarital and marital periods, "the less the religious similarity between partners, the greater the conflict" (pp. 325–326).

There were differences in the degree to which people rejected non-congruent belief systems. Subjects scoring high on a questionnaire measure of "dogmatism" (presumably assessing the extent to which their entire belief system was a closed, interlocking, tightly held affair) typically expressed less liking for the dissimilar religions than did the more "open-minded" people having lower dogmatism scores (p. 300). Southerners, furthermore, had a greater tendency to reject all others— whites as well as Negroes, and those who agreed with them as well as those who disagreed with them—than did Northerners, but they also exhibited a greater preference for those who agreed with them on various issues over those having different views (p. 392).

Rokeach's additional documentation of the relationship between belief congruency and liking is interesting and important. However, his contention that attitudinal similarity is a more important determinant of intergroup harmony than race or ethnic status fails to be convincing. His subjects may have *expressed* the strongest preferences for other people on the basis of their similarity in beliefs rather than because of their racial or ethnic characteristics, as Rokeach reported (1960, Ch. 7), but they would not necessarily have these preferences in an actual situation. Somehow, it is difficult to conceive of a white Mississippi farmer showing a greater willingness to have a Negro than a white for a son-in-law even though the former's religious and economic beliefs were closer to his own. The chances are the prospect of *any* Negro for a son-in-law would be extremely unpleasant to this farmer; unpleasant ideas and feelings are associated with Negroes as a group for him.

*"Family Quarrels."* There are some situations that appear to be an exception to the general rule of greater attraction for similar than dissimilar belief systems. These are the "family quarrels" between factions holding closely related views. Many of these quarrels are characterized by extreme bitterness. For example, there usually is greater enmity between the Stalinist and the Trotskyite than between either of these Communists and a moderately conservative person. Similarly, Rokeach found that Episcopalians rejected Catholics, to whom they were relatively similar, more intensely than they rejected Methodists, whom they resembled much less (p. 303). It is worth examining the reasons for these apparent exceptions to the belief congruence–attraction relationship. In so doing, we can obtain insight into the entire problem of dislike for particular belief systems.

No one hypothesis is satisfactory for all the divergent instances. Three different factors seem to be involved:

1. Some family quarrels evoke hostility because the warring factions are in direct competition with each other. Stalinists and Trotskyites were in conflict over the control of communism; Socialists and Communists (another example of bitter enmity between somewhat similar belief systems) have been in competition for leadership and control of liberal political and economic movements; and Protestants and Catholics have been disputing over the minds of men. Some of the hostility may persist after the competition has ended because attitudes developed in the course of the competition have been learned and transmitted to succeeding generations of group members.

2. In a number of cases the bitterness could have arisen through the nonfulfillment of an expectancy. Many politically conservative members of the upper class regarded Franklin Roosevelt as a traitor to his class. He had not behaved as they had anticipated. Being a descendant of the

aristocracy, he should have aligned himself with "his own kind," these people could have thought. Instead, he implicitly rejected his class (which also could have hurt because it cast doubt on the worth of this class), and did things one did not usually expect from a man of his background.

3. Finally, each side in the controversy may interpret the other side's opposition as a rejection, with this frustration evoking the hostility. Two formulations can help us understand this type of situation. On one hand, as was pointed out in Chapter 3, quarrels between people having close psychological ties can involve the blocking of stronger drives than similar disputes between people who otherwise had little to do with each other. There may be a stronger desire for affiliative satisfactions in the relationship with the other "family" member, and this desire then is obstructed by the threatening difference of opinion.

Festinger's research (1954, 1957) suggests another instigation that also could have been thwarted by differences between the closely related belief systems. The individual who is not sure of the validity of his beliefs frequently attempts to confirm his views by referring them to other people whom he regards as holding a somewhat similar position. If they can come to agreement with him, his uncertainty (dissonance) would be reduced. He then may become angry if these others, whom he had expected to support him, fail to provide this support.

As evidence for this tendency to seek confirmation from similar others, Brodbeck (cited in Festinger, 1957) conducted an experiment in which college students listened to a legal expert speak on the issue of wiretapping. Some of the subjects heard views similar to their own, while other subjects listened to arguments opposing their position. A number of the people in this latter group reacted to the speech by expressing much less confidence in the correctness of their initial beliefs. We can say these people generally had stronger dissonance than any of the others. Then, in a second part of the study, the students were assembled in small groups and each person was given the opportunity to communicate either with others sharing his views or with people who held different beliefs. The subjects presumably experiencing the strongest dissonance indicated the strongest desire to communicate with people having beliefs resembling their own. They apparently sought to reduce their dissonance by talking with others maintaining similar views. These others, by agreeing with them, would provide the desired confirmation.

In this case, dissonance arose from listening to an expert proclaim an opposing point of view. Dissonance can also be the result of maintaining a minority position in some controversy. If there are no independent, objective tests of the merit of some belief, confirmation of this opinion can only be obtained through social consensus (Festinger, 1950). People having an unpopular or minority opinion on some issue will not receive much support, and consequently they may become less sure they are right (although they sometimes attempt to defend themselves against their dissonance by loudly insisting they are correct). Thus, not surprisingly, people in the minority in a group-discussion situation are much more inclined to communicate with others whose opinions are close to their own than are the group members holding the majority view (Festinger, Gerard, Hymovitch, Kelley, & Raven, 1952). The deviates apparently were the ones most wanting confirmation or support for their beliefs, and they sought contact primarily with those people they thought were most likely to provide this support.

The above analysis yields one reason for Freud's bitterness toward Jung and Adler after they had defected from the main body of the psychoanalytic movement. Freud was under attack from many people in the worlds of psychology and medicine. Being an opinion deviate, he probably needed all the support he could get in order to maintain the assurance he was right. The departure of his former disciples could have been a serious blow to his confidence. (If people whose views were somewhat similar to his own in many respects could not support him on the important issues, there might well be a cause for doubt.) Freud had expected support from Adler and Jung, but when it did not come, was frustrated and consequently felt these men had betrayed him.

*Hostility toward One's Former Group.* We now have a mechanism The above analysis yields one reason for Freud's bitterness toward the group he had rejected. This type of hostility occurs frequently. Ex-Communists are among the most violent opponents of communism, and revolutionaries of bourgeois origin typically are harsher toward the *bourgeoisie* than are revolutionaries coming from the ranks of the proletariat (Merton, 1957, p. 295). Several writers have hypothesized that the person rebelling against his original group has a "double orientation"; he must develop a substitute group attachment and also cope with his attraction to his former membership group (Merton, 1957, p. 295). In a sense, he could well still be in a state of ambivalence. If he were truly free of his origins, he would be indifferent to the former group. But he is not free; there still may be some bond of attachment to his past. The aggression toward the former group serves as a defense against these tendencies pulling him back (Parsons, 1951, pp. 254–255). From the point of view of dissonance theory, we would say that the rebel is upset by the incompatibility between (1) his earlier beliefs and behavior (and perhaps the vestiges of these beliefs

still within him) and (2) the diametrically opposed views and behavior he is now expressing. In order to reduce the dissonant state
arising from this incongruity, he leans over backward, so to speak,
disparaging the former group, making it less attractive, and, if the
dissonance is strong enough, even becoming hostile toward it.

*Opposing Beliefs and Dissonance.* This type of reasoning also accounts for our general dislike of dissimilar belief systems. If we are
heavily committed to a particular point of view (as Freud was to
psychoanalytic theory and as Communists often are to their doctrines),
opposing attitudes and values can be greatly disturbing when there is
no objective way of testing the validity of these beliefs. The persistent
assertion of divergent beliefs by other people produces further discomfort (i.e., increases dissonance). Since this state is frustrating, aggressive
tendencies are aroused and directed toward the perceived source of the
frustration—the people proclaiming the opposing opinions.

Evidence from a number of laboratory experiments indicates that the
magnitude of the dissonance created by disagreements with other people is a direct function of (1) the importance of these others to the
individual, (2) the importance and relevance of the issue on which
the controversy exists, and (3) the extent of the disagreement. Opinion
differences produce increased dissonance as each of these factors becomes greater (Festinger & Aronson, 1960). Relatively little is known
about the conditions affecting the particular behavior a person will exhibit in response to the dissonance, but a variety of reactions have
been obtained: (1) reducing the magnitude of the disagreement by
changing one's belief; (2) obtaining additional confirmation for the
disputed belief from others likely to give support; (3) eliminating further contact with the dissonance-producing agent; and (4) disparaging
or derogating the source of the dissonance, making the latter's disturbing communications now less worthy of attention (Festinger, 1957).
There is a good possibility that this last-mentioned reaction, derogation
of the disagreeing source, tends to become increasingly prevalent as
the extent of the disagreement becomes greater (Festinger & Aronson,
1960; Hovland, Harvey, & Sherif, 1957). Thus, the greater the difference
between a person's own beliefs and the opinions advocated by another
individual on some important issue, the more likely it will be that the
former person will respond with contempt for his opponent. If this opponent seriously frustrates the individual, the contempt can easily be
transmuted into open hostility.

## Competition for Scarce Goods

Our basic attitudes toward competition as a form of social interaction
seem to be in the process of change. American society, drifting from a

Darwinistic social philosophy, is no longer as certain as it was in the days of the great industrial barons that competition is "good" or that the people who gain the greatest rewards necessarily deserved to succeed. This attitude change (if it exists) cannot be traced to any one set of factors. We certainly feel a greater sense of social responsibility for the "losers" in the race of life; witness the growth of the welfare state. But is this trend toward the welfare state the cause of decreased competitiveness or the effect of still more basic underlying conditions? The almost completed urbanization and the rapid homogenization of our society probably contribute to the decreased emphasis upon competition as a proper form of interaction. But modern parents, particularly those from the middle class, probably also are more inclined than *their* parents were to have their children avoid anxiety-provoking situations, and they may discourage their children from entering competitions. It may even be that people have learned that competition leads to anger and aggression.

*Competition as a Frustration.* Competition must be regarded as a frustration by most definitions of these terms. Writers, of course, have differed in the details of their analyses of competition, but all are agreed as to the essentials. These involve (1) two or more units, either individuals or groups, engaged in pursuing the same rewards, with (2) these rewards so defined that if they are attained by any one unit, there are fewer rewards for the other units in the situation. The losing unit clearly is frustrated. In a contest between two people, for example, the loser is a person instigated toward a particular goal, who then is prevented from reaching this goal by the other individual's victory. The contest may have been a fair one, and the loser may know he is supposed to be a good sport, but he still is thwarted (although this can be defined as a "reasonable" or "nonarbitrary" frustration). Aggressive tendencies are frequently the result.

Deutsch (1949) showed that the resentment created by a competitive college-classroom situation can produce lower liking for the other members of the classroom group and interferes with effective group functioning. Sections of an introductory psychology course were organized into either cooperative or competitive five-man groups. The members of each cooperative group were to be evaluated as a group, and any rewards obtained in the experimentally established weekly competition with other groups would be divided equally among the group members. Thus, to use Deutsch's phrase, the members of each group were "promotively interdependent"; each person's progress toward the goal also aided the goal attainment of the other group members. In the competitive groups, on the other hand, each of the students in the five-man group would receive a ranking as to how good his individual performance had been. The person having the best scores in the weekly within-group competitions would get the greatest rewards. The people in these groups, then, were "contriently interdependent"; good performance by any one member interfered with the others' chances of gaining substantial rewards.

There generally was better and more harmonious performance within the cooperative groups. The people in these groups, in contrast to their competitive peers, apparently communicated more effectively with each other and more readily accepted each other's ideas. They developed greater liking for the other students in their class and had a stronger desire to win their respect. Competition within a group for mutually exclusive goals seems to have disrupted the communication, coordination, friendliness, and pride in one's group generally conducive to effective group performance, presumably because of the anger toward the other members (and possibly other emotions as well) engendered by the frustrations.

Deutsch also obtained some indications that the students in the competitive situation expected hostile behavior from their rivals. These expectations probably were a reflection of aggression anxiety within the group members created by their own hostile tendencies. They could have felt aggression was not justified in this situation and, therefore, as we saw in Chapter 4, the stronger the hostile inclinations aroused in them under such conditions, the greater was their resulting aggression anxiety. Evidence from later research by Deutsch and Solomon (cited in Thibaut & Kelley, 1959, p. 229) is consistent with this analysis. There were two competitive conditions in this experiment, differing in the degree of drive interference produced by the rival's winning. In one condition if the subject lost, he would receive no score, while he would suffer a sizeable score reduction for losing in the other conditions. Since there was a greater deprivation, stronger anger undoubtedly was aroused in this latter condition. A relatively intense attitude of rivalry apparently developed, and the subject often was especially vindictive toward his competitor. This condition, furthermore, sometimes caused the subject to regard his rival as being "motivated by malevolence." In such a case he probably anticipated hostility from his partner, perhaps because of his anxiety regarding his own hostile inclinations.[4] At any rate, this last experiment indicates why competitive situations sometimes breed intense aggression. Not only is the loser severely frustrated, but he may also attribute his own strong hostile tendencies to his rival,

---

[4] Janis and Katz (1959), also discussing this type of phenomenon, hypothesized that this perception arises as a guilt reaction. Aggression produces guilt, and in order to reduce these guilt feelings the aggressor attributes immoral or evil intentions to his victim, justifying the aggression.

perceiving the competitor as having been motivated by hostility toward him. Such a perception would then strengthen and justify further aggression toward the rival.

Sherif and Sherif (1953) reported an experiment with twelve-year-old boys in a more naturalistic setting also demonstrating aggressive consequences of competition. The experiment, carried out at an isolated summer-camp site, was divided into three stages. In the first phase, lasting three days, the boys engaged in camp-wide activities enabling the adult observers to determine the friendship groupings. These friendships then were deliberately broken in the second stage lasting five days. The boys were divided into two groups, with care being taken to assemble the youngsters with other boys for whom they had relatively little liking. Each newly formed experimental group carried out its activities independently of the other group, and rewards were given to each group as a unit. By the end of this second period the boys had developed fairly strong ties to the other youngsters with whom they were assembled which even overrode their attraction to their earlier "best friends" in the other group. A strong group consciousness (or identification with the group) also developed within each unit. In this connection, Sherif and Sherif made an observation consistent with my previously expressed doubts (in Chapter 6) regarding the supposed emotional effects of the growth of group consciousness. It will be recalled that Schmidt (1960), in summarizing the results of an experiment at a Jewish boarding school, had concluded that the development of group consciousness produces aggressiveness toward outgroups. Sherif and Sherif, in essence, disputed this contention. They explicitly noted (1953, p. 261) that there were no signs of enmity between the two clubs as group identification developed.

Hostility did arise in the last phase of the study, however, after the groups had competed against each other. A series of competitive games was organized, with the winning group receiving extremely attractive prizes. At first, the strongest overt reaction toward the rival was one of derogation, but as the games continued over the five-day period (i.e., as the frustrations were repeated), the rivalry became more intense and overt hostility became more common. A planned frustrating situation added to the aggressiveness between the two groups. The violence finally became so intense—for example, flaring up into a fight in the mess hall in which the boys threw things at each other—that the adults had to terminate the experiment.

*Perception of the Rival.* The aggressive tendencies produced by competition may not be revealed in overt behavior, but whether they are or not, each party's perception of its competitor is generally affected. We saw this in the research by Deutsch and Solomon mentioned above.

Seriously frustrated subjects often regarded their rivals as being intensely hostile and malevolent. Avigdor (1952) obtained essentially similar findings in a field study conducted with girls' clubs. The girls tended to attribute much more unfavorable characteristics to the members of the organization with whom they were in competition than to the other outgroup girls with whom they were cooperating.

Osgood (1960) pointed out that these unfavorable interpretations of one's rival can be the result of a tendency to make judgments of a person consistent with other negative attitudes toward him. If we do not like someone, we must also attribute undesirable properties to him in order to be consistent (or, to use Festinger's terminology, to reduce dissonance by bringing one set of cognitions into line with other cognitions). Thus, according to Osgood, investigations have shown that Americans often attribute favorable characteristics to the British, whereas they frequently judge the Russian people (our competitors) in an unfavorable manner, perceiving them as being cruel, backward, and domineering (pp. 364–365).

Such anger-induced perceptions of the rival obviously can heighten the chances of open conflict with him in the future. There are at least two ways in which this might happen. For one, the individual locked in a prolonged and serious competition often interprets his rival's behavior in a manner consistent with his generally unfavorable impression of him. The competitor's actions, therefore, could mistakenly be interpreted as being aggressive when, in reality, no hostility was intended. Furthermore, as we saw in the last chapter, the unfavorable perception of the competitor could facilitate the generalization of aggressive tendencies from some other frustrater to him.

The above findings demonstrate that competition is frustrating. This frustration is obvious when the individual loses, but even if the contest has not been decided, frustrations are produced by (1) the anxiety arising from anticipating possible defeat and (2) the demands upon one's behavior—such as the need to work for long hours—created by the competitive conditions. *Those features of a frustrating situation generally determining the intensity of the resulting anger also should govern the strength of the anger stemming from competition.* These are: (1) *drive strength,* i.e., the strength of the satisfactions to be obtained by winning the competition, or the intensity of the punishment caused by losing; (2) *the degree of interference* with one's activities resulting from the conditions of the competition; and (3) *the number of thwarted response sequences,* i.e., the duration of the competition. It may be that competition should be differentiated from aggressive conflict on certain conceptual grounds. Where aggression is aimed at injury, competition is not. Competition is usually characterized by established rules limiting what the competitors can do to each other and defining some relatively scarce goal as the proper concern of the rivals, not the injury of one another (cf. Mack & Snyder, 1957, p. 217). Nevertheless, the competitive situation breeds at least some anger and resentment toward one's rival. The resentment is not always revealed in aggressive actions; the rules of the situation often prohibit such behavior. Even in the absence of overt hostility, however, the competitor is frequently perceived in an unfavorable if not extremely derogatory manner, with this interpretation of the rival sometimes serving to justify the aggressive inclination toward him.

The present analysis can be extended to competitive bargaining situations in which each party can inflict injury on the other. The rival units in such situations often are severely frustrated. Not only is the competition itself thwarting, but the threat in the rival's power to cause additional damage also is a frustration. Each side, then, is relatively strongly angered by the other. But on top of this, each competitive party has the ability to hurt the other side. Being angered, there is an inclination to use this power and aggress against the rival. Such inclinations, however, would provoke aggression anxiety; aggression undoubtedly would give rise to retaliatory aggression. And this aggression anxiety is also frustrating. The only form the anger can take, however, is in being stubborn and difficult in dealing with the competitor. As we can see, competition between rivals who can injure each other is all too likely to raise barriers against achieving some reconciliation and may even lead to an impasse. Deutsch and Krauss (1960) obtained results in line with this reasoning in a laboratory experiment. Adults in a bargaining situation who could injure each other took longer to reach an agreement, even when such delays were to their detriment, than did similar competitive adults who did not threaten each other. (The reader is invited to ponder the implications of this study for the present world situation.)

## Strategic Aggression

Not every hostile act is necessarily the result of frustration, of course. Many people become aggressive when they think such behavior will help them achieve particular goals. Both businessmen and labor unions have employed violence as an economic weapon, not only because they were thwarted but because they believed the open hostility was necessary to reach their desired ends. A revolutionist may employ aggression in the pursuit of his philosophical-economic goals, and a counter-revolutionist can retaliate, not because he is angry but in order to preserve his social position. Aggression, in other words, is at times a stratagem in the competition between groups for incompatible goals.

Planned aggression has been used as a technique for maintaining the status quo in race relations. Authorities are agreed some instances of racial violence in the South were instigated by white community leaders as a matter of deliberate policy. Indeed, such occurrences have taken place frequently enough that writers have established concepts separating these acts of instrumental aggression from other forms of interracial hostility. Raper, one of the more eminent of these authorities, for example, proposed that a distinction should be drawn between *Bourbon* and *proletariat* lynchings (cited in Cantril, 1941, p. 94). The former term refers to those acts of deliberate aggression generally "engineered by leading citizens with the knowledge of law-enforcement officers" in order to preserve community norms, particularly regarding white supremacy. Proletariat lynchings, in contrast, "are led by members of the poorer classes . . . and disapproved by the better citizens of the community." They seek to persecute Negroes in general rather than to punish a specific crime.

Hitler's violently anti-Semitic policies apparently were carried out for political purposes. According to one student of modern German affairs (Needler, 1960), "Hitler used his anti-Semitism to achieve a reconciliation, on the ideological plane, of intrinsically contradictory appeals." He could tell the German middle class there would be no more labor troubles after Jewish agitators were removed and still say to the workers their economic difficulties would be lessened when Jewish capitalists were exterminated. Anti-Semitism itself did not necessarily gain votes for Hitler, but the expression of these hostile attitudes supposedly made it possible for the Nazis to say other things that did attract followers. Hitler certainly believed many of the accusations leveled against Jews. Nevertheless, he employed anti-Semitism primarily for political ends. Needler maintained that Hitler also was strongly opposed to Christianity as a religion, but did not express these sentiments because he knew there was little to be gained by doing so.

*Facilitating Conditions.* Jews historically have served as a convenient scapegoat for many groups inclined to employ violence as a political technique. They can readily be blamed for difficulties actually originating from other sources. As was pointed out in the previous chapter, such scapegoating is feasible because of the stimulus properties that Jews have for many non-Jews. Hitler was only one of the more recent political leaders who realized this. Not a few European politicians and government authorities (such as those in Czarist Russia) have attempted to divert their people's attention from their own shortcomings to the supposed wicked machinations of the "evil Jews."

Political leaders, however, cannot lead where their followers are unwilling to go. Mobs cannot be directed to attack a particular group unless they already are angry at someone. *If a particular minority is to become the target of displaced aggression, (1) the people to do the attacking must be angry and (2) the intended victims must have appropriate stimulus characteristics.* A leader may be able to create both of these conditions (if times are right) but, nevertheless, they are necessary before the actual violence can occur. As an illustration, imagine how difficult it would be for some demagogue to inflame the citizens of a prosperous, peaceful community into persecuting their fellows who are of French descent. He probably would be thrown out of the community as a public nuisance without attracting any substantial following.

Czarist officials instigated riots and pogroms against Jews on some occasions but, according to Dahlke (1952), these cases of mob violence would not have occurred if predisposing historical conditions had been absent. In order to isolate these factors, Dahlke compared the events leading up to the Kishinew riot of 1903 and the Detroit race riot of 1943 and suggested that there were a number of features common to both: (1) a historical period of transition, with unusual stresses and strains accompanying considerable horizontal and vertical mobility; (2) a visibly different and strongly disliked subordinate group which, in its struggle to improve its status, "is regarded as an undesirable competitor"; (3) law and established authorities assigning the minority group a subordinate status, so that in its struggle for social betterment the minority group behaves in a manner contrary to the wishes of the authorities, producing hatred and suspicion between this group and the authorities; (4) one or more organizations advocating violence against the minority group; (5) the press and news media reporting the minority group in an unfavorable light, even indulging in minority baiting; (6) upper- and middle-class people supporting and contributing to the defamation of the minority group, but young students and marginal workers initiating the violence.

We can readily see the significance of each of these conditions. Transitional periods, of course, would produce severe frustrations. It is not easy to determine who is to blame, however, and the minority group is perceived as a major source of thwartings because of the second condition, prior dislike for a visibly different group. There is little fear of legal punishment for attacking the minority group since established authorities also oppose the group (condition 3), and more than this, appropriate reference groups have even defined the violence as morally proper and socially necessary (conditions 4, 5, and 6), lessening guilt-induced restraints against hostility. However, aggression anxiety and guilt would still be strong enough in most members of the middle and upper classes to prevent them from participating in the mob violence. They have learned not only that physical aggression is often wrong, but that they also have the most to lose if, by chance, they should be punished for joining in the mob activity. The first people to break through their restraints—the ones most likely to initiate the hostility—are those who either are generally impulsive (Lippitt et al., 1952), because they have not developed strong inhibitory tendencies, or who have not learned to regard physical aggression as "bad" (e.g., some members of the lower classes). This last explains why most of the people actually participating in riot mobs are usually relatively young and from the lower social strata, sometimes even having long histories of previous antisocial aggression (Cantril, 1941, pp. 106–108).

The stage has to be right for strategic aggression. Politicians or government officials can strike a spark, but they must have a flint and material ready to be ignited. Only when these factors combine can there be the sort of violence occurring in Kishinew, when 44 were killed, 583 wounded, and thousands of families financially ruined, or in Detroit, when 34 were killed, hundreds more injured, and 2 million dollars, worth of damage done to property (Dahlke, 1952).

## REDUCING HOSTILITY

There has been a tremendous concern in the Western world, and particularly within the United States, as to how men of goodwill might proceed to lessen aggression between groups. Thus, not only is there the UNESCO "tensions project" mentioned earlier, but also agencies (to name a few) such as the Social Science Research Council Committee on Techniques for Reducing Group Hostility, and the Antidefamation League. These organizations have sought ways and means for reducing conflict between groups. There obviously is no simple solution to this problem, and no one technique would be effective in all situations. The above discussion should have made this clear. We have seen, for example, that many difficulties between groups cannot be removed by dispelling misconceptions; some hostilities arise from all-too-realistic competition.

The most direct procedure for reducing intergroup conflict, of course, would be to lessen the occurrence of frustrations. How this might be done is not for us to say here, but obviously, little actually can be achieved along these lines; even if competition between groups could be minimized somewhat, there is no real prospect for eliminating more than a few of the many sources of anxiety and insecurity in our society. The following discussion, therefore, will assume there are tensions within people. From a nonutopian point of view, the major problem is to prevent the frustration-induced anger from bursting into open aggression against more or less innocent victims. This may be an attainable goal. Hostility against people stemming solely from their group membership can perhaps be lessened fairly easily.

## Communications Advocating Peace and Harmony

We saw earlier in this chapter that information programs may strengthen peaceful group relations under some circumstances. Minorities sometimes are the target of displaced aggression because they are disliked blindly and because of the characteristics they are believed to possess. Lessening this dislike and/or altering the perceived qualities of the subordinate group can reduce the probability that this group will become the victim of generalized aggressive tendencies.

There is an extensive literature on the use of the mass media for attitude change. Some of these writings deal specifically with the implications of communication techniques for the lessening of intergroup conflict (e.g., Williams, 1947; Klineberg, 1950), but many more of the studies, reviews, monographs, and books in this field provide general information conceivably relevant for a wide variety of purposes. Any adequate survey of this voluminuous research literature is well beyond the scope of the present book. Nevertheless, some of the findings obtained in these investigations are of particular interest for our purposes and should be mentioned.

For one thing, messages advocating views on important issues that are greatly discrepant from the beliefs held by the members of the audience generally will meet with a great deal of resistance (Hovland et al., 1957), particularly if the communicator is not a close friend (Zimbardo, 1960). The argument presented by the communicator, we might say, produces dissonance within the audience holding opposite beliefs, and the audience reduces this uncomfortable state by disparaging the communicator and rejecting his message. Obviously, then, a communication advocating a peaceful course of action toward a particular group will tend to be rejected by people strongly committed to aggression against this group. The message will differ too greatly from their beliefs justifying the aggression. This may be one of the reasons why mediators often have a thankless job. Each side in the conflict looks at the would-be peacemaker from an extreme position so that (because of the resulting judgmental contrast effect) both warring parties see him as supporting the *other* side. But in addition, he may be urging behavior incompatible with the combatants' strongly held beliefs about each other. Dissonance would be created, possibly arousing antagonism toward the source of this discomfort.

The communication studies also show the futility of trying to scare people into changing their behavior. Messages arousing strong fear often prove to be less effective in modifying attitudes than communications creating only weak fear or no fear at all (Janis & Feshbach, 1953). This can readily be explained. Dissonance theory suggests that the strong fear-producing message might also be greatly discrepant from the audience's other beliefs (e.g., that the behavior opposed by the message is safe and enjoyable). Suppose the audience is committed to the actions the communication seeks to change. The greater the fear arousal, then, the greater would be the incompatibility between the communication and the initial beliefs, and again, the greater would be the resistance to these emotion-arousing messages.[5] Thus, it does little good to tell some people that the only alternative to world peace is atomic catastrophe; they might still advocate belligerent or absolutely noncompromising international policies. References to nuclear holocausts for them are fear-producing communications entirely inconsistent with their strongly held opinions, and as such are disregarded.[6]

## Minimizing Group Differences

While the perception of another group as being different from one's own does not necessarily incite aggressive tendencies, reduction of these perceived differences may lower the chances that the group will become the target of hostility. There are several reasons why this might be true. For one, similarity generally means psychological "closeness"; the extent to which we associate someone with ourselves is a function of our resemblance to that person on some important dimension. Restraints against attacking the self also would be manifested in inhibitions against attacking others strongly associated with the self, i.e., others seen as similar to us in important ways.

But more than this, group differences can be threatening under some conditions. Reducing these differences lessens the threat. The existence of other groups can be disturbing in a crisis. If problems were to arise in a society that could not be overcome by the established social structure with its existing rules and regulations, each segment of the society could well feel it was on its own, so to speak. Since it was impossible to predict what actions would eliminate the crisis or otherwise bring rewards, each of the social units would attempt to attain these rewards through its own behavior (Mintz, 1958). Moreover, there might even be suspicion of these other units as potential competitors. People who are different often have different opinions and values. They could have

---

[5] Festinger is now engaged in testing a related hypothesis.

[6] The fear-arousing communication probably is not "avoided" when the individual thinks there is a very high probability that he will suffer the noxious consequences referred to in the message.

aims incompatible with one's own desires. When everyone can get what he wants, all is peaceful, but if rewards are scarce, people tend to believe that dissimilar groups might oppose their needs and desires.

Some such process may account for the increased relationship between social class and voting behavior in times of economic recession (Converse, 1958); the members of the different classes become aware of their own particularistic interests when economic goods are scarce, while the other classes, seen as having opposing aims, are regarded as competitors. If the social crisis were to become extremely severe, with a resulting breakdown in the societal organization, class conflict could even flare into violence, as it did in Russia in 1917 and in Germany after World War I. Perceiving society as a relatively homogeneous collection of people not segmentalized into different social classes having divergent interests obviously would lower the likelihood of class conflict. American political history undoubtedly owes much of its calm to such a relative lack of awareness of social-class differences.

### External Threats and Perceived Interdependence

All crises, however, do not have socially disintegrating effects. As a number of writers have observed (cf. Williams, 1947, p. 58), threatening situations at times promote harmony within the social structure. Thus, social-class differences in voting preferences apparently lessen in the United States during times of international trouble (Converse, 1958). But yet, contrary to the beliefs of some authorities (e.g., Alexander, 1938), a common external enemy does not always cement relations among the various segments of a nation. France was torn by dissension in 1940 even though it was locked in battle with its enemy Germany. There *are* conditions under which an external threat to the entire group enhances group-integrative tendencies, but these conditions are not always present.

Lanzetta (1955) showed experimentally that dangers external to the group at times can promote harmony and friendliness among the group members. In his study, varying degrees of external stress were imposed upon four-man groups working on reasoning and mechanical assembly tasks, with the severest stress being created by the experimenter's interferences and by his badgering and belittling the group's performance. Lanzetta found that this harsh treatment coming from outside the group produced a decrease in "negative-social emotional behaviors" within the group and an increase in signs of friendliness, cooperativeness, and other group-oriented behaviors. Leighton (cited in Cartwright & Zander, 1960, p. 82) has reported essentially similar observations; the American Japanese assembled in wartime relocation centers drew together more closely when external authorities seemed to threaten things

they valued highly. The problem now is to determine how these situations differed conceptually from the situation of France in 1940 and
Russia in 1917.

From the writer's point of view, the major differences have to do
with (1) the perceived source of the frustration confronting the group
and (2) the extent to which each group member believes the others in
his group can help him overcome this frustration. It is important here
to recall the definition of a frustration, i.e., an interference with some
*goal-directed* activity. People who have met with continued failures
often change their aims so that they become concerned with altogether
different goals. Erecting a barrier blocking attempts to reach the goal
they already had forsaken obviously would not be too upsetting to
them. But assuming a group is in pursuit of a given goal, the present
formulation maintains that *the individual members become more highly
attracted to each other when they believe their fellow members can and
will help them satisfy their desires.* The presence of an external threat
can make the other group members much more important to the individual; he may need them to overcome the external frustration, and so,
these others become more attractive to him. In the Lanzetta experiment,
then, the group members under stress presumably felt a greater need
for emotional support and assistance from the others working along-
side them and this made them more attractive.

But such support is not always forthcoming in crisis situations. The
collapse of a social structure rendering established modes of conduct
ineffective for reward attainment can heighten the feeling of competitiveness with others, as was pointed out earlier. Other people become
additional sources of frustration instead of help, and as a result they
arouse aggressive tendencies. Thus, the external crisis confronting France
presumably increased dissension when different groups in the country
saw each other as competitors rather than as partners. Another important
aspect of this unstable, ambiguous situation is that the different segments of the society could regard each other as contributing to the
nation's defeat. Other group members are attractive only as long as they
can help the individual attain some rewards. *If a social organization
cannot cope with its tasks and it is not clear who is the source of the
frustration, the members may blame each other.* In one study (Hamblin,
1958), laboratory groups were placed in a crisis situation by, unknown
to them, constantly changing the rules of the game they were playing.
The group members consequently could not achieve their goals. Not
recognizing that the experimenter was the cause of their difficulties, they
apparently came to see each other as the frustration source, and
group integration declined. Similarly, Pepitone and Kleiner (1957) found
that boys' teams experienced a substantial decline in cohesiveness after

they were told they would probably lose their attractive high-status position because they (supposedly) would almost certainly be defeated in future athletic contests. The youngsters presumably thought the others on their team would be the cause of the defeat.

This reasoning can be extended to a variety of intergroup relationships. Members of different groups may become more attractive to each other if they believe they are interdependent, i.e., if they think they need each other and must cooperate in order to overcome shared frustrations. Threats and crises are frustrating and should produce aggressive tendencies. In some cases such aggression may be displaced onto minority groups or other disliked people. However, if the threat were to confront everyone, majority and minority, liked and disliked, it is conceivable that scapegoating would be reduced substantially. Feshbach and Singer (1957a) tested this notion in an experiment in which college students were assigned to either personnel-threat or shared-threat conditions. In both cases the subjects read written communications describing threatening occurrences, but under the former condition the crises were personal events (e.g., referring to mental illness), while in the latter condition they were shared catastrophes (e.g., referring to floods or hurricanes). There apparently was a greater increase in hostility toward ethnic minority groups, as measured by a social-prejudice questionnaire, after the personal threat than following the shared threat. If this is a reliable phenomenon (the experiment should be repeated using other than hypothetical crises), the reduced scapegoating after the shared danger may stem from the "common fate" (perceiving that everybody was in danger) and/or from a perceived need for cooperation among the groups experiencing the common threat.

This perceived need for cooperation is clearly an important determinant of the results in a more realistic experiment. Some time after his summer-camp study described above, Sherif conducted another field experiment designed to investigate the reduction of intergroup hostility (reported in Sherif & Sherif, 1956, pp. 301–331). As before, the experimenters instigated hostility between two boys' groups by staging a series of competitions between them. Then, in order to reduce the conflict, the psychologists established a number of problem situations relevant to both groups and requiring cooperation between them. All the boys had to work together on such tasks as removing an obstacle to their water supply, obtaining a feature-length movie, and pulling a supposedly stalled truck. The psychological barriers between the two groups did not break down easily. But, according to observations and sociometric devices, by the end of the last joint endeavor the rival clubs had lost much of their resentment toward each other. Intergroup friendships developed to a considerably greater extent than before. Cooperation in successfully removing the barriers to their shared goals apparently did much to lessen the earlier enmity between the groups.

Some years ago one of the mass-circulation magazines published a science-fiction story making use of this friendship-through-cooperation theme. In this story a number of scientists eliminated the possibility of nuclear war between the United States and Russia by leading both nations to believe the Earth was confronted by a threat from outer space. The two countries had to cooperate in order to remove the danger. It is unlikely that the real world would accept the notion of "extraterrestrial threats," but the principle illustrated by this plot apparently does have a basis in fact.

## Equal Status Contacts

Several investigations have shown that contact with minority group members sometimes lowers prejudice against them. In some cases this aggression reduction can be traced to successful cooperation between the different groups. People from different ethnic backgrounds had worked together to overcome a shared threat so that the resulting "glow of success" decreased the hostility between them. Perhaps the most dramatic example of such an effect is found in the results of the United States Army's experiment with mixed Negro-white rifle companies during the last stages of the war in Europe. According to an opinion survey conducted several months after the onset of the experiment, the racial mixing under the dangerous conditions of combat had decreased the white soldiers' desire to keep apart from the Negroes; where only 18 per cent of the men in segregated divisions thought it would be a good idea to have Negroes in their companies, 64 per cent of the white enlisted men in the integrated divisions believed this was a good general policy. Furthermore, most of the men in the non-Negro divisions indicated they would dislike to serve in companies having Negro platoons, but only 7 per cent of the men who had fought side by side with colored soldiers expressed this feeling (cited in Harding et al., 1954, p. 1051).

Cooperation in removing frustrations is not the only factor involved in the increased friendliness stemming from contact and acquaintance. Just getting to know someone better often seems to heighten the liking for him. Studies of the effects of residential contact between different ethnic groups have revealed such favorable attitude changes. For example, Deutsch and Collins (1951) found that white housewives living in interracial housing projects tended to express much friendlier attitudes toward Negroes than did similar women residing in segregated projects. The investigators claimed that this was not solely a function of differences in prior attitudes toward Negroes; the experience of interracial living itself presumably had produced much of the decreased enmity toward Negroes.

Such enhanced liking resulting from increased contact has been observed so frequently that some writers (e.g., Homans, 1950) have made it a fundamental principle of human interaction. We have seen, however, that reduced enmity need not always follow increased acquaintance. Bringing people together who are in competition with each other, who have incompatible aims or values, is more likely to intensify the dislike between them than to produce peace and harmony. Putting it simply, they probably will frustrate each other. This certainly is apparent in many residential areas undergoing a socioeconomic transition. Minority ethnic groups moving into a neighborhood are often greeted with hostility, and this hatred increases rapidly the faster the influx of the visibly different newcomers.

What is the difference between such aggression-intensifying situations and the type of situation existing in the harmonious interracial housing projects? For some authorities the key factor is whether the groups in contact have equal status. Negroes and whites are most likely to live together in peace when they see each other as equals. The present writer believes, however, that a more general principle is involved here. Equality of status undoubtedly is important, but it is important because it minimizes frustrations. Thus, the whites living in the interracial project did not feel threatened by their Negro neighbors. They did not see themselves in competition with the colored people for status, housing, or jobs. Increased acquaintance with someone who previously had been a stranger gives rise to increased liking for him when this contact is not frustrating. It may even be, as Deutsch and Collins suggested, that the informality of the contact is an important determinant of this enhanced friendliness. People who come together in more formal work or school situations may become more tolerant of each other, but they do not necessarily develop greater liking. Friendships result primarily when the contact is informal (cf. Harding et al., pp. 1051–1052).

The personality characteristics of the people involved in the intergroup situation can determine the extent to which the interaction is nonfrustrating. Mussen (1950) studied 106 white boys before and after they had relatively intimate contact with Negro boys at an interracial summer camp. Many of the white youngsters did become friendlier to the Negroes by the end of the month, but some did not. Projective tests given to the boys indicated that the children who increased in prejudice had relatively strong "needs to defy authority and strong aggressive feelings." On the basis of these and other findings, Mussen hypothesized that these boys did not find the camp experience satisfying in many different ways. These frustrations then produced aggressive tendencies which presumably were displaced onto the Negroes. Another possibility is that the boys exhibiting an increase in hostility generally operated with hostile, unfriendly expectations (this also is suggested by Mussen's data), so that they interpreted the Negro boys' actions toward them in an unfriendly manner. That is, as far as they were concerned, they were frustrated by the colored boys. Consistent with such an explanation, Berkowitz and Holmes (1959) have shown that people trained to be angry with another person increased in unfriendliness toward him after increased contact with him. They probably interpreted his behavior as being unfriendly or otherwise frustrating to them.

## SUMMARY

Conflict between groups is ultimately a problem for the psychology of the individual, but there is no real incompatibility between group-level considerations of social conflict and individualistically oriented discussions. Differences of opinion and competition between groups can incite anger because of the frustrations they create. The antagonists can also believe aggression is instrumental to attaining their individual goals.

Some of the factors that must exist before there can be intergroup conflict are: (1) People are categorized together as a unit and collectively regarded as a frustrating agent; (2) the group is visible, i.e., there is awareness of it and a perception of it as being "different"; and (3) there is some frustrating contact with the group. The rapid influx of a group into an area is particularly likely to breed antagonism toward the group if (1) it is visibly different and (2) the older residents of the area are in real or imagined competition with the new group, resulting in the group being seen as a frustrater.

Frustrations can arise from knowledge of the existence of opposing belief systems and from competition for scarce goods or values. World history documents how frequently opposing ideological systems have come into open conflict. In many instances, of course, the combatants thought there were direct gains to be achieved through attacking advocates of the opposing belief system (e.g., entering Heaven). But the people espousing beliefs incompatible with the individual's own views could also be disliked because their ideology makes the individual uncertain that his own beliefs are correct. In other words, the opposing beliefs are a source of dissonance within the individual. Intense dissonance produced by wide disagreement on important issues elicits aggressive tendencies because the dissonance itself is frustrating and/or the hostility toward the advocate of the opposing view removes this person (and his beliefs) from consideration as being possibly correct, i.e., the hostility is a mechanism for reducing dissonance.

As support for the dissonance theory interpretation of belief-engendered conflict, evidence is cited demonstrating that attitudinal similarity tends to be directly associated with friendship. People generally assume that their friends hold beliefs similar to their own, and this assumption seems to be correct more often than not. Furthermore, attitudinal similarity often precedes friendship development as well as being the result of such relationships. The intense hostility provoked by "family quarrels" can also be readily explained by dissonance theory. The aggression here is directed against people maintaining beliefs somewhat similar to the individual's own opinions (and thus, whose views are relevant to his beliefs), but who disagree with the individual in certain important ways. In some cases these other people are competitors, but even in the absence of such a thwarting competition, hostility may arise because (1) the important differences in the opposing belief systems increase dissonance and/or (2) these people have failed to provide the person (who is not certain his opinions are correct) with the belief support he wanted and expected.

As both terms are defined, competition must be regarded as a frustration. Consistent with such an analysis, several experiments have shown that competition breeds dislike between the rival parties even though the rules of the situation may prevent the dislike from flaring into open hostility. This enmity is sometimes accompanied by guilt or aggression anxiety, as if the competitive individual were aware that his aggressive inclinations were morally "wrong" or were afraid that his anger would evoke counteraggression. As one manifestation of the dislike, the person also perceives his competitor in an unfavorable manner. This unfavorable perception of the rival might also serve to justify the individual's hostile inclinations and therefore reduce his guilt feelings.

Authorities have sometimes fomented aggression against particular groups because they believed such hostility would help them achieve other, nonaggressive goals. This instrumental or "strategic" aggression, however, requires the necessary predisposing conditions. If people are to be incited to attack a group they must (1) be angry, (2) see the given group as being responsible for their frustrations, (3) believe the attack upon the group is ethically justified, and (4) think they will not be punished for the aggression.

Theoretically, the best way to decrease the likelihood of intergroup conflict is to lessen the occurrence of frustrations and to eliminate the gains that might be accrued through attacking other groups. From a more practical point of view, however, the wisest course probably is to try to block the generalization of frustration-created aggressive tendencies to more or less innocent groups. A number of procedures might be employed in pursuing such an aim. The easiest is to spread communications advocating peace and harmony. However, such communications would encounter a great deal of resistance if they aroused dissonance, i.e., if they opposed action to which the audience was heavily committed. Messages that attempt to persuade through creating fear are generally ineffective, perhaps because such communications are also dissonance provoking.

Minimizing the perception of group differences might also lessen intergroup conflict, but research findings suggest that such hostility can be significantly reduced by demonstrating that the groups are interdependent if they are to cope with a common threat. Inability to overcome these threats could heighten the intergroup conflict, however, if it is possible for each group to blame the other for the failure. Equal status contacts between groups also lower intergroup enmity, particularly if informal social relationships are involved, but strong unfavorable attitudes toward the other group existing prior to the contact can prevent the development of friendships and may even increase the hostility by giving rise to perceived frustrations.

# chapter 8

# Catharsis

A television husband attempted to justify his aggressive outburst to his wife by claiming his display of anger had been beneficial to him. Medical science, he told his story wife, has proved that it's harmful to hide your feelings. "Medical science," of course, has "proved" no such thing, but many people would agree with another statement made by the husband. Having shown his anger, he insisted he now felt better than he would have if he had kept his hostility locked up within him. Indeed, a number of authorities would go even further than the husband did. They would maintain that the display of aggression not only lowered the husband's feeling of tension but also effectively weakened the strength of his aggressive inclinations.

This is the catharsis hypothesis, surely one of the most widely accepted doctrines in the folklore of both the man in the street and the social scientist. For centuries, going back to the ancient Greeks, people have believed that the exhibition of an emotion can purge an individual of that emotion. Bringing this thesis up to date, many laymen, social scientists, psychiatrists, and psychoanalysts contend that expressing hostility reduces the strength of the aggressive tendencies within the individual or somehow makes him feel better.

Quantitative research, however, has not been consistently kind to the catharsis hypothesis. The theoretical formulations of this proposition must be revised, or at least specified in more detail. The present chapter will examine some of the more common versions of the catharsis doctrine and then consider the pertinent evidence bearing upon these formulations. As will become all too clear, the matter is much more complicated than is generally assumed. For one thing, two different kinds of phenomena have been given the label "catharsis," and we cannot be certain with our present knowledge that these phenomena necessarily always occur together. "Catharsis$_1$" may not be equal to or even correlated with "catharsis$_2$."

The most common version of the catharsis hypothesis in the psychological literature maintains that the performance of an aggressive act reduces the instigation to aggression, assuming there is no further frustration. This decrease in the strength of the remaining aggressive tendencies, furthermore, supposedly is not due to the elimination of the frustration evoking the hostility. Orthodox psychoanalysts, together with Dollard and his colleagues (1939, p. 50), insist that the expression of aggression results in at least a momentary reduction of the instigation to aggression regardless of the hostile act's effectiveness in removing the obstacle to the goal-directed activity. Instrumental aggression leading to frustration removal can lessen the strength of the aggressive drive, but this is not "catharsis" in the usual sense of the word.

A second relatively frequent usage of the catharsis doctrine deals primarily with the individual's feelings of pleasantness after performing a hostile act. People (including the previously mentioned TV husband) have such a process in mind when they say they feel better after exhibiting the aggression they formerly had inhibited. They supposedly have "let off steam" or have "gotten something off their chests" and as a consequence are now happier. But do such increased feelings of pleasantness necessarily stem solely from anger reduction? There are a good many possible reasons why someone may feel relief after exhibiting hostility, and tension reduction does not inevitably signify a lessened likelihood of further aggression. The catharsis process must be analyzed in greater detail.

## THEORETICAL FORMULATIONS

### Catharsis and Reduction of the Instigation to Aggression

*"Draining the Reservoir."* It is impossible to develop a really complete picture of the instigation to aggression without considering the phenomenon of catharsis. Drives, whether toward aggression, sex, or hunger, are not fully understood if there is uncertainty as to the conditions decreasing the strength of the instigation. Freud certainly realized this. His analysis of catharsis was clearly part and parcel of his general conception of the nature of aggression. As was discussed in Chapter 1, aggressive behavior for him ultimately was in the service of the death instinct, the endeavor to return to the quiescence of the inorganic world (Freud, 1959d). Human beings—all living things—continually attempt to reduce the level of both aggressive and sexual excitation within them, he maintained. This excitation (or energy) must find a means of discharge. The individual must turn the aggression outward in attacks upon other people, or in seeking to control and have power over them, if he is to avoid killing himself in fulfillment of the death instinct. If hostile energies are not directed outward, they would at the very least turn back upon the self as intensified masochism or guilt feelings (1959a).

The expression of aggression provides an outlet for the destructive impulses. Someone may be attacked, or the hostility may be displayed in more socially acceptable forms. But however it is done, the performance of a hostile act presumably lessens the intensity of the aggressive excitation within the individual. Employing the hydraulic model so aptly applied to the psychoanalytic conception of motivation, we can say that aggressive actions drain the internal reservoir of aggressive energy for a short period of time.

Chapter 1 indicated that Freud's hypothesis concerning the genesis of aggressive behavior is today accepted by some (e.g., K. Menninger, 1942) but by no means all psychoanalysts (e.g., Fenichel, 1945). Some of Freud's present-day disciples, particularly Hartmann et al. (1949), it was pointed out, view aggression as an innate force independent of sex but still somatically rooted and showing many of the characteristics of the sexual drive. Thus, for these writers aggressive as well as sexual behavior is primarily oriented toward the reduction of physiological tensions engendered solely by the biological conditions of the organism. (An external danger, frustration, or unpleasant person, according to Hartmann et al., only "invites" the discharge of the aggressive impulses.) But whatever psychoanalytically influenced writers see as the source of the instigation to aggression, all contend that the hostile behavior is primarily in the interests of tension reduction and should result in a weakening of the aggressive drive until or unless the individual is "stirred up" again.

Hartmann and his colleagues believed that the discharge of aggressive impulses can be pleasurable if guilt or anxiety does not arise. In this respect also, aggression presumably is like sex. Just as there is sexual forepleasure, in which tension increases prior to the pleasure of the sexual act, so may there be an aggressive forepleasure stemming from the preparation for aggressive discharge (Hartmann et al., 1949, p. 17). Furthermore, both libidinal and aggressive tensions supposedly can be reduced by motor activity (p. 17). But however such discharges occur, the tension reduction is pleasurable.

*Catharsis as the Result of Goal Responses.* Dollard and his coworkers at Yale accepted the assumption of a cathartic process in hostile behavior. Following psychoanalytic theory, they hypothesized that aggressive acts reduce the strength of the instigation to aggression (1939, p. 50). However, the reduction would be only temporary if the original frustration persisted. Although the Yale writers did not suggest why catharsis should take place, a possible explanation for catharsis can be formulated which is generally compatible with their theoretical approach. This hypothesis employs a broad principle applicable to all drives. Along with a number of psychologists (e.g., Lewin, 1935), I would maintain that there is an instigation to complete activated response sequences. Once an organism has initiated a particular course of activity, he possesses an instigation to complete this activity. Doing injury is the goal response terminating the aggressive response sequence, and it is not until such a response is made that the "instigation to completion" is satisfied.

This process and its relevance to hostility catharsis will be discussed more fully later. All that need be said now is that this "completion tendency" is in accord with at least some learning-theory analyses of behavior (e.g., Miller, 1959; Sheffield, 1954).

*Equivalent Forms of Aggression.* Learning-theory concepts as we have seen in other chapters, are invaluable in the study of aggressive behavior. The application of the learning model to the problem of hostility catharsis readily permits consideration of substitute forms of aggression. "Equivalence of forms," to employ the phrase used by Dollard et al. (1939, p. 50), is a fairly important matter in aggressive behavior generally and in the catharsis process in particular. To what extent can the angered person obtain gratification and "release" through attacking objects other than the anger instigator?

Psychoanalytic writings make frequent use of this notion of gratifications through substitute forms of aggression. Anna Freud, for example, has reported the case of a young woman who had strong but unconscious hostility toward her mother (cited in Miller & Swanson, 1960, pp. 290–291). She apparently could love her mother only after she succeeded in projecting her hostility onto other people.

There are at least two problems involved in such cases of substitute aggression. One of these, pertaining to the determinants of the target for the displaced aggression, was discussed in Chapters 5 and 6. Putting it briefly, this book contends that the target has some degree of association with the anger instigator on one or more stimulus dimensions. The second problem deals with the effects of the hostility displacement upon subsequent aggressive tendencies. Does the generalization of aggression to objects other than the original frustrater effectively reduce the strength of the instigation to aggression? A negative answer to this question, it might be noted, does not necessarily require rejecting the possibility of the cathartic reduction of hostility. Catharsis may still be brought about by direct attacks upon the instigator.

A learning-theory analysis of the equivalence-of-aggressive-forms concept indicates this matter is more complex than some authorities have suggested. Hartmann et al. maintained that displacement does not necessarily limit the discharge of aggression. Full discharge is possible, they proposed, if the "substitute object is conveniently chosen, particularly if it is inanimate" (1949, p. 20). Here is a place at which learning theory, as exemplified by Neal Miller's (1948) stimulus-response generalization model, and psychoanalytic theory part company.

Miller's formulation at least points to an important qualifying condition. As we saw in Chapter 5, the strength of the aggressive response declines, the weaker the association between the attacked object and the original anger instigator. Substitute objects, then, should receive less intense acts of hostility than the instigator would receive if he were available as a target for aggression and/or if the frustrated individual were not inhibited. Inanimate stimuli, being very dissimilar to the thwarting agent, certainly are not likely to evoke strong attacks. Since they presumably elicit only relatively mild hostility, substitute objects theoretically are comparatively ineffective for "discharging" anger.

## Aggression as a Source of Pleasure

*Pleasure from Tension Reduction.* Several authorities have proposed reasons why people may experience pleasure after displaying aggression. Hartmann and his colleagues hypothesized that the pleasure stems from the reduction of the tension of the aggressive drive, but other tension sources have been suggested as well. For one, McClelland differentiated between aggression, defined as an attack upon the frustrating agent, and emotional anger or rage responses, which supposedly are not directed against particular objects (1951, p. 513). [Saul (1956) has advocated a somewhat similar distinction.] The expression of anger, according to McClelland, can result in some relief even before a given object is attacked. Displaying the emotion supposedly lowers its intensity.

Sears et al. believed the aggressive individual also might obtain a feeling of relief if his overt hostility signified the reduction of an internal conflict (1957, p. 225). Children learn to fear the consequences of their showing aggression, and this learning persists into adulthood. For most people, then, the arousal of aggressive tendencies gives rise to concern about displaying aggression. The angered person wants to hit out but is afraid or reluctant to do so; he is in conflict.[1] If the aggression were to occur, he might well experience relief, although perhaps only temporarily, as the tension engendered by the inhibitions against hostility dissipates. For the time being at least, his internal conflict is over,[2] and he feels better.

[1] Sears, Maccoby, and Levin here advanced a hypothesis similar to a proposition I first introduced in Chapter 4: the stronger the individual's aggressive inclinations, the more intense his aggression anxiety. I have suggested that such a relationship arises when the individual anticipates punishment from others and/or guilt feelings for any hostile actions by him.

[2] Research findings stemming from Festinger's (1957) dissonance theory suggest that the postconflict behavior may itself contribute to a further lessening of the remaining doubts and inhibitions. The person more or less justifies his actions to himself when he is uncertain that he had done the correct thing. His hostility then becomes the "right" course of action.

The earlier-mentioned instigation to completion is another source of tension resulting from the blocking of aggressive responses. The angered person who wants to injure someone could well feel some internal pressure to achieve his aggressive goal if he has to inhibit his hostility. There may be some tension arising from his conflict as to whether to aggress or not, as Sears et al. (1957) claimed, but the failure to perform the consummatory response—inflicting injury—presumably also causes some discomfort. When he finally does act in a hostile manner, the initiated aggressive response sequence is terminated and the "interruption tension" disappears.

*Gratifications through Aggression.* Sears and his collaborators proposed another reason (in addition to conflict reduction) why hostile acts may be pleasurable at times. Aggression, they suggested, may become an acquired motive. The concept of "acquired motives" is a familiar one in psychology. As employed by Sears et al. (1957), this notion contends that behaviors producing need satisfaction come to be valued in their own right. Just as rats who had been fed by a noisy device will later work to produce only the noise, so will children learn to regard doing injury to others as gratifying in itself if they had repeatedly eliminated frustrations through hurting others (pp. 225–226). The cues (seeing signs of pain in another) associated with need satisfaction (removal of the frustration) presumably become desired for their own sake. Childhood aggression was often rewarded, and as a consequence the person may learn to hurt merely for the pleasure of hurting.

Whether or not the desire to injure others can become an acquired motive through the process of secondary reinforcement, there is little doubt that hostile behavior may be instrumental to a wide variety of gratifications. Chapter 2 pointed out that some people try to reach their goals through actions involving injury to others. Fiction continually reminds us of the person who has no qualms about hurting other people in his ruthless climb to the top of the economic ladder. This type of individual inflicts injury in order to achieve his aims, but he is not predominantly concerned with aggression for its own sake.

There are times in which goal attainment may require hostility, at least from the attacker's point of view. Nations have gone to war believing this was the only way to protect their national interests; advocates of certain ideologies have felt that nonbelievers were the legitimate and even necessary targets for their aggression. Essentially the same phenomenon, psychologically, occurs when a person employs hostility to maintain or enhance his self-esteem. Some psychologists, such as White and Lippitt (1960) and Worchel (1960), have hypothesized that hostility is aroused primarily when self-esteem is threatened. These hostile tendencies supposedly are not reduced until self-esteem is restored. But even if ego threats are not the sole cause of anger arousal (as this book maintains), it is true that aggression can restore a wounded ego. We all know people who act aggressively in order to convince themselves or others of their superiority. They feel better if others can be belittled or shown to have clay feet.

Secondary gratifications can also be obtained through warfare and military actions. Jobs and money become plentiful during wartime. If you are not in immediate danger of being killed, war may be exciting and provide an escape from monotony and drabness. Uniforms can bring glamour, status, and trips to exotic countries. But more than this, according to some social observers writing at a safe distance from the battlefield and long before the advent of the hydrogen bomb, war puts " 'iron' in the bloodstream of a nation" (cf. the views summarized in May, 1943, pp. 7–11). War is supposed to stimulate invention, develop leaders, increase hardihood and patriotism, and generally bring out the best in a nation. William James, America's great philosopher-psychologist, accepted much of this argument. Like McDougall and others of his time, he believed man had an instinct toward pugnacity and that a society achieved many positive gratifications (other than conquest) in the course of fighting a war.[3]

The validity of James's analysis need not concern us here. For our present purposes the important feature of his thesis lies in his recognition of the benefits that at least some people may gather through war and military life. Aggression in general, whether in ordinary interpersonal relations or in socially sanctioned military combat, can result in a variety of pleasures. When a person says he feels good after displaying hostility, he may or may not have reduced tension within him. But he also could have reached a nonaggressive goal, expressed an acquired motive, removed a threat, or demonstrated his virility and superiority.

## Aggressiveness as a Habit

One final theoretical point should be made at this time. Investigations of the catharsis hypothesis have not always differentiated between the instigation to aggression arising from frustration (i.e., anger) and an individual's characteristic level of aggressive behavior in social situations (i.e., his customary aggressiveness). Writers employing the energy

---

[3] In the last analysis, however, James preferred peace to war. There could be a "moral equivalent of war," he stated in a famous essay (James, 1917). Peaceful activities could provide the "social vitamins" otherwise provided by international conflict. Our ideals of valor and hardihood would be preserved if young men fought natural forces, such as diseases, floods, and the natural elements, in the interests of general human happiness. Although this is not too clear, James did not seem to assume that these peaceful activities would necessarily weaken the aggressive instinct.

model have not felt the need to make such a distinction; they generally assume that the internal stimulus conditions impelling hostile behavior in ordinary social situations must correspond in all respects to the emotional state leading to aggressive responses to objective frustrations. Every time a person acts in a hostile manner, regardless of the immediate circumstances, he supposedly does so because of his aggressive "energy" (cf. Hartmann et al., 1949).

The present book, on the other hand, insists that hostile reactions to recent frustrations must be differentiated from persistent or customary aggressive tendencies. This matter will be elaborated more fully in the following pages, but it is possible to maintain that *aggressiveness* is a learned habit and, like any other habit, is readily elicited by relevant cues. The significance of such a formulation is obvious. *Providing an opportunity to express hostility may lessen the frustration-engendered instigation to aggression (anger), but could also evoke and/or strengthen a person's habitual hostile tendencies.*

## RESEARCH

### Research Findings in "Real-life" Settings

Investigations of the cathartic process can be organized in terms of the conditions under which the subjects express aggression. Some studies attempt to capitalize on "real-life" situations by measuring the strength of aggressive tendencies in young adults after they had participated in athletic contests. Other investigations employ settings in which subjects are permitted or encouraged to display hostility, for example, in the form of play therapy. As we shall see, such "life-like" conditions generally do not provide the degree of control necessary for adequate tests of the catharsis hypothesis, and we will have to resort to formal laboratory experiments for more definitive information.

*Effects of Aggressive Sports.* There are very few quantitative examinations of the effects of combative sports upon the instigation to aggression. However, despite this paucity of data, or perhaps because of it, many psychiatrists, psychologists, and recreation leaders insist that competitive athletic contests provide a necessary release for pent-up aggressive impulses. As an illustration, this view was expressed by two prominent psychiatrists speaking within a few years of each other on the topic of recreation and mental health.[4] Both G. E. Gardner (1952) and William Menninger (1948) stated that play brings about a needed release from the tensions created by "instinctive" aggressive impulses.

---

[4] Needless to say, theirs is not the only psychiatric conception of play and recreation. Alexander (1958), for example, discussed play in terms of the exercise of surplus libidinal energy and mastery attempts.

Menninger went on to claim that "competitive games provide an unusually satisfactory social outlet for the instinctive aggressive drive," but that some discharge could be obtained even from sports involving "sedentary intellectual competition," such as chess and checkers (p. 343). He cited a few cases in which aggressive recreational activities seemed to facilitate the therapeutic progress of patients at the famed Menninger Clinic.

These anecdotes, however, all involved people who apparently benefited from the weakening of inhibitions or the lessening of internal conflicts. Such observations, of course, do not prove that engaging in competitive games is an effective means in itself for reducing hostile tendencies. Indeed, research cited in the preceding chapter suggests that competition is more likely to enhance than to decrease the strength of an individual's aggressive inclinations. It certainly is not necessary to conclude that the Menninger patients' therapeutic gains resulted merely from a cathartic hostility reduction.

There is no conclusive evidence one way or another as to the consequences of aggressive contests. Nevertheless, such findings as are available seem to point more to an aggression-anxiety (and/or guilt) reaction to these games than to pleasant feelings following the discharge of hostile impulses. Husman (1955) obtained the responses of collegiate athletes, including boxers, to several projective tests during the course of the competitive season. Statistically significant differences were found, with the boxers having considerably less fantasy aggression on the TAT than the other students. The projective tests given to the boxers less than two days after a fight showed presumptive signs of tension rather than ease. Where there were no such significant differences on any other occasion, shortly after the contest the boxers displayed a reliably greater level of "super-ego" responses on the Rosenzweig P-F Study than did a nonathletic control group. Husman stated that this increase in "super-ego" was to be expected. The boxers' aggressive behavior during the match presumably made them feel anxious or guilty even though this aggression was socially sanctioned. (We do not know whether the boxers had won or lost, but then, the previously mentioned psychiatrists did not stipulate that catharsis would occur only if the contestant had emerged victorious.) These "super-ego" responses tended to decrease with time so that there again were no significant differences between the boxers and controls on this measure after the end of the season.

In another study, Stone (1950) also found suggestive indications of guilt or anxiety following a socially sanctioned athletic contest. The TAT was given to football players both during and after the athletic season, and their responses were compared with the stories told by a matched control group. There was no difference between the two groups in fantasy aggression during the football season, but the football players showed significantly less manifest aggression on the TAT following the completion of the season. Interestingly enough, however, the aggression that the athletes did display tended to be of a "projective" nature. That is, the hostility was attributed to an impersonal source. Stone argued that this aggression was projected onto an impersonal source because of the football players' anxiety concerning aggression.[5] The football players may not have been anxious about their aggressive behavior during the athletic season; they had been rewarded for such socially approved hostility. Anxiety may have arisen because they now (after the season) had to inhibit aggression (McClelland, 1951, p. 500). If so, this would mean their aggressive tendencies probably had not been diminished by the football games.

These findings are relatively ambiguous but, all in all, they offer little support for the Menninger-Gardner thesis. Most nondisturbed people do *not* seem to have either (1) weaker aggressive inclinations or (2) less concern about their hostile tendencies after engaging in socially sanctioned aggressive sports. If hostile behaviors are less apparent following such competitive activities, the above studies suggest, these actions may have been inhibited by game-induced guilt or anxiety.[6]

On the face of it, these negative results would appear to question only the proposition that aggressive "energy" can be channeled off in a variety of basically equivalent ways. Several authorities have objected to the equivalent-forms-of-aggression concept, arguing that hostile acts are not interchangeable for draining the "reservoir of free-floating energy" (e.g., G. W. Allport, 1954; McClelland, 1951). However, it also may be a mistake to postulate the existence of persistent pent-up hostility. There may not be a continual, years-long anger constantly impelling internal aggressive responses. The hostile person may have only a strong predisposition to become angry—a predisposition that is dormant in many situations. Where short-term anger might subside after an injury is inflicted, the long-lasting predisposition (the aggressiveness habit) would not necessarily be weakened, and may even be strengthened, by aggressive behavior. The Husman-Stone studies involved aggressiveness rather than an immediate frustration-elicited hostility, and aggressive sports probably do not eliminate aggressive habits. Thus, Mc-

---

[5] Clark (1955), in a study reported in Chapter 4, also found a high proportion of "projective hostility" TAT responses and relatively few manifest aggression themes in an experimental condition presumably arousing guilt.

[6] Aggressive tendencies resulting from feelings of inferiority may be weakened if the individual wins a series of competitive contests and, consequently, no longer sees himself as inferior to others, i.e., if the competition removes the frustration.

Clelland, in discussing Stone's findings, observed that the football players who showed high aggression on the field also tended to be high on TAT aggression (1951, p. 517). There apparently were aggression-evoking cues both on the football field and on the TAT cards. The men with strong aggressive habits had a low threshold and high amplitude of response to these cues so that they showed relatively intense hostility in both situations.

*Expressive Therapies.* It probably is fair to say that contemporary psychoanalytic therapy does not emphasize catharsis—the expression of inhibited responses—to the extent that such a process was stressed in the first years of this therapeutic movement. A number of early Freudians (e.g., Ferenczi) contended that the beneficial effects of therapy largely arose from the release of repressed energy. Today, however, catharsis seems to be valued primarily for any contribution it might make to the development of insight and reeducation. There is good reason for such a deemphasis. Patients engaged in expressive forms of psychotherapy do not appear to improve solely because they had performed responses they previously had inhibited. Slavson, a disciple of the psychoanalytic movement, for example, has flatly stated, "Catharsis may give the patient temporary relief, but emotional maturity is achieved through insight" (1951, p. 50).

Whether the patient's hostile outbursts are therapeutically beneficial or not, of course, depends in part upon the nature of his difficulties. Redl and Wineman (1957), in discussing the treatment of extremely aggressive children, advocated permissiveness within certain limits, not to discharge a pent-up hostile energy, but in order to change the youngsters' perception of the world about them. Hostile behavior is all right, the writers said, but only in the proper place. Destructiveness has to be contained within some bounds. In other cases, however, the patient is actively encouraged to express hostility. Menninger referred to such a therapeutic technique in the previously cited paper (1948). Cameron (1951) maintained that people exhibiting excessive passivity can become more normally self-assertive through practicing aggressiveness. By being encouraged to display hostility, they presumably will recognize the powerful but inhibited aggressive impulses within them, will see the sources of this hostility, and will learn how to cope with their anger in a more adequate manner.

But, in general, little is said of the value of catharsis for the sake of catharsis and, indeed, remarkably few contemporary experts in the area of psychotherapy place any stress on the doctrine of cathartic emotional purges. As I stated before, there is no evidence that the expression of aggression in the course of the therapy results in a prolonged reduction of hostile tendencies. More than this, two experiments indicate that the support given aggressive behavior during play therapy-like situations can even enhance the likelihood of later hostile actions.

Kenny (1953) provided an experimental group of fifteen first-grade children with two supposed catharsis sessions involving a play-therapy technique. A control group spent an equal time playing on the swings or with a jigsaw puzzle. Employing a projective test given at the start and conclusion of the study as a measure of the strength of the children's hostile tendencies, the investigator actually obtained results contrary to the catharsis hypothesis. The *control* group had a significantly greater decrease in hostility scores than did the play-therapy group. We might wonder whether the play-therapy experience had retarded the lessening of hostile inclinations. Feshbach (1956) also found no evidence of a cathartic reduction of aggression as a function of the usual play therapy. He observed that boys (but not girls) initially low in aggressive behavior showed a significant increase in overt hostility after a series of permissive free-play experiences. [This, the reader will recall, is somewhat similar to the findings in the Iowa doll-play studies and in the experiments by Siegel (1957, 1958) reported in Chapter 4.]

Feshbach argued against the equivalence-of-aggressive-forms notion on the basis of his negative results, contending that "displaced aggression toward a spouse may not reduce aggression toward one's employer." However, as I proposed earlier, the cathartic process may not occur when we are dealing with aggressive habits. *The children in Feshbach's study had not suffered recent frustrations and therefore had relatively little if any active anger to "discharge."* Hostile actions probably weaken frustration-induced instigations to aggression (anger) and not hostility habits. Instead of weakening hostile tendencies, stimuli in the Feshbach play situation apparently evoked aggressive responses within the youngsters (particularly boys) because of their previous learning. Thus, there was the greatest rise in overt hostility when the children had played with aggressive toys such as guns. We might say these objects had the greatest cue value for the boys' habitual hostile responses. The children characteristically low in overt aggression probably had strong internal restraints against hostile actions rather than weak aggressiveness habits. As their inhibitions weakened in the permissive-therapy situation—the adult, in essence, defining aggressive behavior as permissible—they exhibited a greater increase in open hostility than did any of the other children with continued exposure to the hostility-eliciting stimuli.

Expressing aggression does not in itself lessen the probability of further aggressive acts. Aggressiveness habits may even be reinforced. Psychotherapy apparently results in a reduction of hostile behaviors when (1) the frustrating conflicts and anxieties within the patient are eliminated, weakening the sources of internally induced anger, (2) the individual learns to interpret ambiguous external situations as being nonfrustrating, lessening the likelihood of externally caused anger, and (3) he learns to control his aggressive reactions.

Patients at times report feeling better after getting something "off their chests" in expressive therapy. Here again, there is a question of whether the relief results solely from the purging of pent-up emotions. On some occasions, according to Rogers (1939), the very act of talking about one's problems serves to clarify them. The patient is less confused and feels better. In other cases the relief may stem from the lessening of anxiety, the reduction of internal conflict, and/or the implicit approval provided by the nonderogating therapist. The patient's pleasant feelings are certainly not necessarily the result of his having discharged repressed energy.

### Experimental Investigations of a Cathartic Effect on Aggressive Response Strength

*Design Requirements.* If the present analysis has any validity, hostility catharsis is most likely to be obtained when the individual has experienced a recent frustration and is angry. The following pages will therefore be concerned with experimental investigations of the catharsis hypothesis in which subjects are deliberately angered, given the opportunity to express aggression, and then are compared with an appropriate control group. The first part of this summary will deal with studies of cathartic effects upon aggressive response tendencies. After this, we will examine the tension-reduction possibilities of hostile behavior.

The basic research design just described seems fairly simple and straightforward but, in actuality, is susceptible to a number of major pitfalls. Research on hostility catharsis has more than its share of problems (Berkowitz, 1958, p. 279). Three of these difficulties are particularly important:

1. Open acts of hostility may be followed by weaker or less frequent aggressive responses because of guilt or anxiety evoked after the attacker's first hostile actions.

2. Hostile tendencies may not be weakened after aggression is expressed if the attacker is frustrated further or stimulates himself to continued aggression.

3. A hostile act can lead to weaker residual hostility if it eliminates the original anger-inciting frustration. Since the barrier to the goal-directed activity is overcome, the earlier anger may dissipate quickly.

*Inhibited Aggression.* Chapter 4 cited several studies indicating that aggressive behavior is often directly associated with signs of aggression anxiety (and/or guilt). I suggested there that the strength of an individual's hostile inclination is related to the intensity of the aggression anxiety or guilt subsequently aroused in him to the extent that he anticipates punishment or disapproval for aggression from himself or others. Thus, anxiety and/or guilt following the first intense acts of hostility conceivably could account for negative correlations between initial and final aggression toward frustrating agents (cf. French, 1944; Pepitone & Reichling, 1955).

Perhaps the clearest indication of an aggression-anxiety reaction following hostile behavior can be found in the experiment by Berkowitz and Holmes (1960). As the reader will recall, strongly provoked college women who had inflicted the greatest injury upon a peer (one of their frustraters) by means of electric shocks were the only subjects showing a reliable tendency to make amends in their ratings of this peer at the end of the experimental session. The subjects were given questionnaires at the start and conclusion of the hour-long period in which they were to rate the peer's performance and also to say how fair she had been in her treatment of them during the experiment. The severely frustrated, highly aggressive women were the only ones in the study whose expressed judgments of the peer's fairness were significantly *more favorable* at the end of the experiment than they had been at the start. They were not only less unfriendly than any of the other subjects, they apparently also made the greatest attempt to avoid condemning her for unethical behavior. Such an extreme "leaning over backward" reaction seems indicative of guilt and/or anxiety.

These findings may be exactly analogous to the questionnaire results obtained by Pepitone and Reichling (1955). The men in this latter study who expressed the strongest hostility toward the absent instigator later tended to give him the most favorable questionnaire ratings. They might have come to feel guilty and/or anxious about their earlier aggressive remarks and then, in essence, said they were sorry by giving the frustrater friendly ratings.

Several experiments attest to the aggression-inhibiting complexities involved in hostile behavior. One of these, reported in Chapter 4, suggests that strong anger arousal may delay the time at which the individual comes to feel guilt or anxiety, particularly if the provocation enables him to regard his behavior as being justified (Berkowitz, 1960a). The latency and amplitude of aggression-anxiety responses vary from person to person as well as from one situation to another. Rosenbaum and deCharms (1960) observed that college men who were low in self-esteem (but not those with high self-regard) expressed less resentment against a peer-frustrater after they heard someone else attack him than after this third person had been neutral toward the instigator. The lowest overt hostility toward the frustrater, however, came after the low self-esteem men had been given an opportunity to communicate back to this instigator themselves. The psychologists had predicted such condition differences on the basis of the catharsis hypothesis. But they were puzzled about one aspect of their findings. The statements made by the subjects in rebuttal to the attacks upon them were almost invariably mild. With such little retaliatory aggression being shown, the researchers questioned whether the low residual hostility displayed by the low self-esteem people could be attributed to a catharsis effect in the direct communication condition.

Rather than purging their anger, it seems much more likely that the communication conditions elicited aggression anxiety in the low self-esteem men. This type of person generally doubts his ability to obtain social rewards and, therefore, may well become anxious at events signaling possible rejection. Overt hostility is dangerous for him, when the aggression is performed by others, and particularly when he himself can act aggressively; hostile behavior might bring the rejection he anticipates and fears. Evidence obtained in the writer's laboratory suggests that people who are low in self-esteem have a relatively strong predisposition toward hostility, but frequently refrain from exhibiting such behavior in social situations (Berkowitz, 1960c), perhaps because of aggression-anxiety arousal (Hokanson, 1961b).

*Persistent Stimulation to Aggression.* While aggressive acts may lessen anger somewhat, this instigation to aggression could build up again fairly rapidly if the anger-arousing frustration continued or if the individual somehow stirred himself up to further hostility. Differences in the persistence of a frustration may be responsible for Thibaut's (1950) demonstration of a lessening in aggression following hostile actions. After thwarting the status aspirations of boys assembled in groups, the investigator succeeded in having these subjects direct aggression against the high-status teams. Half of the low-status groups then won high status, while the remaining teams remained low in status. Since the thwarting did not continue for the successful groups, they are the only ones who should have displayed a cathartic reduction of hostility, and the findings seem to bear out this expectation. The correlation between pre- and poststatus-alteration aggression was significantly negative (−.69) for the upward mobile groups, but not for the teams remaining in the low-status position (−.22). The greater the hostility they had expressed previously, the less aggression the boys displayed after their status frustration had ceased. Moreover, while the persistently thwarted groups exhibited a sizeable drop in their indicated liking for the high-status teams from the start to the end of the session, there was no similar decrease in liking for the other high-status boys in the no longer thwarted, upward mobile groups.

As usual, there are any number of ways in which these condition differences may be interpreted. It may be that the mobile youngsters had shown a lowered resentment toward their former superiors when their frustrations were removed because they had cathartically purged themselves of their anger. But there are at least two other possible explanations as well. The decrease in aggressive behavior by the no longer frustrated boys could have resulted from their judgment that their behavior had been at least partly responsible for their rise in status. As a result of their hostility, their status aspirations were now fulfilled and they were no longer angry. They also may have developed guilt feelings when their frustration was shown to be only temporary, i.e., when they were elevated to the high-status position. But however the Thibaut findings are explained, they do highlight the importance of ascertaining whether the hostility-provoking frustration continues in existence. *Overt hostility is relatively unlikely to weaken to any great extent if an obstacle to need satisfaction continues to elicit anger.*

The aggression-arousing situation in the Thibaut experiment derived from external conditions. A person's hostile tendencies may also remain in full force if there is a consistent source of stimulation to aggression operating within him. To illustrate, Berkowitz (1960a) hypothesized that people may stimulate themselves to continued resentment against a frustrater, even after aggressing against him, if they continually remind themselves of the provocations they have received. In order to test this notion half of the subjects in each condition were given a task in which they presumably would readily think of the treatment they had received from a peer; they were to describe themselves on an adjective checklist—reminding themselves while they did this (the experimenter assumed) of the peer's previously expressed attitude toward them. The remaining subjects responded to four TAT cards during the same interval of time. As was mentioned earlier, some of the students experienced two frustrations (insulting communications) at the hands of a peer. In this extreme provocation condition only, the subjects describing themselves on the checklist were reliably more unfriendly toward the instigator at the end of the session than were the subjects taking the TAT cards, supposedly because the former, in responding to the checklist, had stirred themselves up.

Another finding in this experiment lends some additional credence to this self-stimulation hypothesis. The subjects in two other conditions completed the self-description task after receiving a very friendly communication from the peer. These people should have stimulated themselves to an increased liking for the peer, and such seems to have been the case. In both conditions the adjective-checklist subjects became significantly friendlier to the peer the more hostile they had been to him before getting the message. These correlations were virtually zero for the TAT group. The previously aggressive checklist subjects presumably had reminded themselves that the peer had been friendly to them while they had been unkind to him.

Berkowitz argued against the notion of a cathartic anger reduction in the strongly provoked students responding to the TAT cards. There were indications of a decrease in overt hostility in this TAT group, but the total pattern of changes in expressed attitude to the peer in the various conditions suggested that these changes were due to an aggression-anxiety reaction rather than a catharsis. Thus, as was reported earlier, the TAT subjects who had increased in open hostility to the peer after getting a friendly communication from him showed a relatively early reduction in hostility: *prior* to taking the TAT. These people, I have hypothesized, felt guilt or anxiety fairly early because a strong insult had not justified their aggressive behavior. The strongly aroused subjects, on the other hand, displayed this decrease in overt hostility later: *after* responding to the projective test. For these people the greater the level of hostility exhibited on the TAT, the greater the change toward friendliness to the peer from the questionnaire completed before the TAT to the final questionnaire at the end of the session. The relatively extreme insults they had received may have justified their earlier aggressive ratings somewhat and therefore delayed the onset of the guilt-anxiety reaction.

The self-stimulation-to-aggression process has one very important practical implication. Some people advocate the free expression of feelings when barely submerged resentment impedes harmonious relationships. "Get it off your chest," they say. "Reveal your anger. You'll feel better and the air will be cleared." Unfortunately, however, such a philosophy sometimes leads to enhanced anger. Mutual recriminations may develop. Each side accuses the other of being at fault and only arouses heightened anger in the other party. But more than this, when a person vents his feelings, he may also excite himself even more. Morlan (1949) criticized the all-too-frequent uncritical acceptance of the catharsis hypothesis because of this possibility of a self-stimulation. An individual might incite himself to further resentment against his frustrater by performing a hostile act, he argued, and he pointed out that Dollard himself had raised this possibility in an article appearing just before the publication of *Frustration and Aggression* (Dollard, 1938).

We are now faced with two questions before we can go on. Does this "vicious-circle" phenomenon (in which a heightened instigation to aggression follows the performance of an aggressive act) occur with any real frequency, and if so, under what conditions is this self-stimulation to aggression most likely to arise? To deal with the first of these problems, several experiments indicate that the vicious-circle reaction occurs often enough to be a major difficulty confronting the catharsis hypothesis.

Kahn (1960) reported increased hostility after the display of aggression. In his study individual subjects participating in a physiological investigation were insulted by a relatively low-status laboratory technician and then placed in one of two conditions. The experimental group was encouraged to express any angry feelings by a sympathetic "physician" who approved whatever hostile remarks were made about the instigator. In the control group, on the other hand, this "physician" only praised the student for being a good subject. Questionnaire ratings obtained at the end of the session showed that the experimental subjects expressed a significantly stronger dislike for the frustrater than did the control subjects who had not voiced their resentment.

Berkowitz, Green, and Macaulay (1962) obtained a somewhat similar finding in another experiment dealing with the catharsis process. As in other studies done in the writer's laboratory, male university students, assembled in pairs, were led to believe the other pair-member was going to rate their performance on an assigned task by administering electric shocks. Half of the subjects were made to be angry with their partner by giving them an inordinate number of shocks, ostensibly from the partner but actually administered by the experimenter. The others received a much friendlier "evaluation," the minimum one shock. Then, within each of these conditions, half of the men were told to rate what was supposedly the partner's performance by giving him electric shocks. The remaining students were shown the partner's work but were given another task and were not permitted to shock their peer. An adjective-checklist description of the partner completed at the beginning and conclusion of the session assessed each subject's attitude toward his peer.

As a result of the experimental manipulations, in other words, one group of angered men had an opportunity to retaliate against their tormenter in kind, while this opportunity was not provided for the other aroused students. Analysis of the checklist scores revealed that only one of the four experimental conditions did *not* show an over-all trend toward increased friendliness for the partner from the beginning to the end of the session. This was the angered group permitted to aggress against the instigator. *The counteraggressing, frustrated men exhibited an increased dislike for the instigator and ended up reliably more hostile to this peer than were their controls, but the similarly insulted, nonaggressing students displayed a slight change toward friendliness for the partner, as did their controls.*

Why did these results occur? Why did aggression toward a frustrater produce increased dislike for this person? One possible answer had been suggested earlier in this section. The hostile behavior might in some way cause the thwarted individual to remember and even brood upon the injuries he had received from the other person. Because of these recollections the frustration persists symbolically, and its severity might even be exaggerated in the remembering.

Two other somewhat related reasons for the hostility increase can also be advanced. In his pre-*Frustration and Aggression* paper, Dollard (1938) reminded us that hostile behavior can lead to a fear of retaliation. The frustrated person is carried away by his rage, lashes out at his tormenter, and then fears the consequences of his action. Since the aggression anxiety is frustrating, the instigation to aggression remains and may even be heightened. Hokanson (1959) obtained evidence of a heightened instigation to aggression in subjects led to believe there might be retaliatory aggression for any hostility they exhibited.

Guilt arousal can also enhance aggressive tendencies. Guilt implies a frustrating experience. The individual feels he has done something he should not have done and, in essence, has thwarted his need to think well of himself. Anger probably results, some of it directed against himself, but some may also add to the resentment against the original anger instigator; the attacked object may be seen as at least partly responsible for his unethical behavior. Guilt arousal, of course, also can lead to attempts to justify the guilt-producing behavior. The person who thinks he has done something wrong may then try to convince himself that his victim really deserved the attack upon him. His perception of the victim changes, and this person is now seen in a much more unfavorable light. Kahn suggested that such a process might account for the heightened unfriendliness toward the insulting lab technician in his experimental group, although he used the terminology of dissonance theory. The subjects' hostile remarks about the technician were incompatible with their supposed desire not to get the man into trouble with his superior, the "physician." Dissonance arose, and the subjects sought to reduce the discomfort by altering their perception of the technician. They convinced themselves that his behavior really warranted the hostile comments.

Guilt or dissonance will also be evoked if the individual believes he had chosen to aggress against someone when such behavior was not really necessary. Davis and Jones (1960) had their subjects indicate their first impressions of a stranger, and then gave some of the subjects the option of saying derogatory things to the stranger over a telephone system or of making more favorable remarks to him. However, they were encouraged to say the unfriendly things, and nearly all did so.

Other subjects were required to make the derogatory statements. Within each of these conditions, some of the people were led to believe they would meet the stranger after the experiment, while the others were told they would not see him again. The investigators had predicted that the subjects would feel most disturbed when they had chosen to express the hostile statements but would not see the stimulus person again so that they could make amends. This expectation seems to have been fulfilled. The subjects who thought they had voluntarily attacked the stranger and would not meet him again showed a significantly greater increase toward dislike for their victim than did the people in any of the other conditions.

Internal reactions to one's own hostile behavior can prevent a cathartic anger reduction. These inner responses—guilt, dissonance, or aggression anxiety—may even enhance the aggressor's hatred for his victim. The injured person is disliked even more, as Dollard commented, for the crime of having been the object of the aggressor's hostility.

Self-stimulation might also result in later aggression against a frustrater because of the learning process. The angered person might develop an unfavorable attitude toward his frustrater so that even after aggressing against the instigator, and temporarily weakening his anger, later sight of the frustrater could remind him of his thwartings and stimulate him to renewed resentment. The unfavorable attitude also could cause the person to interpret the instigator's behavior at some later time as a frustration.

*Instrumental Aggression.* I pointed out at the beginning of this chapter that instrumental aggression is not relevant to the catharsis hypothesis. Hostile actions that eliminate the frustration lessen anger because the emotion-inducing obstacle to goal attainment has been surmounted and not necessarily because the behavior has resulted in an emotional "purge." Voicing a somewhat similar opinion, Thibaut and Riecken (1955) hypothesized that aggression toward a frustrater will increase liking for him if the behavior succeeds in controlling or eliminating the unpleasant aspects of that person's activity. The behavior has removed the barriers to need satisfaction.

Several studies have demonstrated that such instrumental aggression does lessen open enmity toward the thwarting agent. In an investigation by Horwitz et al. (1954), for example, students who were angered by a teacher's violation of the established rules wrote notes complaining of his illegitimate behavior. The teacher read these notes in one of the experimental conditions and then proceeded to act according to the rules. The hostile complaints eliminated the frustration. In a second condition the teacher's supervisor read the notes and directed the teacher to act legitimately. Finally, in the remaining condition the teacher did not read the notes and the frustrating behavior continued. The subjects in this last condition, of course, really experienced two frustrations: their notes were disregarded and the illegitimate actions persisted. It is not surprising, then, that the students receiving this treatment expressed the greatest dislike for the teacher. Open hostility toward the frustrater decreased with cessation of the disturbing rule infractions, but there was more indicated dislike for the teacher when the supervisor had directed him to behave "properly" than when the teacher had changed of his own volition.

This last finding points to an important source of gratifications sometimes obtained through hostile actions: ego enhancement. When the teacher altered his behavior supposedly of his own free will after reading the complaints, he indicated he was a reasonable person. Moreover, he also implied that he respected the students enough to accede to their demands. By complying with the notes, the teacher essentially enhanced the worth of the students. The teacher who had to be directed to behave legitimately by his superior, however, seemed less reasonable and, also, did not show respect for the students. He himself did not indicate their importance by altering his actions. Thus, there was greater liking for the "nice" teacher who implicitly indicated the worth of the students than for the frustrater who did not show this respect. A study by Magaziner (1961) yields further information on the hostility-reducing effects of ego-enhancing experiences. Subjects who were angered by creating a threat to their self-esteem displayed less hostility after their self-worth had been increased again.

### Two Notable Tests of the Catharsis Hypothesis

*Reduction in Overt Hostility after Communication with the Instigator.* The previous discussion has highlighted some of the difficulties confronting tests of the catharsis hypothesis. These problems, however, are not the only ones facing the researcher. He must also be prepared to recognize and (hopefully) to overcome some additional sources of uncertainty. Two interesting and provocative articles can be used in illustrating some of these difficulties.

One of these papers, by Thibaut and Coules (1952), has already been mentioned on a number of occasions. Male undergraduates, taken singly, were made to be angry with a peer (actually the experimenter's confederate) by having the peer send them an insulting message as the culmination of an exchange of notes. Two experimental treatments were created after the provocation. In one, the experimenter prevented the subjects from replying to the note by telling them the time was up. In the other condition, on the other hand, the subjects were permitted to write a reply to the instigator after they had received the attack. The strength of the residual hostility toward the insulting peer was assessed by comparing the subjects' written descriptions of the instigator's personality at the start and conclusion of the study.

Thibaut and Coules obtained data consistent with the catharsis hypothesis. The sketches written by the men who had been prevented from communicating back to the instigator showed a significantly greater decrease in the number of friendly units than did the descriptions composed by the people permitted to reply. In comparison with their first impressions, the *no communication* group ended up seeing the insulting peer in a much less favorable light.

But what could have produced this difference? The investigators were well aware that they had not really demonstrated the existence of a hostility catharsis. *Preventing the occurrence of a hostile reaction to a thwarting,* as I have noted before, *theoretically is a frustration capable of increasing the instigation to aggression* (Dollard et al., 1939, p. 40). Thus, the experimenter's interruption blocking a reply to the instigator actually might have heightened anger in the *no communication* condition. This frustration could have produced the condition difference rather than some cathartic hostility reduction in the other treatment. To test such a possibility, Thibaut and Coules conducted a second experiment similar to the first in all but one important respect. After the anger arousal the subjects in the communication condition could write one note to the instigator as before, but the remaining subjects this time were interrupted by the experimenter for three minutes before they were permitted to reply.

Analysis of the messages sent to the frustrater confirmed the *Frustration and Aggression* hypothesis. The people who had had to wait three minutes before replying sent a reliably greater volume of hostility to the frustrater than did the students who could respond to the provocation more rapidly. As the researchers concluded, "the thwarting of communication back to the instigator immediately after instigation increases the level of hostility, in spite of the fact that the instigator is not responsible for the interruption" (p. 773).

We can now easily see the problem faced by the investigator. His basic design typically will involve a comparison between a group permitted to aggress against some frustrater and a group not given this opportunity. Greater residual hostility in the former condition may then be interpreted as evidence for the catharsis hypothesis. But, as Thibaut and Coules observed, it also may be attributable to increased hostility in the people prevented from attacking the anger instigator.

*Symbolic Aggression.* Another experiment, by Feshbach (1955), is also cited frequently for its relevance to the catharsis doctrine. The findings reported in Feshbach's study appear to offer some striking evidence of an emotional "purge" following aggression, but again other considerations point to difficulties in the interpretation of the results.

The researcher sought to determine whether angered people could satisfy their aggressive drive through symbolic satisfactions obtained in a fantasy task. Could they reduce hostility by expressing aggression symbolically in a projective test? Two experimental treatments were applied to introductory psychology classes angered by an insulting lecturer. In one of these conditions the students responded to a fantasy task, i.e., four TAT cards, and then were given the aggression-measuring instruments, a questionnaire and a sentence-completion test. The other experimental group had to complete a nonfantasy task, a mildly challenging intellectual test, after they were angered and before responding to the aggression measures. Finally, as a control, there was a noninsulted fantasy group.

Several results seem to indicate that there had been a symbolic anger catharsis. For one thing, the insulted fantasy group had significantly lower scores on the final hostility-assessing instruments than did the insulted nonfantasy group. The former subjects may have "drained" their anger in taking the projective test. Of course, the condition differences may also be due to the frustrating nature of the nonfantasy task, and a noninsulted, nonfantasy condition is needed to see if the intellectual test could have aroused some resentment under the conditions of this study. But there is further support for the catharsis hypothesis in other findings. The insulted TAT subjects, not surprisingly, did express more hostility in the stories they told to the projective test than did the noninsulted group. As the catharsis doctrine requires, there was a significant negative correlation between the level of hostility the aroused students displayed in the TAT protocols and the hostility they expressed on the final questionnaire ($-.25$). The greater the anger they had shown previously, the less there seemed to remain at the end of the session.

However, every psychological study can be explained in a number of different ways, and the present experiment is no exception. Several factors might have been operating to affect the results (cf. Berkowitz, 1958; McClelland, 1956). I have already suggested that the control group might have experienced some degree of frustration. This is true even if the "neutral" task had been fairly enjoyable for the subjects; the Thibaut and Coules study suggests such a task might be thwarting merely by preventing the occurrence of hostile responses. In addition, there also is the possibility that aggression anxiety arose in the insulted subjects as a consequence of their expressing hostility to the TAT. They could have become aware of their aggressive inclinations in responding to the projective test, thus provoking the guilt or anxiety inhibiting aggression on the final questionnaire. My previously described experiment (Berkowitz, 1960a) obtained findings consistent with such a possibility.

Perhaps more important than any of these alternative explanations, two more recent experiments, also testing the symbolic catharsis hypothesis, have yielded negative results. One of these (Hokanson & Burgess, 1962) will be discussed later. The more relevant investigation was conducted by Hornberger (1959) as an attempted replication of the Feshbach experiment. Groups of male college students were angered by derogating their performance on a series of arithmetic problems. Following this, one-third of the subjects completed an intellectual task similar to the one used by Feshbach, and the remaining angered people responded to two TAT cards during the same period of time. Nonprovoked students also worked on each of these tasks.

There were indications that the arousal was not too strong in the angered groups, although the insulted students were more aggressive than the control groups on the final hostility measures. The only significant differences among the various interpolated activity conditions occurred on the sentence-completion test. On this measure the people who had spent ten minutes in nail hammering had reliably higher scores than did the fantasy group, regardless of whether there had been anger arousal or not. Hornberger attributed this difference to the physical activity in the hammering task, maintaining that the activity stimulated aggressive responses from the subjects. [But even if this is not true, his results cast serious doubt on the previously mentioned contention by Hartmann et al. (1949, p. 17) that vigorous motor activity *in itself* is an effective means of discharging aggressive energy. I would suggest that nonaggressive activities lead to a lessening of anger only by distracting the thwarted individual so that he does not think of his unpleasant experience and incite himself.] Continuing with the findings, the insulted intellectual group was only slightly higher than the insulted fantasy group on the sentence-completion hostility measure, but here again the psychologist believed the difference could be traced to task characteristics other than their "cathartic value."

The present section can be summarized in just a few words. In general, there is no unequivocal evidence of a cathartic lessening in the strength of aggressive tendencies following the performance of hostile acts. Such a phenomenon may well exist, but the studies that have been conducted to date have not been altogether convincing.[7]

[7] A more recent experiment conducted by Feshbach (1961) also should be reported here. Extending his investigations of the possibility of a cathartic reduction in "aggressive drive" through symbolic or vicarious activity, Feshbach had experimentally angered and nonangered male college students watch a ten-minute film

*Tension Release through Aggressive Behavior*

*Completion of an Instigated Aggressive Response Sequence.* No one hypothesis can satisfactorily explain every instance of pleasure obtained from hostile activity. We already have seen that aggression can be gratifying because it involves the expression of an acquired aggressive motive, and/or it signals the reduction of internal conflict, and/or it may restore self-esteem. But, as mentioned at the beginning of this chapter, it also may be that some of the pleasure following the display of aggression results from the completion of a previously interrupted aggressive response sequence. The interruption created tension, and the completion of the sequence brought about a decrease in the disturbing internal excitement.

The notion of a "completion tendency" certainly is not new in psychology. Lewin had discussed such a proposition in the 1920s, and two of his students have published supporting data. Thus, we have Zeigarnik's demonstration that there is better memory for incompleted tasks than for completed ones and Ovsiankina's study indicating that people are more inclined to resume interrupted activities then to take up tasks again that they had recently completed (Lewin, 1935, pp. 242–244). Failure to complete the tasks presumably created the tension leading to

---

clip of either a violent prizefight or a more neutral scene. He found, on two aggression measures administered after the movie, that the angered men seemed to have a lower level of hostility after seeing the aggressive film than after the neutral movie, while there were only negligible differences between the nonangered subjects shown these movies.

These results certainly are consistent with the aggressive drive-reduction version of the catharsis doctrine, but further research is definitely needed before this thesis can be accepted. There are at least two main reasons for these doubts:

1. I had suggested earlier, particularly in Chapter 4, that the intensity of the anxiety and/or guilt resulting from the arousal of a socially disapproved drive often is in direct ratio to the strength of the disapproved inclinations (cf. Berkowitz & Holmes, 1960; Clark, 1955; Thibaut & Coules, 1952). Thus, the angered men shown the prizefight could have been excited still more, perhaps to the point where a strong anxiety-guilt reaction took place. Or they may have become aware of their own aggressive wishes in the course of watching the aggressive movie so that anxiety and/or guilt was provoked which inhibited their expressions of aggression.

2. An experiment by Berkowitz and Rawlings to be described in the next chapter has yielded contradictory findings. Angered subjects shown a brutal prizefight scene and who believed the aggression they witnessed was justified gave reliably *unfriendlier* ratings to their frustraters than did similarly insulted subjects shown the same movie but who believed the filmed aggression was unjustified. Feshbach probably would have predicted a greater "drainage" through watching justified aggression.

their better recall and the tendency to resume them. An activity will tend to continue, of course, until the activity goal is reached. Preventing the organism from reaching this goal, i.e., interrupting the activity, can be a source of tension. Sheffield (1954), more recently, has hypothesized that there is "an increase in excited emotion" when a consummatory response—completing the activity sequence—is stimulated but not allowed to occur completely.

I believe these formulations also apply to aggressive behavior. *Inflicting injury on the anger instigator is the goal response completing the aggressive response sequence.* When a person is thwarted, anger is aroused and he wants to see his frustrater hurt (perhaps, originally, destroyed), preferably by himself (if this is safe), although there may be satisfying substitute aggressors. The anger has initiated a sequence of responses whose goal or consummation is the perception that the frustrater has been injured. *As long as the anger lasts and the individual is set to aggress, he does not obtain "completion" until he sees that he has injured his frustrater or that someone else has done so.*

Sheffield also proposed, in a manner altogether consistent with the theoretical formulation presented in this book, that when the consummatory response is stimulated but prevented from occurring, internal tension is induced which is "channeled into whatever response happens to be underway at the time." Several writers have advanced somewhat similar views (e.g., Brown & Farber, 1951; Mowrer, 1960). Extending this argument to aggressive behavior, we have the frustration-aggression notion that blocking aggressive reactions increases the instigation to aggression.

Furthermore, the lessening of the excitement arising from the interruption of the consummatory response can be enjoyable. The angered person who had to delay committing an aggressive act but then is able to injure his frustrater gets pleasure from completing the hostility sequence and reducing tension—as long as he does not feel guilt or anxiety.

Some implications of this analysis should be made explicit. First, along with Dollard and his colleagues, the present formulation suggests (tentatively) that heightened aggressive response tendencies will result from even a relatively brief delay before hostile acts can be performed. The Thibaut-Coules (1952) experiment seems to support this expectation, but there are contrary indications in the Hokanson studies to be reported later, and additional research is needed.

Second, while a hostile act may lessen the probability of further aggression by completing the instigated hostility sequence, the present reasoning insists that such a catharsis would not occur at all if the anger persists or is rearoused, and further goal responses are elicited. Thibaut's

(1950) investigation, cited earlier, documents the importance of considering the persistence of the frustration.

Third, resumption of an interrupted aggressive sequence is tension decreasing only for those people who had been angry during the interruption period and set (i.e., prepared) to make an aggressive response to the thwarting agent.

Fourth, "completion" is said to be achieved only to the extent that the anger instigator is seen to be injured. Kicking a can or beating some other inanimate object would not provide gratifications unless the object is somehow associated with the frustrater. The aggression against the inanimate object might even enhance hostile tendencies if the activity reminded the individual of his frustrations without causing him to believe the instigator had been injured. Hornberger (1959), the reader will recall, employed a somewhat similar argument to explain the heightened hostility following his hammering task.

Finally, another point can also be made which derives more from experience than from theory. There is a suggestion in some of the studies just reviewed that anger may decrease fairly soon after it is aroused if the frustration does not continue in the external environment or if the individual does not stir himself up by thinking of his unpleasant experience. Magaziner (1961), for example, obtained a relatively rapid decline in overt hostility after an anger-arousing loss of self-esteem was countered by a rewarding event. Assuming the decrease in aggressive behavior was due to anger reduction and not to inhibitions, Magaziner's subjects seem to have quickly gotten over their anger once the frustration was removed. The behavior of young children also illustrates the rapid dissipation of anger. Preschoolers are easily aroused, but their emotional excitement can vanish just as quickly. The children may not stimulate themselves to continued emotionality by thinking of the instigating situation. Once distracted their mood changes rapidly. Adults might also exhibit such shifts in mood if the instigating events did not remain symbolically in their thoughts.

*Experimental Evidence.* Perhaps the best demonstrations of tension reduction following aggression have been reported by Hokanson. In the first of his experiments (Hokanson & Shetler, 1961), male and female university students were placed into one of eight conditions created by the experimental manipulations. The students knew they were subjects in a psychological investigation (their blood pressure was being measured), but they were led to believe either that the experimenter was a high-status person—in this case, a middle-aged "university professor"— or that he was a low-status person—a fellow student. Half of the people in each of these two conditions, while working singly, were deliberately angered by the experimenter, while the remaining subjects received a kindlier treatment from him. The systolic blood pressure obtained at this time showed that physiological tension[8] increased in all of the insulted groups independently of the instigator's status. Following the arousal, half of the subjects in each of the now four conditions were given an opportunity to shock the experimenter; the experimenter said he would try to guess what number the subject had in mind, and the subject would give him a shock to tell him if he was wrong. The nonaggressing group simply flashed a light instead of shocking the experimenter. There were ten "guessing trials."

Physical aggression against the low-status instigator appeared to be tension reducing. The systolic blood pressure in the angered, aggressing students decreased to the level existing in the nonaroused group, but the pressure remained high in those people not shocking their insulting peer. They presumably believed they had not injured the instigator and therefore did not complete the aggressive sequence.

The results are somewhat puzzling for the high-status-experimenter condition. In this case, systolic pressure decreased in *both* the nonaggressing and aggressing angered students to the level within the nonprovoked groups. We might conjecture that the insulted nonaggressing students had quickly given up the idea of attacking the high-status professor. They no longer wanted or expected to aggress against him so that, in essence, an instigated aggressive sequence was no longer in operation.[9]

A second experiment (Hokanson & Burgess, 1962) showed that the findings obtained in the low-status-experimenter condition are reliable and in addition highlight the importance of perceived injury to the instigator. Only a low-status experimenter was employed this time but, as before, half of the subjects, male and female college students, were deliberately angered and half were not. Also as in the earlier experiment, one group of subjects could shock the experimenter for making

---

[8] Many neurophysiologists feel that one particular conscious state cannot always be attributed to a given physiological pattern. Thus, high systolic blood pressure is not necessarily indicative of the same conscious emotion in all people. The most parsimonious interpretation is to regard the high blood pressure as indicative of physiological tension.

[9] Tension may arise only when the instigator is set to aggress against his tormenter but cannot do so. In the Rosenbaum and deCharms (1960) modification of the Thibaut-Coules study, the high self-esteem subjects not permitted to attack their frustrater were *not* more hostile at the conclusion of the session than were the other high self-esteem groups given an opportunity for aggression. *But* the nonaggressive group in this later experiment had not expected to retaliate against the instigator, while the aroused people in the Thibaut-Coules study had expected to be able to reply. Not anticipating an opportunity to aggress, the Rosenbaum-deCharms subjects were not set to make an aggressive response and therefore were not frustrated aggressively.

incorrect guesses, while another group could only signify this by flashing a light. Two other treatments were also carried out. One group created a story in response to a TAT card, and a final condition rated the experimenter's capabilities as an experimenter in his presence. Since the experimenter could see the questionnaire, unfavorable ratings are taken as verbal aggression. Deliberately angered and nonangered students were included in each of the four experimental treatments.

Systolic blood pressure and heart rate measures again indicated that there was a significant physiological arousal following the provocation. The frustrated subjects given an opportunity to injure their tormenter, either physically (by shocks) or verbally (through the questionnaire ratings), then showed a lessening in physiological tension so that their final scores were not different from those in the nonfrustrated groups. The tension remained high, however, in the insulted TAT and light-flashing conditions.

Clearly, the angered individual must believe he has injured his frustrater in retaliation for the injury he has received if there is to be a physiological relaxation. Fantasy aggression in response to the TAT card in this study did not provide "closure." Fantasy aggression in general, I believe, is relatively unlikely to be satisfying. Gratifications may be achieved through such symbolic behavior (or through watching movie or television violence) only when the *victim* of the fantasy aggression is associated strongly with the individual's own frustrater. When the fantasy target is injured, the observer symbolically injures his own tormenter. Since the association between fantasy target and real-life frustrater is usually very weak, I doubt whether fantasy aggression could ever be a really satisfactory means for reducing the audience's frustration-engendered anger.[10] Furthermore, as we shall see in the next chapter, if the observing individual identifies with the fantasy aggressor (i.e., associates this fantasy figure with himself) and does not see his own frustrater as having been hurt, fantasy cues may even strengthen his aggressive tendencies.

Hokanson's studies contain no indications of a tension increase following the blocking of hostile activity. Nonetheless, they show there is a decline in physiological excitement when the provoked subject has an opportunity to injure his frustrater under conditions in which guilt or aggression anxiety is unlikely to be elicited.

The next link in our theoretical chain is to prove that the tension created by interruption of the aggressive sequence is often uncomfort-

---

[10] The symbolic catharsis notion seems to be based on the energy conception of aggression regardless of the exact terminology employed in discussing this thesis. Release is said to be obtained by expressing a quantum of aggressive energy no matter what is the target of the symbolic aggression.

able. Some evidence on this matter was provided by Worchel (1957). Discomfort probably can be inferred from signs of disrupted performance after anger is provoked, while a decrease in this uncomfortable excitement might be indicated by improved performance after the expression of aggression. In Worchel's study, college students who aggressed against a frustrating experimenter, either directly to him or indirectly to his assistant, performed reliably better on a digit-symbol test than did similarly insulted subjects not given an opportunity for catharsis. It may well be that the lessening of the work-disrupting tension was pleasant.

There is more direct evidence of the gratifications that might be obtained by displaying hostility when guilt or anxiety is not anticipated in an investigation by Festinger et al. (1952). College students assembled in twenty-three groups were given the task of describing their "true" feelings toward their parents and were strongly encouraged to express their resentments. The discussion was sometimes so active the group members could not always recall who had made the various statements recorded by the experimenter during the session. The investigators assumed the subjects felt they were anonymous ("deindividuated") to the extent that the group members were focused on the content of the remarks and could not remember the source of the statements. As was noted in Chapter 4, the greater the presumed anonymity in the group, the more the group discussion was dominated by hostility toward the parents. But what is more important here, the reduction of restraints against aggression toward the parents apparently was pleasant. The more the discussion concentrated upon resentment against the parents, the greater the average attraction to the discussion group.

From my viewpoint the emotional gratifications these students felt did not stem from the discharge of a lifelong or even years-long volume of hostile energy. I would prefer to say that the discussion had elicited anger toward the parents, perhaps by reminding the students of the frustrations they had suffered at the hands of their mothers and fathers. Tension then arose in the men; they wanted to aggress against their parents because of their now conscious resentment toward them and because of the other cues present in the discussion situation. Since these men did not fear punishment or disapproval (and the situation also defined attacks upon the parents as being permissible), they obtained pleasure from expressing their hostility.

One possible explanation for these findings is to suggest that the subjects experienced pleasure when their aggressive behavior restored or enhanced their self-esteem. But yet, can such a hypothesis adequately account for the results? The Festinger et al. men expressed hostility and felt happy about the group situation presumably only to the degree they believed they were anonymous. Ego enhancement appears unlikely when attention is focused on the content of the discussion rather than on the individuals doing the talking. The aggressive people in this study obtained gratifications but probably not from increasing their self-regard. It may be that the pleasure resulted from the completion of aggressive response sequences.

The previously described study by Berkowitz et al. (1962) also contains some tentative evidence for the tension-reduction thesis. After the subjects were shown their partners' performance and either were given an opportunity to shock them or were deprived of this opportunity, they were asked to describe their mood by rating how "good" they felt. Considering only those men led to believe their partners had done well on the assigned task, the angered subjects permitted to retaliate against the instigator were reliably happier than the similarly insulted group not given this opportunity to attack their tormenters in kind.[11] This difference was in the opposite direction for the less angered condition.

## SUMMARY

The theoretical analysis of hostility catharsis requires several important distinctions. Some formulations of this widely accepted social science doctrine are couched in terms of the instigation to aggression, and it is held that the performance of a hostile act decreases the strength of the remaining instigation to aggression. Other versions of the catharsis hypothesis maintain that aggressive behavior results in a reduction of internal tension so that the individual feels better after acting aggressively. Various discussions of hostility catharsis are reviewed, and it is pointed out that according to some theoretical analyses, tension reduction need not signify a decrease in the instigation to aggression. The hostile act might be instrumental to the attainment of a nonaggressive goal, or might be an expression of an acquired aggressive motive, or might indicate there has been a resolution of an internal conflict as to whether to aggress or not. For any of these reasons, the hostile act

---

[11] When the men were told their peers had done a bad job on the assigned task, the angered group *not* permitted to aggress against them indicated they felt reliably better than did the people in any other condition. The provoked people may have been pleased to learn the instigator had done so poorly. In other words, they may have believed that the experimenter had injured the frustrater symbolically by "showing him up." Some support is given this interpretation by the findings in a more recent experiment from the writer's laboratory. Under conditions similar to those in the present experiment, angered subjects shown that their instigators had done a very poor job had a reliable increase in the "goodness" of their mood. Such a change did not occur in any of the nonangered groups or in the provoked people who were led to believe the instigator had done good work.

could bring pleasure without lessening the probability of further aggressive behavior. Indeed, the reinforcement value of the tension-reduction effect could even increase the likelihood of further aggression.

A second distinction involves the difference between anger-induced aggressive behavior and customary or habitual aggressiveness. Providing an opportunity to express hostility may lessen the frustration-engendered instigation to aggression but could also evoke and/or strengthen a person's habitual hostile tendencies.

Research findings pertaining to the catharsis hypothesis are summarized. There is no evidence that competitive games in themselves either weaken aggressive inclinations or decrease concern about hostile tendencies. Modern psychotherapists generally deemphasize the therapeutic value of catharsis, i.e., the expression of previously inhibited responses, usually contending that such a breakdown in inhibitions is helpful in achieving insight and reeducation rather than for the "discharge of pent-up energy."

Because of the need for adequate controls, catharsis formulations ultimately must be tested in the experimental laboratory. However, experimental investigations (and field research as well) are subject to a number of major difficulties. Among these problems are:

1. Open acts of hostility may be followed by weaker or less frequent aggressive responses because of guilt or anxiety evoked by the first hostile actions.

2. Hostile tendencies may not be weakened after aggression is expressed if the frustration continues or if the attacker stimulates himself to continued aggression.

3. A hostile act can lead to weaker residual hostility if it eliminates the original anger-inciting frustration, resulting in a lessening of anger without "catharsis."

4. Preventing the occurrence of a hostile response to a thwarting theoretically is a frustration capable of increasing the instigation to aggression.

Demonstrations of a supposed decrease in the instigation to aggression following aggressive behavior are not altogether convincing because they generally have failed to take these problems into consideration.

There is better evidence, however, that an angered individual often obtains some tension reduction if he can injure his frustrater in some way (i.e., if he can aggress against him) without feeling guilty or anxious. The pleasure signifying such a tension reduction may arise from the fulfillment of a "completion tendency." As long as he is angry and set to aggress against the instigator, the individual has within him an "activated" aggressive response sequence. Injuring the instigator is the goal response terminating the aggressive sequence. Interrupting the sequence may heighten tension, or at least prevent (or perhaps delay) the lessening of the internal excitement, and the individual does not complete the sequence—which will lower tension—until he perceives that he has injured the instigator physically or psychologically, or that an acceptable substitute has done so.

# chapter 9

# Violence in the Mass Media

INTRODUCTION

In October, 1960, a team of investigators made a tally of the program content on the five television channels in a large metropolitan area of the United States. Approximately 24 per cent of the shows during the Monday through Friday period specialized in aggression (i.e., they were either westerns or crime programs). This is a heavy concentration of violence for any audience. However, since the researchers had made their observations between 4 and 9 P.M., when children were most likely to be watching TV, this could even be regarded as an extreme amount of aggression. Disregarding cartoons, there were 12 murders, 16 major gunfights, and 42 other violent scenes with gunplay during the 100 hours of the investigation (Schramm et al., 1961, p. 139). These statistics are not unusually high. Other monitors have reported seeing over sixty-eight hundred aggressive incidents depicted on television in the New York area in only one week in 1954.

While some counts of the frequency of TV violence, employing exceedingly broad definitions of aggression, may be questioned (see the critique by Klapper, 1960, pp. 136–138), there can be little doubt that shootings and sluggings are a prominent feature of much of television programming. Such a heavy dosage of aggression is not unique to the United States. Abundant violence seems to characterize British television as well. Himmelweit, Oppenheim, and Vince noted that hostility was a dominant theme in about 20 per cent of the plays shown over British TV channels during children's peak viewing hours (5 to 9 P.M.) in 1956 (1958, p. 176).

But television is not the only communications medium portraying aggression. Crime and violence pour from the pages of children's comic books (Wertham, 1954) and are frequently depicted on the movie screen. Unless his watching and reading are highly selective, it is practically impossible for the modern child to escape scenes of aggression and lawlessness in the mass media.

There are nagging uncertainties in our society as to the possible effects of all of this violence. A 1954 Gallup poll found that seven out of ten American adults attributed the postwar rise in juvenile delinquency at least in part to the high incidence of criminal acts shown in comic books, television, and radio (cited in Klapper, 1960, p. 135). Some authorities agree with them. Dr. Frederic Wertham, senior psychiatrist for the Department of Hospitals in New York City, has insisted (1954) that crime comics definitely contribute to youthful lawlessness. These magazines supposedly "seduce the innocent," "causing, stimulating, and encouraging" socially improper attitudes and behavior in some children. Crime comics, Wertham stated, degrade taste and sensibility and convey unrealistic if not harmful views of the external world. But more than this, they presumably suggest socially undesirable outlets for youngsters' sexual and aggressive drives, as well as incite such impulses.

Somewhat similar charges have been leveled against crime and violence on television. Dr. Ralph Banay, a psychiatrist at Columbia University, told a subcommittee of the United States Senate investigating juvenile delinquency that "TV is a preparatory school for delinquency" (United States Senate, 1955, p. 83). Emotionally secure children probably are not seriously affected by TV aggression, he said. However, the gravely disturbed child, exposed to persistent scenes of violence "creating false images and conceptions of life," can undergo "an unfavorable unconscious conditioning" which directs his energies into destructive and even vicious actions (p. 81).

Newspaper stories seem to document the charges made by Wertham and Banay. Despite protestations by comic-book publishers and television and movie producers that their codes prohibit presenting crimes in such a way as to foster the desire to imitate criminals, stories continually crop up telling of aggressive incidents apparently precipitated by violence in the mass media. Wertham (1954) reported a number of such events presumably traceable to comic books, and Chapter 1 told of a triple murderer who admitted slaying one of his victims after he had seen a movie about a deranged killer. To cite another incident, there is the story of a Los Angeles housemaid who caught a seven-year-old boy sprinkling ground glass into the family's meal. The boy supposedly was experimenting to see if the trick would really work as well as it did on television (Schramm et al., 1961, p. 161).

These admittedly are unusual cases—but even these have to be explained. And what are the usual effects of media violence? Parental concern about aggression in the mass media—which apparently varies directly with the parents' educational level—commonly focuses on the frightening aspects of such violence (Schramm et al., 1961, pp. 55–56). But there may be other consequences of hostility in TV, movies, books, and magazines as well. To what extent does the display of crime in the media constitute a "school for delinquency"? Is it true that aggression shown in movies, television, or comic books can stimulate hostile behavior in other social situations? Can scenes of violence depicted on the screen or printed page produce undesirable attitudes and values?

Many authorities doubt whether the communications media can be held responsible for all the sins attributed to them. A survey of eighteen prominent experts revealed a widespread unwillingness to blame juvenile delinquency on TV crime and aggression (United States Senate, 1955, pp. 49–54). The few who thought television might be at least partly responsible for youthful lawlessness admitted they had no definite proof. There also seemed to be general agreement that television violence might provoke mild emotional upsets in children, but that the basic causes of serious disturbances probably lie elsewhere.

On the positive side, some observers are even willing to attribute beneficial social effects to media depictions of crime and violence. "A considerable number of psychiatrists and psychologists" interviewed by Klapper in 1953 (Klapper, 1960, p. 143) thought that the display of aggression in the communications media could provide an opportunity for hostility catharsis, lessening the hostile tendencies which otherwise might find an outlet in asocial behavior.

Such uncontrolled observations as these obviously are inadequate for tracing the effects of aggression in the mass media. To deny that TV violence and crime is a major cause of juvenile delinquency is *not* to say that aggressive scenes have no influence on a child's behavior. Only systematic quantitative research can determine what these effects might be. After reviewing such research we will see that we cannot be altogether sanguine about media violence. Scenes of crime and aggression in television, movies, or books heighten the probability that some child in the audience will behave in a hostile fashion, particularly if he has aggressive predispositions.


## RESEARCH

### Immediate Effects of Fantasy Violence

*Functions of the Mass Media.* One way to organize our discussion of fantasy aggression is in terms of the possible functions served by the entertainment media. Social practices, whether in the communications industry or in any other human endeavor, persist because they are rewarding to the practitioners. If aggression is a dominant theme in comic books, television, and movies, this is so because it "works"; scenes of violence are attractive to many viewers. Magazines, programs, and movies featuring aggression are often highly popular. But why does fantasy aggression appeal to so many people?

As Schramm et al. pointed out (1961, p. 61), there are essentially two different types of theories concerning the psychological functions of art and entertainment. One school of thought emphasizes the wish-fulfilling nature of such endeavors, contending that art satisfies frustrated desires. This type of theory obviously has a strong psychoanalytic bent. In contrast, other doctrines see art and entertainment primarily as agencies for social learning, creating and strengthening habits, values, and expectations. Both approaches can be employed in dealing with the effects of the communications media.[1] We can ask (1) is the depiction of crime and violence attractive to some people because this is need satisfying for them, and (2) can aggressive scenes influence the audience's beliefs and values? In addition, we want to know whether the mass media can evoke and shape particular classes of behavior, such as hostility.

*Fantasy and Frustration.* Several studies attest to the possible wish-fulfilling function of television, movies, and comic books for children. In one of the first of these investigations, Eleanor Maccoby (1954) found that television viewing by upper-middle-class five- and six-year-old children tended to increase, the more frustrated these children were in their current home life. Upper-lower-class youngsters, on the other hand, showed no relationship between home frustrations and amount of television watching. Mrs. Maccoby explained the social-class differences by suggesting that parents from the two social levels had somewhat different attitudes toward TV. Parents in the upper-socioeconomic status families generally engage in relatively little television viewing themselves so that their frustrated children can do what the parents do not do: escape from harsh reality into the fantasy world of television. The parents in the poorer homes, however, characteristically watch TV a great deal. The loved child from this background presumably will spend a good deal of time before the television screen in order to be with his family and imitate them, while the frustrated child indulging in TV daydreams also will be a frequent watcher of television.

Schramm et al. obtained virtually the same results in a survey of adolescents in the Rocky Mountain area. Teen-agers from the higher

---

[1] Analyzing the consequences of particular communications in terms of these psychological functions does not imply, of course, that there are no other fruitful approaches to the study of the mass media. Sociological analyses employing other concepts undoubtedly are necessary as well. Thus, Schramm and his colleagues reported that socioeconomic status and its behavioral concomitants (e.g., willingness to defer gratifications and readiness to plan ahead) were directly related to a high use of the printed word and a low use of TV in tenth-grade school children (Schramm et al., 1961, pp. 114–115).

social strata made greater use of TV if they were in conflict with their parents over their occupational and educational plans than if they lived in more complete harmony with them. There were no such differences for the adolescents in the lower social strata (p. 131).[2] Various types of frustrations may lead to heavy use of television by children. A survey of British children reported by Himmelweit et al. demonstrated that insecure youngsters, particularly those having difficulty in making friends, spent a longer time watching television than did more secure, socially successful children (1958, p. 388). In all these instances it appears as if thwarted children tended to withdraw as much as possible from the frustrating agents, whether these were parents or peers, and sought gratifications in television fantasies.[3]

Other evidence further strengthens this thesis of a frustration-fantasy activity relationship in children. If, as this book argues, thwartings engender aggressive tendencies, we might well expect characteristically hostile children to be especially attracted to the make-believe material. There are several reasons why youngsters may have developed strong aggressiveness habits, but one important factor undoubtedly is a history of persistent frustrations in the home. Hostile children, presumably often thwarted in the past and possibly encountering relatively strong frustrations at present, should be frequent television viewers if this reasoning is correct.

Schramm and his collaborators have reported just such findings in their survey of Rocky Mountain children. In addition to determining the frequency with which the youngsters watched television and read books, magazines, and newspapers, the investigators administered the six aggression scales developed by R. R. Sears (referred to in Chapter 5). Aggressive tendencies within tenth-grade children, as measured by these scales, were related to usage of the mass media. Fantasy-oriented adolescents—who spent a great deal of time before their TV sets but did relatively little book and newspaper reading—were significantly higher than any of the other children on the measure of antisocial ag-

---

[2] Bandura (personal communication) has suggested that the middle-class youngsters, in spending many hours before the television set, may actually have been rebelling against their frustrating parents. Middle-class parents generally frown on excessive TV viewing.

[3] There can be little doubt that excessive television viewing by children is largely fantasy-oriented behavior. Schramm et al. have shown that the introduction of TV into a community results in a decrease in the number of children engaging in such clearly fantasy activities as the reading of comic books, but does not lessen their reality-oriented usage of the communications media, such as newspaper reading. Moviegoing also declines (1961, pp. 70–71). Maccoby (United States Senate, 1955, pp. 6–7) stated that children who watch TV a great deal also tend to read many comic books, but do little other reading.

gression. (Thus, they were more likely to say such things as, "I don't see anything especially wrong about a fight between two gangs of teen-agers; it's their business, and adults should stay out of it.") Children who read a lot and did little television viewing, i.e., who supposedly were reality-oriented, on the other hand, had the lowest antisocial aggression scores. They also were reliably higher than any of the other groups on the index of aggression anxiety. These differences, further-more, tended to persist when socioeconomic status was controlled statis-tically. Additional findings reported by the authors suggested that the aggression measures were not affected by TV viewing (Schramm et al., 1961, pp. 121–123).

All in all, then, there is ample evidence that socially frustrated chil-dren frequently withdraw to a world of fantasy—a world often created by television but one that can also exist in movies and comic books. But we must go even further in this analysis. The frustrated youngsters do more than retreat from harsh realities; they apparently also seek par-ticular forms of pleasure in the fantasy media. Since thwarted children probably have strong aggressive inclinations, it is not surprising to learn that they generally like aggressive action in the television and movies they watch and in the comic books they read.

Riley and Riley (1954) ascertained the kinds of radio and television programs favored by 400 schoolchildren. The younger the child, they found, the greater was his preference for programs characterized by violence, action, and aggression (p. 394). However, among the older children, those boys and girls who had relatively few friends but who were attracted to their peer groups expressed the strongest liking for the violence-action programs. This relationship, furthermore, was not confined to the older groups. Socially frustrated younger children also were more likely than their nonthwarted peers to prefer the aggressive programs (pp. 395–396).

Bailyn (1959) obtained somewhat similar findings for boys (but not girls) in the fifth and sixth grades of Massachusetts schools. In part of this investigation the children responded to a questionnaire by indicat-ing their frequency of exposure to six different media: radio, TV, movies, comic books, comic strips, and books. As we have assumed throughout this section, the researcher noted that children who spent a relatively great amount of time with the pictorial media (TV, movies, and comic books) tended to spend little time reading and listening to the radio. Certain sociological characteristics were associated with high exposure to the pictorial media (e.g., having less intelligent fathers in the worker or service occupations), but these factors, by and large, did not account for the type of content the children preferred in these media. According to Bailyn, personality characteristics are important determinants of preference for at least one kind of story, i.e., the "aggressive-hero" story, whose protagonist aggressively defends innocent people and himself from hostile actions initiated by others. Unlike the somewhat older girls studied by the Rileys, the girls in Bailyn's survey generally did not care for this type of program, and there was relatively little variation among them. For the boys, however, liking for the aggressive-hero story was associated with (among other things) an attitude of "rebellious independence." These youngsters probably had met with considerable frustration in their family life and therefore indicated they wanted to have relatively little contact with their parents. In summarizing her findings, the investigator concluded that certain children were particularly likely to employ the mass media for escapist purposes. These were the boys who had high rates of exposure to the pictorial media, but also were relatively aggressive as well as being rebelliously independent (pp. 33–34).

As far as the present writer is concerned, these children did more than merely escape. They probably obtained vicarious pleasures through the aggressive fantasies. Consistent with such an interpretation, Berkowitz and Rawlings found that deliberately angered college students scored higher than their nonangered peers on a disguised measure of the degree to which they had enjoyed a filmed, violently aggressive prizefight scene. Such pleasure from witnessing filmed aggression or reading aggressive-hero comic books does not necessarily mean, however, that the hostile inclinations have been cathartically weakened. The previous chapter suggested that catharsis occurs only when an angered individual perceives that his frustrater has been aggressively injured. The frustrated person may enjoy fantasy aggression because he sees characters doing things (acting aggressively) that he wants but fears to do.[4] In seeing the fantasy aggression, however, he probably is not purging himself of his emotion.

*Effects on Aggressive Behavior.* Assuming that the child does attempt to gratify his suppressed desires (including his hostile wishes) vicariously, how does this fantasy activity influence his subsequent behavior? Wording the question somewhat more generally, we can ask, does hostility in the mass media alter the likelihood that a child in the audience will behave aggressively on some future occasion? An answer to this

[4] Another possibility is that the pleasure derived from viewing TV or movie violence stems from changes in internal tension. The individual watching fantasy aggression is first aroused or excited and then experiences a pleasing tension reduction when the conflict situation is terminated by the hero's victory. The intensity of the pleasure is proportional to the magnitude of these tension shifts. People with strong aggressive predispositions would be aroused relatively strongly by the fantasy aggression and, therefore, would feel a relatively strongly pleasing reduction in excitement when the fighting ends.

question can be attempted. The evidence is not overwhelming in every study of this problem, but it is consistent. The research will suggest media violence is more likely to incite children to acts of overt aggression than to "drain" them of their hostile energy. Before proceeding any further, however, one important aspect of this research should be made clear. *The studies only demonstrate short-range effects. They do not show media-induced changes in persistent modes of conduct.*

Two experiments indicate that media violence can enhance the degree to which the child prefers to witness and even engage in hostile behavior. In one of these investigations, Lövaas (1961a) showed two different animated cartoons to nursery school children. One of the cartoons depicted a great deal of aggressive action. The film exhibited in the other condition, in contrast, was much more peaceful in content. After the movie was over, each child was given an opportunity to play with two mechanical toys requiring bar pressing for their activation. One was an ordinary and relatively neutral toy, but the bar pressure in the other device caused one doll to strike another doll. The children who had seen the aggressive cartoon activated the fighting doll to a significantly greater extent than did the children in the neutral movie condition. Both groups made the same total number of responses. The difference between them was in the time spent with the aggressive toy. There are at least two explanations for these findings. The children exposed to the aggressive cartoon may have come to enjoy seeing further acts of hostility, or it may be, as the investigator concluded, "the aggressive film selectively increased behavior that had aggressive consequences."[5]

Another study has demonstrated that children can easily imitate aggressors portrayed in a movie. Bandura and his students have conducted a number of experiments revealing modeling and imitative influences upon children's behavior. In one of these (reported in Chapter 4), Bandura et al. (1961) found that children readily imitated an adult's aggressive behavior even when this adult model was no longer present. A subsequent investigation by the same psychologists (1962) indicated that the same phenomenon occurred when the adult model was observed on a movie screen. The nursery school children in the experimental groups watched either a movie of an adult striking a "Bobo" doll or an aggressive cartoon also depicting such a doll. Control children did not see these films. Later, each child was subjected to a deliberate frustration and placed in a room with the Bobo doll and

---

[5] Such a conclusion may perhaps be unwarranted since the children did not actually injure anyone when they started the fighting doll. However, if the children did obtain pleasure from witnessing aggression, this may be the result of the arousal of aggressive tendencies within them.

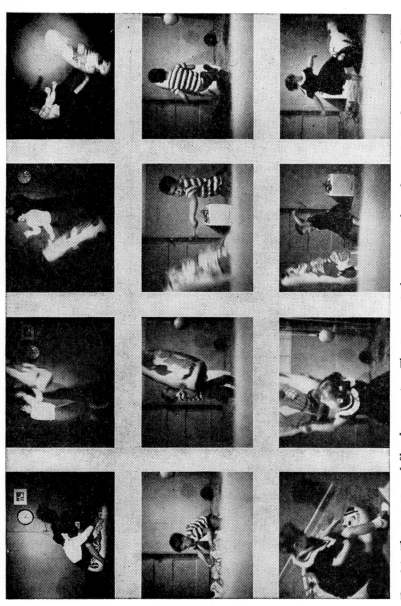

Fig. 9.1. The imitation of filmed aggression. The top row is four excerpts from the movie Bandura, Ross, and Ross showed to their nursery school children in which the adult model aggressed against a Bobo doll. The last two rows of pictures show the behaviors of a boy and girl who saw this film. (*Reproduced with the permission of Albert Bandura.*)

other toys. The preschoolers who had witnessed the filmed aggression (realistic or cartoon) displayed more hostility toward the Bobo than did the control group. A live aggressive model produced more imitative aggression than did the cartoon but not more than the realistic movie.[6]

These hostile aftereffects of filmed aggression may even carry over into an unstructured free-play situation, according to a study reported by Alberta Siegel (1956). Pairs of like-sex nursery school children were observed after the youngsters had watched aggressive and nonaggressive animated cartoons. Although the difference was not significant, trends consistent with the Bandura findings were obtained. There was more hostility in the children's play after the aggressive than the nonaggressive cartoon.

One way to explain these results is in terms of the learning analysis employed in the earlier chapters. Putting it simply, we might say the filmed aggression had set previously learned aggressiveness habits into operation. The depicted aggression was a cue, stimulating hostile tendencies within the children, and as a result, they were readily instigated to overt aggression in a subsequent situation. This approach, furthermore, suggests a number of mediating factors governing the probability that hostile actions will occur in these later situations: (1) *the strength of the aggressiveness habits;* (2) *the intensity of the hostile tendencies evoked by the media violence;* (3) *the degree of association between the fantasy situation and* (a) *the situations in which the hostile habits were learned, and* (b) *the postfantasy setting; and* (4) *the intensity of the guilt and/or aggression anxiety also aroused by the fantasy violence.*

The importance of these determinants can easily be demonstrated by everyday experiences and research findings. The first two factors generally (but not always) go together; youngsters who are characteristically extremely aggressive are fairly likely to show an extreme reaction to media violence. Other things being equal, these habitually hostile children are the ones most readily instigated to copy the aggressive actions depicted in the mass media. However, the second factor also proposes that many preschoolers can be incited into action if the media aggression is intensely stimulating—as may have been the case in the Bandura and Lövaas experiments. In most instances, of course, there is only a very mild arousal resulting from the fantasy cues. But this moderate drive state can be strengthened so that overt behavior occurs if there are appropriate stimuli in the later situations.

[6] Where the present analysis suggests that the filmed violence could have "aroused" aggressive tendencies, Bandura et al. (1962) emphasized two other effects of the fantasy aggression: lowering of inhibitions and the "shaping" of the aggressive responses. We agree, however, that seeing models "portraying aggression on film . . . increases . . . the probability of aggressive reactions to subsequent frustrations." (All the Bandura subjects were frustrated after viewing the aggressive films or aggressive models.)

As for the third determinant, association between the fantasy and real worlds, younger children probably are particularly susceptible to the type of modeling effects shown by these investigations because they do not discount the fantasy situations to any great extent. The make-believe scenes are fairly real to them. They do not draw as sharp a differentiation between the events witnessed in the media and their own circumstances as do the older children, and so, there is a stronger association between these two settings for them. This association will also be enhanced by very prominent features common to both the real and make-believe situations. In the Bandura et al. experiments, for example, the Bobo doll employed by the adult model was also present in the room with the child. The response tendencies activated by observation of the model striking this doll could then be readily evoked later by the sight of the same object.[7]

Finally, inhibitory tendencies can prevent the occurrence of aggressive acts. Since preschoolers and their older but very hostile peers are both typically deficient in behavior controls (Redl & Wineman, 1957), these youngsters would not inhibit all of the hostile tendencies evoked by the violent scenes they have witnessed.

The operation of these determinants can be illustrated by a story appearing in a March, 1961, issue of the *San Francisco Chronicle* after a local TV station had shown a movie about juvenile delinquents.[8] Two high school youths, apparently carried away by the film, had reenacted a switchblade knife fight occurring in the movie. As a consequence, one of the boys ended up in the hospital, requiring emergency surgery. If a little speculation is permitted, we can see some of the hostility-inciting factors at work in this case. The weapon is a good starting point. Since one of the teen-agers had gone out of his way to acquire an illegal knife (and later was arrested for possessing it), it is at least conceivable that he had relatively strong aggressiveness habits. He certainly did not have strong aggression anxiety. When this boy exhibited the knife in school the day after the movie, the other adolescent evidently was instantly reminded of the fight scene (the knife cue present in the movie also was present in this later situation, producing an association between the two settings) and at once began to imitate the violent actions he had witnessed in the film. The two youngsters were quickly swept up into the make-believe fight. But they did not stop at fantasy. Relatively uncontrolled hostility rapidly emerged, and the knife was thrust into the other boy's body. A cue in the school situation that also had been present in the aggressive movie scene evoked and shaped the young-

[7] To refer to the concepts employed in other chapters of this book, the fantasy situation provides cues *arousing* (predisposing) aggressive responses, while the cues in the later situation *evoke* these aroused tendencies.

[8] Dr. Albert Bandura called this story to the writer's attention.

sters' aggressive actions. In the absence of controlling inhibitions, this violence soon got out of hand.

The present formulation obviously rules out the possibility of a cathartic process resulting from the passive observation of violence in television, movies, or comic books. There is no need for theoretical twisting or turning on this point; there simply is no adequate evidence that hostility catharsis occurs through vicarious aggression (despite the near consensus among the previously mentioned psychiatrists and psychologists interviewed by Klapper). Fantasy violence may be pleasant and gratifying to the observer, particularly if he imagines himself in the place of the virile, powerful make-believe aggressor. But this pleasure does not necessarily mean his own aggressive inclinations are weakened. He does not have a reservoir of hostile energy to discharge in fantasy. Hostile tendencies would persist to the extent that the individual's real problems and frustrations persist. If aggressive inclinations do weaken after viewing a film or reading a book, this may mean only that the viewer was sufficiently distracted so that he forgot his frustrations and ceased stimulating himself to continued anger.

As we saw in the preceding chapter, the one investigation supposedly demonstrating a cathartic reduction of hostility through symbolic aggression (Feshbach, 1955) has not stood the test of replication, and its findings can be explained in other ways. But in addition to these negative results, other experiments to be reviewed in this chapter have yielded results directly contrary to the catharsis hypothesis.

*Effects on Attitudes, Beliefs, and Values.* Entertainment media do more than provide pleasure and symbolic gratification of suppressed desires. Mass communications also convey information about the external world. Children can learn a great deal from television, movies, and comics, including what other people are like and how to act toward them. In general, the media provide much of the information that a child should have in his task of learning to become a functioning member of his society.

However, the information television, radio, movies, and comic books bring to the child can also enhance the likelihood that he will behave in an aggressive and even lawless manner. Frequent portrayals of aggression on film or the printed page can adapt the impressionable observer to the idea of violent action. Seeing hostility so often, he may be less inclined to regard hostile behavior as "wrong." His attitude toward his own hostile urges is particularly likely to be affected. To return to the theoretical analysis of factors governing aggressive responses to media violence, the reader will recall that guilt and/or aggression anxiety can prevent the occurrence of overtly hostile behavior. Not surprisingly, the setting in which the fantasy violence takes place apparently can affect his interpretation of aggressive behavior generally and, therefore, determine the degree to which the youngster will feel guilty or anxious about his own hostile inclinations.

Such a finding was obtained by Albert (1957) in a study in which eight- to ten-year-old children were shown different versions of a western film. Three forms of this movie were constructed by changing the order in which some of the scenes were presented. In one condition the usual, stereotyped order was employed so that it appeared as if the hero had "won." In other words, the movie sanctioned the hero's aggression. Things were reversed in the second condition. Here, the organization of scenes made it seem as if the hero was shot and the villain had emerged victorious. Finally, in the third condition, no one gained the upper hand, and the aggressive conflict was left unresolved. A control group did not see any of these versions. The Rosenzweig P-F test was administered at the start and conclusion of the experiment as the measure of hostile tendencies.

The pattern of changes in extrapunitive hostility scores following the cowboy film can be readily understood if we assume (as was discussed in Chapter 4) that aggressive responses to projective tests can be effected by inhibitory tendencies. Such inhibitions, of course, are likely to be relatively weak if aggressive behavior is defined as morally correct. The hero's victory in condition 1 justified aggression to a certain extent, and therefore it is not surprising to see that this was the only condition in which there was an over-all increase in hostility scores (although the change was not significant statistically). Guilt-induced restraints against hostility may have weakened somewhat as a result of viewing the film.

The stereotyped movie apparently had the greatest effect upon the older children. Fourth graders witnessing the socially sanctioned aggression exhibited a significantly greater increase in extrapunitive hostility scores than either the younger children in this condition or the same-age children in the control condition, perhaps because the justification of aggression was more important to these older children.

There is a somewhat clearer demonstration of the influence of the context in which the fantasy aggression occurs in an experiment conducted by Berkowitz and Rawlings. In this study groups of male and female college students were assembled supposedly as part of a survey of student reactions to filmed violence. Before they were shown the scheduled movie scene, however, it was announced that someone else wanted to take a few minutes of their time to collect normative data on an intelligence test, and that this had nothing to do with the survey. This new person, a male graduate student, then distributed the brief IQ test to the group. His manner varied depending upon the condition to which the group had been assigned. He behaved in an insulting and thoroughly obnoxious fashion toward half of the groups, succeeding in arousing a good deal of anger toward him. He acted in a neutral fashion to the remaining groups.

The examiner left the room as soon as the test papers were completed and collected, and the original experimenter then introduced the film, saying they were to see a fight scene from a movie about a prizefighter. The introductory statement about the movie also varied with the experimental condition. A synopsis of the story was provided in each group, but half of the cases within each of the conditions created up to this point heard, in essence, that the protagonist was a downright scoundrel. They therefore presumably would conclude that the beating the protagonist would receive in the fight was *justified aggression*. The other subjects were given information much more sympathetic to the protagonist, and they supposedly would regard the punishment administered to him as *unjustified aggression*. A questionnaire was distributed to all of the subjects as soon as the nine-minute-long film had ended. Relevant items on this form indicated that all of the experimental manipulations had succeeded in creating the intended effects.

The findings again indicate that media violence is most likely to strengthen the audience's own hostile tendencies when the make-believe aggression seems justified. The angered students expressed the greatest hostility toward the test examiner on the final questionnaire after they had seen an "evil" person receive a deserved beating. Since there was relatively little sympathy for the movie protagonist in this condition (as was clearly demonstrated by one of the questionnaire items), this result essentially is analogous to that obtained by Albert; fantasy violence that can be justified or sanctioned by the audience evidently heightens the probability of overtly hostile actions by the audience.

As least three explanations may be offered for the Berkowitz-Rawlings findings.

1. As I already have proposed, the story context may have influenced the observer's interpretation of his own circumstances. Seeing morally proper aggressive behavior in the fantasy world, the observer may have become at least momentarily convinced that there was nothing "wrong" if he attacked his own frustrater.

2. The sight of the ethically unwarranted aggression may have aroused aggression anxiety, or perhaps made the audience aware of moral standards of conduct. Now conscious of "right" and "wrong" behavior, the socialized observer presumably felt the need to behave in a socially proper fashion. In other words, scenes of unjustified hostility decreased the likelihood of hostile actions by the audience.

3. The third possibility is that the justified aggression in the story somehow reminded the observer of the injuries *he* had received and

stirred him up to even stronger anger against his frustrater. Without any additional evidence we cannot choose among these alternatives, but the first two hypotheses seem to be more convincing.

Contrary to the findings in the Albert experiment (where no provocations were employed), justified fantasy aggression in the Berkowitz-Rawlings study did not increase the college students' unfriendliness toward the test examiner when they had not been insulted by him. The previous theoretical analysis of media violence suggests several reasons for this difference. For one, the Berkowitz-Rawlings subjects, being considerably older than Albert's third and fourth graders, undoubtedly were more likely to have discounted the movie scene as make-believe. That is, they established a somewhat greater differentiation between the fantasy and real-life worlds so that for them there was less generalization from the film to the audience's own situation. In addition, the older students probably had stronger inhibitory tendencies restraining the activation and operation of their own aggressive habits. Having stronger internal controls, they were less likely to become impulsively excited by what they saw.

But it should be remembered that the hostility-augmenting effect of filmed violence was relatively slight even in Albert's study. A plausible hypothesis can be derived if the two sets of findings can be combined: *Media aggression depicted as being justified has the greatest probability of leading to overt hostility when the audience is already angry, or is otherwise strongly predisposed to make aggressive responses, particularly if the observers are older, intellectually discriminating and controlled adults rather than children.*

More evidence obviously is needed before we can accept the thesis that the context in which the fantasy aggression occurs alters the individual's interpretation of his own hostile inclinations.[9] There is reason

[9] The experiment by Feshbach (1961) on the effects of viewing an aggressive movie briefly described in the preceding chapter appears to contradict the present analysis. As the reader will recall, Feshbach showed either an exciting prizefight scene or a more neutral scene to angered and nonangered male college students. Significant effects were found only among the angered men, as generally was the case in the Berkowitz-Rawlings investigation. However, contrary to this latter study, there seemed to be indications of a "catharsis" in Feshbach's insulted students viewing the fantasy aggression; there was a lower level of overt hostility expressed by the men shown the aggressive scene than by the men who had watched the neutral movie.

The Berkowitz-Rawlings findings cast serious doubt on Feshbach's catharsis interpretation of his results. The "purge" notion surely would predict a greater weakening of the instigation to aggression through watching justified aggression than through observing a scene of nonjustified hostility—but the opposite findings were obtained. Further research clearly is needed, but there still is no good evidence that the "aggressive drive" can be diminished by viewing fantasy aggression.

An experiment by Mussen and Rutherford (1961), published just as this footnote

to believe, however, that filmed stories can produce at least a short-lived change in children's perceptions of their environment. Emery (1959) found a significant increase in boys' feelings of being threatened by a powerful and hostile world after they had watched a so-called "adult western."

This type of changed outlook undoubtedly is only temporary for the majority of children seeing crime and violence depicted in TV, movies, and comic books. Most youngsters (we can hope) probably find relatively little reinforcement in the real world for the belief that the world is a hazardous place populated by evil beings. The media-induced perceptions usually weaken and give way under the more powerful impact of the child's dealings with his parents and friends.

However, television, movies, and comic books can have a lasting influence if (1) the themes presented in the communications media are repeated often enough and (2) the information imparted by the media is not clearly contradicted by other agencies (parents, peers, teachers, etc.). Indeed, not a few of the lessons the child learns from the screen or printed page may be supported, either explicitly or implicitly, by the statements and actions of his parents. Adults do not always frown on immorality. The child may see his parents occasionally approve illegal behavior, or hear them condone someone's minor violation of the law. Some fantasy crimes may then be regarded as permissible in the real world. Zajonc (1954) found that children often approve the actions of the fantasy heroes in the make-believe stories told by the media solely because these actions "work." For many youngsters a course of behavior is "right" because it enables the hero to reach his goal and not because of its conformity to moral standards. Moral infringements that may help them obtain what they want cannot be so bad, and their parents, frequently enough, will support this view. Any such ethical compromises advocated even indirectly by TV, movies, or magazines will find a receptive audience in many children in our society.[10]

---

was written, also has produced results contrary to Feshbach's catharsis hypothesis. First-grade school children displayed a reliably higher level of aggression on an oral projective test after watching an aggressive cartoon than after viewing a nonaggressive cartoon, whether they had been experimentally insulted or not.

[10] After this book went to press, Bandura (1962) reported an experiment demonstrating that nursery school children had a stronger tendency to imitate successful than unsuccessful adult aggression portrayed on a TV screen. (Successful aggression is aggression that "worked," that led to goal attainment.) The children also showed a greater preference for the successful than for the unsuccessful aggressor. Interestingly enough, when the youngsters were interviewed later it was found that many of them characterized the successful aggressor's actions in strongly negative terms. Such judgments—assuming they had been formed at the time the fantasy aggression was witnessed—nevertheless did not prevent the children from patterning themselves after the successful aggressor.

The mass media obviously may also be the child's major source of information about particular groups and, therefore, can exert some influence on his attitudes toward these groups. Peterson and Thurstone (1933) reported what probably are the best known demonstrations of such an attitude modification. School children were surveyed before and after seeing well-known silent films, such as "The Birth of a Nation" (which portrayed Negroes in an unfavorable light). The investigators found that even one exposure to some of the films resulted in a substantial attitude change apparently lasting over a considerable period of time. They also noted that continued exposure to movies dealing with similar topics could produce a cumulative effect.

These alterations in the favorability of the children's attitudes toward groups involved in the movies undoubtedly came about because their conceptions of the groups had changed. The communications media can change our expectations as to how members of given groups will behave, particularly if little is known about these groups beforehand. Siegel (1958) has shown that young children may form beliefs as to how certain people are likely to act in given situations from the stories they encounter in TV, movies, and books. In her study second-grade school children heard one of two versions of a previously prepared radio drama involving a taxi driver. In the story presented to the experimental group the driver resolved the dramatic conflict by means of physical aggression, while the control children heard this character adopt a nonaggressive solution to the same conflict. The next day the children were given a supposed achievement test in which they ostensibly were to demonstrate their ability by completing news stories from current editions of the local newspaper. Mrs. Siegel made sure that the children in her sample understood the "reality-reporting function of a newspaper"; i.e., in responding to the test the children presumably revealed what they actually supposed would happen. As she had predicted, the experimental children wrote more aggressive endings in the newspaper stories featuring taxi drivers than in the other stories, while such a difference did not arise in the control group. The former children also attributed more aggression to taxi drivers than did the controls but only when the situation depicted in the news story resembled that involved in the radio drama. They apparently had learned that taxi drivers are likely to become hostile in that type of setting.

*Relevance and Identification with the Fantasy Figures.* Relatively little is known about the particular qualities of the film or printed page that are most likely to incite aggressive behavior from the audience or alter its attitudes and values. However, one reasonable assumption is that the fantasy scenes will have the greatest impact when they are relevant to the observers' own circumstances. (I have already suggested that the instigational effect of media violence is a direct function of the association between the fantasy scene and the audience's real-life situation. Relevance certainly would affect this association.)

A witnessed event may be relevant to the viewers because it has a direct and immediate bearing on their own lives. Relevance also may be created, however, by the process of *identification*. Audience members may, in their thoughts, identify with, i.e., put themselves in the place of, characters appearing on the screen or in the book, so that the things happening to these characters seem to be happening to them. As Maccoby and Wilson (1957) described this phenomenon, the observers covertly match their own actions with those of the fantasy character with whom they identify.

What affects this identification process? Psychoanalytic writings deal at length with the determinants of identification, but one important factor probably is the perceived similarity between the character and the observer. Zander (1958, p. 108) reported an experiment in which youngsters' degree of identification with a "deep-sea-diver" storyteller was manipulated by leading them to believe the "diver" was more or less similar to them on certain biographical characteristics. Later, after the "diver" had told the story of his life, the children rated themselves on abilities totally unrelated to deep-sea diving. Those children who had identified with the storyteller were most likely to have been affected by his life story. They covertly matched their own self-image with what the "diver" had said about himself; if his life had been successful they were more favorable to themselves than if his life had been a failure.

Maccoby and Wilson (1957) hypothesized that identification with fantasy figures would influence the amount and nature of the material learned from observing a fantasy scene. The viewer, in putting himself in a particular story character's place, supposedly would have the best memory for that figure's actions and the things that had happened to him. This expectation was generally confirmed. When movies were shown to seventh-grade school children, it was found the youngsters identified with the like-sexed leading characters (according to their questionnaire responses) and that the boys also tended to identify with characters from their own social class. (The social-class data obtained from the girls were inadequate.) The viewers also had a tendency to remember somewhat better the words and actions of the figure with whom they identified.

However, similarity was not the only determinant of identification choice or of memory. As far as social class was concerned, the viewers identified most strongly with the fantasy character coming from the social class to which they aspired. This preferred character, we might say, was most relevant to the audience's needs. Similarly, the best-learned film content appeared to be most "need-relevant." Boys remembered aggressive content better than did the girls, provided the boy hero was the aggressor, while girls had the better memory for scenes depicting boy-girl interactions. In both cases, the children were most likely to remember that material of greatest relevance to their culturally defined roles.

Such learning of need- and role-relevant information may not become much apparent until much later. Maccoby (1959) also has suggested that children may covertly practice the actions portrayed in the communications media that are appropriate to some future status rather than the one they presently occupy. The little girl can see in the fantasy world of the screen or page how grown women dress and act, and not use this learning until she herself has matured.

The material attended to and remembered by the viewer has a particular cue value for this viewer. The material elicits thought responses from him so that it can be learned. Similarly, emotional responses may also be evoked. Fantasy material that is relevant to the observer's social role and needs, or that is especially significant to him because of his identification with a story character, can produce emotional reactions in him. Dysinger and Ruckmick (cited in Maccoby & Wilson, 1957, p. 86) found that movie scenes of conflict evoked a greater physiological reaction from boys than girls, again because aggressive material probably is more relevant to the former, but that romantic movie scenes produced stronger reactions in the girls. Relevance and identification, in other words, can affect not only what the audience learns from the communications medium, but also what it feels and, therefore, what actions the audience might take.

## Effects of the Media on Crime and Lawlessness

*Media Exposure and Crime Rates.* The preceding discussion of media violence seems to support the arguments raised by Wertham, Banay, and other critics of the mass-communications industry. All in all, the experimental research just reviewed indicates that the depiction of aggression in television and movies can incite aggressive behavior in the audience under certain conditions. If we were to extrapolate freely from some of these studies, such as the experiments by Bandura and by Lövaas, we might even expect to find definite delinquent trends among ardent TV- and movie-viewing children. Since aggression is a prominent feature of many shows, children who have a high degree of exposure to these media may exhibit a relatively high incidence of hostility themselves in imitation of the aggression they have witnessed. Survey research (in contrast to anecdotal case histories), however, has failed to uncover any evidence that television and films cause persistent aggressive lawlessness.

Shuttleworth and May (1933), in conducting one of the first of these studies, compared grade school students who attended the movies from four to five times a week on the average with a matched group of other youngsters who typically attended only about twice a month. Although the frequent moviegoers generally had somewhat poorer reputations with their teachers and peers, there were no significant differences between the two groups on a number of measures of moral conduct, such as honesty in out-of-school situations. More recently, Lewin (cited in Klapper, 1960, p. 151) found that twelve- and thirteen-year-old boys who were greatly interested in comic books were no more truant in school attendance, deficient in school achievement, or delinquent than other comparable boys who were less interested in these magazines.

Himmelweit et al. (1958) extended these negative results to television in their survey of British children. They did note that approximately one in four children reported fear and anxiety reactions to certain TV programs, but as far as lawlessness was concerned, "found no more aggressive, maladjusted, or delinquent behavior among viewers than among [their matched] controls" (as indicated by teachers' ratings and the children's responses to personality inventories). The English researchers' conclusion seems to summarize all of the findings in this area: "Seeing violence on television [or in any of the other communications media] is not likely to turn well-adjusted children into aggressive delinquents" (p. 215).

Such a statement should be stressed. Observers of the social scene all too frequently offer oversimplified explanations of human behavior, singling out particular villains as the sole or primary cause of complex social ills. Some years ago, Thrasher and Blumer failed to find any indications that movie attendance contributed to youthful crime rates and concluded that a simple cause and effect relationship does not prevail. Movies are not solely responsible for antisocial conduct (Charters, 1935, p. 13). No one "whipping boy" should receive the blame rightfully due to a host of agencies.

Nevertheless, the communications media have *some* influence on antisocial conduct. The media are not all black or all white. Himmelweit et al. have contended that children typically do not "translate television experience into action" except in extreme cases, but that even in such cases "the influence of television is small" (1958, p. 215). The present writer is not this optimistic. All that the empirical research in this area has done essentially is to minimize the persistent day-after-day influence of the mass media upon youthful behavior. Juvenile delinquency, or any other form of aggressive lawlessness, typically is an outgrowth of long-lasting determinants operating throughout the formative years. Juvenile delinquents are not like Minerva, emerging fully developed after just a short period of gestation; their personalities usually require years of development. The media apparently have only a minor role in governing this long-term socialization. However, they can arouse and shape *specific* acts of violence under certain conditions. The remaining section of this chapter will indicate what these conditions may be.

*Predisposition to Make Aggressive Responses.* While the evidence is far from unequivocal, most authorities are cautious in their estimates of the social damage done by the media. They generally believe that fantasy aggression elicits strong overt hostility only from youngsters who already have aggressive predispositions. Some writers, e.g., Wertham (1954), of course do not care to emphasize such possible limitations and maintain that TV, movies, or comic books might incite socially undesirable behavior from almost anyone, or at least from any child. But this is not a popular view. The experts tend to confine extreme media effects to only a small proportion of the audience (cf. Klapper, 1960). The theoretical analysis of aggressive behavior presented throughout this book also essentially favors the more restricted conception. Aggression, I have noted, typically arises when the individual (1) has experienced a recent frustration and perceives some stimulus associated with the frustrater and/or (2) responds to a relevant cue activating previously learned aggressiveness habits. But more than this, people in our society usually develop fairly strong inhibitions against displaying aggression. What all this means, then, is that only a small proportion of the audience is susceptible to aggressive influence; the predisposing conditions necessary for effective arousal probably are weak or absent in most of the people exposed to media aggression.

The previously cited experiments by Lövaas and by Bandura and his colleagues, seemingly demonstrating a fairly widespread tendency to imitate hostile actions depicted on film, do not really contradict such an analysis. The most parsimonious interpretation of Lövaas' findings, as was mentioned earlier, suggests that the movie had influenced only what the children preferred to see. They were not necessarily instigated to injure others. Similarly, the Bandura subjects who clearly imitated the hostile actions they observed were experimentally frustrated and therefore, it might be argued, were predisposed to make aggressive responses. Further, to add to the reasons for caution in generalizing the Lövaas-Bandura results, there probably were only weak inhibitions against aggression operating in these studies. Both investigations employed children, who undoubtedly were too young to have strong internal controls, and their targets were dolls, objects unlikely to arouse strong guilt or aggression anxiety if attacked.

These experiments cannot be dismissed entirely, however. They do indicate that filmed violence can have cue value for whatever aggressive tendencies already exist in the audience. Aggression portrayed on the screen or printed page can arouse aggressive responses from people inclined to make these responses.

Perhaps the clearest demonstration of the importance of predispositions to aggression can be seen in the previously reported experiment by Berkowitz and Rawlings. As the reader will recall, this study showed that filmed hostility was most likely to incite aggressive responses when the fantasy hostility seemed justifiable to the audience. In actuality, however, it was the experimentally frustrated subjects who exhibited the strongest hostile reactions under the sanctioning of the filmed aggression. The film-elicited overt hostility apparently was most intense when the subjects' guilt-induced restraints against aggression presumably had also been weakened by the movie, and the subjects were ready to make hostile responses because they had been angered.

This type of influence is analogous to one of the most frequently observed effects of exposure to the mass media. Children often get ideas as to what they should do in their games from material they see in books, television, or the movies. Adults interested in obtaining certain goals sometimes learn the actions instrumental to goal attainment from the media. The young woman who wants to look attractive learns about makeup and dress, while the young man aspiring to be the successful young executive sees what to wear and how to act. *In each of these cases there is a drive state in operation* (the child wants to play, the adults want to achieve a certain appearance), *and the communications media shape the nature of the behavior occurring in the attempts to satisfy these drives.*

But *television, movies, magazines, and books can also arouse drives.* The communications industry is often accused of inciting crime and lawlessness by exciting desires for easy money, luxury, and sex, as well as by suggesting antisocial methods for gratifying these drives. From the present writer's viewpoint *the media are most likely to instigate a particular course of behavior* (in addition to shaping the nature of this behavior) *when they provide cues activating previously learned habits.*

According to this formulation, then, people with strong aggressiveness habits are prone to show relatively strong aggressive reactions to media violence. All of us have learned to respond aggressively to certain stimuli (e.g., the sight of someone we regard as a frustrater). Cues on the movie screen associated with these aggression-provoking stimuli will therefore also have a tendency to arouse hostile reactions. Similar association processes have been discussed earlier in this book, but the point to be made here is this: Highly aggressive personalities have learned to respond aggressively to many different cues. They interpret many objects as threatening or, more generally, frustrating and are relatively quick to use hostility to gain their ends or as a source of pleasure. Since many things incite hostility in them, there is a relatively wide variety of media situations that also are capable of evoking aggressive responses from them (i.e., there are many media situations associated with the broad range of situations to which they have learned to become hostile). There is another important characteristic of hostile personalities that should also be mentioned. Not only do they show frequent aggressive responses but these reactions typically are unusually strong. Thus, the highly aggressive youngster will respond often and in an extreme manner to the relevant cues provided by the media.

Newspaper stories again can be used as an illustration. Schramm et al., for example, have reported the case of two California teen-agers arrested for sniping at pedestrians with a BB pistol from a car. When they were caught after having shot two people, the boys said they got the idea from a television program (1961, p. 164). These youngsters probably had fairly strong aggressiveness habits which were readily activated by the fantasy violence they had witnessed and then gave rise to unusually intense hostile reactions. Quite clearly, to contradict Himmelweit and her colleagues, television experience may be translated into action—if the viewers (1) have strong hostile habits, (2) possess weak inhibitions against aggression, and (3) associate the TV setting with their real-life circumstances.

There is another consideration we should also keep in mind when contemplating the potential effects of media violence: the nature of the audience. An earlier section of this chapter has reported that frustrated children—who presumably have hostile inclinations—are particularly attracted to programs featuring aggressive content. This relationship can be extended to people with delinquent or criminal histories. Bailyn (1959) noted that boys with a strong liking for "aggressive hero" content in the pictorial media seemed to resemble the portrait of the juvenile delinquent drawn by the Gluecks (1950). More important, in their pioneering investigation of movies and conduct in the early 1930s, Blumer and Hauser found that crime movies were especially popular with people having criminal records, while Hoult, more recently, has reported that juvenile delinquents read a greater number of comic books dealing with crime and violence than did nondelinquents, although this difference was not always significant (cited in Klapper, 1960, p. 153).

Such findings have profound implications. Those people who are most strongly attracted to media featuring aggressive content evidently possess qualities resulting in their being particularly susceptible to influence by this type of content. A comment made by a prominent educational researcher seems appropriate here. After reviewing the studies by Blumer and his colleagues, W. W. Charters remarked: "To say that the movies are solely responsible for anti-social conduct, delinquency, or crime is not valid. To assert contrariwise that delinquents and criminals happen to frequent the movies and are not affected by them is clearly indefensible" (1935, p. 13). If nothing else, lawbreakers can (and often do) learn criminal techniques from the media. Indeed, from their point of view the lessons provided by TV, movies, and books can be very profitable. Blumer has observed that delinquents may learn such things as how to open a safe by the feel of the dial, force open a house window or a car door, put burglar alarms out of commission, burglarize a house, and pick pockets, merely by going to the movies (Charters, 1935, p. 54).

The motion pictures in this case govern the exact nature of the lawless, aggressive responses made by people prone to antisocial conduct. All the media can exert this type of influence. They often tell the delinquent, criminal, or aggressive child just how to go about satisfying his already existing illegal or hostile desires. But TV, movies, and books may also do more than shape behavior. Research and theory suggest that the media can also instigate such drives.

*The Association between the Fantasy and Real-life Settings.* If this analysis is correct, someone might ask, why don't the media evoke violence more frequently? Why is the provocation restricted to such a small number of incidents? There are, I believe, at least two principal answers to these questions. For one thing, the instigational effects of the media (i.e., the drives they arouse in contrast to the neutral information they provide) probably do not last too long. The aggressive inclinations evoked by cues from the screen or printed page usually weaken and then vanish as the individual enters different stimulus situations. The duration of these elicited hostile tendencies undoubtedly is in direct ratio to their intensity, so that the aggressive effects of media violence are short-lived except when the observer has strong aggressive habits (as presumably is the case in those boys arrested for translating TV violence into action). Even the information acquired from the media can be forgotten or contradicted by other sources.

The second and primary reason, somewhat related to the first, involves the degree of association between the scenes depicted on the screen or page and the observer's own real-life circumstances. As was mentioned earlier, fantasy violence can activate aggressiveness habits only to the extent that there is an association between the make-believe setting and the situations in which these habits were learned. Further, in most cases when the habits are aroused they operate only in "low gear," and do not go into full force, effecting overt behavior, unless there are relevant cues in the postfantasy settings. We saw this type of phenomenon in the newspaper report of the boys who imitated the knife fight they had witnessed on TV.

These all-important associations between fantasy and life vary in strength from situation to situation and from individual to individual. One of the most important determinants of this associative strength, of course, is the degree to which the observer discounts what he sees as "not true." When a person realizes that the figures moving on the television screen are paid actors portraying fictitious roles, he makes a discrimination differentiating the make-believe setting from the observer's own situation. As a consequence, the association is weakened if not abolished altogether, and the observer is relatively unaffected by the images before him.

Such discounting reactions are much more frequent in older children and adults than they are in young children. Youngsters, as every parent knows, often become involved in the dramatic scenes flashed before them. They become what Blumer has termed "emotionally possessed," identifying with the plot and characters, forgetting their surroundings, losing control of their feelings and thoughts and, as a result, easily aroused emotionally (Charters, 1935, pp. 38–43). The discriminations necessary to prevent this media-induced emotional arousal generally come with age and parental training. Dysinger and Ruckmick showed such changes with age in an investigation of children's physiological reactions to motion pictures. Scenes of danger, for example, produced the greatest effect on the youngest age group (from six to twelve years), with the magnitude of the reaction declining steadily with maturity. Romantic and erotic scenes, on the other hand, usually evoked the greatest reaction in the twelve- to eighteen-year-old group—probably because this material did not have any significance (i.e., cue value) to the younger children—but here again, older people seemed to be less affected physiologically. The more mature observers evidently were more prone to discount what they saw and therefore were not as strongly aroused (Charters, 1935, pp. 25–27).

Emotional possession, producing intense attention to the communications medium, could well enhance the learning of the information conveyed by the story. But it probably also is a reflection of the degree to which the medium has succeeded in instigating response tendencies in the observer. The intensely emotionally aroused person can translate his TV, movie, or comic-book experience into action if his inhibitions are weak. Older members of the audience, being more detached, generally have only weak associations (if any associations exist) between the make-believe world of the medium and their own circumstances and thus are usually not instigated to action by the fantasy story.

Young children, however, are not necessarily the only ones to make inadequate differentiations between the fantasy and real worlds. According to Bailyn's (1959) observations, the somewhat aggressive and rebellious boys who are particularly attracted to media material featuring aggressive content may be relatively likely to accept what they see as true and real. They show a tendency to oversimplified, stereotyped thought patterns that readily accommodate make-believe stories. The fantasy world does impinge upon them to a relatively great degree and, consequently, if the conditions are right, can excite action.

## SUMMARY

There is a good deal of controversy and greater uncertainty as to the possible effects of the heavy concentration of crime and violence in the mass media. Some authorities insist that this dosage of fantasy aggression can be extremely harmful to many children, inciting and conditioning them to antisocial modes of conduct; other specialists take the opposite view, contending that children and adults can obtain a socially beneficial cathartic release for their own hostile inclinations through identifying with the make-believe aggressor. Most specialists, however, are relatively cautious in their evaluations of media aggression. Extreme aggression or anxiety reactions do occur in response to scenes of violence in TV, movies, and comic books, they acknowledge, but they also generally agree that such extreme reactions happen only if the individual is already strongly aggressive or anxious.

Quantitative research consistently indicates that frustrated children and young adults are particularly likely to make heavy use of the pictorial media: television, movies, and comic books. But these socially thwarted individuals also do more than seek an escape from harsh reality in withdrawing to the world of fantasy; they frequently look for particular kinds of satisfactions, and so they seem to be especially drawn to media content featuring crime and lawlessness. On the basis of these findings we can hypothesize that people with strong aggressive predispositions will display a relatively strong liking for aggression in TV, movies, and comics. There is no evidence, however, that their hostile predispositions are weakened by viewing fantasy aggression. If anything, experimental results suggest that scenes of violence depicted on the screen will have a much greater tendency to incite children to later aggressive acts than to "drain" them of their aggressive "energy."

By and large, there are no convincing data that the mass media can be included among the major determinants of delinquency and crime. Aggressive lawlessness usually is the outgrowth of many interacting factors operating throughout much of the individual's formative period, and the communications media apparently have only a minor part in this long-term socialization process. Under certain conditions, however, they can influence specific actions in specific situations.

Experimental findings point to at least three different ways in which television and movies (and perhaps comic books as well) can affect behavior: (1) through shaping the nature of the aggressive responses made by people already instigated to behave in a hostile manner; the delinquent or criminal can learn techniques for fulfilling his lawless desires through observing scenes of criminal activity in the media; (2) through instigating hostile behavior; the fantasy aggression may provide cues arousing previously learned aggressiveness habits; (3) through affecting the individual's interpretation of his own hostile inclinations; the story context within which the fantasy aggression is portrayed may determine whether the observer will regard his own hostile wishes as being morally justified or not.

In addition, information imparted by the media may also modify the observer's attitudes toward specific groups, particularly if he knows relatively little about them and, therefore, if nothing else, can affect the observer's likelihood of displacing hostility onto these groups.

According to the present writer's theoretical analysis, the probability that media aggression will evoke hostile behavior in later situations is a direct function of (1) the strength of the observer's aggressiveness habits, (2) the intensity of the hostile tendencies elicited within the observer by the fantasy violence, (3) the degree of association between the fantasy situation and (*a*) the situations in which the hostile habits were learned and (*b*) the post-fantasy setting, and (4) the intensity of the guilt and/or aggression anxiety also aroused by the media violence.

Aggressive scenes in television, movies, and comic books excite only a small number of extremely aggressive incidents because these predisposing factors are weak or nonexistent. Thus, only a small proportion of the audience is easily instigated to aggression because of prior anger arousal or the possession of strong aggressive habits. There also is a strong tendency to discount the observed fantasy situations as "make-believe" or "not true," weakening the necessary association between the fantasy setting and the observer's real-life circumstances.

The present analysis obviously has important social implications. While it may be true that television, movies, and comic books will excite antisocial conduct from only a relatively small number of people, we can also say that the heavy dosage of violence in the media heightens the probability that someone in the audience will behave aggressively in a later situation. This might not be so bad if the observer indulging in the fantasy aggression were the only person to suffer. He had chosen to expose himself to the influence of TV, movies, and comic books. Unfortunately, however, the observer instigated to carry out hostile acts usually injures an innocent bystander.

# chapter 10

# The Operation and Development
## of Aggressive Personalities

In this chapter we finally come to the matter probably of greatest concern to those who must deal with aggression regularly: the problem of aggressive personalities. Many people, adults as well as youngsters, exhibit frequent hostility. Some are quickly angered and lash out explosively at those they believe have injured them. Other people seem to take sadistic delight in inflicting injury, while still others are almost constantly carping, criticizing, or insulting—aggressing against more or less innocent bystanders apparently without consciously realizing what they are doing. Anyone who would understand human behavior must be able to explain why these people act as they do. How did these aggressive personalities develop, and why do they perform hostile acts in some situations and not in others?

The present chapter will attempt to answer these questions. Relatively little will be said of extreme examples of aggressive personalities, such as the pathological killer; and our discussion of crime, suicides, and homicides is reserved for Chapter 11. Rather, by focusing on the more usual instances of persistent hostility—for example, boys judged to be troublemakers by their teachers—we will be able to make use of the available quantitative data in formulating an analytic scheme that may then, perhaps, be extended to extreme cases.

## THE OPERATION OF THE AGGRESSIVE PERSONALITY

### Aggressiveness as a Habit

*Aggressiveness as a Latent Disposition.* The conception of aggressive personalities to be spelled out here has been anticipated in some of the earlier chapters. The section on catharsis, for example, proposed that frequent aggressive behavior can be regarded as arising from aggressiveness habits and that such habits may be strengthened by whatever rewards the attacker receives through injuring others. Similarly, in analyzing the effects of television and movie violence, I suggested that the hostile acts depicted on the screen can arouse aggressiveness habits within the viewers and thereby lead to aggressive behaviors in a later situation if appropriate aggression-evoking cues are present on the later occasion. The fantasy aggression presumably would not give rise to the subsequent hostile action if the audience lacked strong aggressiveness habits.

This formulation does not picture the characteristically hostile person as having a storehouse of "aggressive energy" pent up within him. To put it another way, the frequently aggressive individual is not always angry; he does not possess a constantly operating "aggressive drive" which, when not revealed in overt behavior, is still active "unconsciously." What he does have is a predisposition to be readily aroused. He is relatively quick to respond aggressively to suitable cues because of his prior learning experiences and probably will not perform aggressive actions in the absence of such cues. His hostile behavior, when it is not precipitated by a recent frustration, stems from the activation of a habit by an appropriate stimulus.

An increasing number of writers in the field of personality theory have advanced somewhat similar propositions. In their work on the achievement motive, for example, McClelland and his colleagues (McClelland, Atkinson, Clark, & Lowell, 1953) suggested that the number of achievement associations the individual gives to TAT cards is a function of the cues in the situation (including those in his thought processes and everyday environment), cues specifically introduced by the experimenter, and those in the TAT pictures. More recently, Atkinson (1954) maintained that the "need achievement" scores derived from responses to TAT cards are significantly related to performance primarily when subjects believe the performance is instrumental to the attainment of some self- or other-imposed label of excellence. The motive is a latent state put into operation by environmental cues (e.g., instructions that performance on the given task can lead to a sense of achievement).

Scores on paper-and-pencil instruments assessing an individual's characteristic level of anxiety apparently are also related to the number or intensity of anxious actions largely when such performances occur in the presence of anxiety-evoking cues (e.g., threats). Taylor, the developer of one of the most widely known of such tests, the Manifest Anxiety Scale, reported (1956) a considerable body of evidence indicating that "MAS scores reflect different potentialities for anxiety arousal" rather than a "chronic emotional state."

Two investigations demonstrate how aggression-evoking cues can affect hostile behavior whether the people involved are clearly frustrated or not. As I mentioned in Chapter 2, Weatherley (1962) found that the anger created by an experimenter's deliberate insults did not give rise to a high level of aggressive TAT responses unless there were relatively many aggression-eliciting cues on the test cards and the subjects had comparatively weak restraints against hostility. Kagan (1956) obtained essentially similar findings in a study involving characteristic rather than frustration-reactive aggression. He gave cards (like those used in the TAT) to boys judged to be either high or low in customary aggressiveness. Some cards had a strong "picture pull" for hostile themes, i.e., they had a relatively strong cue value for hostile responses, while other cards contained few aggressive cues and generally elicited few aggressive themes. The two groups of children gave approximately the same number of hostile responses to the low-cue cards; the highly aggressive boys, we might say, did not demonstrate their typical hostility in the low-cue situation. Habitual aggressiveness was related to the frequency of TAT aggression in the case of the high-cue cards, however. The extremely hostile boys displayed their usually strong aggressiveness only when there were aggression-eliciting stimuli before them.

*A Stimulus-response Analysis of Learned Aggressiveness.* Generally speaking, personality psychologists have emphasized the importance of situational cues in activating the personality determinants of behavior only since the 1950s. However, a theoretical analysis published some years ago can help us understand the nature and operation of at least some of these determinants, particularly those governing habitual aggressiveness. Leonard Doob, one of the authors of *Frustration and Aggression,* suggested (1947) that attitudes can be viewed in stimulus-response terms as habits having drive properties. Putting it briefly, the individual with a particular attitude toward a given class of objects, according to Doob, has learned to make particular internal responses upon seeing these objects or stimuli associated with them. The internal responses, in turn, produce the stimuli evoking the behavioral tendencies. Thus, a person who has a negative attitude toward, say, Turks would habitually respond in a particular way to the sight of these people (e.g., he might automatically label the people—"Those are Turks"— then think, "They are strange"). These ideational responses give rise to an unpleasant emotional state within the individual which elicits, in this case, avoidance behaviors. Learning operates at two places in such a theoretical chain of events: in affecting the first response to the external cue (the attitude object), "Turks," and then determining the reaction to the internal stimuli arising from this initial response.

Many aggressive personalities can be analyzed in a similar manner. We can say the *habitually hostile person is someone who has developed a particular attitude toward large segments of the world about him. He has learned to interpret ( or categorize) a wide variety of situations and/or people as threatening or otherwise frustrating to him. Anger is aroused when these interpretations are made, and the presence of relevant cues—stimuli associated with the frustrating events—then evokes the aggressive behavior. In many instances the anger seems to become "short-circuited" with continued repetition of the sequence so that the initial thought responses alone elicit hostile behavior.*

The perception of a frustration is not necessary in arousing hostile inclinations, however. As Chapter 2 pointed out, aggressive responses can become functionally connected to other drive states. Some people have learned to make hostile actions in striving for nonaggressive ends. To use the illustration employed earlier, a boy may learn that his hostile actions often bring him the attention he desires. He may then come to perform aggressive responses whenever relevant cues (signs of neglect or indifference in important people around him) arouse his desire for attention. The instigating sequence in this case might be as follows: He responds to the external cues with the thoughts, "No one is paying attention to me. I must get their attention." An "attention motive" is aroused, and this produces the hostility in the presence of suitable "releaser cues," the sight of appropriate people who could give him the attention he wants. Findings in a study by Bandura (1960) to be discussed later suggest that the hostile actions of many nondelinquent but extremely aggressive boys may originate in some such process.

We also will see later in this chapter that nonfrustrating experiences can play an important part in the learning of aggressive behavior. Parents sometimes serve as aggressive models for their children. By giving their youngsters an aggressive person to imitate, they in essence teach their children that hostility is often correct behavior outside the home. The hostile adult has defined aggression as the appropriate way of reacting to particular situations. Implicitly or explicitly, an aggressive father may teach his son to respond to people merely as irrational obstacles to be shoved aside if they get in his way. Copying his father, this is the way the son does think of people, and such perceptions readily give rise to aggressive behavior. But whatever the intervening thought reactions might be, Doob's basic model seems to be applicable even to boys learning to be aggressive by imitating their fathers. *The aggressive adult models have taught the children to make the kinds of implicit responses to certain cues which arouse hostile inclinations within them.* The presence of appropriate releaser cues, I would then say, either the arousing objects or other stimuli associated with them, leads to the performance of aggressive acts.

*Aggressiveness as a Trait.* The reader familiar with the history of personality theory will recognize the present scheme as a trait analysis of aggressiveness. The hostile person can indeed be regarded as possessing a strong aggressive trait. Gordon Allport has defined a "trait" as a condition of the individual which (1) "renders many stimuli functionally equivalent" and then (2) "initiates and guides consistent (equivalent) forms of . . . behavior" (1937, p. 295). Both parts of Allport's definition are included within the conception I·have just outlined. The habitually hostile person's first reactions to external cues "render many stimuli functionally equivalent." He has learned to categorize a wide variety of objects or events in fairly similar terms—for example, as being frustrating to him. He then behaves aggressively over a range of objectively different situations.

## Consistency of Aggressive Behavior

Observations of boys between eight and eleven years of age suggest that the characteristically extremely hostile youngster does indeed often respond in much the same manner to different situations (Dittman & Goodrich, 1961). Hyperaggressive boys at a clinic exhibited a much smaller variety of actions over a number of different situations than did matched normal children. The aggressive boys apparently were much more likely to regard the various settings as being essentially alike and therefore behaved in pretty much the same way from one occasion to the next.

Presumably because of this tendency to make similar ideational and affective responses to somewhat different stimulus objects, the highly aggressive person should exhibit a good deal of consistency in his hostile behavior. We are not surprised to find correlations between indices of hostility in one situation and similar measures obtained in another objectively comparable situation (e.g., Yarrow, 1948; Levin & Sears, 1956). Thus, Jersild and Markey (1935) observed that children who had relatively many conflicts in nursery school also tended to be fairly aggressive a year later in kindergarten. More impressive is the evidence of a correlation over situations seeming (to the outsider) to have little in common. Such consistency is found when scores on a psychological test successfully predict behavior in another nontest setting (e.g., Mussen & Naylor, 1954) or when a test appears to elicit the kinds of emotional responses probably affecting behavior in the nontest situations. In this last regard, Funkenstein, King, and Drolette reported that men reacting to experimental frustrations with aggression directed against others generally had fewer signs of aggression anxiety or guilt in their TAT stories than did men displaying anxiety or intrapunitive reactions to the thwartings (1957, pp. 216–219).

Projective tests provide behavior samples. Performance on such tests is representative of the individual's behavior in other settings to the extent that the same kinds of cues are perceived in both the test and nontest situations. As we saw in Chapter 4, inhibitions evoked in a person's usual social environment may also become manifest in his reactions to a personality test (although projective tests often elicit only relatively weak restraints).

Two kinds of generalization processes are involved in behavioral consistency of the sort just described. For one, there is *stimulus generalization* in which the individual responds in somewhat the same manner to different stimuli. The highly aggressive person tends to equate a relatively wide variety of people and then displays similar reactions to these stimuli. But there also is *response generalization;* the actions themselves often show some variation although they remain aggressive in nature (see the discussion of response generalization in Chapter 5).

MacKinnon (1938) uncovered instances of both stimulus and response generalization in his well-known study of the violation of moral prohibitions. College graduates required to solve difficult problems were given an opportunity to cheat while the investigator (unknown to the subjects) observed them from behind a one-way screen. The people who violated the social code against cheating generally were much more aggressive during the frustrating examination period than were the nonviolators. The violators' cheating was an attack upon the examiner and also, in a sense, upon society as a whole; but they also were more likely to have expressed verbal aggression against the problems and physical aggression against the inanimate objects in the room. In other words, the violators exhibited a greater range in both the objects and form of their aggression.

## Factors Affecting Behavioral Consistency

Most of the investigators seeking to test the utility of the trait conception of personality have looked for evidence of behavioral consistency (cf. G. W. Allport, 1937). They have attempted to determine whether an individual who is honest in one situation will also tend to be honest in other settings and whether measures of punctuality are correlated from one occasion to the next. These correlational studies, however, are usually based upon an overly simplified analysis of the trait concept. The same response tendencies are not necessarily revealed in every situation. Whether a person behaves at time $B$ as he had at time $A$ is, among other things, a function of the cues existing in the situations, i.e., how the individual perceives the two settings. Prior learning experiences can affect the nature of these perceptions.

*Prior Rewards and Punishments for Aggression.* Research described in earlier sections of this book, particularly in Chapter 4, has shown how the person's past history can determine the consistency of his aggressive behavior. If his parents and friends have continually rewarded his aggression, he probably will not regard his hostile behavior as being morally reprehensible or very dangerous for him and therefore will have relatively weak restraints against aggression in most situations. Frequent punishment for aggression, on the other hand, may lead to anticipations of punishment for displaying hostility on most—but not all—occasions, giving rise to periodic inhibitions against aggression.

R. R. Sears (1951b) has offered a similar analysis. After first determining that doll-play aggressiveness was only negligibly related to hostility in nursery school play throughout an entire sample of forty preschool children, Sears and his colleagues subdivided the sample for further analysis in terms of the degree to which the children's mothers had punished aggression. Consistency was now revealed in the mildly and moderately punished groups. For these children, the more aggression they exhibited in doll play, the more hostile they were during nursery school activities. The severely punished children, however, did not show any correspondence between doll play and nursery aggressiveness; they displayed a higher level of aggression in the fantasy situation where inhibitions were weak than in the more realistic nursery setting. Lesser (1952) obtained the same sort of results in a study employing a thematic projective test. Aggressive responses to TAT-like pictures were directly associated with reputation among peers for overt aggressiveness for a group of elementary school boys whose mothers had indicated they were relatively supportive of aggression. On the other hand, the correlation between these two aggression measures was negative in the case of children whose mothers had said they discouraged aggression.

In both of these investigations, then, the intensity of a child's fantasy aggression often did not correspond to the level of overt aggression he exhibited in social situations when his parents had generally punished his hostile behavior. He apparently inhibited overt aggression when he anticipated punishment for such actions. Having been punished often in the past, he evidently was likely to expect punishment in the present.

The hostility-inhibiting effects of punishment are not ever-present, however. As I indicated in Chapter 3, the parent who punishes his child's aggression (or any other form of behavior) only causes this behavior to be suppressed rather than eliminated altogether. The child will repeat the given action (e.g., aggression) on some future occasion when punishment is not anticipated. Such a phenomenon has been demonstrated with rats and with human beings. In one animal study, for example, rats who had been the losers in staged bouts—and who, therefore, had experienced relatively severe punishment—were found to make fewer aggressive responses the day after the fight than before to both the winning and other rats. However, contact with a persistently inoffensive rat completely restored the average loser's aggressions (Seward, 1946). The animal's inhibitions against hostile acts probably had weakened when punishment was no longer anticipated. Chasdi and Lawrence (1955) obtained essentially the same results with nursery school children. Youngsters who had been admonished for displaying aggression in the course of their doll play at first decreased in the frequency of such disapproved behavior but then showed a rise in hostile acts when it became clear that no more punishment would be forthcoming.

More will be said of the effects of punishment later in this chapter. The important point to make now is that parental punishment for aggression can lead to inconsistent aggressiveness on the part of the child. He does not necessarily expect punishment for such behavior on every occasion. Indeed, parental punishment for aggression may even lead to a heightened likelihood that the child will behave aggressively in situations distinctly different from the home (Chasdi & Lawrence, 1955; Sears et al., 1957; Bandura & Walters, 1959; Eron, 1960).

*Situational Arousal of Motives Incompatible with Aggression.* Physical punishment, of course, is not the only unpleasant consequence of socially disapproved behavior. A person can be rejected by his friends if he engages in actions they frown upon. Knowing this, he may restrain his hostility in order to avoid incurring their disapproval. Situational cues also are important in this regard. Since aggression is generally frowned on in our middle-class society, the person who is preoccupied with maintaining pleasant interpersonal relationships should tend to inhibit his hostile inclinations. But he is not always concerned with maintaining or enhancing his popularity with other people. Gordon and Cohn (1961) reported that preschool children whose affiliation desires were *not* aroused by the experimenter exhibited a rise in fantasy aggression (from the first to the second session of doll interviews), while such an increase did not occur in the children whose affiliation needs were activated experimentally. The former youngsters, not made to be concerned about their social relationships, apparently had only relatively weak restraints against aggression in the second fantasy situation.

People with strong affiliation needs apparently are generally likely to avoid aggressive behavior. Thus, Bandura et al. (1960) found that psychotherapists rated by their supervisors as having relatively intense desires for social approval were prone to avoid dealing with their patients' hostile remarks, whether the hostility was directed toward themselves or others. As I have said earlier, these people do not necessarily possess an ever-active affiliative drive. Having a strong need for affiliation means they have a low threshold and a high amplitude of response to affiliation cues. They are easily aroused by signs of potential social approval or disapproval and, when aroused, typically react fairly intensely. The psychotherapists rated as having strong social approval needs probably had these desires activated fairly often, and so they were relatively consistent in their avoidance of aggressive behavior. Allison and Hunt (1959) also have presented some evidence that is pertinent here. Subjects presumably strongly oriented toward avoiding social disapproval tended to deny they would react aggressively to frustrations, whether these thwartings were "reasonable" or "unreasonable." In contrast, subjects less interested in always placing themselves in the best possible social light were readier to admit that they would become hostile after an "unreasonable" frustration. Restraints against aggression evidently were operative more often in the former, highly socially concerned group than in the people typically having less of a desire for social approval.

Desires for social approval or affiliation are not the only motives opposing aggressive behavior. Since hostility is so generally prohibited, the individual who engages in such disapproved behavior stands to lose whatever benefits he customarily gains from other people, whether this is friendship or aid in coping with his problems. Rejection sometimes means help will not be forthcoming, and so the person with relatively intense dependency needs will often hide his anger. But the hostility-restraining effects of dependency motivation also are contingent upon situational arousal. Beller (1959) showed that children's dependency strivings increased under a "dependency-stress" condition created by an adult's reduced and inconsistent availability. The more adult help was not forthcoming, the more these particular children seemed to want help from the inconsistent adult. In trying to get this desired aid, furthermore, the youngsters attempted not to offend the adult, and they refrained from acting destructively. The stronger the signs of dependency-need arousal in the child under dependency stress, the less destructive aggression he displayed. Behavioral manifestations of dependency were not associated with reduced aggression in a nonstress situation.

Blocking particular goal-directed activity frequently heightens the instigation to that activity, at least for a short period of time. Thus, the frustration of dependency strivings temporarily increases the incidence of dependency behavior in many youngsters (Beller & Haeberle, 1959). However, as the thwarting continues, the frustration-engendered drive may weaken and other response tendencies become more dominant. These latter tendencies will take over more rapidly, the weaker the predisposition to the frustrated activity. In the Beller and Haeberle experiment, characteristically highly dependent children maintained their dependency behavior longer than did the habitually less dependent children as the dependency deprivation persisted. The thwarted children previously judged to have only weak dependency needs tended to exhibit aggressive behavior much more quickly. Their weak instigation to dependency apparently weakened fairly rapidly in the face of the continued dependency frustration, and the aggressive actions were performed.

In many of the studies just described, the cues eliciting the hostility-inhibiting tendencies were located in the external situation. For example, the experimenter aroused the affiliation needs restraining the expression of hostility in the Gordon and Cohn investigation, while the frustrating adult elicited the dependency motivation in the Beller experiments. However, data first mentioned in Chapters 4 and 8 suggest that the aggressive inclinations evoked in a person can in themselves sometimes lead to inhibitions against aggression. The intensity of the aggression anxiety and/or guilt produced in the individual following anger arousal often is in direct ratio to the strength of his aggressive tendencies, although probably only to the extent that he anticipates disapproval from himself or others for displaying hostility. Consistent with such a proposition, Berkowitz and Holmes (1960) found that the most severely provoked women in their study who expressed the strongest volume of aggression against the anger instigator seemed to be more concerned later with making amends to her than were any of the other subjects. Similarly, the experimentally angered men in the Thibaut and Coules (1952) study manifesting the strongest hostility toward the instigator were also most likely to want to cease participating in the study as if they had the strongest desire to leave the anxiety-producing situation. As these researchers had hypothesized, "internalized tendencies to avoid aggression increase . . . sharply" as hostile inclinations increase in intensity (p. 774).

Such aggression-induced restraints against aggression also affect the persistence of hostile behavior. Some people with relatively strong predispositions to aggressive behavior may actually display inordinately intense hostility on one occasion and then only fairly weak aggression soon afterward (cf. Berkowitz, 1960c), perhaps because their first hostile responses had provoked anxiety and/or guilt (Hokanson, 1961b).

The material just reviewed provides reasons for behavioral inconsistency. Basically, people do not act in the same manner from one occasion to the next because the stimuli governing their actions are not constant across situations. Anger may or may not be aroused; aggression-eliciting cues may be present or not; and situational stimuli may vary in the degree to which they activate motives incompatible with aggressive behavior. The trait concept when viewed from this approach does not and cannot demand unchanging behavior. *A personality trait as a habit involves,* in the words of John Dewey (cited in G. W. Allport,

1937, p. 291), a *"special sensitiveness or accessibility to certain classes of stimuli."* Traits or habits do not necessarily mean incessant repetition of given forms of behavior.

## Characteristics Associated with Individual Differences in Aggressiveness

If we really are to understand the operation and development of aggressive personalities, we must know more than that they possess strong aggressiveness habits. We also have to know which (if any) features of the hostile individual's constitution and personality facilitate the development of such habits and what characteristics help determine the frequency, intensity, and form of his aggressive actions. In general, how does the extremely hostile person differ from the person who rarely exhibits aggression?

*Constitutional Characteristics.* Genetic factors appear to be related to differences in aggressiveness both within and between many species of the animal kingdom. Hall and Klein (1942) observed the fighting behavior of rats under four different conditions: when thirsty and without water; when the thirsty animals were given a water bottle from which only one could drink at a time; after the male rats had been deprived of the company of females for several days; and finally under normal laboratory conditions. Many of the animals behaved consistently throughout the four tests. "Fighters remained fighters and pacifists remained pacifists despite altered test circumstances." Differences in aggressiveness also were fairly stable over a three-month period, a considerable portion of the rats' life-span. Hall suggested that the consistency in aggressiveness was probably due to the animals' genetic inheritance. Rats bred to be fearless in a strange environment were more aggressive than animals bred for timidity.

Genetic factors may operate to influence an animals' readiness to fight in a number of ways, but one possible avenue is through governing the relative intensities of the anger and fear reactions to frustration. According to some authorities (e.g., Funkenstein et al., 1957), a relatively excessive production of norepinephrine in the body is related to, and may even cause, outward-directed aggressive reactions to thwartings, while the production of an excessive amount of epinephrine supposedly is associated with, and may bring out, anxiety or inward-directed aggressive responses. The evidence for such a thesis is still equivocal.[1] But

[1] Ax (1953) and Schachter (1957) maintained that anger is accompanied by a norepinephrine-like physiological pattern, while epinephrine-like reactions presumably predominate with fear. However, their findings demand further checking. Other writers prefer to consider all emotions as involving a high level of physiological arousal or activation. Thus, Schachter and Singer (1962) hypothesized that there is a common state of physiological arousal in the various emotions and that they are differentiated largely through the aroused person's knowledge and understanding of the provoking situation.

it has been reported that typically aggressive animals, such as lions, have a high content of norepinephrine in relation to epinephrine in their adrenal medullas. Customarily "anxious" animals—e.g., rabbits—on the other hand, show a much higher proportion of epinephrine to norepinephrine (von Euler, cited in Funkenstein et al., 1957, p. 82). There is, of course, a long way to go from such correlational findings to the establishment of causal relations. It certainly has not been determined that the ease with which a human being's body manufactures norepinephrine as against epinephrine will govern his likelihood of exhibiting aggressive reactions to frustrations. And even if such relations are uncovered, the question would remain open as to whether genetic factors or prior learning experiences are more important in influencing the rate of production of these secretions.

Other linkages between physical constitution and behavior also have been proposed. Social observers since the time of Hippocrates have contended that a man's physique exerts a profound influence over his actions and temperament. Sheldon and Stevens (1942), among the most recent members of this school of thought, have hypothesized that mesomorphic people—characterized by a predominance of muscle, bone, and connective tissue—tend to be relatively free, uninhibited, and assertive in their bodily actions. Many of these people supposedly exhibit competitive aggressiveness and physical courage, and so they might be expected to have many fights, particularly when they believe they have been frustrated unjustly. Ectomorphic individuals, by contrast—having a "relative predominance of linearity and fragility"—presumably tend to be much more controlled and inhibited and therefore would be expected to perform fewer aggressive acts.

Here again there is some uncertainty as to whether the relationship between constitution and behavior really has been demonstrated. But even if such a correlation exists, it can be interpreted in several different ways. The muscular person may get into frequent fights because he had developed aggressive habits. He might have won many fights and arguments as a child because of his strength. Consequently, he had learned that aggression "pays off" for him, and he now exhibits hostility fairly readily.

*Sex and Aggressiveness.* There is relatively little doubt that a relation exists between aggressiveness and two other physical characteristics: sex and age. *In most species of the animal kingdom*, taking up the first of these factors, *the male tends to be more aggressive than his female counterpart*. To cite but one investigation supporting such a commonplace generalization, a study of thirty adult chimpanzees at the Yerkes Laboratory in Florida demonstrated that the males performed more acts of direct, open hostility than did the females. Complicating matters somewhat, the females seemed to be more "treacherous" in that they more frequently suddenly switched from friendly to aggressive behavior (Hebb & Thompson, 1954, pp. 545–547). The greater frequency of direct hostility by the males, however, suggests they were more strongly and quickly angered.

As for human aggressiveness, much of the relevant empirical data (in contrast to our everyday experiences) come from observations of children. A study by Jersild and Markey (1935) is illustrative. The researchers recorded some fifteen hundred conflicts among fifty-four nursery school children in free play. The conflicts were relatively short-lived, lasting on the average only about thirty seconds. But even so, the boys made more overtly aggressive responses than did the girls. The hostility the girls did display was largely indirect, i.e., somewhat inhibited, for they were more likely to use language instead of making more direct physical attacks. These differences in mode of aggression were particularly greater among the older preschoolers in the sample, probably because they were beginning to learn the forms of behavior appropriate to their sex roles.

Boys also are more aggressive than girls in middle childhood and adolescence. In his follow-up of the children studied by Sears et al. (1957), Sears (1961) found that the twelve-year old boys scored higher than the like-aged girls on a self-report measure of antisocial aggression and were lower than the girls on the questionnaire measures of aggression anxiety and prosocial aggression (the latter presumably an indicator of inhibited hostility). Lansky, Crandall, Kagan, & Baker (1961) obtained comparable results in an investigation of teenagers between thirteen and eighteen years of age. The boys were higher than the girls on self-ratings of aggressive tendencies.

Other studies yielding similar sex differences in aggressive behavior also could be cited. But all we need actually say is that such differences have been reported frequently, not only in social settings, such as the free-play situations observed by Jersild and Markey, but also in comparatively less restrained fantasy tasks, such as doll play and doll interviews (e.g., Gordon & Cohn, 1961; Levin & Sears, 1956; P. Sears, 1951; Yarrow, 1948).

More important than demonstrating what already is widely known, our real problem is to account for the human male's generally greater readiness to display direct, overt aggression. Both learning and biological factors seem to play some part in producing this difference. Research summarized in the first chapter of this book has shown clearly that the male sex hormone enhances the likelihood of aggressive responses in at least the lower animals (e.g., Beeman, 1947). Castrated male animals are usually not as aggressive as their noncastrated peers, but the formers' hostile tendencies can be restored by the administration of androgen. Rather than directly stimulating aggressive responses, it seems much more likely that the male hormone acts to increase physiological excitability (Beach, 1942), and thus frustrations may produce a stronger arousal state in males than females. In addition to this type of hormonal influence, males also may exhibit greater aggressiveness in some situations because of their greater size and muscular strength. (Size differences, of course, cannot account for the differences in the behavior of nursery school children.)

These constitutional factors, however, are by no means the complete explanation. Prior learning also is important, perhaps through affecting three different processes: (1) by determining the strength of the frustrated instigations, (2) by governing the strength of the aggressive reaction to the aggression-evoking cue, and (3) by affecting the strength of the inhibitions against aggression. The first of these processes is sometimes neglected in considerations of sex differences in hostile behavior. *Any given obstruction to goal-directed activity may actually mean more of a deprivation to one sex than to the other.* For example, an experimenter's derogation of the leadership or intellectual capabilities of his college student subjects, intended to raise their ire, can provoke stronger aggressive responses from men than from women because the former typically have stronger ambitions to excel in leadership and intellectual ability (McClelland et al., 1953). Stronger drives are thwarted, producing a more intense emotional reaction. Similarly, women often have stronger needs for affiliation and social success than do their masculine counterparts (cf. Lansky et al., 1961), and consequently attacks upon their popularity with others may be more upsetting to the women.

Such differences in intensity of the frustrated drive also are only part of the story. *Men probably have stronger aggressiveness habits than do women and thus generally make stronger hostile responses to the evoking cue* (holding the anger-arousal state constant for the two sexes). These presumably stronger aggressiveness habits would be an outgrowth of the greater parental reinforcement of aggression by boys than by girls. Boys are encouraged to fight back when attacked, but girls usually are not (Sears et al., 1957).

Finally, *women often have stronger inhibitions against direct aggression than do men.* Berkowitz et al. obtained indications of these sex differences in restraints against overt hostility in an experiment with college students. The subjects were brought together in like-sex pairs supposedly for a study of problem-solving under stress. Each pair member would work on a designated problem, with the stress created by knowing the other person would evaluate him (or her) by means of electric shocks. All the subjects worked on the first problem believing the other pair member was serving as the judge. Half were angered by giving them a large number of shocks (seven), while the others received the minimal one shock implying the most favorable evaluation. Following this, the subjects were shown what was ostensibly the partner's performance on another problem, with half of the students in the provoked and nonprovoked conditions led to believe the partner had done poorly and the remaining subjects being shown an obviously much better product. They now had their first socially sanctioned opportunity to aggress against their partner in the guise of a judgment of the partner's work. Then some minutes later, after completing several questionnaires, the subjects were given a second opportunity to administer shocks. Their partners supposedly had worked on another problem, and they were shown a moderately good product to evaluate by means of the shocks. Table 10.1 presents the mean number of shocks given to

*Table 10.1. Mean Number of Electric Shocks Administered to Partner by Men and Women in the Various Conditions*

|  | Angered subjects | | Nonangered subjects | |
|---|---|---|---|---|
|  | Trial I | Trial II | Trial I | Trial II |
| When partner had done good work: | | | | |
| Men | $3.88_d$ | $3.69_d$ | $1.56_a$ | $1.99_{ab}$ |
| Women | $3.69_d$ | $5.34_e$ | $1.93_{ab}$ | $1.96_{ab}$ |
| When partner had done poor work: | | | | |
| Men | $5.52_e$ | $4.54_{de}$ | $2.37_{bc}$ | $1.44_a$ |
| Women | $4.88_e$ | $2.79_c$ | $2.02_{ab}$ | $1.56_a$ |

NOTE: The actual statistical analysis employed a square-root transformation because of the skewed distribution of scores. Cells having a subscript in common are not significantly different from one another (at the .05 level) by Duncan Multiple Range Test.

the partner on the first and second trials in each of the experimental conditions.

We here are mainly concerned with the differences in the reactions of the men and women subjects. First, how did each sex respond to the provocation (the excessive number of shocks)? In this case there are no differences between the men and women. The shocks they received may have thwarted the achievement ambitions of the men (and possibly of the women to a lesser extent) but conceivably also frustrated stronger affiliation desires in the women. As the table indicates, the subjects in the angered conditions administered significantly more shocks to the instigator on this first occasion than did the noninsulted students, re-

gardless of sex, with the subjects shown a poor product by the instigator sending the greatest number of shocks. The angered people
apparently took advantage of the social sanctioning created by the
poor performance.

Now, how did the men and women respond to the partner's second
performance several minutes later, that is, when they were to evaluate
a moderately good product? I suggested earlier, the reader will recall,
that many people in our society come to feel anxious and/or guilty about
their previous aggressive behavior, with the magnitude of this anxiety-
guilt reaction being in direct proportion to the intensity of their earlier
hostility. As a result, they then exhibit a decrease in overt aggression
upon some subsequent occasion. Essentially this type of process seems
to have occurred in the present experiment. The subjects who had
given their partners the greatest number of shocks—i.e., those who had
been provoked by the partner and then were shown a poor performance
by him (or her)—were the only angered people to show a substantial
decrease in the number of shocks they administered on this second
opportunity. However, the decline in the number of shocks given in this
condition was statistically significant only for the women, and they
ended up expressing reliably less overt hostility on this final measure
than all but the noninsulted subjects. Thus, the women apparently had
developed somewhat stronger guilt and/or anxiety than did the men as
a consequence of their initial hostile behavior.[2] They presumably were
more likely to have regarded their first aggressive acts as "wrong" or
"bad."

It is easy to see why the female students would become relatively
anxious or guilty as a result of their aggression. For one thing, women
generally have stronger conformist tendencies than do men (Janis &
Field, 1959), and consequently they usually are somewhat more concerned with doing what is socially "right" and "proper." Some of the
strongest social demands made upon an individual involve the requirements of his sex role; he has to behave in a manner his society deems
appropriate to his sex. *The average woman*, then, *has a fairly strong
wish to conform to the cultural definition of her sex role, and in our
society this means she is to avoid behaving aggressively.* Those women
students in the Berkowitz et al. experiment who had exhibited intense

[2] Although this cannot definitely be ruled out, I do not believe the decrease in
overt hostility was due to some cathartic process. Note that the nonangered subjects who had been led to believe their partners had done poorly also tended to
decline in overt hostility from trial I to II. I suspect they had felt guilty because
of the higher number of shocks they had given than received on the first trial; in
essence, they may have doubted whether the higher number of shocks they had
given was really warranted. Such doubts presumably were fairly strong in the
comparable angered condition.

overt hostility might well have become anxious and guilty over their departure from the approved mode of feminine behavior.

There is little doubt that our society generally frowns on direct aggression by women. If evidence is needed, some can be found in the widely known study of 379 middle- and lower-class kindergarten children in the Boston area, published by Sears et al. Interviews with the mothers indicated boys were given more freedom to fight with other neighborhood children than were girls. They also, unlike the girls, were frequently encouraged to fight back when they were bullied. Furthermore, while the boys were not allowed more freedom to fight with their siblings, there was even a somewhat greater permissiveness given them to aggress against their parents. Summarizing their findings, the investigators concluded that *parents generally regard some aggression as "natural, and even desirable," in a boy, particularly outside the home* (1957, p. 403). More than this, we might also say *girls are discouraged from displaying aggression in at least its more direct forms.* Women, girls learn, do not hit or curse other people. Direct aggression is not only unladylike, it is unfeminine.

Such a formulation of the relation of aggressive behavior to the sex role in our society has some obvious implications. For one, we would expect the women who typically exhibit a relatively great amount of direct, overt hostility to be somewhat masculine in their values and attitudes. Girls generally inhibiting their aggressive tendencies, on the other hand, should be much more likely to have adopted all of the attitudes and behaviors associated with their sex role. In a word, *aggression-inhibiting women should be more feminine than their more aggressive sisters.*

These expectations are given tentative empirical support by investigations with children. Lansky and his colleagues at the Fels Research Institute assessed the attitudes, values, and personalities of fifty-four adolescents in seeking to determine the personality correlates of habitual aggressive tendencies in boys and girls. Their findings pointed to sex differences in the source of the hostile inclinations. Aggressive dispositions in the boys seemed to be a reaction to unacceptable dependent needs. (Much more will be said about this hypothesis in the later sections of this chapter. Bandura and Walters (1959) have employed a version of this thesis to explain the personality development of aggressively antisocial boys.) In the girls, however, aggressive responses appeared to be "related to 'masculine' interests, behaviors, and needs" (Lansky et al., 1961, p. 56). The girls expressing the greatest hostility (in criticism of their mothers) generally were high on the masculine characteristic of achievement motivation and low on such feminine qualities as concern with affiliation, desire to be similar to the mother, and guilt about aggressive acts directed against a male authority.

Women do exhibit aggressive behavior under some conditions, of course. For example, they express hostility when they snub or criticize someone violating their standards of "correct" behavior. The aggression in these cases is in defense of social codes, at least as the women have defined these approved rules of conduct. To use the terminology employed by Sears (1961), such hostility is "prosocial aggression." Sears, as I reported in Chapter 5, has obtained some evidence suggesting that this hostility in support of propriety usually is an outgrowth of strong internal restraints against direct aggression. Women, having relatively strong inhibitions against direct, over hostility, should therefore tend to be high in this prosocial aggression. But they also should become more antagonistic when the social codes are endangered because propriety generally is more important to them than to men. For both reasons, then, there is no surprise in Sears' finding that twelve-year-old girls score higher than boys on a self-report measure of prosocial aggression. Lending further weight to this finding, Johnson (cited in Levin & Sears, 1956; and in Sears et al., 1957) showed that five- and eight-year-old girls performed more prosocial aggression acts than their like-age male peers.

A woman is not necessarily being "unfeminine" every time she acts in a hostile manner. Many women advocate some form of inhibited aggression in the interests of law enforcement and the maintenance of social rules. This is the sort of behavior involved in Sears's prosocial aggression scale. Sears found that prosocial aggression was also positively related to a measure of femininity in his sample of twelve-year-old children. In general, women do become aggressive—though in an inhibited form—when their strongly held values are threatened.

Going to the determinants of the anxiety-guilt reaction to hostility, Sears (1961) has hypothesized that aggression anxiety[3] does not develop in the same manner in the two sexes. He found that child-rearing conditions, as described by the mothers in 1951–1952, were related differently in boys and girls to a self-report scale of aggression anxiety completed by the children some seven years later. Boys tended to describe themselves as high in aggression anxiety when their mothers had relied on withdrawal of love as a disciplinary technique and had shown relatively little permissiveness toward aggression. Girls, on the other hand, were most likely to have strong aggression anxiety when they had been exposed to child-rearing conditions likely to develop and enhance aggressiveness habits, such as parental permissiveness regarding aggression

[3] Sears's usage of the concept "aggression anxiety" includes the notion of guilt.

against other children and parental encouragement to fight back when attacked by other children. The girls also tended to have high aggression anxiety if their fathers had taken care of them a good deal of the time during their childhood.

Reasoning from the total correlational pattern, Sears suggested that aggression anxiety in boys is "a close relative of conscience." Such anxiety appeared to be a consequence of love-oriented disciplinary methods, and of relatively strong but nonpunitive pressures toward behaving in a socially "correct" manner. The conditions facilitating the development of aggression anxiety in the twelve-year-old girls, however, seemed to him to be "antithetical to appropriate sex typing." Putting it simply, learning conditions resulting in the frequent activation of the disapproved (for women) hostile inclinations tended to produce strong aggression anxiety. Similarly, a high amount of caretaking by the father during the preschool years could have predisposed the girls to a variety of actions not appropriate to their sex role, including aggression, and thus made them anxious about engaging in these behaviors.

All in all, then, the picture is fairly clear. Constitutional factors may enter into the differences in the frequency, intensity, and form of aggression displayed by men and women, but these biological determinants probably are relatively unimportant, at least in human beings. Cultural training, through which the child receives reinforcements for engaging in behaviors appropriate to his sex, or punishments for carrying out disapproved actions, unquestionably is the most important source of sex differences in human aggressiveness.

*Age.* The form and intensity of aggressive reactions to frustrations vary with the child's age. Reflecting the experiences of countless parents, Sears et al. (1957) described the infant's response to a thwarting as a diffuse rage, in which he "just flails his limbs and screams" (p. 222). Only with maturation and learning does the hostility become focused into aggressive behavior—actions intended to injure some object. Such an increase in the specificity of hostile actions is partly due to the direct influence of reinforcement—the child repeats those particular modes of aggressive behavior that have brought him the rewards he desires—and partly to the development of internal controls. Restraints shape the form of the individual's hostility as well as its frequency and intensity.

Goodenough's (1931) study of aggression in young children clearly points to the development of internal controls with age. Her data, based upon forty-five mothers' reports of instances of aggression by their children during a one-month period, showed that violent outbursts within the first two years of life frequently are characterized by displays of undirected energy (*rage* in the Sears et al. terminology). Specific motor and language responses begin to increase as the child grows older, and indirect (presumably inhibited) modes of aggression, such as peevishness and whining, become more frequent. Primitive, diffuse bodily responses are largely replaced by specific, controlled actions often involving language, in which symbolic injury substitutes for physical hurt. Possibly as a function of the rise of inhibitions, the diffuse rage reactions appear to become shorter in duration with age. But emotional aftereffects, such as sulking and brooding, last longer, again probably because of the restraints against aggression and perhaps also because the children, in thinking about their frustrations, continue to stir themselves up.

Rosenzweig and Rosenzweig (1952) obtained essentially similar results in an investigation employing their Picture-Frustration Study. Direct aggression, defined in terms of extrapunitive responses, declined with age from the four-year-olds to the thirteen-year-olds in their sample, while the more inhibited intropunitive responses increased in frequency.

Learning conditions may produce age differences in the instigation to aggression as well as in restraints against aggression. As I suggested in Chapter 3, young children may well be more readily aroused by obstacles in the path of their goal-directed activity than are their older brothers and sisters. Evidence reviewed earlier indicates anger intensity is, among other things, a function of the degree to which the frustration blocks *all* the goal-oriented responses the individual is capable of making in the situation. Older children are more likely to have learned alternative courses of action so that, in essence, any one obstacle generally results in a smaller degree of interference and therefore produces a weaker reaction.

*Internal Controls and Ego Strength.* It is difficult to exaggerate the importance of internal controls as a determinant of aggressive behavior. When a person controls himself, he minimizes the emotional reactions he might have to frustrations. He is capable of acting rationally, lessening the duration and extent of the thwarting by altering his goals or at least the path to his goals. Blocked in one way, he tries something else. But more than this, even if his frustration persists, he can inhibit much of his aggression.

Authorities sometimes employ the term *ego strength* to refer to such a behavior pattern. A person with a strong ego supposedly has the ability to engage in constructive, problem-solving behavior when confronted by frustrations and can restrain disrupting emotional reactions. Clinical observations and more systematic quantitative research agree in suggesting that *highly aggressive youngsters tend to be low in ego strength.* Many hyperaggressive boys, whether actual juvenile delinquents or on the verge of trouble with the law, have serious ego disturbances, according to the portrait drawn by Redl and Wineman (1957). These writers described the ten extremely hostile eight-to-ten-year-old boys sent to them for group psychotherapy as having several signs of ego weakness, such as:

1. *Low frustration tolerance*—even the slightest obstacle or hindrance to their activities frequently provoked the sort of "wild outburst of unstructured bickering, fighting, disorganization, and griping" which, in more normal youngsters, occurred only in the face of extreme frustrations (p. 77).

2. *Inability to cope with insecurity, anxiety, and fear*—the threats that would produce only mild anxiety in other children sometimes resulted in panic or "ferocious attack and diffuse destruction," a "total breakdown in controls" (p. 81).

3. *Low temptation resistance*—they were easily tempted or lured into socially unacceptable behavior by the actions of their fellows (pp. 83–88).

Many other qualities also were listed, but the above three are most relevant for the present analysis. Summarizing the Redl-Wineman observations, we can say these hyperaggressive boys often were unable to cope with frustrations and threats and unable to restrain their emotional reactions to the thwartings they could not eliminate.

Since the concepts *ego strength* and *internal controls* appear to be so important, they should be analyzed more closely. The terms can be thought of in an erroneously oversimplified manner. For one thing, there are different patterns of ego control. Boys may manifest low ego strength, for example, by (1) being passive, timid, and fearful, or by (2) being overly expansive (masking an underlying insecurity), hostile, and dominating, though lacking independence, and craving attention and praise (Livson & Bronson, 1961). We cannot be certain that this latter pattern applies to the Redl-Wineman children in all respects, although there certainly are similarities. Extremely hostile people (such as the youngsters studied by Redl and Wineman) may be different in a number of important ways from those who are only moderately aggressive and who have not been brought to the attention of legal authorities or therapists. Furthermore, there may even be important differences among the people with habitually very strong proclivities to aggression. Nevertheless, many aggressive youngsters do have certain features in common, features which can be summarized by the label *weak ego controls*, and it would be helpful to specify just what seems to be involved in this construct.

Let us first consider two of the three qualities listed by Redl and Wineman: low frustration tolerance and susceptibility to temptation.

First, these characteristics clearly imply that the hyperaggressive person shows an *extremely intense responsiveness to the arousing stimuli.* Confronted by a frustration that would produce only a mild reaction from most people, he typically becomes relatively strongly excited and then exhibits strong aggressive responses to the evoking cues. In addition, both of these factors indicate an *inability to defer gratifications. The extremely aggressive child apparently cannot withstand frustrations; he often wants his pleasures as quickly as he can get them or else he is greatly disturbed.* Being unable to postpone need satisfaction for too long, he cannot establish the inhibitions necessary to control and regulate his behavior, and he is prey to easy temptation by others.

Several studies show the relationship between ego-control capacity and aggressive behavior. Block and Martin (1955) assessed the control capacity of twenty-two preschool children by means of two tasks. One dealt with the child's ability to defer immediate gratification in order to achieve a greater reward in the future (he could accumulate as much candy as he wished, but once he stopped to taste a piece he couldn't get any more), while the other had to do with the extent to which satiating his desire to work on one task extinguished his motivation to work on another similar task (this process is termed *cosatiation*). A composite measure based on both performances was found to be related to the children's reactions to a frustrating play situation. Upon being thwarted, the under-controlled preschoolers exhibited less constructive play and acted aggressively more frequently than did the youngsters having stronger ego control.

Livson and Mussen (1957) employed very similar tasks in another investigation with nursery school children and again found that a composite ego-control score was significantly negatively related to indices of aggressive behavior. The children presumably having a low frustration tolerance and little ability to postpone their pleasures behaved much more aggressively over a two-week observation period than did their "strong ego" peers.

Learning to become an effective member of our society requires the ability to defer gratifications. The person demanding immediate satisfactions will encounter many frustrations and will become angry fairly often. But more than this, he usually is selfish and inconsiderate of others; he doesn't care about the needs of others as long as his own are satisfied. Pursuing pleasures when the mood strikes rather than when it is socially feasible, he may even break laws. Mischel (1961) noted that juvenile delinquents were more likely to prefer smaller, immediate rewards to larger, delayed reinforcement (in their choice of candies) than were comparable but nondelinquent youngsters. In addition, within each of these samples the adolescents favoring the delayed reinforcements tended to have higher scores on an attitude measure of social responsibility than did those insisting on the immediate gratifications. The socially responsible individual avoids hurting others. He does not aggress against other people if he can help it, nor does he seek to injure them by pressing for the satisfaction of his own needs to the detriment of *their* gratifications. But he can behave in such a responsible manner only to the extent that he can postpone his pleasures.

*Psychopathy and Self-esteem.* Since a deficiency in ego controls is one of the prime characteristics of the psychopathic personality, it would be tempting to label all hyperaggressive people as psychopaths. It also would be misleading to do so. Every hostile person is not a psychopath. The term is sometimes used indiscriminately; psychopathy tends to be one of psychiatry's wastebasket categories. Nevertheless, authorities generally agree on the following features of the psychopath. He often is lacking in self-control, impulsively pleasure-seeking, callous, immature, and aggressive when frustrated. He is, in a few words, primarily concerned with getting his pleasures regardless of social norms and the wishes of other people and shows relatively little anxiety about his behavior.

Some criminals and juvenile delinquents can legitimately be said to possess these characteristics, and many extremely hostile people undoubtedly have psychopathic tendencies. But just as psychopathy is not necessarily present in every lawbreaker, so is this category inappropriate for every aggression-prone person. Not a few extremely aggressive people have strong feelings of inadequacy, sometimes leading to depressive moods, while such anxiety states typically are lacking in the classical psychopath.

Several experiments have demonstrated a relationship between adequacy feelings, or what is sometimes termed *self-esteem,* and aggressive behavior. The individual who describes himself as incompetent and inadequate apparently has a stronger predisposition to hostility than does the person with higher self-esteem. Thus, the former is more likely to have an initially negative attitude toward the strangers he encounters (Berkowitz, 1960c) and, when insulted, may show stronger disguised hostility (Rosenbaum & deCharms, 1960). However, the provoked, low self-esteem individual does not always display more open aggression than does his similarly treated but psychologically more adequate peer (Berkowitz, 1960c; Hokanson & Gordon, 1958; Rosenbaum & deCharms, 1960). It could be that the low self-esteem individual is also more prone to aggression anxiety (Hokanson, 1961b) and fears retaliation for any overt hostility he might exhibit.

Low self-regard, of course, can also be taken as indicative of a weak ego. But, as I have just indicated, people having such a personality characteristic are not necessarily lacking in inhibitions. Their restraints may even be quite strong when they believe particular actions are likely to bring them some form of punishment. They seem to be easily aroused to hostility (although the aggressive responses may not be performed), but they are too conflict-ridden, anxious, and restrained to be thought of as psychopaths.

*Social Class.* Constitutional and biological factors clearly have only a small part in determining individual differences in frequency, form, and intensity of hostile behavior. If John Smith loses his temper easily upon being thwarted, while Joe Jones remains calm and unruffled, we cannot attribute the difference (at least not with any certainty) to the direct influence of inherited characteristics possessed by one but not the other. Human nature is too malleable to be fixed at birth. Our personalities seem to be shaped more by our learning experiences, possibly in interaction with our genetic qualities, than by these genetic factors alone. John Smith and Joe Jones grew up in different families; their friends and teachers were not the same; they may even have come from different social classes.

Social scientists generally agree that a family's position in the social stratification system has a considerable effect on the behavior patterns, attitudes, and values of the family members. A social class is a restricted learning environment to a considerable extent. The people within any one social stratum have more frequent contact with each other than they do with members of other social levels (A. Davis, 1944). Many important learning experiences are shared by people from the same social class but not by people from the other strata. The child of a middle-class family greatly concerned with maintaining its social "respectability" will probably acquire aspirations, codes of conduct, and attitudes not possessed by children whose families are exceedingly wealthy and secure in their status or by children from the lowest social strata. Sociologists have even suggested that children growing up in the different social classes often also learn different attitudes toward aggression. The classic formulation of such a thesis can be found in Davis's (1944) discussion of social factors in the development of the adolescent personality. Probably thinking of youngsters similar to the "Dead End" children made famous in the movies and plays of the 1930s and 1940s, Davis maintained that lower-class culture generally rewards aggressive behavior on the part of children and adolescents. Youngsters from these social strata supposedly learn "to strike out with fist or knife and to be certain to hit first" (p. 209).

Empirical evidence indicates, however, that the influence of social class on aggressive behavior is somewhat more complicated than Davis's observation would suggest. Consistent with the Davis argument, McKee and Leader (1955) have reported that working-class preschoolers displayed more aggression in an experimental play situation than did their middle-class peers. However, the working-class and middle-class mothers interviewed by Sears et al. (1957) did not differ in the extent to which they described their children as behaving aggressively, while Levin and Sears (1956) found no social-class differences in doll-play aggression. Davis's observation apparently holds in some situations but not in others. Lesser (1959) also has pointed out that Davis did not adequately specify just what kinds of hostility are socially rewarded in lower-class culture. In Lesser's study of white boys from the lower social levels, reputation for engaging in unjustified aggression was associated with little popularity with classmates, much as undoubtedly would be the case in a sample of middle-class youngsters. The working-class culture may reward aggressive acts that seem justified, but it will punish other forms of hostile behavior. Comprehensive formulations of social-class influences on aggressive behavior must be able to identify the situations in which particular hostile actions are likely to occur and be rewarded.

Such formulations probably will have to distinguish between instigational and inhibitory effects. Thus, a working-class individual, having experienced more economic deprivations throughout his lifetime, might have a lower frustration tolerance than the economically more fortunate middle-class person. He, therefore, could be more easily aroused by any one thwarting. Social-class differences in this case are due to differences in ease of arousal and not necessarily to lower inhibitions against hostility in the working class. Davis suggested another instigational effect when he contended that youngsters from the lower classes are more likely to employ instrumental aggression, i.e., using hostility as a means to particular ends, such as gaining approval from peers. There are no good data bearing on these possibilities, but suggestive findings in a study by B. Allinsmith (in Miller & Swanson, 1960, pp. 315–336) indicate that the social strata may differ in the degree to which they provide aggressive models for their children. Mrs. Allinsmith obtained measures of the directness with which seventh- to ninth-grade boys habitually expressed aggression and related these scores to characteristics of their mothers derived from interviews with the mothers. Among other things, the investigator noted that the middle-class women were more controlled than those from the working class; when frustrated, the latter apparently were much more likely to show their emotions. This emotional control was related to the boys' behavior. The very controlled women had youngsters who typically restrained their aggression and usually showed only indirect hostility, while absence of emotional control in the mothers was associated with a relative absence of inhibitions in their sons so that these boys tended to display very direct aggression. As the psychologist commented, the children were more likely to follow their mothers' actual behavior than their admonitions (p. 329). It may well be that lower-class culture in general provides more aggressive models than does middle-class culture. Working-class boys may be more likely to see adults (including their parents) and other youngsters behaving aggressively and consequently are more likely to copy these hostile models. As a result they would have stronger aggressiveness habits.

We probably can assume that the above-mentioned factors exert a direct effect on the occurrence of aggressive acts by either heightening anger or enhancing the development of aggressiveness habits. But class cultures also differ in the degree to which they give rise to internal restraints against aggression. Davis's analysis also assumes such a difference, and his contention is shared by other social scientists. Miller and Swanson (1960, pp. 28, 263) have argued, for example, that middle-class parents are more concerned with teaching their children to inhibit their aggression and otherwise restrain their emotions than are working-class parents, since self-control presumably is necessary for advancement in the social order.

Research results suggest, however, that social-strata differences in the learning of inhibitions against aggression are not due solely to class differences in the punishment of hostility. People from the middle and upper levels of society often are more restrained emotionally than are working-class people; the former may have stronger inhibitions against expressing *any* feelings. Funkenstein et al. have reported that the Harvard University men in their sample who were fifth generation Americans (and who probably came from upper-class backgrounds) tended to show inhibited, intropunitive responses to the experimental frustrations, whereas only a minority of the other subjects displayed such a reaction (1957, p. 149). Similarly, working-class boys in the earlier-mentioned Allinsmith investigation apparently were more likely than their middle-class peers to indicate they would respond to frustrations with the most direct forms of aggression: direct attacks on the instigator (Miller & Swanson, 1960, p. 330). Working-class youngsters may have habitually weaker restraints against extremely direct aggression than do middle-class children. But, we might ask, are such class differences in inhibitions against hostility only the result of greater cultural approval of direct aggression in the working class? These differences may also arise from differences in the extent to which parental training successfully erects restraints against disapproved behavior. Working-class parents may be relatively unsuccessful in controlling their children's hostile behavior because, on the whole, they employ less effective disciplinary techniques than do middle-class parents.

Findings in the Allinsmith study are consistent with such a possibility.

In order to assess the directness of the aggression customarily expressed by the teenagers in her sample, the psychologist administered a projective test in which the boys were to complete stories all telling how a boy was frustrated by an older person he either loved or feared. The endings supplied by the youngsters were then coded for the directness of the aggression exhibited by the hero, presumably indicative of the strength of the storyteller's own restraints against aggression. With the exception of the most direct hostile acts (which, as I reported earlier, showed a class difference), there were no reliable differences between the middle-class and working-class boys in this sample. The working-class boys seemed to be almost as inhibited as their middle-class peers when all of the hostile incidents were taken into consideration. But although social level was not significantly associated with aggression directness, parental discipline (as inferred from interviews with the mothers) was reliably related to this measure. Parents favoring psychological disciplinary techniques—attempting to manipulate by expressing disappointment, appealing to the child's pride, or arousing guilt or shame—tended to have children displaying predominantly inhibited, indirect hostility. In contrast, the aggression in the story endings composed by the physically punished youngsters was typically much more direct and unrestrained. All in all, then, *type of parental discipline appears to be a stronger determinant of the directness with which the teenagers expressed aggression than does social class.* This is not to say that social class is unimportant. *The mothers' social level often affected the type of discipline they favored.* Middle-class women, on the average, preferred psychological techniques, while the working-class mothers were more likely to favor physical punishment (pp. 324–327). Summarizing these findings, we can say that, contrary to the notions of many social scientists, the working-class boys apparently did not show substantially weaker restraints against *all* forms of aggression than did the middle-class adolescents. The lower-class culture may not of itself lead to habitually weak inhibitions against hostility. *If working-class boys do exhibit more open and unrestrained aggression than do middle-class boys, such a difference may arise, at least in part, from differences in the disciplinary techniques generally favored by working-class and middle-class parents.*

This thesis obviously requires further testing before it can be accepted with any confidence. There seems to be a good deal of evidence, however, that working-class parents are more likely than their middle-class counterparts to be punitive toward their children, although this difference may diminish in time with the spread of information about child rearing (Bronfenbrenner, 1958). The love-oriented or psychological discipline techniques preferred on the average by middle-class parents probably facilitate the development of fairly stable attitudinal prohibitions against aggression. The punitive techniques employed by many working-class parents, on the other hand, apparently are less likely to produce such moral prescriptions against hostility so that the working-class youngster subjected to corporal punishment may tend to inhibit his aggression primarily when he fears punishment from others for such behavior.

## THE DEVELOPMENT OF AGGRESSIVE PERSONALITIES

### Frequent Frustrations

There is a very common answer to the question of how the extremely hostile person got to be that way. Most of the specialists in the mental health disciplines seem to agree that aggressive personalities are the product of many severe emotional thwartings. But as we saw in the section on catharsis, a high degree of consensus among the experts is not sufficient proof. We want to know if there is any substantial body of quantitative evidence in support of this formulation. Is it true that a child who had been frustrated often in the course of his formative years is likely to become a generally hostile individual?[4]

According to several empirical investigations, parental frustrations frequently do lead to strong aggressive tendencies in children. Radke's (1946) summary of the research literature up to the end of World War II suggests that a variety of socialization conditions which probably can be regarded as frustrating to the child, such as parental rejection and parental disharmony, seem to be related to aggressiveness in the child (Child, 1954, p. 669). Such findings are not surprising. Psychoanalytic conceptions and the frustration-aggression hypothesis of Dollard and his colleagues maintain that frequent thwartings yield a heightened instigation to aggression, and parents tend to be fairly consistent in their actions toward their children. Youngsters treated with hostility by their mothers when they are infants are usually still treated in this manner as they approach adolescence (Schaefer & Bayley, 1960). Many emotionally thwarted children experience a consistent pattern of frustrations throughout their formative years, and there is ample opportunity for them to develop habitual modes of reaction to these deprivations.

But yet the question remains whether every persistently hostile person has undergone a history of frustrations. The theoretical analysis

[4] The following review, of necessity, is confined to the development of aggressive personalities in boys. Research cited earlier in this chapter, particularly that by Sears (1961), suggests that aggressiveness habits develop differently in boys and girls, and very little is known about the formation of hostile tendencies in girls.

described earlier suggests that there are many avenues through which aggressive personalities can develop. We certainly cannot satisfactorily explain the development of every hostile boy merely by saying he has been frustrated (Bandura, 1960). Frequent deprivations throughout childhood may lead to withdrawal reactions or apathy as well as to habitual aggression. Frequent frustrations are not sufficient; other factors may also be necessary for the development of extremely hostile reaction tendencies. More recent research will have to be reviewed before we can attempt to assess the role of frustrations in the development of hostile personalities. In the course of this review we will see that many hyperaggressive individuals *have* suffered severe emotional deprivations throughout their childhood. Such thwartings have had an important part in shaping the life patterns of at least these particular people.

*Frustration of Needs for Affection and Nurturance.* Maternal coldness and lack of affection is undoubtedly frustrating to the child, and many characteristically aggressive individuals seem to have had such a loveless relationship with their mothers. Sears et al. (1957) have found that affectionally cold mothers tend to describe their children as highly aggressive, while the college-student offspring of this type of mother generally show a relatively high frequency of aggressive responses on the Rosenzweig P-F test (Bornston & Coleman, 1956).

The child must find the care and protection he is too young and helpless to provide for himself before he can function as an independent being. Being dependent upon his parents, he wants to be valued by them, and he desires their nurturance and protecting warmth. Should his parents be cold and inattentive to him, however, his dependency needs would not be satisfied, and hostility could result (Redl & Wineman, 1957; Saul, 1956). Bandura and Walters (1959) contended that habitual antisocial aggression in boys is often the result of the thwarting of their dependency needs. Dependency strivings are not innate, these psychologists maintained; children have to learn to want help and nurturance from their parents. If they do have strong dependency wishes, the frustration of these desires for help and emotional support, particularly "through a lack of affectional nurturance on the part of one or both . . . parents," supposedly leads to a "continuing instigation to aggression" and weak internalized controls against hostile behavior (pp. 32–41).

Bandura and Walters cited the results of several earlier investigations in support of their analysis. Thus, observations published by Glueck and Glueck (1950) suggest that delinquent boys are more likely to have a history of inadequate affectional relationships with parents than are their less aggressive, more law-abiding peers, while Bender (1947) found that many psychopathic children had neglectful or rejecting mothers, or were separated from their mothers.

In their own study, Bandura and Walters compared psychological test and interview data for a group of twenty-six hyperaggressive adolescent boys who had been in trouble with authorities for antisocial aggression with a matched group of youngsters who were "neither markedly aggressive nor markedly withdrawn." The aggressive boys apparently had received enough love and attention from their mothers during infancy to develop further desires for aid and comfort (i.e., they had acquired fairly strong dependency needs). As they grew older, however, the boys experienced coldness and neglect from their fathers and, to some extent, from their mothers as well. Supposedly because of this rejection and their mothers' inconsistent reactions to their earlier dependency behavior, they developed not only strong aggressive inclinations but also relatively intense dependency anxiety.

This last-mentioned fear of dependency theoretically leads to another characteristic frequently observed in aggressively antisocial youngsters: Such boys generally are reluctant to enter into close attachments with other people (see, for example, Redl & Wineman, 1957). The highly aggressive group in the Bandura-Walters sample tended to have little affection for either parents or schoolmates. Possibly as the result of their strong dependency anxiety and hostility toward their parents, highly aggressive preadolescents have been found to construct relatively few stories containing themes of dependency upon parents when given TAT-like pictures (Kagan, 1958).

To return to dependency frustrations, McCord, McCord, and Howard (1961) have also obtained indications of little emotional warmth in the mothers and fathers of aggressive boys. After an intensive examination of the case histories of both aggressive (but nondelinquent) preadolescents and more "normal" youngsters, the investigators reported that the parents of the aggressive boys were more rejecting of, and punitive to, their children than were the parents of the nonaggressive boys. Parents of assertive and occasionally aggressive children were generally given ratings between these two extremes.

Since dissension between the mother and father is disturbing and prevents the child from getting the nurturance he desires, we also find a history of parental disharmony in the backgrounds of many highly aggressive children. Conflict within the family is a frequent characteristic of the home lives of juvenile delinquents and other aggressively antisocial youngsters (cf. Glueck & Glueck, 1950; Bandura & Walters, 1959), but is by no means confined to the lawless. McCord and his collaborators have reported (1961) that the parents of the aggressive but nondelinquent boys in their sample typically had more frequent fights and less respect for each other than did the mothers and fathers of the nonaggressive children.

*The Role of Frequent Frustrations.* Clearly, many extremely aggressive children have experienced fairly severe emotional deprivations. Nevertheless, we cannot say that such persistent frustrations will necessarily lead to the development of habitually strong overt aggressiveness. Some researchers have *not* obtained relationships between various forms of parental frustration and aggressiveness in the child (cf. Child, 1954, p. 670). What part do frequent parental thwartings play in the development of aggressive personalities? How can we explain these apparently inconsistent results?

One possibility, of course, is that *the objective situations recorded or observed by the investigators are not actually frustrating to the child.* Home conditions considered to be frustrating by the researchers may not be too much of a deprivation to the children living in these settings. The youngsters may not have the drives the psychologists attribute to them so that their unfortunate family situations do not seriously block their need satisfaction. Bandura and Walters have made essentially this point. According to these writers, boys objectively experiencing little parental nurturance are unlikely to become extremely aggressive if they have not learned to want their parents' affection. Some children do not seek their parents' love and attention (in their overt actions and/or their thoughts), perhaps because they have never received much love from them. For these boys, parental coldness does not block many ongoing response sequences oriented toward the attainment of parental love. In the words of Chapter 2 of the present book, anger results only when such activated response sequences are thwarted; children who are uninterested in their parents' love for them—or, more generally, who are not concerned with reaching a particular goal—are not aroused by their failure to get this love (or goal).

But even if the youngsters are frustrated by the situations surrounding them, *they may have developed response tendencies incompatible with aggressive behavior.* Their frustrating parents may have taught them, implicitly or explicitly, to inhibit their hostility. Bandura and Walters suggested that the child will refrain from engaging in aggressive behavior, even though the mother and father he loves are often cold to him, if he has learned that he cannot gain the affection he desires unless he conforms to his parents' demands. In this latter case the child experiences relatively frequent thwarting of his dependency wishes but has learned that the satisfaction of these wishes is contingent upon acceding to his parents' dictates (1959, pp. 39–41). He then hides whatever aggressive inclinations he might have.

There is another important principle that also should be taken into consideration. The theoretical position taken here maintains that *frustrations in themselves create only a predisposition to aggression;* obstructions to goal-directed activity are not the sufficient cause of hostile behavior. Aggressive cues (stimuli associated with the anger instigator) must be present if such behavior is actually to occur. *Prior learning to behave aggressively,* through which the individual learns to perceive aggression-evoking cues readily and also to make strong aggressive responses to these cues, *may also be necessary in order to produce the habitually extremely hostile person.*

Bandura (1960) has obtained some evidence indicating that a history of frequent frustrations in childhood is not sufficient to explain childhood aggressiveness, and indeed, may not even be necessary in the formation of such behavior patterns. In this study nondelinquent boys judged by observers to exhibit frequent hostility were compared with demographically similar inhibited and withdrawn boys. There was little difference between the two groups of boys in the extent to which they had been deprived of affection by their parents. If anything, the parents of the aggressive schoolchildren had been somewhat *more* affectionate during early childhood than the parents of the withdrawn youngsters. The aggressive boys also seemed to have much less dependency anxiety than the more withdrawn children; the former sought their parents' attention more frequently, were more likely to ask their fathers for help, and generally sought the company and attention of their teachers and peers more often. Bandura concluded that the relatively frequent aggression shown by the habitually hostile youngsters in his sample did not arise from the frustration of their dependency needs but, rather, was the result of their parents' intermittent reinforcement of aggression outside the home. Many of the parents of the aggressive group also had served as aggressive models for their boys to copy. In one way or another, the aggressive youngsters had been taught to behave aggressively outside the home.

There are several ways in which frequent frustrations throughout childhood might affect the growing individual's behavior. He is not necessarily chronically angry, constantly steaming with pent-up rage and resentment. Instead, he is quick to become strongly enraged because of two processes:

1. *He readily interprets many events as frustrations.* Thus, he tends to define someone's ambiguous behavior toward him as threatening or as a personal affront, or he may often feel that he is unable to cope with a difficult situation. In a sense, he expects unpleasant events to occur, and consequently for him these anger-arousing events *do* frequently take place.

2. *He has a low frustration tolerance so that his emotional reactions*

*to any one thwarting usually are relatively intense.* Through either or both of these processes, then, he often is angered, or at least he is predisposed to make aggressive responses to suitable cues.

3. When aroused, the often frustrated individual may be quick to perceive such cues; i.e., *he readily associates people and objects with his frustraters, so that there are many stimuli functionally equivalent to his frustraters and capable of "drawing" hostile behavior from him.*

4. In addition, although this probably is not a necessary consequence of many frustrations, *he may have learned to make strong aggressive responses to the aggression cues.* I would like to propose that the strength of the aggressive actions exhibited by a person is a joint function of the intensity of his anger, the strength of his restraints against aggression, the degree of association between the initial instigator and the aggression cues in the situation, and the strength of his habitual tendencies to respond aggressively to aggression cues.

### Punishment and Disciplinary Techniques

*Punishment as an Inhibitor of Aggression.* An earlier section of this chapter has discussed some of the complex effects of parental punishment of the child's hostile behavior. Summarizing the available evidence, we can say the frequently punished child (1) is likely to inhibit his aggressive inclinations when he anticipates punishment for hostile behavior, (2) may readily expect such punishment for hostility, particularly in situations resembling the punitive home environment, but (3) will not restrain his aggressive actions if he believes punishment will not be forthcoming, and (4) is likely to have fairly strong aggressive tendencies since his prior punishments had acted like other frustrations to increase the strength of his predisposition to aggression.

Looking at the effects of punishment in this way permits us to reconcile the apparently contradictory findings obtained in several different investigations. Some studies have found that frequent parental punishment of aggression by the child is associated with a high level of child hostility, while other research has yielded the opposite results. Thus, according to Sears et al. (1957, p. 259), mothers reporting they tended to severely punish their children's hostility also generally described their offspring as showing a relatively high amount of aggression. Similarly, Eron and his colleagues (1960) found that the third-grade school children whose parents, when interviewed, indicated they severely punished their children's aggression usually displayed a greater volume of aggression in school (as reported by their peers) than did the children of less punitive parents. Assuming the parental punishment preceded the full development of the child's habitual aggressiveness, we have here evidence consistent with the frustration interpretation of punishment: Punishment, by occasionally thwarting the occurrence of hostile acts, presumably increases the likelihood of further hostility.

However, somewhat in opposition to such a thesis are the findings in two other studies. For example, in Lesser's (1952) previously cited TAT investigation there are indications that frequently punished children generally tended to inhibit their aggressiveness in social situations. Indeed, the stronger their habitual aggressive tendencies (as inferred from their TAT responses), the *less* open hostility they showed. Sears's (1961) follow-up of the children surveyed seven years earlier by himself, Maccoby, and Levin also seems to demonstrate an inhibitory effect of punishment. There was a negative correlation between maternal punishment of aggression at age five and the children's scores on a scale of antisocial aggression obtained when they were twelve years old. The more severely their mothers had punished their aggression in early childhood, the less the youngsters appeared to engage in anti-social aggression as they entered adolescence.

I am inclined to interpret these differences in terms of differences in anticipations of punishment. The severely punished children in the latter studies were somewhat older than the similarly treated youngsters in the first-mentioned investigations. The older group conceivably could have come to expect punishment for aggression in most situations, while the younger children might not have generalized their anticipations of punishment much beyond home-like settings. Aggressive tendencies probably were not eliminated in either group, however; punishment serves to suppress rather than eliminate the disapproved response tendencies. Thus, angered children could well exhibit a great deal of hostility in a particular situation, even though their parents had persistently discouraged such behavior, if they believed punishment would not be forthcoming in that situation. The punitive treatment they had received may even lead to a heightened intensity of aggressive behavior in this situation.

*Disciplinary Techniques for Controlling Aggression.* The present analysis of the effects of parental punishment is consistent with the reasoning employed in earlier chapters of this book. For example, in discussing the generalization of inhibitory tendencies (in Chapters 4 and 5), I cited Miller's (1959) contention that the slope of the generalization gradient will vary with the extent to which the restraining responses are evoked solely by external cues. The fear of punishment theoretically arises from just such situational stimuli, and consequently restraints produced by fear of punishment will decline sharply in strength with increasing psychological distance from the punishing agent. In other words, the fear-engendered inhibition of aggression tends to be confined to the situations in which punishment is anticipated. Inhibitory tendencies will be generalized over a relatively wide range of situations, however, when they arise from internalized prescriptions.

Clearly, parents seeking to lessen certain forms of behavior by their offspring are ill-advised to rely on frightening their children. A child will be most likely to comply with his parents' wishes—that is, when they are not around to observe him—when he has accepted their standards as his own. If his parents are extremely punitive, there is a greater chance that he will resent them as frustraters than adopt their attitudes and mode of conduct. What can the parent do to have his youngster take over his behavioral standards?

Whiting and his colleagues at the Harvard University Laboratory of Human Development have hypothesized that *love-oriented* disciplinary methods facilitate the degree to which the child internalizes his parents' values (cited in Bandura & Walters, 1959, p. 191). Parents using such disciplinary techniques generally reward their children by giving love (for example, by praising them) and punish noncompliance by threatening to withhold love (by showing they are hurt or disappointed). They usually also explain to the child how he has behaved incorrectly. *Nonlove-oriented* methods, on the other hand, are based on punishment: physical punishment and/or the deprivation of privileges.

There seems to be little reason to doubt the greater efficacy of the psychological, love-oriented methods for the development of conscience and internalized behavior controls. The cheaters in MacKinnon's (1938) previously mentioned examination of the violation of moral prohibitions evidently were much *less* prone to guilt feelings than were the non-cheaters; the former, we can say, had weaker consciences. Consistent with the Whiting analysis, a higher proportion of cheaters than non-cheaters reported that their fathers had relied primarily upon physical punishment rather than psychological techniques informing the child (1) he had fallen short of some ideal and/or (2) he had disappointed and hurt his parents and therefore might be less loved. Sears et al. also have published data suggesting that the formation of conscience in children is associated positively with parental use of praise and reasoning and negatively with their use of physical punishment (1957, pp. 386–388).

Proceeding further in our chain of evidence, Allinsmith's study, described earlier (Ch. 14 in Miller & Swanson, 1960), demonstrated that seventh- to ninth-grade boys with weak internal controls against socially disapproved behavior—in this case, aggression—tended to have parents who had favored corporal punishment in enforcing their demands. The parents of the youngsters exhibiting habitually strong inhibitions against aggression, in contrast, were more likely to have employed psychological discipline in which they attempted to make their children feel guilty about, or ashamed of, moral transgressions.

Bandura's investigations also have obtained significant relationships between parental discipline and the degree of aggressiveness customarily exhibited by the child. In his study with Walters (1959) he noted that the parents of the boys high in antisocial aggression, in comparison with the parents of the control youngsters, were more likely to resort to physical punishment and deprivation of privileges, and made less use of reasoning, in trying to get compliance with their demands. The two groups of parents did not differ in the extent to which they explicitly threatened the child with loss of love, and the authors suggested that such a disciplinary technique is relatively ineffective for achieving control over adolescents. Finally, in his later comparison (1960) of nondelinquent but highly aggressive school children with markedly withdrawn and inhibited youngsters, Bandura observed somewhat the same pattern. The parents of the aggressive boys, as seen by the children themselves, seemed to be more punitive and made less use of reasoning than did the parents of the inhibited boys.

There is a remarkable consistency to these findings. The studies reviewed here agree in noting that *punitive parental disciplinary methods* (such as physical punishment and depriving children of privileges) *tend to be associated with a high level of aggression and other forms of antisocial behavior by the children. Love-oriented disciplinary methods,* on the other hand, *evidently facilitate the development of conscience and internalized restraints against socially disapproved behavior.* Praising the child when he complies with parental standards and reasoning with him when he does not apparently are among the most effective of these love-oriented techniques.

### Parental Affection and Standards for Behavior

The parents' use of love-oriented methods of control of course assumes that the child cares for his parents and wants to gain and keep their love for him. Actually, we should find that the most effectively trained children (from society's point of view) are those whose parents (1) have consistently prescribed firm standards for their behavior, (2) have employed love-oriented disciplinary techniques in seeking obedience to these standards, and (3) are affectionate and nurturant to the children.

*Parental Affection.* Setting the problem of parental standards aside for the moment, we would expect loving parents to have relatively non-aggressive children for several reasons. For one, affectionate care is need gratifying for the child. The youngster whose parents are cold and rejecting is a child who has been frustrated often and thus should be relatively prone to aggressive behavior. But in addition, parental affection seems to go with the use of love-oriented control methods according to Sears et al. (1957), and Bandura and Walters (1959). In the former study, the investigators found that maternal warmth and acceptance of the child was associated with infrequent use of physical punishment (1957, pp. 335–336). Bandura and Walters observed that the warm and nurturant parents in their sample characteristically tried to reason with their children, while the rejecting, punitive parents resorted more frequently to such punitive disciplinary measures as physical punishment, deprivation of privileges, ridicule, nagging, and scolding (1959, p. 245). Thus, in dealing with his child, *the average affectionate parent probably will employ those disciplinary techniques that capitalize most effectively on the love his child bears for him.* In one way or another, the loving parent will teach his child that the maintenance of this love is contingent upon the child's compliance to his demands. Learning this, the youngster usually also adopts the parent's rules and regulations as his own standards of conduct.

As I already have reported, several studies have obtained a fairly clear-cut relationship between parental rejection or lack of warmth, on one hand, and a high level of aggressive behavior by the child, on the other hand (e.g., Bender, 1947; Glueck & Glueck, 1950; Bandura & Walters, 1959; McCord et al., 1961). Rejecting people as they themselves have been rejected in early childhood, hyperaggressive boys theoretically do not fully internalize social norms, although they may show occasional and aperiodic flashes of guilt. The highly aggressive but nondelinquent boys in Bandura's later (1960) study conceivably refrained from engaging in actually lawless behavior because their dependency needs were not seriously thwarted. Their affectional ties with their parents were strong enough so that they could adopt parental and societal standards to some extent. Nevertheless, their internal controls against hostility apparently were based primarily upon fear of punishment rather than upon generalized moral prescriptions against aggressive behavior, and such inhibitions were none too strong outside the home.

*Identification with Parents.* One of the reasons the child adopts his parents' attitudes and values is because of his desire to be similar to them. Loving his parents, he wants to emulate them, to say what they say, and particularly, to do what they do. He does not have to be actively trained by his parents to copy them; more frequently, he models himself after his parents as he sees them going about the daily business of living. This is the process of *identification*. When the child identifies with another person, he tries to take over this other's qualities and obtains satisfactions from acting like him. According to Sears and Whiting (cf. Sears et al., 1957; and Bandura & Walters, 1959), the identification process originates in the dependency relationship. The child, wanting to obtain more parental love and attention than is granted him, presumably seeks to get these rewards by imitating his parents. (Thus, the aggressively antisocial boys studied by Redl and Wineman, and by Bandura and Walters, supposedly did not adequately identify with their parents because of their intense dependency anxiety.)

We still do not know all of the factors involved in identification. Why does a boy take on his father's qualities when the mother is his main caretaker? Part of the explanation, of course, is that he is rewarded for behaving in a masculine manner and punished in one way or another for behaving like a girl. Nevertheless, such rewards and punishments do not seem to be the complete story by any means (cf. A. Freud, 1937). But however identification occurs, most boys do seek to model themselves after their fathers. If they do not, if they fail to identify sufficiently with their fathers, their learning to become mature, responsible members of society generally suffers. Among other things, the boys' internal controls against socially disapproved behavior may not develop adequately if the youngsters resist accepting the fathers' moral standards.

According to several studies (cf. Bandura & Walters, 1959, p. 256), the strength of the love the boy has for his father is an important determinant of the degree to which he will identify with his father. Thus, we are not surprised to learn that many extremely aggressive boys seem to have a much stronger enmity for their fathers than for their mothers. The aggressively antisocial youngsters in the Bandura-Walters investigation, for example, generally expressed almost as much warmth toward their mothers as did the less aggressive boys but were much more hostile toward their fathers (p. 278). As a consequence of this dislike, they also were much less inclined to identify with their fathers (p. 28). Mackinnon's (1938) finding that the father's predominant disciplinary technique was more strongly related to whether university men cheated or not than was the mother's chief disciplinary method also can be understood from this point of view. If a father had relied primarily upon physical punishment, his son could well have grown to dislike him and as a result failed to identify adequately with the father. Strong moral restraints against unethical behavior, such as cheating, then did not develop.

Consistent with our argument so far, it also appears that the feelings college men have for their fathers are associated with the type of reaction they show to experimental frustrations. In the Funkenstein et al. (1957) experiment, one group of men had responded to the thwarting with aggression directed outward (the *anger-out* group), while another had tended to blame themselves (*anger-in*). The men in both groups later reported that their mothers were the chief source of affection, but the *anger-in* subjects apparently had a more affectionate and closer relationship with their fathers than did the *anger-out* subjects. Perhaps because of this close relationship, the *anger-in* men seem to have developed relatively strong inhibitions against aggression and conceivably other forms of asocial behavior as well.

*Parental Demands.* The child's identification with his parents will lead to his behaving in a moral manner only if his parents actually demand such "correct" behavior. Here is another reason why some children persistently deviate from social norms. Their parents may not insist upon socially proper action, or if they do, are inconsistent or half-hearted about it. Even if the children fully wanted to obey their parents —which they frequently do not—the parents do not provide clear and consistent lessons as to what is right and what is wrong.

Observers have often noted the absence of firm behavioral standards in the home lives of delinquent or aggressively antisocial youngsters (Glueck & Glueck, 1950). Bandura and Walters (1959) found that the parents of their "normal" children, particularly the mothers, imposed stronger restrictions and demands upon their sons than did the parents of the hyperaggressive adolescents. But despite their relative freedom from parental control, the habitually hostile youngsters were much more inclined to resent whatever demands their parents did make. Compliance with parental demands frequently means that the child must sacrifice his own wishes. As the investigators commented (1959, p. 214), the aggressive boys did not receive enough affectional compensation from their parents to make this an easy sacrifice. McCord et al. (1961) have obtained similar results. Their nonaggressive boys typically were more likely than either the highly aggressive or assertive children to come from families demanding polite and responsible behavior. Further, the nonaggressive children apparently were more closely supervised than either of the other two groups.

In reporting these findings, I of course do not advocate that the parent impose strict, rigidly unyielding restrictions upon his child or establish unrealistically severe standards for him. The restrictions and demands obviously should be within the child's abilities and also should be sufficiently permissive so that the child can satisfy (to some degree at least) his developing needs for independence. The parents' demands should be enforced, but they should be enforced with understanding and affection rather than punitively. Equally if not more important, the parent must be consistent in his demands.

Inconsistent prescriptions for behavior are probably frustrating to some extent; the child faced by such shifting standards does not know what to expect. Further, ambiguously vacillating parental rules cannot become the basis for strong internal restraints against disapproved behavior. Sears et al. (1957) observed that inconsistent maternal handling was associated with above average aggressiveness in the child.

McCord et al. (1961) obtained the same results. The mothers of the nonaggressive boys in their sample tended to be fairly consistent in their discipline, while the assertive and aggressive youngsters had much more erratic mothers. The fathers did not differ in the consistency with which they enforced rules. More relevant for our analysis of moral development, the mothers of the "normal" boys in the Bandura and Walters investigation not only imposed stronger demands for obedience on their youngsters but also were more consistent in enforcing these demands than were the mothers of the highly aggressive and socially rebellious boys. Again, there were no significant differences between the two groups of fathers. The Gluecks (1950) also have reported greater behavioral inconsistency in parents of juvenile delinquents than in the mothers and fathers of nondelinquents.

### The Parent as an Aggressive Model

*Investigations in Naturalistic Settings.* Whether or not the child deliberately seeks to pattern himself after his parents, the mother and father can serve as models for him. Their actions may define the appropriate modes of behavior in particular situations. He may love or hate his parents, but he copies their actions in a given situation because he has seldom, if ever, seen anyone else act differently. Bandura and Huston (1961), in an experiment reported previously in Chapter 2, have shown this type of process at work. Nursery school children first interacted with either a nurturant or less nurturant adult and then were given an opportunity to watch this person (the adult model) work on a task. In some of the cases the adult model displayed a good deal of verbal and physical aggression as well as other forms of behavior and in other instances did not exhibit any aggression at all. The results indicate fairly convincingly that children can acquire hostile forms of behavior merely by observing the aggressive actions of an adult; the children clearly imitated the adult's reactions. Interestingly enough, although the adult model's prior nurturance affected the degree to which the children copied many of his behaviors, aggression was readily imitated regardless of the quality of the adult-child relationship.

This last finding seems to have a parallel in the home lives of many highly aggressive youngsters. These children often copy their parents' habitual forms of behavior even though they harbor a strong resentment toward them.

Quite a few studies attest to the frequency with which the parents' actions set an example for their children to follow. Allinsmith's previously mentioned investigation, for example, suggested that boys' typical modes of response to aggression-evoking stimuli were affected by their mothers' characteristic way of reacting to emotion-arousing situations; emotionally controlled mothers tended to have children with relatively strong restraints against aggression, while less controlled mothers had less inhibited boys. Similarly, Bandura and Walters found that the fathers of the aggressively antisocial youngsters in their survey could have served as aggressive models for the boys to emulate since these men were often fairly hostile and punitive themselves. Bandura has also hypothesized, as I have reported earlier, that this type of modeling influence was one of the chief sources of the differences between the aggressive and inhibited children in his second study (1960). Thus, the mothers and fathers of the inhibited boys were themselves particularly anxious and inhibited, and the aggressive children usually had aggressive parents.

Fathers can serve as aggressive models for their children without being exceptionally aggressive. Aggressive behavior is associated with the masculine role in our society. A man must be able to display *some* aggression. He usually is expected to fight back when attacked, for example. This means, then, that boys can learn to exhibit some hostility merely through identifying with their fathers and taking over their roles. However, if their fathers are absent from the home during the formative years of their early childhood (because of death, divorce, or military service) and no suitable adult male substitute is present, they may not learn to act in a thoroughly masculine fashion. According to Sears, Pintler, and Sears (1946) the nursery school–age boys of such absent fathers had a reliably lower level of aggressive doll play than boys whose fathers were not away. A similar difference was not obtained between the father-present and father-absent girls. It may be that the father is particularly likely to be a frustrater to his boy during these preschool years (perhaps because of Oedipal rivalry), and there is some evidence in the study consistent with such a thesis. However, Sears and his collaborators also suggested that the fathers' absence from the home for considerable periods of time resulted in an inadequate masculine identification and that this deficient identification had produced relatively strong restraints against hostile behavior in their sons.

Tentative support for this latter notion can be found in the data published by Funkenstein et al. (1957). Some of the men in this study became so anxious about the aggressive inclinations provoked by the experimental frustration that they were extremely reluctant to admit to being angered (although they did make this admission in later interviews). In contrast to the situation existing in the families of the *anger-out* and *anger-in* men (who had been somewhat less anxious about aggression), the mother was the chief source of authority as well as affection in the family of the typical highly anxious subject. Indeed, approximately half of the anxious men had no father because of death or divorce. Possibly because of this absence, or because of the father's submissiveness, many more of the aggression-anxious men also indicated that they had not identified with their fathers. Their deficient masculine identification could have caused their exceptionally strong anxiety about aggressive behavior.

Sears et al. (1957, p. 266) have warned against punishment as a disciplinary technique partly because of modeling influences. The punitive parent can actually set an aggressive example for his child to copy, they noted. A field study by Levin and Sears (1956) illustrates how such a modeling process might work. They employed the mothers' descriptions of the degree of conscience development in their children to construct an index of the strength of the youngsters' identification with their parents. Since the formation of a conscience theoretically presupposes identification, children seeming to have strong consciences (they often acted guilty when naughty, for example) were assumed to have identified strongly with their mothers and fathers, while the youngsters showing no or little evidence of a superego (who did not seem to be unhappy when bad and/or who appeared to be affected only by fear of punishment) were said to have little identification with their parents. The investigators further assumed that the children in their sample also would be most likely to take over the qualities of their same-sex parent. If punitive parents served as aggressive models for the children who had identified strongly with them, these youngsters, the researchers reasoned, should display a relatively high frequency of aggression in doll-play sessions. Their results generally confirmed this hypothesis. For the girls, those showing the greatest proportion of aggressive responses over the two doll-play sessions were the ones who were presumably strongly identified with severely punitive mothers and who lived in families having the mother as the usual punisher. It appears as if aggressive mothers had produced relatively strong aggressiveness habits in girls strongly identifying with them. The severity of home punishment for aggression was a relatively unimportant determinant of doll-play aggression for the boys, however, perhaps because aggression is characteristic of the masculine role. But acceptance of this role in the form of presumed identification with the father did seem to make a difference. In the case of boys, identification was positively related to doll-play aggression only when the father was the chief punitive agent in the family. When the father was the usual punisher, in other words, high identification (probably largely with him) seemed to have resulted in strong aggressiveness habits.

*Some Laboratory Research.* The present discussion, of course, only assumes a modeling influence. We do not have any direct evidence in the above-mentioned correlational studies that the children had imitated their parents. Properly designed and sufficiently sophisticated field investigations can give us a good deal of information about the modeling process, but whenever possible we must look to laboratory experimentation for answers to some of the difficult questions concerning modeling effects. Thus, one conceivable question involves the generalization of the reinforcement of the child's hostile behavior. Bandura (1960) has noted, as was reported earlier, that the parents of his nondelinquent aggressive boys often rewarded their children's aggressive behavior outside the home. Does such parental reinforcement strengthen only those specific forms of hostility practiced by the boys at home?

An experiment by Lövaas (1961b) strongly indicates that parental rewards for aggression can enhance the likelihood of a broad spectrum of hostile behavior. The psychologist reinforced aggressive verbal responses by children in a typical verbal conditioning session and found there was a subsequent increase in the number of nonverbal, aggressive motor responses made by these youngsters while working on another task.

Other research, conducted by Bandura et al. (1961; 1962) points to a possible limitation in modeling effects. The Levin and Sears study just reviewed suggested that girls might copy their aggressive mothers. The Bandura et al. laboratory findings imply, however, that it is relatively unusual for girls to imitate an adult woman's aggressive behavior. Identification with the aggressive woman could be an important contigency condition determining whether aggressive modeling occurs. Thus, in the first of these studies (1961), as in the earlier Bandura-Huston experiment, nursery school children were found to readily imitate the behavior of an aggressive adult model. But the sex of the model and of the potential imitator made a difference. The aggressive male model was imitated more frequently than the aggressive female, particularly in the case of masculine-typed activity such as physical aggression. Moreover, boys exhibited a greater imitation of physical aggression than did girls. Both of these results may have been affected by sex-typing. The adult female probably was less readily copied when she behaved aggressively because the children regarded her aggression as being inappropriate to *her* sex role, and similarly the girls undoubtedly did less imitating of physical aggression because such activity was not consistent with *their* sex role.

## SUMMARY

The present book regards the highly aggressive person as an individual who has a latent disposition to make hostile responses to relevant, aggression-evoking cues rather than as someone who is chronically angry. Continuing with the stimulus-control theme espoused in earlier chapters (e.g., those on hostility generalization), the habitually extremely aggressive individual is said to (1) render many people and objects as functionally equivalent (usually as frustraters), making them capable of evoking hostile behavior from him, and (2) have firmly learned habits of making aggressive responses to the aggression cues. Internal emotional states (anger) only predispose aggressive behavior, as do hostility habits, according to the present view; aggression cues—stimuli associated with anger instigators—are necessary if hostile responses are to be performed. These evoking stimuli may be outside or within the aggressor. The strength of the aggressive responses an individual performs following a frustration is considered to be a joint function of four factors: (1) the intensity of his anger, i.e., the intensity of his emotional predisposition to aggression, (2) the degree of association between the initial anger instigator and the aggression cues in the situation, (3) the strength of his habitual tendencies to respond aggressively to aggression cues, and (4) the strength of the inhibitory tendencies elicited in the situation.

Because of his readiness to perceive relatively many aggression cues in the external environment, the extremely hostile person displays aggressiveness in a wide variety of situations. However, he is not necessarily consistently aggressive because (1) aggressive cues may not be present in some situations, (2) he may on occasion anticipate punishment for hostile actions, and/or (3) motives incompatible with aggressive behavior, such as desires for affiliation or dependency, may be activated in some situations but not in others.

Several characteristics are frequently associated with a high level of aggressiveness in human beings. The customarily highly aggressive person usually is a male with a weak ego-control capacity, i.e., he is relatively unable to defer gratifications and typically shows intense emotional reactions to frustrations. Women are less likely than men to exhibit frequent direct hostility because such behavior deviates from their culturally defined sex role. They may, however, display much "prosocial aggression," inhibited, indirect hostile actions in defense of their codes of social propriety. If working-class youngsters have a greater likelihood of performing very direct aggressive acts than do their middle-class counterparts (as is suggested by one study), this may stem from (1) more frequent frustrations, perhaps because of their greater economic privations, (2) stronger aggressiveness habits because of the encouragement of supposedly justified hostile behavior by parents and/or peers and their greater contact with aggressive models, and (3) weaker restraints against hostile behavior. These weaker inhibitions may be traced, at least in part, to the less effective disciplinary techniques generally employed by working-class parents in comparison with middle-class parents; the former are more likely to rely on physical punishment rather than love-oriented disciplinary methods.

A history of frequent frustrations does not necessarily give rise to aggressive personalities, although many characteristically extremely hostile boys have suffered at the hands of emotionally cold and rejecting parents. (Indeed, many such aggressive boys have experienced severe frustration of their dependency needs.) I have suggested that home conditions regarded as frustrating by investigators may not actually be too much of a frustration to the children. For example, a rejecting mother may not be upsetting to the boy who has never learned to want his mother's love. Frustrations are said to create a predisposition to aggressive behavior, and many thwartings throughout childhood theoretically (1) cause the person to expect frustrations in the future so that he readily interprets ambiguous situations as frustrations, (2) produce strong emotional reactions to any one thwarting, and (3) cause him to associate many people and objects with his previous anger instigators so that they are capable of evoking hostility. However, the person may also have acquired strong response tendencies incompatible with aggression.

The present chapter also has discussed parental training behaviors related to the development of internal controls against aggression and other forms of socially disapproved behavior. From the viewpoint of society, the most effectively trained youngsters are those whose parents (1) have consistently prescribed firm standards for the children's behavior, (2) have employed love-oriented disciplinary techniques, especially relying on praise and the use of reason rather than physical punishment and the deprivation of privileges, and (3) have been affectionate and nurturant to the children throughout childhood.

Parents employing punitive disciplinary methods may cause their children to expect further punishment for disapproved behavior on many, but not all, occasions. They may also heighten their youngsters' aggressive tendencies, because the punishment is frustrating, and also, because by punishing their children they have provided their children an aggressive model to copy. The parents' use of punishment probably also interferes with the children's acceptance of the parents' attitudes and values.

# chapter II

# Aggression in Crime,
## Homicides, and Suicides

Most readers probably will not be surprised that the present book includes a discussion of criminal behavior. Many crimes are acts of deliberate violence, perpetrated primarily to do injury. Juvenile delinquency often is of this sort. Teen-agers may beat up members of rival gangs, break store windows, slash automobile tires, or demolish schoolrooms because they are angry and somehow associate the targets of their aggression with their frustraters. Similarly, adults usually commit murder in a fit of uncontrolled rage. There is little doubt that such behavior is aggressive. But yet, what about thefts and other property crimes? Most major violations of the criminal law fall into this category. According to the Uniform Crime Reports published by the FBI, some 1.4 million of the approximately 1.6 million major crimes committed in the United States in 1958 involved robbery, burglary, larceny over $50, and auto thefts (cited in Tappan, 1960, p. 37). In what sense, someone might ask, are such actions aggressive? They are carried out in order to obtain some valued object and not necessarily to injure.

At least two reasons can be advanced for the inclusion of criminal behavior within the scope of the present work:

1. Aggression can serve aims other than the desire to hurt or destroy. The thief may want only money (a noninjurious aim), but in striving for this goal he attacks the property owner, the insurance company, and, in a larger sense, society as a whole. Without necessarily intending to be hostile the lawbreaker is aggressive in that he does do injury. (But of course in many cases he does seek to hurt others.)

2. Even disregarding such considerations of injury, crime is similar to aggression in one important respect: Both activities are socially disapproved. The criminal usually knows that most people regard lawbreaking to be wrong (even though a small peer group may approve of his actions). Aggressive behavior also is strongly discouraged in

many segments of our society and sometimes leads to social if not legal punishment.

Thus, aggression, as a violation of social standards, may be affected by many of the same factors governing violations of the norms against crime. Many criminals, in other words, may possess characteristics generally held by people with strong aggressive tendencies.

This final chapter will indeed attempt to draw a parallel between the conditions leading to habitually extreme aggressiveness as formulated in the preceding chapter and those conditions apparently affecting the individual's likelihood of becoming a criminal.[1] I will try to show that some of the same factors may be at work in developing both types of deviant behavioral dispositions, particularly in schoolchildren and adolescents.

The theoretical propositions offered in the earlier sections of this book are applicable to a variety of illegal actions. After reviewing several investigations into the genesis of criminality, we will consider some of the determinants of two other extremely aggressive forms of illegal behavior: murder and suicide. Particular attention will be given to the role of frustrations in producing such cases of violence.

## CAUSES OF CRIMINALITY

Given the present status of research into the wellsprings of crime, any attempt to develop one all-inclusive explanation for all delinquent actions would be decidedly premature. There are many complex and difficult problems confronting the criminologist, and the present chapter cannot hope to offer a definitive, detailed analysis of the origins of crime.[2] Rather than attempting a comprehensive survey of the voluminous literature on the topic, I will try to show that some of the theoretical generalizations employed earlier in this work also can be applied to the problem of illegal behavior. A variety of factors contribute to the development of criminal tendencies (cf. Glueck & Glueck, 1950), but many of these can be understood in terms of the concepts used throughout this volume: frustrations creating an emotional arousal predisposing to aggressive behavior, aggressiveness habits also predisposing to such behavior, external cues evoking the hostile actions, and inhibitions against these socially disapproved responses.

---

[1] As also was the case in Chapter 10, the present discussion is restricted to the development of criminal tendencies in males. Women probably take somewhat different roads to crime.

[2] The reader interested in pursuing this topic further can consult a number of excellent texts, such as those by Tappan (1960) and Sutherland and Cressey (1960).

## Personalities of Criminals and Delinquents

*Criminal and Delinquent Types.* One important caution should be raised before we embark on the analysis per se. The present formulation will list several conditions that may lead an individual into criminal behavior, such as recurrent frustrations, group norms approving illegal actions, etc. We cannot say what weight is to be given to each of these factors in every case. There are different kinds of lawbreakers, and each type may have taken a different road to crime. Some delinquents, for example, engage in criminal actions primarily because of their personality characteristics. They may assault their victims in a fit of rage or commit a robbery because of an uncontrolled urge. Although this is not certain by any means, strong frustrations at the hand of parents, particularly of the child's dependency needs, appear to play an important part in forming this type of individual. Other delinquents, however, seem to be more strongly influenced by the behaviors and opinions of their friends and associates. Their peers have defined thefts or violence as "correct" or even necessary behavior, and so they steal a car, rob a store, or beat someone up in order to validate their membership in a group (as well as because of the intrinsic attractiveness of these activities for them).

Several authorities have insisted criminals must be differentiated along some continuum of social versus personality determinants of crime. As an illustration, Lindesmith and Dunham (1941) have established a system of categories ranging from the "individual" criminal at one end of the continuum to the professional and career criminals who are strongly affected by their deviant subcultures at the other extreme. Similarly, Hewitt and Jenkins (1946) have divided juvenile delinquents into three groups: "neurotics" whose behavior supposedly is an outgrowth of strong emotional disturbances and anxiety, "unsocialized delinquents" possessing little anxiety and guilt for engaging in socially disapproved actions, and "pseudosocial delinquents" who presumably are identified with their peer groups but not the larger society.

The same factors may have gone into the formation of each of these offender types, but not necessarily always in the same way or to the same degree. Most lawbreakers may have been exposed to some combination of frustrations and aggressively antisocial role models, with the thwartings being particularly important in the development of "individual" offenders and the antisocial models being more influential in the formation of the "socialized" criminals.

Empirical evidence is consistent with such a possibility. Jenkins (1957) has reported several investigations which succeeded in differentiating socialized delinquents from other, aggressively unsocialized youngsters. In the first of these studies, conducted with Hewitt (1946), socialized offenders showing characteristics such as bad companions, gang activities, and cooperative stealing were distinguished from less socialized and more aggressive youngsters possessing such traits as strong assaultive tendencies, defiance of authority, and inadequate guilt feelings. A statistical cluster analysis of the traits of five thousand children examined at the Institute for Juvenile Research appears to support the existence of these two different syndromes; socialized delinquents, characterized by stealing, truancy, and associating with bad companions, did not emerge in the same cluster as an unsocialized aggressive type displaying a great deal of open hostility.

Other evidence also is available. Peterson, Quay, and Cameron (1959) factor-analyzed a number of personality questionnaire items which had successfully differentiated delinquents from "normals" in other research. The first of the five factors obtained, describing tough, amoral, and rebellious qualities, and labeled "psychopathy," is clearly similar to the unsocialized aggression identified by Jenkins and his colleagues. Some of the other factors conceivably could have predisposed the children to socialized aggression.

Jenkins (1957) also has suggested that his two types of delinquents had different experiences with their families. The typical socialized delinquent supposedly has had a background of "gross lack of supervision . . . in an overcrowded, often impoverished, and usually disorganized home in a high delinquent area." The unsocialized aggressive boy, on the other hand, has suffered from extreme parental rejection, particularly maternal rejection, and may also have been provided with many examples of antisocial, deviant behavior in the actions of his parents and peers. More will be said about these antecedent conditions later, but the reader will note the similarity between Jenkins's description of the unsocialized delinquent and the portrait of the aggressively antisocial youngster drawn in the preceding chapter.

*Personality Functioning.* The reader also should be reminded of the present conception of personality functioning. This book does *not* conceive of the individual as a storehouse of repressed energies constantly striving for expression. His personality is largely (but not exclusively) composed of traits (or habitual tendencies) which, as was discussed in the preceding chapter, do at least three things: (1) They make the individual sensitive to particular classes of stimuli; (2) they associate a relatively wide range of stimuli with the cues to which he is sensitive, in essence rendering "many stimuli functionally equivalent"; and (3) they give rise to certain action tendencies in response to these cues. Many extremely aggressive people, for example, are quick to perceive threats or frustrations in their external environment, interpret a great variety of events as frustrating to them, and display strong, hostile reactions after making these interpretations.

Contrary to the conception of traits held by many writers, the present formulation does not contend that personality habits are exhibited in every situation. A trait is a latent disposition to respond to particular cues; the response is not revealed in overt behavior if these cues are not present or if stronger responses incompatible with the trait response are also evoked. There is a great deal of consistency in a person's behavior across different situations but not an ever-present fixedness of response.

Such an analysis suggests additional features in the operation of at least some criminal personalities. As I pointed out in Chapter 10, behavioral consistency involves both stimulus and response generalization. The individual tends to exhibit a given action to a wide variety of stimuli (which for him have some degree of association with each other) and also shows some variation in the form of this action. Thus, if many delinquents have habitually strong aggressive tendencies, they should display both stimulus and response generalization in their aggressive behavior. This seems to be so according to observations published by Sheldon Glueck and Eleanor Glueck (1950). The five hundred boys in their sample of delinquents apparently showed more frequent hostile actions across a broader range of situations, and also a greater variety of aggressive actions, than did the five hundred matched but nondelinquent boys.

One decided advantage to viewing personality as a constellation of habits is the explicit recognition of the possibility of change. Habits are learned. They also may be forgotten or extinguished through the operation of other learning. Again, this applies to delinquency and criminality. The juvenile delinquent does not necessarily grow up to become the older, full-fledged, hardened criminal. Tappan (1960, pp. 62, 72–73) has reviewed several investigations demonstrating such transformations of young lawbreakers into mature, law-abiding citizens. The Gluecks, for example, have reported that only 32 per cent of a large sample of reformatory inmates studied over a fifteen-year time span persisted in crime, while 34 per cent seemed to have reformed entirely.[3] In another investigation, only approximately 31 per cent of a sample of Detroit juveniles followed for five years after they had reached seventeen years of age were subsequently arrested as adults. As Tappan concluded, many delinquents cease committing offenses when they at-

[3] For many reasons, all of which need not be gone into here, we would expect the earliest learning to be the strongest and longest-lasting. Thus, children developing delinquent tendencies at a relatively early age may have been exposed to extremely strong (and persistent) conditions predisposing to unlawful behavior. Whatever the reasons, the younger the delinquent at time of first arrest, the less likely he is to reform (Glueck & Glueck, 1959, pp. 82–83).

tain maturity. Many adult criminals are "unregenerated juvenile delinquents," but some had waited until they were "of age" before seriously breaking the law.

The two reasons just advanced—the requirement that relevant situational cues be present if the habitual tendencies are to be "activated" and the possibility of changes in habit patterns—can explain the frequent failures to predict delinquent behavior from social and personality measurements. Attempts have been made to employ the research findings concerning the biographical and personality characteristics differentiating young offenders from other boys in forecasting whether children will become delinquent or not, but these attempts have not been met with a high degree of success (despite some extravagant claims to the contrary). As an example, the Gluecks (1959) have constructed several "prediction tables" for the identification of potential delinquents. A study conducted in New York City reported "89 per cent accuracy" in forecasting delinquency from these tables. More sober examination of the data, however, casts serious doubt on such claims (cf. Herzog, 1960, pp. 2–3). The "accuracy" stems predominantly from the correct forecasting of boys who do *not* become offenders. There was no more than a 37 per cent accuracy in predictions (and probably much less than this if the criterion is restricted to legal offenses rather than "delinquent traits") for the group rated as having the highest probability of delinquency. A good many children have been labeled as potential delinquents without, so far at least, actually engaging in illegal actions. Similar failures of prediction in at least two out of three cases have been obtained with other instruments such as the Minnesota Multiphasic Personality Inventory (Herzog, 1960, pp. 4–5). From the present viewpoint the boys not realizing their delinquent "potential" could have failed to encounter the kinds of situations "activating" this potential and/or their personality habits may have changed.

*Conjectured Personality Characteristics of Persistent Lawbreakers.* Many delinquents and criminals seem to possess the following characteristics in varying degrees during the period of their lives in which they commit crimes:

1. They are relatively unable to defer gratifications. [There are exceptions, of course; some lawbreakers do control themselves in order to prepare and plan for a crime. Many juvenile delinquents, however, evidently are unable to postpone their pleasures for too long (cf. Mischel, 1961).]

2. They are fairly easily frustrated and, when aroused, typically show a relatively strong emotional reaction.

3. They feel alienated and apart from many other people, often viewing them with hostility and resentment.

4. They have relatively strong aggressive inclinations—which, however, may be expressed only indirectly, such as in property crimes, if punishment for direct aggression is anticipated or if inhibitions against direct hostility are strong enough.

5. They possess insufficiently developed moral standards so that criminal actions, and possibly other socially disapproved behaviors as well, do not produce intense guilt feelings and therefore are frequently not restrained—again, unless punishment is anticipated for carrying out these actions.

6. They hold attitudes justifying antisocial behavior.

The first two qualities—inability to defer gratifications and strong emotional reactivity to thwartings—often are described as denoting a "weak ego control." Research reviewed in the preceding chapter indicates aggressively antisocial youngsters typically are weak in such control. When combined with the next three characteristics—hostility toward much of the outside world, strong aggressive dispositions, and weak moral standards—we have the picture of the unsocialized delinquent as drawn by Jenkins (1957) and the "psychopathic" individual isolated by Peterson and his colleagues (1959). Many of the delinquents studied by the Gluecks (1950) also seemed to possess these impulsive, hostile characteristics, but often in combination with the sixth trait—attitudes justifying socially deviant behavior. These latter attitudes presumably are relatively predominant in the personalities of criminals and delinquents influenced by criminal subcultures, the so-called "socialized" criminals. Socialized criminals probably also have a somewhat stronger ego control than the more psychopathic criminals and delinquents. They also have relatively intense resentment toward the frustrating middle-class agencies of society, usually regarding such agencies as the legitimate target of their aggression.

Assuming these descriptions are at least partly correct, how do the criminal personality characteristics develop? The following section will be concerned with this question. Sociological and psychological investigations will be considered from the viewpoint of effects on individual behavior.[4]

## Frustrations

The present book has taken a definite stand on the frustration-aggression hypothesis. Frustration, i.e., interference with a person's ongoing goal-directed activity, arouses anger and thus can lead to

---

[4] There is no implication in such an analysis that sociological formulations dealing with group- or cultural-level variables are inferior to psychological formulations. The discussion must be restricted and is here confined to the level of individual behavior.

aggressive reactions if suitable aggression-cues (stimuli associated with the frustrater) are present. But since the anger probably decreases with time, the frequently thwarted individual does not possess a life-long-accumulated pool of aggressive energy. He is not in a constantly active drive state. Rather, I have argued, his past history of frustrations increases his sensitivity to further deprivations. He is quick to perceive thwartings, perhaps even when other people would not see them, and displays relatively uncontrolled, intense emotional responses. These intense reactions to real or imagined frustrations predispose him to extreme hostile behavior. However, the predisposition to aggression is not necessarily reflected in antisocial aggression even given the presence of hostility-evoking cues. The thwarted person may have learned other, nonaggressive modes of response which inhibit illegal hostile actions. *Before we can predict the likelihood of antisocial aggression, we have to know* (1) *whether the individual blames people other than himself for the frustration,* (2) *the extent to which his hostile behavior has been reinforced in the past by parents and/or peers,* (3) *the particular forms of aggression that had been reinforced most frequently, and* (4) *the extent to which he has interiorized moral standards opposing antisocial conduct.* Frustrations are important in the development of delinquency and criminality but are not the sufficient cause of such behavior.

The probability of an aggressive reaction to a frustration, I also have suggested, following Dollard et al. (1939), varies with certain quantitative aspects of the thwarting (e.g., the intensity of the blocked instigation, the degree to which all alternative nonaggressive responses are thwarted, etc.). But to emphasize such quantitative aspects is not to say the qualitative nature of the frustration is unimportant in the formation of the offender personality. We will see that the perceived source of the deprivation may determine whether the individual becomes a socialized lawbreaker susceptible to influence by a delinquent subculture or an unsocialized, individual criminal. As was discussed in Chapter 5, aggressive responses aroused by a frustration tend to be directed toward the perceived frustrater. *If the individual is thwarted by middle-class agencies, such as teacher, employer, or vague business forces, his hostility will be vented against people associated with these middle-class frustraters and not against his peers. The boy who has been exposed to severe parental rejection in early childhood, on the other hand, may generalize his feelings beyond his parents to many other people including his peers.* In a sense, he does not differentiate too well among the people around him; all are frustraters (real or potential), and all are not to be trusted.[5]

---

[5] The failure to differentiate among people as frustraters or nonfrustraters may be due at least in part to the immaturity of the child when he was first rejected by

*Culturally Induced Deprivations.* The immediately preceding outline of frustration effects implies there should be a relationship between economic conditions and crime rates. People seeking work and other economic goods are, by definition, frustrated when they are unable to attain these goals. Crime should be one of the aggressive consequences of such a thwarting. Of course, there is nothing new to this reasoning; social observers have long believed in the linkage between crime and economic deprivations. What is more surprising is the actual empirical evidence on this matter. Several studies suggest economic conditions in reality may play only a minor role in the rise of criminal behavior. Thus, business indices have been found to be only negligibly associated with crime rates (cf. Tappan, 1960, pp. 210–212).

At least two reasons can be advanced for such low obtained correlations: (1) the heterogeneity of the criminal population and (2) an inadequate analysis of the effects of economic deprivations. In regard to the first of these possibilities, Glaser and Rice (1959) have demonstrated unemployment does not have the same effect on criminality at all age levels. Adult crime rates, particularly property offenses by people between twenty and forty-five years of age, varied directly with unemployment in this investigation utilizing data for the United States as a whole as well as more adequate data for three large American cities. In contrast, there was a tendency for poor economic conditions to depress crime rates in the younger group. Temporary economic stress might reduce juvenile delinquency by cementing family relationships.

But in addition to there being such divergent reactions to economic hardships, these privations are not necessarily always frustrating. Frustrations involve interference with *ongoing,* goal-directed activity. The person who is relatively apathetic economically and socially should be fairly indifferent to poor business conditions. If he does not care about having a good job he will not be too disturbed by his failure to obtain such a position. Anger, then, would be relatively weak if it arises at all, and he would not have any resulting strong predispositions to unlawful behaviors.

Wood (1961) has employed an essentially similar view in an investigation of socioeconomic correlates of criminal activities in Ceylon. Crimes result, he contended, not from "objective external restraints," but from "conditions *subjectively* defined as undesirably limiting behavior." For one reason or another, the offenders could not do what they wanted to

---

his parents. He was not old enough to have learned that people can differ in their behavior toward him. The youth frustrated by teacher or employer, however, presumably has already learned to distinguish between potential friends and nonfriends.

do. Thus, in comparison with nonoffenders, Ceylonese lawbreakers were more likely to have career ambitions out of line with their actual occupational achievements. The criminals also had a greater frequency of other forms of status frustrations.

A number of contemporary sociologists have pointed to still other frustrations as causes of socially deviant behavior. Taking his lead from Durkheim (1951), Robert Merton has maintained that deviant behavior ensues when there is an "acute disjunction" between culturally prescribed goals and institutionalized means for attaining these goals (1957). As the result of such a disjunction, Merton stressed, regulatory social norms tend to break down; traditional rules lose their authority for the person who, for one reason or another, is denied the means to the satisfaction of his wishes. A state of anomie exists for him. Albert K. Cohen (1955) extended this reasoning to the formation of delinquent subcultures. He essentially viewed much juvenile delinquency (but by no means every case) as arising from status deprivations. Growing up in a society dominated by middle-class attitudes and aspirations, the lower-class child is taught that ambition, hard work, self-control, respect for property, and the postponement of gratifications lead to academic success, financial achievement, and the rewards of high social status. By and large, however, his social-class background does not equip him to meet the terms for success established by middle-class institutions, and he experiences a serious status deprivation together with a decline in self-esteem. The result supposedly is a "reaction formation." Middle-class norms are repudiated, and "nonutilitarian, malicious, and negativistic" values are substituted.

Professor Cohen's thesis is altogether consistent with the theoretical approach taken in the present book.[6] Any status deprivations felt by working-class children could certainly be regarded as frustrations capable of arousing anger. Since middle-class agencies—schools, teachers, employers, legal authorities, etc.—are instrumental in producing these frustrations, they, or other people and institutions associated with them, should tend to evoke hostile responses from the boys. The hostility is

---

[6] Some doubts have been expressed as to whether the status deprivation postulated by Cohen is as widespread or intense throughout the working class as his argument insists (cf. Tappan, 1960, p. 182). Social-psychological research suggests most people do not aspire to faraway goals. A person's social aspirations usually are affected by comparisons between his own social standing and that of his friends and acquaintances, the people around him with whom he associates most intimately, i.e., his reference groups. The working-class individual typically wants to be at least as well off as those with whom he comes into relatively close and frequent contact and rarely compares himself with the banker or successful businessman. But whether such status deprivations are widespread in the lower class or not, they are only a few of the many frustrations to which the urban working class is heir.

not directed against peers—other youngsters just like themselves also suffering from status frustrations; these other boys are victims like themselves, not frustraters.

*Family Induced Frustrations.* The child is affected by thwartings at the hands of his mother and father as well as by economic and status deprivations. Some of these parental barriers to the youngster's goal-directed activity probably do not prevent him from developing close friendships with peers, although they may predispose him to criminal activities. Quarrels among the family members can thwart the boy's need for a secure, stable home life (as well as provide aggressive models for the boy to copy). Not surprisingly, as I reported in Chapter 10, family conflicts are common in the home lives of many delinquents and other aggressively antisocial children (Glueck & Glueck, 1950; Bandura & Walters, 1959; McCord, McCord, & Zola, 1959). Similarly, the mother and father may pay relatively little attention to the boy, not actively rejecting him but still, through neglect, refusing to recognize his worth and importance as a unique individual. Again, studies show parents of juvenile delinquents are more likely to be neglectful toward their children than are parents of more law-abiding youngsters (e.g., Glueck & Glueck, 1950; McCord et al., 1959). Children exposed only to such frustrations evidently do form close attachments with peers. These peers are not seen as frustraters. Indeed, some of the people the thwarted boy meets on the street may even become particularly attractive to him. If they engage in aggressively antisocial activities, they will permit him to expresss his own hostile inclinations.

Other parental deprivations, however, can obstruct the development of close friendships. Chapter 10 pointed out that parental thwarting of the child's dependency needs apparently has such an effect. The rejected child has not obtained the love and protection he desired from his mother and father. He wanted to be cared for by them but, instead, received only harsh rebuffs. Growing up not trusting and even fearing his parents, he regards everyone around him as a potential frustrater (Redl & Wineman, 1957; Bandura & Walters, 1959). The boy then goes out into the streets and to school with a "chip on his shoulder." He expects unfriendliness from others and this is what he frequently gets. If he becomes a delinquent or criminal, he will be an unsocialized or individual offender rather than a socialized gang member (Jenkins, 1957). The frustration of his dependency needs presumably made him anxious about forming emotional attachments to other people (Bandura & Walters, 1959). On top of this, his aggressive inclinations probably are heightened even more by the disciplinary techniques employed by his rejecting parents. The preceding chapter also has reported, the reader will recall, that such parents tend to rely on punitive rather than love-oriented methods of controlling their children (Bandura & Walters, 1959; McCord et al., 1959). Punitive treatment has at least two unfortunate effects from the point of view of society (and probably the parents as well): (1) Punishment is a frustration and increases the child's resentment; (2) the punitive parents also serve as aggressive models for their children to emulate.

The consequences of parental rejection can be summarized in a few words. The severely punished, rejected child generally has the wrong kind of learning experiences. He does not adopt societal moral standards too readily. Nor does he develop ego controls strong enough to enable him to withstand serious frustrations. He does, however, learn to imitate his parents' aggressive behavior, and his aggressiveness habits are strengthened even further. Finally, he does not trust most people, and this also leads to continued frustrations.

Consistent with such reasoning, Bandura and Walters (1959) have noted that parents of aggressively antisocial youngsters were much harsher and more rejecting toward their children than parents of demographically comparable, nonviolent children. Many of the delinquents studied by the Gluecks also had such rejecting mothers and fathers. Similar findings have been published by McCord et al. (1959) in a comparison of the home lives of law-abiding and lawbreaking individuals (described before the crimes were committed). Warm, loving fathers and mothers in this latter study had fewer criminal children than did cruel, rejecting parents. The mother's behavior evidently was particularly important in the development of criminal tendencies. Her son was not too likely to become a criminal if she was a loving parent, regardless of the father's attitude toward the boy, but had a good chance of being convicted for some offense if she was rejecting, especially if the father also was a rejecting parent.

Tentative findings published by McCord et al. suggest that parental treatment also affects the choice of criminal act. Many of the people convicted of property crimes in their investigation evidently had been seriously neglected as children, while offenders guilty of crimes against the person appeared to have suffered primarily from the frustrations of maternal domination or paternal rejection. Also in line with the present formulation, the investigators noted that love-oriented discipline "seemed to be a strong preventive" for crimes against the person (1959, p. 151).

Parental frustrations probably also influence the likelihood of reform. Rarely establishing close relations with others, the severely rejected child will not have too many chances to learn that some people can be warm, friendly, and trustworthy. Consequently, his harsh, resentful attitude toward the world typically persists as he grows into manhood, and adult criminality becomes all too probable. Only 45 per cent of the juvenile delinquents with nonloving mothers in the McCord et al. study seemed to have reformed as they matured, but fully 68 per cent of the young offenders with loving mothers were not arrested for any further crimes by the end of the investigation.

## Criminal Standards of Behavior

Severe frustrations of intense desires are not the only causes of aggressive behavior (cf. Bandura, 1960), and such thwartings are by no means the sole determinants of criminal or delinquent activity. People generally have to find some social support before they can translate their hostile inclinations into persistent actions. *Unless a person is extremely susceptible to intense emotional arousal and possesses unusually weak inner controls, he will not engage in recurrent criminality without the approval of some friends or associates.* The unsocialized offender governed by strong emotional urges may not need such encouragement, but other lawbreakers, particularly unsupervised delinquents, probably do. They must believe illegal actions are "right," are the things to do in certain situations. The shared opinions of their peers define law violations as appropriate and even necessary behavior for them in some circumstances. Offenders also must have the aid and encouragement of friends if they are to overcome their fear of punishment, and their membership in delinquent or criminal gangs provides such support. They may even need special training in particular illegal activities, and this can be obtained only through association with other offenders. Social influences clearly play an important part in many crimes.

*Cultural Determinants.* Sociologists have long emphasized the contribution of neighborhood and community to criminal and delinquent behavior. Thus, according to Thrasher's (1936) well-known study of Chicago gangs, gangland is concentrated in a "geographically and socially interstitial area," in a twilight zone of factories, deteriorated housing, poverty, and cultural change. Other research by Clifford Shaw and his followers has demonstrated that these deteriorated, poverty-stricken areas have extremely high delinquency and crime rates. The social disorganization and culture conflicts among Negroes and native- and foreign-born whites in such neighborhoods supposedly result in a failure to develop adequate social controls, and the values held by delinquent groups take the place of more traditional social values (Shaw & McKay, 1942). Criminal traditions arise to steer and encourage criminal behaviors.

*Social Associations.* The ecological approach pays relatively little attention to the specific ways in which social disorganization affects the individual residing within the high crime areas. How, we might want to know, do the delinquency values develop and how are they transmitted to the boys growing up in these criminal subcultures? There is an obvious explanation to this last question. As the eminent criminologist Edwin Sutherland first propounded in his "differential association" theory (cf. Sutherland & Cressey, 1960), youngsters often adopt the values and behavior patterns of their associates. When a person becomes delinquent, Sutherland maintained, he does so because he has had frequent contacts with criminal behavior patterns and has been isolated from anticriminal patterns. He absorbs the attitudes and values of his surrounding delinquent culture much as a Southerner learns not to pronounce the *r*'s in words because the people around him also fail to make these sounds (p. 78).

There is little doubt that people are affected by the company they keep, whether they are law-abiding citizens or not. Most youthful offenders, for example, seem to associate primarily with other delinquents (Glueck & Glueck, 1950). Nevertheless, criminal associations do not provide the complete explanation for all illegal activities. Sutherland himself had recognized (cf. Cloward, 1959, p. 169) that the commission of a crime often depends upon *both* "differential associations favoring the acquisition of criminal values and skills, and conditions encouraging participation in criminal activity."

The factors listed by Sutherland are not entirely independent. *Frustrations may predispose a person to associate with lawbreakers and also make him ready to accept their values.* We do not automatically adopt whatever views our peers may happen to advocate. We are quickest to accept someone else's beliefs if these values coincide with our own inclinations. We may not assimilate another's hostile values, for example, unless we ourselves have strong aggressive tendencies. Laboratory experimentation has documented this point. In one study college students accepted the aggressive views expressed by a communicator when they had been angered by deliberate frustrations, but did not adopt these beliefs if they had not been provoked (Weiss & Fine, 1956).

A. K. Cohen (1955) also has emphasized the role of frustrations in the development and acceptance of delinquent values. He argued that lower-class youngsters suffering from the disjunction between culturally prescribed goals and the means available to them for reaching these goals often band together in a common rebellion against middle-class norms. They develop a delinquent subculture emphasizing "nonutilitarian, malicious, and negativistic" values that serves to protect them from further status punishments and loss of self-esteem. But such status deprivations common to many working-class children are again not the complete story. Youngsters are not equally attracted to delinquent groups.

Empirical research has shown that differential associations do not arise entirely by chance. To a considerable extent people select their friends and companions. Thus, in the study by the Gluecks (1950) mentioned throughout this chapter, only about 7 per cent of the five hundred nondelinquents had persistent lawbreakers as friends. Most of the law-abiding children seem to have avoided all but the most superficial contact with their delinquent peers. Indeed, the Gluecks' findings suggest the young offenders had themselves exerted a good deal of selectivity in their friendship choices. More frequently than the "normal" children, the delinquents had gone out of their way to play in distant neighborhoods and had sought out older boys rather than same-aged peers as companions. Their gang membership could have had an important part in strengthening their aggressive tendencies and in weakening their restraints against socially disapproved behavior, but their friendships had not always come about fortuitously. The delinquents could well have selected aggressively antisocial youngsters as friends because of their own hostile inclinations.

McCord et al. (1959) also stressed this selectivity in associations. Their study had uncovered strong indications of the operation of deviant subcultures. Three-quarters of the boys associating with delinquent gangs in childhood subsequently developed criminal records, while only 30 per cent of the children who "looked to their homes or to nondelinquent peers as their reference group became criminal" (pp. 71–72). Again we can ask, why did this selectivity arise?

*Parental Influences.* For the McCords the explanation for the particular choice of friends was to be found in the boys' home lives. They contended that children coming from cohesive homes (characterized by warm, affectional relationships among the family members, and where the members participated together in recreational activities) had little "need for the attractions of delinquent life" (p. 86). Jackson Toby (1957) had come to a somewhat similar conclusion after reviewing juvenile court data. "The better integrated the family," he maintained, "the more successful it is as a bulwark against antisocial influences . . . from the neighborhood or the peer group."

Family cohesiveness counters delinquent neighborhood and peer influences in at least three ways. We have already touched upon one of these. Home life can determine the extent to which the boy becomes attracted to aggressively antisocial activities outside the home. Those youngsters not exposed to frequent severe frustrations in their homes probably do not have strong aggressive urges, and so they are not drawn to groups encouraging the expression of hostility. Nor are they too interested in obtaining adventurous (if not reckless) outlets for their emotional tensions. Delinquent activities have comparatively little attraction for them. In addition, a secure, emotionally satisfying family life probably facilitates the development of law-abiding self-conceptions. Seeing himself in a certain way, the youngster cannot conceive of himself as engaging in unlawful activities. Delinquent behavior is incompatible with the standards he has set for himself. Reckless, Dinitz, & Kay (1957) have demonstrated that boys living in high delinquency areas who were regarded by their teachers as probable nondelinquents were more likely than potential delinquents (as judged by their teachers) to have self-concepts which would "insulate" them from criminal behavior.

Finally, the family, and particularly the parents, may teach the child —implicitly or explicitly—either to engage in socially disapproved actions or to avoid such behaviors. Part of this training stems from the parents' explicit demands and prohibitions. If the mother and father consistently label aggressive and delinquent actions as "bad," their children may also learn to look at these behaviors in this light, especially if they love and are identified with their parents. Should parents punish antisocial behavior on one occasion but not do so at another time, however, their children will not be certain delinquent activity is "wrong"; the parental lapses tell them such behavior may be permissible in some situations. (The inconsistency can even be frustrating.) Sheldon Glueck and Eleanor Glueck (1950) observed that the mothers and fathers of their delinquent group displayed extremes of both laxity and harshness in attempting to control their children, or were careless and neglectful in supervising them.

But as was discussed in the preceding chapter, parents also train their children to conform to particular moral standards through the examples they provide by their own behavior. Such modeling influences were evident in both the Glueck (1950) and McCord (1959) investigations. The earlier researchers reported a greater incidence of socially deviant behavior, such as alcoholism and criminalism, in the parents of the delinquents than in the parents of law-abiding youngsters, while McCord et al. (1959) also noted that such deviant behavior on the part of the parents led to later criminal records. The mother's conformity to socially approved modes of conduct seemed to be a stronger influence for good than was the father's behavior. A combination of two socially deviant parents produced the highest crime rates in the children.

## Alienation

Some final comments also should be made regarding the habitual criminal's feeling of being estranged from respectable society. A considerable number of sociologists have maintained that the offender generally is alienated from his social order and that this alienation impels his lawbreaking (cf. Nettler, 1959). He supposedly does not possess the values of middle-class society, is uninterested in, and may even be hostile toward this society and its representatives. A. K. Cohen's (1955) analysis of juvenile delinquency, summarized earlier, makes use of such an argument.

Many offenders, of course, do reject the predominant values and standards of the cultural majority. Wood's (1961) study of Ceylonese lawbreakers showed, to cite but one example, that most of these people had unfavorable attitudes toward their home villages and also had rejected the ethical and moral code of their Buddhist society. Such feelings of estrangement are not limited to Asiatic criminals. The juvenile delinquents described by the Gluecks (1950) also typically possessed hostile, defiant, resentful, and suspicious attitudes toward the world about them.

This alienation can lead to illegal behavior in several ways. Obviously, the person estranged from society is not likely to accept its standards of behavior and consequently probably will not have strong moral restraints against socially disapproved behavior. But in addition to this, his hostile, resentful attitude toward the dominant social agencies may even justify the aggressively antisocial actions he is inclined to carry out. "They deserve it," he tells himself, and again his inhibitions against disapproved behavior are weakened.

The two processes just described involve the offender's inner controls against unlawful actions rather than the urge toward such behaviors. However, alienation conceivably can also affect the instigation to attack particular targets. As was demonstrated in Chapter 6, a disliked object tends to be associated with the individual's more immediate frustraters so that the former can become the recipient of aggression aroused by the latter. We can see such a phenomenon in operation in many juvenile delinquents. Suffering from some recent thwarting, say at the hands of their parents, they might pass a middle-class institution such as a school. The school is associated with their parents—both are strongly disliked—and consequently evokes aggressive acts. Windows are smashed. The alienated youngsters committed the vandalism because (1) they did not have strong internal inhibitions against such behavior, (2) they believed the resented, hated school authorities deserved such treatment, and (3) since they were disliked, these latter middle-class authorities could evoke aggressive responses aroused by other disliked people.

## MURDER AND SUICIDE

We now have come to the ultimate in aggressive behavior: the destruction of human life. This topic can be approached dispassionately. Novelists and playwrights have told of the hopes, ambitions, desires, and torments leading to violent death, of the twisted, complicated thread of incidents ending finally in murder or suicide. Dramatic though these events might be, a good deal—but not all—of the complexity can be reduced to simple, highly abstract, bloodless formulations. Countless factors may have contributed to the chain leading to final death, and one person's story—whether he takes his own life or someone else's— is never similar in all details to the biography of any other killer. Nevertheless, people who kill can be described with a relatively small number of concepts. They have not been exposed to exactly the same conditions, but *all have suffered extreme* (for them) *frustrations*. Further, although their personalities vary in important respects, *their reactions to the intense thwartings can be understood in terms of* (1) *the perceived source of the frustration* and (2) *the strength of their inhibitions against overt hostility*. The formula to be discussed here is essentially a simple one. The person who kills generally does so because he has been frustrated. Whether he kills someone else or himself depends partly upon whom he blames for the thwarting and partly upon the strength of his controls against socially disapproved behavior.

## Murder

Despite the attention given to homicides in fiction and the popular press, such crimes constitute only a tiny fraction of the illegal actions committed in this country. One-tenth of 1 per cent of the arrests reported by the police of some fifteen hundred American cities in 1958 were for homicide, and most of these probably were due to negligence rather than deliberate intent (Sutherland & Cressey, 1960). Too many lives are taken violently, but murder is a relatively rare phenomenon in our complex society. It apparently is a fairly unusual response to unusual circumstances.

Most of the people displaying these extreme reactions, furthermore, probably would never commit murder again if released from jail. With the exception of hired killers, they typically are not hardened criminals. One study of ninety-six convicted murderers found only about half of the men had ever been arrested before. Two-thirds of the sex offenders and over 90 per cent of the property offenders surveyed, in comparison, had such prior records.[7] Murderers, by and large, are not habitual law-breakers and once released from prison are relatively good parole risks (Clinard, 1957, p. 210). They have taken a life, in most cases at least, not because of a persistent urge to kill, but because their emotions flared up out of control in response to an extreme thwarting. "Most murders," says one authority (cited in Clinard, 1957, p. 210), "are crimes of passion—explosive reactions to a difficult situation."

[7] According to at least one study (Berg & Fox, 1947), Negro murderers are more likely than white murderers to have prior convictions for assaultive crimes.

*Individual Characteristics.* To say that the violence was provoked by frustrating circumstances is not to rule out the importance of personality characteristics. Experts generally are agreed that the killer's life history has made him susceptible to such "explosive reactions." Another person exposed to the same final instigating condition might have exerted better control over his emotions or may not have been as strongly aroused by the thwarting.

Not surprisingly, many murderers have had a history of frequent frustrations. Palmer (1960) interviewed the mothers of fifty-one male murderers in order to determine how the life experiences of these men had differed from those of their nearest-age nonhomicidal brothers. He found the murderers had apparently suffered many more physical and psychological frustrations, such as illnesses, accidents, and harsh treatments. Because of these relatively frequent thwartings (as I suggested earlier), they conceivably developed a fairly great readiness to perceive further frustrations in the world about them, tended to exhibit relatively intense anger in response to these thwartings, and did not learn strong restraints against socially disapproved actions. Any one frustration, then, was likely to provoke an extreme reaction, and so Palmer also reported the murderers had shown more frequent socially unacceptable aggression than their brothers as they matured. The nonhomicidal siblings probably had stronger inhibitions against antisocial behavior, and what aggression they exhibited tended to be of the controlled, socially acceptable variety.

Homicides may be more common in lower socioeconomic groups than in the higher social strata (Henry & Short, 1954; Falk, 1959) partly because of the greater number of deprivations to which the lower-class individual is typically subjected throughout his lifetime. Lower-class existence is relatively frustrating. Research summarized in the present and preceding chapters has indicated some of the areas in which the lower-class person is often seriously thwarted. For example, he is frequently prevented from satisfying his economic and status wishes, and his parents probably were also somewhat more punitive toward him in childhood than would have been the case if his had been an average middle-class family. Living in such an environment, he is all too likely to show the consequences of these deprivations: a tendency to intense emotional outbursts as well as to psychoses.

Berg and Fox (1947) have made use of the frustration-aggression hypothesis in explaining the relationship between intelligence and homicides. Consistent with other researchers, they observed that a sample of two hundred murderers had reliably lower school achievement and intelligence than did a control group of other prison inmates and suggested that the former's low intelligence level had led to their being frustrated relatively severely by their victims. But if the killers had been thwarted on this one occasion (presumably in an argument with the victim), they probably had also experienced a good many frustrations in other situations throughout their lifetimes. These recurrent frustrations could have led to the final violent outburst when the murder was committed.

Another reason for such an extreme emotional flare-up can be found in the murderers' occasionally weak inhibitions against socially disapproved behavior. Murderers generally violate criminal laws less frequently than do most property offenders or people guilty of nonhomicidal assaults. They can restrain their antisocial inclinations in most situations. These inner controls, however, may not be too strongly rooted and can give way under periods of severe emotional stress. Wood (1961) has published evidence in accord with this analysis in his previously mentioned study of crime in Ceylon. In contrast to robbers and burglars, the murderers in his sample tended not to be regular gamblers or rowdies. They also were less likely to have a police record. But, attesting to their tenuous controls, almost as many murderers as robbers and burglars used alcohol. Their religion and village customs frowned on intoxicating beverages, but they tended to drink more often than most of the noncriminals around them.

*Sociological Determinants.* Social conditions producing frequent severe frustrations together with comparatively weak inhibitions against socially disapproved behavior should give rise to a disproportionately high incidence of murders if the present reasoning is correct. Such seems to be the case. We already have seen, for example, that there are high homicide rates in poor and deteriorating city areas. The people living in these urban areas usually experience a good many serious thwartings and in many instances, as was pointed out earlier, have not learned strong inhibitions against unlawful behavior. Frustrations and weak inhibitions are particularly characteristic of lower-class Negroes and may explain why the Negro homicide rate is much higher than that of whites (Sutherland & Cressey, 1960, p. 140; Falk, 1959).

Much the same argument can also account for regional differences in the incidence of homicides. Thus, there were only 1.5 homicides per 100,000 population known to the police in New England in 1958, while this rate rose to 9.5 in the South Atlantic states (Sutherland & Cressey, 1960, p. 152). Many Southerners, of course, have been seriously thwarted throughout their lives because of the poverty of their part of the country. But in addition, the lower-class Southerner is more likely than his New England counterpart to feel that he must seek personal retribution for any "wrongs" done to him. His social code often justifies striking out on his own against the people harming him.[8]

[8] Several authorities have suggested that homicide rates are high in the South

We must remember, however, that recurrent frustrations and weak inner controls only create a predisposition to extreme aggression. They do not actually impel such behavior. The frequently thwarted person is easily aroused, and not constantly angry. He does not attack just anyone for the sake of releasing some supposed pent-up "hostile energy." But he can become enraged fairly easily in the course of his daily life. This is why killers and their victims generally come from the same groups, why, for example, whites usually kill whites, Negroes kill primarily other Negroes, and the victims often are relatives or acquaintances of their murderers (Clinard, 1957; Falk, 1959). The murder victim probably had frustrated his slayer in some argument or fight, thereby precipitating the violent, uncontrolled emotional reaction leading to his death.

Frustrations also account for changes in homicide rates as business conditions alter. Henry and Short (1954) have demonstrated that murders committed by whites tend to be most frequent when business conditions are bad. Negro homicides, on the other hand, decrease in such times of depression and are most common when the country is relatively prosperous. Along with Henry and Short, I would say the variation in homicide rates stems primarily from differences in frustrations. But contrary to these writers, it seems to me the thwartings arise, at least in part, from comparisons the individual makes with others in his own group.[9] When a low-status white person loses his job in a depression, he finds himself deprived of status and economic goods relative to those of his friends and acquaintances who still have jobs. However, since Negroes are generally the first to be fired in hard times, poor business conditions act as a leveler in this group. Nearly all lower-class Negroes suffer from economic privations in a depression, and they do not see themselves as being much worse off than their peers. Prosperous times, however, permit some Negroes to get economically well ahead of their peers. Those not doing too well conceiv-

---

because "cultural definitions call for personal violence in some situations" (Clinard, 1957, p. 214). Along similar lines, Wolfgang (1958) has contended after an analysis of almost 600 cases of criminal homicide in Philadelphia, that many murders take place in a "subculture of violence" which gives social approval to "quick resort to physical aggression."

[9] Henry and Short have contended that the individual is most likely to compare his own status with that of people in other social strata. If he is in a high stratum, he supposedly wants to be better off than the low-status group, while the low-status individual presumably wants to be closer to the higher social levels. The present book argues, on the other hand, that such comparisons tend to be primarily with others in one's own social level. The same objection was raised earlier against A. K. Cohen's (1955) conception of the status deprivations presumably felt by lower-class boys.

ably feel greatly deprived in comparison with wealthier Negroes; they are frustrated, and anger results.

*Effects of Death Penalties.* Restraints against socially disapproved behavior are most effective, I have indicated on a number of occasions throughout this book, when they are based upon relatively stable moral attitudes rather than on the fear of punishment. The person who believes criminal actions are morally wrong will refrain from engaging in such behavior in most situations, whether he anticipates punishment for the criminal activity or not. However, as Chapter 5 proposed, inhibitions based primarily upon fear of punishment are likely to be operative only when the individual expects to be caught and punished for carrying out the disapproved activity.[10]

This reasoning explains why the threat of a death penalty does not reduce the incidence of murders (cf. Cressey & Sutherland, 1960, pp. 292–297). When a person commits a murder, he usually has done so in a fit of violent rage. He certainly does not think of being apprehended by the police at such times. There are few if any cues in the situation to remind him of the police. The only thing that could have restrained his violence in the absence of such external danger stimuli would have been strong internal prohibitions against antisocial aggression. *Stable and strong internal controls are more likely to prevent murders than are death penalties; the latter often are out of sight and out of mind.*

## Suicide

Few human actions seem to be as difficult to understand as suicide. A 50-year-old industrialist committed suicide supposedly (according to the newspapers) because he recently had sold his firm and was despondent at no longer controlling its destiny. He left an estate of over 2 million dollars. Did he feel there was nothing left in life for him? Such an explanation probably is much too simple to be true. Suicide is a highly complex phenomenon, and there is relatively little agreement among authorities as to its cause or even how the potential self-killer should be treated.

Some of the confusion in the study of suicidal behavior arises from the multiplicity of reasons for self-destruction. The eminent French sociologist Emile Durkheim (1951) listed three types of suicides: *altruistic, egoistic,* and *anomic.* In the first of these the person takes his own life in order to benefit other people. A good example of this

---

[10] People undoubtedly differ in the extent to which they expect to succeed in a risky undertaking. One person may characteristically expect not to get caught if he carried out a crime, while another, more pessimistic, individual may anticipate only the worst and thus would be less likely to commit a crime.

is seen in the World War II Japanese kamikaze pilots who dived their planes into American warships. The egoistic suicide, on the other hand, is concerned primarily with himself rather than with others. Not bound to other people by close personal ties, he is wrapped up in his own personal problems and kills himself when he cannot attain his individualistic goals. Finally, the anomic type of suicide presumably occurs when social values disintegrate in a crisis situation and the individual feels "lost." The disruption of the collective order stimulates men's appetites, making them "less disciplined precisely when they need more disciplining." Some people are "declassified" as they are thrown into lower social levels by the cultural turmoil. They must restrain their needs, but they cannot do so. The new social conditions forced on them may be regarded as intolerable, and feeling all is hopeless and meaningless in a world bereft of values, they may take their own lives.

Other writers also insist it is wrong to account for suicides in terms of a single type of motivation. Thus, one authority (Jackson in Shneidman & Farberow, 1957) established a continuum ranging from "irrational" suicides—such as the psychotic who kills himself because he believes the world is coming to an end—to "rational" self-destruction as in the case of the cancer victim suffering from extreme pain. An analysis of over seven hundred notes written by white, native-born suicides also points to the desirability of distinguishing among suicide types. Shneidman and Farberow (1957) found a much higher incidence of direct aggression references (either against the self or others) in the notes written by the younger self-killers, while the "wish to die," characterized by hopelessness, fear, and despair, was predominant in the majority of notes written by suicides over 60 years of age. The younger victims apparently were angrier than the older group and probably did not commit suicides for the same reasons.

*Individual Considerations.* Chapter 4 has advanced one possible explanation for suicides: the inhibition of outward-directed aggression. Following a line of thought essentially similar to the orthodox Freudian conception summarized in the first chapter of this book, Dollard et al. (1939) suggested that aggression against the self was a consequence of the blocking of all other aggressive reactions to frustration. Just as "aggressive energy" supposedly turned inward if not discharged in attacks upon other people (cf. Hartmann et al., 1949), aggressive responses to the frustrater, the Yale psychologists contended, presumably heightened the instigation to self-aggression. Suicide, then, could conceivably be regarded as an extreme manifestation of inhibited aggression.

There is some evidence that suicide victims do have stronger internal controls against unlawful behavior than do murderers. Wood (1961) reported, for example, that Ceylonese who had taken their own lives were less likely to use alcohol, have a police record, or a reputation as a neighborhood bully than the people charged with killing someone else. But whether such strong restraints were primarily responsible for the self-destruction is, of course, open to question. Other factors are also involved in suicides. According to several psychiatrists (cf. Chs. 2 and 3 in Shneidman & Farberow, 1957), suicidal actions often stem from several complex motives, such as:

1. *A wish to punish some frustrater.* Many victims apparently delighted in the belief that a particular person, someone who supposedly had hurt or tormented them, would feel sorry and—more important—guilty when learning of the suicide.

2. *Yearning for self-punishment and rebirth.* Self-destruction often is self-punishment for crimes the suicide victims thought they had committed. (In some cases the "crime" supposedly arose from "death wishes.") Fenichel (1945) has maintained that self-destruction during fits of melancholia is typically instigated by desires for forgiveness. This self-punishment could then lead to a new start by alleviating guilt. Children and schizophrenics are said to feel that if they can kill the "bad me" they could then achieve a rebirth as a less wicked person.

3. Paradoxically, suicide victims may believe their self-destruction will not really mean the end of their existence. Potential suicide victims sometimes develop grandiose fantasies in compensation for the frustrations they have suffered, and according to psychiatric observations, such fantasies often include ideas of immortality and omnipotence (Shneidman & Farberow, 1957, p. 27). They will punish themselves, and perhaps other people as well, by taking their lives, but they will still exist to enjoy the after-effects of their action. Consistent with this, Shneidman and Farberow (1957, p. 39) have reported that suicide notes frequently contain admonitions and instructions perhaps "indicative of unrealistic feelings of omnipotence and omnipresence." The victims presumably "cannot successfully imagine (their) own death and . . . complete cessation."

We cannot say how often such beliefs and desires occur in the incipient suicide or, for that matter, how important these feelings are in the instigation of the self-murder. But it is clear that many suicides are extreme attacks upon the self arising from guilt and self-blame. Inhibitions against attacks upon others may be present and may have had an important role in the sequence of events leading to suicide. Self-killers evidently are frequently angry with other people; their strong inhibitions could have interfered with earlier, milder angry outbursts. Nevertheless they are extremely angry with themselves as well, and this is important. *Hostility is directed toward the self, at least in part, because the self is regarded as a frustrater.*

*Sociological Considerations.* Henry and Short (1954) have employed the frustration-aggression hypothesis in explaining social-status differences in suicide rates, assigning the notion of self as frustrater a prominent place in their theorizing. In almost every status hierarchy, and regardless of the basis for the stratification, members of high-status groups tend to kill themselves at a greater rate than do lower-status people. Thus, while suicides are relatively common at both ends of the economic scale, they occur most often among the well-to-do. Similarly, more whites than nonwhites kill themselves, commissioned officers are more prone to take their own lives than are enlisted men of the same race, and men are greater suicide risks than women (pp. 135–136). (In this last regard it is assumed men have a higher status than women because of their positions in the economic system of our society.)

To account for these differences in self-destruction, the sociologists made use of two sets of empirical findings. First, the inverse correlation between business conditions and suicide rates is generally highest for the higher-status groups (p. 41). Depressions lead to more suicides in the upper than the lower social strata. The people in the upper strata probably suffer greater deprivations than their lower-status peers as a result of harsh business conditions; there is a greater discrepancy between their predepression and depression conditions, and consequently they are frustrated more severely. But in addition to such greater frustrations in higher-status levels, social relationships also affect the likelihood of committing suicide, as Durkheim stressed (1951). People having close ties with others are a lesser suicide risk than people living in emotional isolation. Married people, for example, are not as prone to kill themselves as single, widowed, or divorced individuals of the same age (p. 73), and city dwellers, often having only relatively anonymous and impersonal contacts with others, have a higher suicide rate than people living in the more tightly knit rural communities (p. 76).

Henry and Short used the concept of "external restraints" to integrate these data. The lower-status person typically does not have the freedom possessed by the members of the higher social groups. He has to accede to the demands of his supervisor and/or employer, and he lacks the financial wherewithal even to think of becoming his own master. In general, his actions are subject to relatively great restraints by his social superiors. Similarly, the individual enmeshed in close relationships with other people also experiences restraints. He has obligations to his family and friends. He must conform to their expectations. He often has to comply with their wishes.

These external restraints, as hampering as they might be, serve an important function in times of stress, according to Henry and Short. They "provide immunity from suicide" presumably because they permit the individual to blame others for his troubles. The individual cannot attack himself for the frustrations he suffers if other people must share in the responsibility for his actions.

The Henry and Short argument is an intriguing one. Their reliance on the concept of "external restraints" might appear forced but actually is in complete accord with scientific tradition. Scientists must seek to develop unifying principles capable of showing that apparently diverse phenomena (e.g., the suicidal deaths of a wealthy person and of a lonely city dweller) are special cases of a more general phenomenon (self-blame for a frustration). The present writer does not reject the Henry-Short emphasis upon external restraints altogether but would prefer to add to this argument. High social status in our society produces more than a relative freedom from restraints. (Indeed, in many cases well-to-do families feel they have a good deal of responsibility and obligations to others. Witness the Rockefellers.) What may be more important is the greater emphasis upon self-reliance and self-accomplishment in the upper social levels. Middle-class parents frequently teach their children that a person is primarily responsible for whatever happens to him (cf. Kohn, 1959). The lower-class individual, on the other hand, tends to see himself as the hapless victim of forces beyond his control. Thus, *since the people from the upper social levels generally regard themselves as masters of their own fate, they also must blame themselves for their social and economic failures.* In extreme cases such self-blame can lead to suicide.

## SUMMARY

The present chapter is a highly selected review of factors involved in crime, homicide, and suicide. Because of the complexity of the subject matter, the picture drawn here is bound to be greatly oversimplified, but frustrations are said to have an important part in the genesis of all criminal activity (including murder and suicide).

"Unsocialized" or "individual" criminals, who are subject to strong and at times uncontrolled emotional reactions and who have relatively little regard for other people, are differentiated from more "socialized" criminals, who are more strongly influenced by criminal subcultures. The first type supposedly arises primarily from extreme parental rejection, but socially deviant role models may also play some part. The parental rejection presumably thwarts the child's dependency needs and, by producing dependency anxiety, disrupts the youngster's capacity to form close personal ties with other people. The so-called "socialized" criminal, on the other hand, while frustrated by parents and middle-class society, has not experienced such parental rejection and can develop friendships with his peers. He may form attachments to criminal groups and adopt many of their values.

The recurrent frustrations to which these people have been exposed generally result in (1) a readiness to perceive further frustrations, (2) intense emotional reactions to such thwartings, and (3) weak restraints against socially disapproved behavior. Such frequent frustrations are also held to affect the socialized criminal's friendship choices. He presumably is attracted to people who feel as he does and who will permit the expression of aggression. Because of his aggressive inclinations, he also readily accepts their criminal values and attitudes. Criminal or delinquent groups increase the likelihood of the members' criminal activity by (1) weakening inhibitions against socially disapproved behavior—by both (*a*) lessening fear of punishment, such as by minimizing the fear of being caught, and (*b*) justifying the unlawful actions—and (2) by reinforcing and strengthening the dispositions to the criminal behavior.

Frustrations are not the only factors involved in criminal activity. In many cases the delinquent or criminal has also had his unlawful behavior reinforced by parents and/or peers and has learned attitudes justifying such behavior.

These criminal tendencies are viewed as habits. The habits are latent response dispositions which must be "activated" by suitable situational cues if the relevant behavior is to occur, and which may be extinguished by other learning experiences. This means the aggressively antisocial actions will not necessarily be revealed in every situation. The relevant cues may not be present; responses incompatible with the aggressive behavior may be evoked; and the aggressiveness habits may have weakened through the operation of the laws of learning and forgetting.

Murderers theoretically have suffered from relatively persistent frustrations through a good part of their lives. Ordinarily they possess restraints against illegal behavior, and most murderers are not habitual criminals. But their inner controls are not strongly rooted, and an intense frustration can provoke an extreme emotional outburst leading to someone's death.

Suicide victims, on the other hand, generally have much stronger inhibitions against socially disapproved behavior. For a number of reasons, such as their socialization experiences in a particular social class and their financial and social circumstances, they are prone to blame themselves for any serious frustrations they suffer. Suicide often is punishment the individual inflicts upon himself because of such intense self-blame.

# Bibliography

Adorno, T., Frenkel-Brunswik, Else, Levinson, D., & Sanford, R. *The authoritarian personality.* New York: Harper, 1950.

Albert, R. S. The role of mass media and the effect of aggressive film content upon children's aggressive responses and identification choices. *Genet. Psychol. Monogr.*, 1957, **55**, 221–285.

Alexander, F. Discussion of "Hostility and fear in social life" by John Dollard. *Soc. Forces*, 1938, **17**, 27–29.

Alexander, F. The psychiatric aspects of war and peace. *Amer. J. Sociol.*, 1941, **46**, 504–520.

Alexander, F. A contribution to the theory of play. *Psychoanal. Quart.*, 1958, **27**, 175–193.

Allee, W. C. *Animal aggregations.* Chicago: Univer. of Chicago Press, 1931.

Allee, W. C., Nissen, H. W., & Nimkoff, M. F. A re-examination of the concept of instinct. *Psychol. Rev.*, 1953, **60**, 287–297.

Allison, J., & Hunt, D. E. Social desirability and the expression of aggression under varying conditions of frustration. *J. consult. Psychol.*, 1959, **23**, 528–532.

Allport, F. H. *Social psychology.* Boston: Houghton Mifflin, 1924.

Allport, G. W. *Personality.* New York: Holt, Rinehart & Winston, 1937.

Allport, G. W. *The nature of prejudice.* Reading, Mass.: Addison-Wesley, 1954.

Allport, G. W., & Kramer, B. M. Some roots of prejudice. *J. Psychol.*, 1946, **22**, 9–39.

Anastasi, Anne, Cohen, Nadia, & Spatz, Dorothy. A study of fear and anger in college students through the controlled diary method. *J. genet. Psychol.*, 1948, **73**, 243–249.

Aron, R. Conflict and war from the viewpoint of historical sociology. In int. Sociol. Ass., *The nature of conflict.* Paris: UNESCO, 1957.

Arsenian, Jean M. Young children in an insecure situation. *J. abnorm. soc. Psychol.*, 1943, **38**, 225–249.

Atkinson, J. W. Explorations using imaginative thought to assess the strength of human motives. In M. R. Jones (Ed.), *Nebraska symposium on motivation, 1954.* Lincoln, Nebr.: Univer. of Nebr. Press, 1954.

Avigdor, R. The development of stereotypes as a result of group interaction. Unpublished doctoral dissertation, New York Univer., 1952. Cited in M. Sherif & Carolyn Sherif, *Groups in harmony and tension.* New York: Harper, 1953.

Ax, A. The physiological differentiation of fear and anger. *Psychosom. Med.*, 1953, **15**, 433–442.

Bach, G. R. Young children's play fantasies. *Psychol. Monogr.*, 1945, **59**, No. 2.

Bailyn, Lotte. Mass media and children: a study of exposure habits and cognitive effects. *Psychol. Monogr.*, 1959, **73**, No. 471.

Bandura, A. *Relationship of family patterns to child behavior disorders.* Progress report to Nat. Inst. of ment. Hlth on grant M-1734. Stanford Univer., 1960.

Bandura, A. Social learning through imitation. In *Nebraska symposium on motivation,* 1962. Lincoln, Nebr.: Univer. of Nebr. Press, 1962.

Bandura, A., & Huston, Aletha C. Identification as a process of incidental learning. *J. abnorm. soc. Psychol.,* 1961, **63**, 311–318.

Bandura, A., Lipsher, D. H., & Miller, Paula E. Psychotherapists' approach-avoidance reactions to patients' expressions of hostility. *J. consult. Psychol.,* 1960, **24**, 1–8.

Bandura, A., Ross, Dorothea, & Ross, Sheila A. Transmission of aggression through imitation of aggressive models. *J. abnorm. soc. Psychol.,* 1961, **63**, 575–582.

Bandura, A., Ross, Dorothea, & Ross, Sheila A. Imitation of film-mediated aggressive models. *J. abnorm. soc. Psychol.,* 1962, in press.

Bandura, A., & Walters, R. H. *Adolescent aggression.* New York: Ronald, 1959.

Bateson, G. The frustration-aggression hypothesis and culture. *Psychol. Rev.,* 1941, **48**, 350–355.

Beach, F. A. Analysis of factors involved in the arousal, maintenance, and manifestation of sexual excitement in male animals. *Psychosom. Med.,* 1942, **4**, 173–198.

Beach, F. A. Bisexual mating behavior in the male rat: effects of castration and hormone administration. *Physiol. Zool.,* 1945, **18**, 390–402.

Beeman, Elizabeth A. The effect of male hormone on aggressive behavior in mice. *Physiol. Zool.,* 1947, **20**, 373–405.

Beller, E. K. Exploratory studies of dependency. *Trans. N.Y. Acad. Sci.,* 1959, **21**, 414–426.

Beller, E. K., & Haeberle, Ann W. Dependency and the frustration-aggression hypothesis. Paper presented at 1959 meetings of East. Psychol. Ass., Atlantic City, N.J., April, 1959.

Bender, Lauretta. Psychopathic behavior disorders in children. In R. Lindner & R. Seliger (Eds.), *Handbook of correctional psychology.* New York: Philosophical Library, 1947.

Berg, I., & Fox, V. Factors in homicides committed by 200 males. *J. soc. Psychol.,* 1947, **26**, 109–119.

Berkowitz, L. The expression and reduction of hostility. *Psychol. Bull.,* 1958, **55**, 257–283.

Berkowitz, L. Anti-Semitism and the displacement of aggression. *J. abnorm. soc. Psychol.,* 1959, **59**, 182–187.

Berkowitz, L. Some factors affecting the reduction of overt hostility. *J. abnorm. soc. Psychol.,* 1960, **60**, 14–21. (a)

Berkowitz, L. Repeated frustrations and expectations in hostility arousal. *J. abnorm. soc. Psychol.,* 1960, **60**, 422–429. (b)

Berkowitz, L. Manifest hostility level and hostile behavior. *J. soc. Psychol.*, 1960, **52**, 165–171. (c)

Berkowitz, L. The judgmental process in personality functioning. *Psychol. Rev.*, 1960, **67**, 130–142. (d)

Berkowitz, L. Anti-Semitism, judgmental processes, and displacement of hostility. *J. abnorm. soc. Psychol.*, 1961, **62**, 210–215.

Berkowitz, L., & Daniels, Louise R. Responsibility and dependency. *J. abnorm. soc. Psychol.*, 1963, in press.

Berkowitz, L., & Green, J. A. The stimulus qualities of the scapegoat. *J. abnorm. soc. Psychol.*, 1962, in press.

Berkowitz, L., Green, J. A., & Macaulay, Jacqueline R. Hostility catharsis as the reduction of emotional tension. *Psychiatry*, 1962, **25**, 23–31.

Berkowitz, L., & Holmes, D. S. The generalization of hostility to disliked objects. *J. Pers.*, 1959, **27**, 565–577.

Berkowitz, L., & Holmes, D. S. A further investigation of hostility generalization to disliked objects. *J. Pers.*, 1960, **28**, 427–442.

Berkowitz, L., & Macaulay, Jacqueline R. Some effects of differences in status level and status stability. *Hum. Relat.*, 1961, **14**, 135–148.

Berkowitz, L., & Rawlings, Edna. Effects of film violence on inhibitions against subsequent aggression. *J. abnormal soc. Psychol.*, 1963, in press.

Berlyne, D. E. *Conflict, arousal, and curiosity.* New York: McGraw-Hill, 1960.

Bernard, Jessie. The sociological study of conflict. In Int. Sociol. Ass., *The nature of conflict.* Paris: UNESCO, 1957.

Bettelheim, B., & Janowitz, M. *Dynamics of prejudice.* New York: Harper, 1950.

Bevan, W., Daves, W. F., & Levy, G. W. The relation of castration, androgen therapy and pre-test fighting experience to competitive aggression in male C57BL/10 mice. *Anim. Behav.*, 1960, **8**, 6–12.

Block, J., & Block, Jeanne. An investigation of the relationship between intolerance of ambiguity and ethnocentrism. *J. Pers.*, 1951, **19**, 303–311.

Block, J., & Martin, B. C. Predicting the behavior of children under frustration. *J. abnorm. soc. Psychol.*, 1955, **51**, 281–285.

Bogardus, E. S. Racial distance changes in the United States during the past 30 years. *Sociol. soc. Res.*, 1958, **43**, 127–134.

Bornston, Frieda L., & Coleman, J. C. The relationship between certain parents' attitudes toward child rearing and the direction of aggression of their young adult offspring. *J. clin. Psychol.*, 1956, **12**, 41–44.

Bowlby, J. An ethological approach to research in child development. *Brit. J. med. Psychol.*, 1957, **30**, 230–240.

Bronfenbrenner, U. Socialization and social class through time and space. In Eleanor Maccoby, T. M. Newcomb, & E. L. Hartley (Eds.), *Readings in social psychology.* (3rd ed.) New York: Holt, Rinehart & Winston, 1958.

Brown, J. S. Principles of intrapersonal conflict. *Conflict Resolution*, 1957, **1**, 135–154.

Brown, J. S., & Farber, I. E. Emotions conceptualized as intervening variables —with suggestions toward a theory of frustration. *Psychol. Bull.*, 1951, **48**, 465–495.

Brown, R. W. A determinant of the relationship between rigidity and authoritarianism. *J. abnorm. soc. Psychol.*, 1953, **48**, 469–476.

Brown, R. W. Mass phenomena. In G. Lindzey (Ed.), *Handbook of social psychology.* Vol. 2. Reading, Mass.: Addison-Wesley, 1954.

Bruner, J. S. Going beyond the information given. In J. S. Bruner et al., *Contemporary approaches to cognition.* Cambridge, Mass.: Harvard, 1957.

Bucher, R. Blame and hostility in disaster. *Amer. J. Sociol.*, 1957, **62**, 467–475.

Buss, A. H., & Durkee, Ann. An inventory for assessing different kinds of hostility. *J. consult. Psychol.*, 1957, **21**, 343–349.

Cameron, D. E. The conversion of passivity into normal self-assertion. *Amer. J. Psychiat.*, 1951, **108**, 98–102.

Cantril, H. *The psychology of social movements.* New York: Wiley, 1941.

Cantril, H. The invasion from Mars. In Eleanor Maccoby, T. M. Newcomb, & E. L. Hartley (Eds.), *Readings in social psychology.* (3rd ed.) New York: Holt, Rinehart & Winston, 1958.

Carpenter, C. C. Aggressive behavior and social dominance in the six-lined racerunner. *Anim. Behav.*, 1960, **8**, 61–66.

Cartwright, D., & Zander, A. (Eds.), *Group dynamics.* (2nd ed.) Evanston, Ill.: Row, Peterson, 1960.

Charters, W. W. *Motion pictures and youth: a summary.* New York: Macmillan, 1935.

Charters, W. W., Jr., & Newcomb, T. M. Some attitudinal effects of experimentally increased salience of a membership group. In Eleanor Maccoby, T. M. Newcomb, & E. L. Hartley (Eds.), *Readings in social psychology.* (3rd ed.) New York: Holt, Rinehart & Winston, 1958.

Chasdi, Eleanor Hollenberg, & Lawrence, Margaret Sperry. Some antecedents of aggression and effects of frustration in doll play. In D. McClelland (Ed.), *Studies in motivation.* New York: Appleton-Century-Crofts, 1955.

Child, I. L. Socialization. In G. Lindzey (Ed.), *Handbook of social psychology.* Reading, Mass.: Addison-Wesley, 1954.

Clark, G., & Birch, H. G. Hormonal modifications of social behavior. I. The effect of sex hormone administration on the social status of a male castrate chimpanzee. *Psychosom. Med.*, 1945, **7**, 321–329.

Clark, R. A. The effects of sexual motivation on phantasy. In D. McClelland (Ed.), *Studies in motivation.* New York: Appleton-Century-Crofts, 1955.

Clinard, M. B. *Sociology of deviant behavior.* New York: Holt, Rinehart & Winston, 1957.

Cloward, R. A. Illegitimate means, anomie, and deviant behavior. *Amer. sociol. Rev.*, 1959, **24**, 164–176.

Cohen, A. K. *Delinquent boys.* New York: Free Press, 1955.

Cohen, A. R. Social norms, arbitrariness of frustration, and status of the agent of frustration in the frustration-aggression hypothesis. *J. abnorm. soc. Psychol.*, 1955, **51**, 222–226.

Cohen, A. R. Upward communication in experimentally created hierarchies. *Hum. Relat.*, 1958, **11**, 41–54.

Collias, N. E. Aggressive behavior among vertebrate animals. *Physiol. Zool.*, 1944, **17**, 83–123.

Collias, N. E. Problems and principles of animal sociology. In C. P. Stone (Ed.), *Comparative psychology.* (3rd ed.) Englewood Cliffs, N.J.: Prentice-Hall, 1951.

Converse, P. E. The shifting role of class in political attitudes and behavior. In Eleanor Maccoby, T. M. Newcomb, & E. L. Hartley (Eds.), *Readings in social psychology* (3rd ed.) New York: Holt, Rinehart & Winston, 1958.

Cowen, E., Landes, J., & Schaet, D. E. The effects of mild frustration on the expression of prejudiced attitudes. *J. abnorm. soc. Psychol.*, 1959, **58**, 33–38.

Dahlke, H. O. Race and minority riots—a study in the typology of violence. *Soc. Forces*, 1952, **30**, 419–425.

Davie, M. R. *The evolution of war.* New Haven: Yale, 1929.

Davies, J. C. Toward a theory of revolution. *Amer. sociol. Rev.*, 1962, **27**, 5–19.

Davis, A. Socialization and adolescent personality. In *Adolescence, Yearb. nat. Soc. Stud. Educ.*, 1944, 43.

Davis, D. E. Aggressive behavior in castrated starlings. *Science*, 1957, **126**, 253.

Davis, K. E., & Jones, E. E. Changes in interpersonal perception as a means of reducing cognitive dissonance. *J. abnorm. soc. Psychol.*, 1960, **61**, 402–410.

Davitz, J. R. The effects of previous training on postfrustration behavior. *J. abnorm. soc. Psychol.*, 1952, **47**, 309–315.

De Soto, C. B. Learning a social structure. *J. abnorm. soc. Psychol.*, 1960, **60**, 417–421.

Deutsch, M. The effects of cooperation and competition upon group process. *Hum. Relat.*, 1949, **2**, 129–152 and 199–231.

Deutsch, M., & Collins, Mary E. *Interracial housing: a psychological evaluation of a social experiment.* Minneapolis: Univer. of Minn. Press, 1951.

Deutsch, M., & Krauss, R. M. The effect of threat upon interpersonal bargaining. *J. abnorm. soc. Psychol.*, 1960, **61**, 181–189.

Dinwiddie, F. M. *An application of the principle of response generalization to the prediction of displacement of aggressive responses.* Washington: Catholic Univer. of America Press, 1955.

Dittes, J. E., & Kelley, H. H. Effects of different conditions of acceptance upon conformity to group norms. *J. abnorm. soc. Psychol.*, 1956, **53**, 100–107.

Dittman, A. T. & Goodrich, D. W. A comparison of social behavior in normal and hyperaggressive preadolescent boys. *Child Develpm.*, 1961, **32**, 315–327.

Dollard, J. Hostility and fear in social life. *Soc. Forces*, 1938, **17**, 15–25.

Dollard, J., Doob, L., Miller, N., Mowrer, O., & Sears, R. *Frustration and aggression*. New Haven: Yale, 1939.

Dollard, J., & Miller, N. *Personality and psychotherapy: an analysis in terms of learning, thinking, and culture*. New York: McGraw-Hill, 1950.

Doob, L. The behavior of attitudes. *Psychol. Rev.*, 1947, **54**, 135–156.

Doob, L., & Sears, R. Factors determining substitute behavior and the overt expression of aggression. *J. abnorm. soc. Psychol.*, 1939, **34**, 293–313.

Durbin, E. F. M., & Bowlby, J. *Personal aggressiveness and war*. New York: Columbia, 1939.

Durkheim, E. *Suicide*. (Originally published in France in 1897.) New York: Free Press, 1951.

Easterbrook, J. A. The effect of emotion on cue utilization and the organization of behavior. *Psychol. Rev.*, 1959, **66**, 183–201.

Einstein, A. *Why War?* Letter to Professor Freud. Int. Inst. of Intellectual Cooperation, League of Nations, 1933.

Elliott, D., & Wittenberg, B. Accuracy of identification of Jewish and non-Jewish photographs. *J. abnorm. soc. Psychol.*, 1955, **51**, 339–341.

Emery, F. E. Psychological effects of the western film: a study in television viewing. *Hum. Relat.*, 1959, **12**, 195–232.

Eron, L. D. *Psychosocial development of aggressive behavior*. Progress report to Nat. Inst. of ment. Hlth on grant M-1726. Hudson, N.Y.: Rip Van Winkle Foundation, 1960.

Estes, W. K. An experimental study of punishment. *Psychol. Monogr.*, 1944, **57**, No. 263.

Ewer, R. F. Ethological concepts. *Science*, 1957, **126**, 599–603.

Falk, G. J. Status differences and the frustration-aggression hypothesis. *Int. J. soc. Psychiat.*, 1959, **5**, 214–222.

Fenichel, O. *The psychoanalytic theory of neurosis*. New York: Norton, 1945.

Fenichel, O. Elements of a psychoanalytic theory of anti-Semitism. In E. Simmel (Ed.), *Anti-Semitism: a social disease*. New York: International Universities Press, 1946.

Ferguson, D. C., & Buss, A. H. Operant conditioning of hostile verbs in relation to experimenter and subject characteristics. *J. consult. Psychol.*, 1960, **24**, 324–327.

Feshbach, S. The drive-reducing function of fantasy behavior. *J. abnorm. soc. Psychol.*, 1955, **50**, 3–11.

Feshbach, S. The catharsis hypothesis and some consequences of interaction with aggressive and neutral play objects. *J. Pers.*, 1956, **24**, 449–462.

Feshbach, S. The stimulating versus cathartic effects of a vicarious aggressive activity. *J. abnorm. soc. Psychol.*, 1961, **63**, 381–385.

Feshbach, S., & Singer, R. The effects of personal and shared threats upon social prejudice. *J. abnorm. soc. Psychol.*, 1957, **54**, 411–416. (a)

Feshbach, S., & Singer, R. The effects of fear arousal and suppression of fear upon social perception. *J. abnorm. soc. Psychol.*, 1957, **55**, 283–288. (b)

Festinger, L. Informal social communication. *Psychol. Rev.*, 1950, **57**, 271–282.

Festinger, L. A theory of social comparison processes. *Hum. Relat.*, 1954, **7**, 117–140.

Festinger, L. *A theory of cognitive dissonance.* Evanston, Ill.: Row, Peterson, 1957.

Festinger, L., & Aronson, E. The arousal and reduction of dissonance in social contexts. In D. Cartwright & A. Zander (Eds.), *Group dynamics.* (2nd ed.) Evanston, Ill.: Row, Peterson, 1960.

Festinger, L., Gerard, H., Hymovitch, B., Kelley, H., & Raven, B. The influence process in the presence of extreme deviates. *Hum. Relat.*, 1952, **5**, 327–346.

Festinger, L., Pepitone, A., & Newcomb, T. M. Some consequences of deindividuation in a group. *J. abnorm. soc. Psychol.*, 1952, **47**, 382–389.

Fiedler, F., Warrington, W., & Blaisdell, F. Unconscious attitudes as correlates of sociometric choice in a social group. *J. abnorm. soc. Psychol.*, 1952, **47**, 790–797.

Fletcher, R. *Instinct in man, in the light of recent work in comparative psychology.* London: G. Allen, 1957.

Frederiksen, N. The effects of frustration on negativistic behavior of young children. *J. genet. Psychol.*, 1942, **61**, 203–226.

Fredericson, E. Time and aggression. *Psychol. Rev.*, 1951, **58**, 41–51.

French, J. R. P., Jr. Organized and unorganized groups under fear and frustration. In K. Lewin et al., *Authority and frustration. Univ. of Iowa Studies in Child Welfare.* Iowa City: Univer. of Iowa Press, 1944.

Freud, Anna. *The ego and the mechanisms of defence.* London: Hogarth, 1937.

Freud, S. The economic problem in masochism. In J. Strachey (Ed.), *Collected papers of Sigmund Freud.* Vol. 2. New York: Basic Books, 1959. (a)

Freud, S. Instincts and their vicissitudes. In J. Strachey (Ed.), *Collected papers of Sigmund Freud.* Vol. 4. New York: Basic Books, 1959. (b)

Freud, S. Why war? Letter to Professor Einstein. In J. Strachey (Ed.), *Collected papers of Sigmund Freud.* Vol. 5. New York: Basic Books, 1959. (c)

Freud, S. *Beyond the pleasure principle.* New York: Bantam. 1959. (d)

Funkenstein, D. H., King, S. H., & Drolette, Margaret E. *Mastery of stress.* Cambridge, Mass.: Harvard, 1957.

Gardner, G. E. Recreation's part in mental health. *Recreation*, 1952, **45**, 446–448.

Gatling, F. P. Frustration reactions of delinquents using Rosenzweig's classification system. *J. abnorm. soc. Psychol.*, 1950, **45**, 749–752.

Glaser, D., & Rice, K. Crime, age, and employment. *Amer. sociol. Rev.*, 1959, **24**, 679–686.

Glueck, S., & Glueck, Eleanor. *Unraveling juvenile delinquency.* New York: Commonwealth Fund, 1950.

Glueck, S., & Glueck, Eleanor. *Predicting delinquency and crime.* Cambridge, Mass.: Harvard, 1959.

Goodenough, Florance L. Anger in young children. *Inst. Child Welf. Monogr. Ser.*, No. 9. Minneapolis: Univer. of Minn. Press, 1931.

Gordon, J. E., & Cohn, Fay. The effects of affiliation drive arousal on aggression in doll interviews. Unpublished experiment, 1961.

Graham, Frances K., Charwat, W. A., Honig, A. S., & Weltz, P. C. Aggression as a function of the attack and the attacker. *J. abnorm. soc. Psychol.*, 1951, **46**, 512–520.

Hall, C. S., & Klein, S. J. Individual differences in aggressiveness in rats. *J. comp. Psychol.*, 1942, **33**, 371–383.

Hamblin, R. Group integration during a crisis. *Hum. Relat.*, 1958, **11**, 67–76.

Haner, C. F., & Brown, P. A. Clarification of the instigation to action concept in the frustration-aggression hypothesis. *J. abnorm. soc. Psychol.*, 1955, **51**, 204–206.

Harding, J., Kutner, B., Proshansky, H., & Chein, I. Prejudice and ethnic relations. In G. Lindzey (Ed.), *Handbook of social psychology*. Reading, Mass.: Addison-Wesley, 1954.

Harlow, H. F. Mice, monkeys, men, and motives. *Psychol. Rev.*, 1953, **60**, 23–32.

Hartley, E. L. *Problems in prejudice*. New York: Kings Crown, 1946.

Hartmann, H., Kris, E., & Loewenstein, R. M. Notes on the theory of aggression. *Psychoanalytic Study of the Child, 1949*. Vols. 3–4. New York: International Universities Press, 1949.

Harvey, O. J., & Consalvi, C. Status and conformity to pressures in informal groups. *J. abnorm. soc. Psychol.*, 1960, **60**, 182–187.

Haward, L. R. C. The effect of chlorpromazine on verbal aggression. *Indian J. physiol. Pharmacol.*, 1958, **2**, 367–373.

Hebb, D. O., & Thompson, W. R. The social significance of animal studies. In G. Lindzey (Ed.), *Handbook of social psychology*. Vol. 1. Reading, Mass.: Addison-Wesley, 1954.

Henry, A. F., & Short, J. F., Jr. *Suicide and homicide*. New York: Free Press, 1954.

Herzog, Elizabeth. *Identifying potential delinquents*. Washington: GPO, 1960.

Hewitt, L. E., & Jenkins, R. L. *Fundamental patterns of maladjustment: the dynamics of their origin*. Springfield, Ill.: Green, 1946.

Himmelweit, Hilde T., Oppenheim, A. N., & Vince, Pamela. *Television and the child*. London: Oxford, 1958.

Hokanson, J. E. Behavioral and physiological concomitants of frustration. Unpublished doctoral dissertation, Univer. of Wisconsin, 1959.

Hokanson, J. E. Vascular and psychogalvanic effects of experimentally aroused anger. *J. Pers.*, 1961, **29**, 30–39. (a)

Hokanson, J. E. The effects of frustration and anxiety on overt aggression. *J. abnorm. soc. Psychol.*, 1961, **62**, 346–351. (b)

Hokanson, J. E., & Burgess, M. The effects of three types of aggression on vascular processes. *J. abnorm. soc. Psychol.*, 1962, in press.

Hokanson, J. E., & Gordon, J. E. The expression and inhibition of hostility in imaginative and overt behavior. *J. abnorm. soc. Psychol.*, 1958, **57**, 327–333.

Hokanson, J. E., & Shetler, S. The effect of overt aggression on physiological tension level. *J. abnorm. soc. Psychol.*, 1961, **63**, 446–448.

Holmes, D. S., & Berkowitz, L. Some contrast effects in social perception. *J. abnorm. soc. Psychol.*, 1961, **62**, 150–152.

Holzberg, J. D., Bursten, B., & Santiccioli, A. The reporting of aggression as an indication of aggressive tension. *J. abnorm. soc. Psychol.*, 1955, **50**, 12–18.

Homans, G. *The human group.* New York: Harcourt, Brace & World, 1950.

Hornberger, R. H. The differential reduction of aggressive responses as a function of interpolated activities. Paper presented at meetings of Amer. Psychol. Ass., Cincinnati, Ohio, September, 1959.

Horowitz, E. L. The development of attitude toward the Negro. *Arch. Psychol.*, 1936, No. 194.

Horowitz, E. L., & Horowitz, Ruth E. Development of social attitudes in children. *Sociometry*, 1937, **1**, 301–338.

Horwitz, M., Goldman, M., & Lee, F. J. *Effects of two methods of changing a frustrating agent on reduction of hostility.* ONR Technical Report, 1954.

Horwitz, M., Lee, F., & Goldman, M. Power over decision making and the response to frustration by group members. Cited in A. Zander, Group membership and individual security. *Hum. Relat.*, 1958, **11**, 99–111.

Hovland, C., Harvey, O., & Sherif, M. Assimilation and contrast effects in reactions to communication and attitude change. *J. abnorm. soc. Psychol.*, 1957, **55**, 244–252.

Hovland, C., & Sears, R. Minor studies in aggression: VI. Correlation of lynchings with economic indices. *J. Psychol.*, 1940, **9**, 301–310.

Hull, C. L. *Principles of behavior.* New York: Appleton-Century-Crofts, 1943.

Husman, B. F. Aggression in boxers and wrestlers as measured by projective techniques. *Res. quart. Amer. Ass. Hlth. phys. Educ.*, 1955, **26**, 421–425.

International Sociological Association (in collaboration with Jessie Bernard, T. H. Pear, R. Aron, & R. C. Angell). *The nature of conflict: studies on the sociological aspects of international tension.* Paris: UNESCO, 1957.

James, W. The moral equivalent of war. In *Memoirs and studies.* London: Longmans, 1917.

Janis, I. L. *Air war and emotional stress: psychological studies of bombing and civilian defense.* New York: McGraw-Hill, 1951.

Janis, I. L. *Psychological stress: psychoanalytic and behavioral studies of surgical patients.* New York: Wiley, 1958.

Janis, I. L., & Feshbach, S. Effects of fear-arousing communications. *J. abnorm. soc. Psychol.*, 1953, **48**, 78–92.

Janis, I. L., & Field, P. B. Sex differences and personality factors related to persuasibility. In I. L. Janis, C. I. Hovland, et al., *Personality and persuasibility.* New Haven: Yale, 1959.

Janis, I. L., & Katz, D. The reduction of intergroup hostility: research problems and hypotheses. *Conflict Resolution,* 1959, **3**, 85–100.

Jenkins, R. L. Motivation and frustration in delinquency. *Amer. J. Orthopsychiat.,* 1957, **27**, 528–537.

Jensen, A. R. Aggression in fantasy and overt behavior. *Psychol. Monogr.,* 1957, **71**, No. 445.

Jersild, A. T., & Markey, F. V. Conflicts between preschool children. *Child Develpm. Monogr.,* 1935, No. 21.

Johnson, W. R., & Hutton, D. C. Effects of a combative sport upon personality dynamics as measured by a projective test. *Res. quart. Amer. Ass. Hlth. phys. Educ.,* 1955, **26**, 49–53.

Jones, E. E., Hester, S. L., Farina, A., & Davis, K. E. Reactions to unfavorable personal evaluations as a function of the evaluator's perceived adjustment. *J. abnorm. soc. Psychol.,* 1959, **59**, 363–370.

Kagan, J. The measurement of overt aggression from fantasy. *J. abnorm. soc. Psychol.,* 1956, **52**, 390–393.

Kagan, J. Socialization of aggression and the perception of parents in fantasy. *Child Develpm.,* 1958, **29**, 311–320.

Kahn, M. A polygraph study of the catharsis of aggression. Unpublished doctoral dissertation, Dep. of soc. Relat., Harvard Univer., 1960.

Kardiner, A., & Spiegel, H. *War stress and neurotic illness.* New York: Hoeber-Harper, 1947.

Katz, D., & Braly, K. W. Racial stereotypes of 100 college students. *J. abnorm. soc. Psychol.,* 1933, **28**, 280–290.

Keister, M. E., & Updegraff, R. The behavior of young children in failure: an experimental attempt to discover and to modify undesirable responses of pre-school children to failure. *Univer. Iowa Stud. Child Welf.,* 1938, **14**, 27–82.

Kenny, D. T. *An experimental test of the catharsis theory of aggression.* Ann Arbor: University Microfilms, 1953.

Klapper, J. T. *The effects of mass communication.* New York: Free Press, 1960.

Klineberg, O. *Tensions affecting international understanding.* SSRC Bull. 62. New York: soc. Sci. Res. Council, 1950.

Kohn, M. L. Social class and the exercise of parental authority. *Amer. sociol. Rev.,* 1959, **24**, 352–366.

Kris, E. Psychoanalytic propositions. In M. Marx (Ed.), *Psychological theory: contemporary readings.* New York: Macmillan, 1951.

Kuo, A. Y. The genesis of the cat's response to the rat. *J. comp. Psychol.,* 1930, **2**, 1–35.

Lansky, L. M., Crandall, V. J., Kagan, J., & Baker, C. T. Sex differences in aggression and its correlates in middle-class adolescents. *Child Develpm.,* 1961, **32**, 45–58.

Lanzetta, J. T. Group behavior under stress. *Hum. Relat.,* 1955, **8**, 29–52.

Lesser, G. S. Maternal attitudes and practices and the aggressive behavior of children. Doctoral dissertation, Yale Univer., 1952. Published as, The relationship between overt and fantasy aggression as a function of maternal response to aggression. *J. abnorm. soc. Psychol.*, 1957, **55**, 215–221.

Lesser, G. S. Extrapunitiveness and ethnic attitude. *J. abnorm. soc. Psychol.*, 1958, **56**, 281–282.

Lesser, G. S. The relationships between various forms of aggression and popularity among lower-class children. *J. educ. Psychol.*, 1959, **50**, 20–25.

Levin, H., & Sears, R. R. Identification with parents as a determinant of doll-play aggression. *Child Develpm.*, 1956, **27**, 135–153.

Levin, H., & Turgeon, Valerie F. The influence of mother's presence on children's doll-play aggression. *J. abnorm. soc. Psychol.*, 1957, **55**, 304–308.

Levy, D. M. The hostile act. *Psychol. Rev.*, 1941, **48**, 356–361.

Lewin, K. *A dynamic theory of personality.* New York: McGraw-Hill, 1935.

Lindesmith, A. R., & Dunham, H. W. Some principles of criminal typology. *Soc. Forces,* 1941, **19**, 307–314.

Lindzey, G. An experimental examination of the scapegoat theory of prejudice. *J. abnorm. soc. Psychol.*, 1950, **45**, 296–309.

Lindzey, G., & Borgatta, E. F. Sociometric measurement. In G. Lindzey (Ed.), *Handbook of social psychology.* Reading, Mass.: Addison-Wesley, 1954.

Lippitt, R., Polansky, N., Redl, F., & Rosen, S. The dynamics of power. *Hum. Relat.,* 1952, **5**, 37–64.

Livson, N., & Bronson, Wanda C. An exploration of patterns of impulse control in early adolescence. *Child Develpm.*, 1961, **32**, 75–88.

Livson, N., & Mussen, P. H. The relation of ego control to overt aggression and dependency. *J. abnorm. soc. Psychol.*, 1957, **55**, 66–71.

Lövaas, O. Ivar. Effect of exposure to symbolic aggression on aggressive behavior. *Child Develpm.*, 1961, **32**, 37–44. (a)

Lövaas, O. Ivar. Interaction between verbal and nonverbal behavior. *Child Develpm.*, 1961, **32**, 329–336. (b)

Lundberg, G. A., & Dickson, L. Selective association among ethnic groups in a high school population. *Amer. sociol. Rev.*, 1952, **17**, 23–35.

Lundy, R., Katkovsky, W., Cromwell, R., & Shoemaker, D. Self-acceptability and descriptions of sociometric choices. *J. abnorm. soc. Psychol.*, 1955, **51**, 260–262.

McClelland, D. C. *Personality.* New York: Holt, Rinehart & Winston, 1951.

McClelland, D. C. Personality. In P. R. Farnsworth & Q. McNemar (Eds.), *Annual review of psychology.* Vol. 7. Stanford: Annual Reviews, 1956.

McClelland, D. C., & Apicella, F. S. A functional classification of verbal reactions to experimentally induced failure. *J. abnorm. soc. Psychol.*, 1945, **40**, 376–390.

McClelland, D., Atkinson, J. W., Clark, R. A., & Lowell, E. L. *The achievement motive.* New York: Appleton-Century-Crofts, 1953.

Maccoby, Eleanor E. Why do children watch television? *Publ. Opin. Quart.,* 1954, **18**, 239–244.

Maccoby, Eleanor E. Role-taking in childhood and its consequences for social learning. *Child Develpm.*, 1959, **30**, 239–252.

Maccoby, Eleanor E., & Wilson, W. C. Identification and observational learning from films. *J. abnorm. soc. Psychol.*, 1957, **55**, 76–87.

McCord, W., McCord, Joan, & Howard, A. Familial correlates of aggression in nondelinquent male children. *J. abnorm. soc. Psychol.*, 1961, **62**, 79–93.

McCord, W., McCord, Joan, & Zola, I. *Origins of crime.* New York: Columbia, 1959.

McDougall, W. *An introduction to social psychology.* (Rev. ed.) Boston: Luce, 1926.

Mack, R. W., & Snyder, R. C. The analysis of social conflict—toward an overview and synthesis. *Conflict Resolution*, 1957, **1**, 212–248.

McKee, J. P., and Leader, Florence B. The relationship of socioeconomic status and aggression to the competitive behavior of preschool children. *Child Develpm.*, 1955, **26**, 135–142.

McKellar, P. The emotion of anger in the expression of human aggressiveness. *Brit. J. Psychol.*, 1949, **39**, 148–155.

MacKinnon, D. W. Violation of prohibitions. In H. A. Murray, *Explorations in personality.* New York: Oxford, 1938.

McNeil, E. B. Psychology and aggression. *Conflict Resolution*, 1959, **3**, 195–293.

Magaziner, D. The reduction of hostility without catharsis. Paper presented at meetings of East. Psychol. Assn., Philadelphia, April, 1961.

Malinowski, B. An anthropological analysis of war. *Amer. J. Sociol.*, 1941, **46**, 521–550.

Marx, M. H. Some relations between frustration and drive. In M. R. Jones (Ed.), *Nebraska symposium on motivation*, 1956. Lincoln, Nebr.: Univer. of Nebr. Press, 1956.

Maslow, A. H. Deprivation, threat, and frustration. *Psychol. Rev.*, 1941, **48**, 364–366.

Maslow, A. H. Conflict, frustration, and the theory of threat. *J. abnorm. soc. Psychol.*, 1943, **38**, 81–86.

Mason, W. A. Socially mediated reduction in emotional responses of young rhesus monkeys. *J. abnorm. soc. Psychol.*, 1960, **60**, 100–104.

May, M. A. *A social psychology of war and peace.* New Haven, Conn.: Yale, 1943.

Menninger, K. *Love against hate.* New York: Harcourt, Brace & World, 1942.

Menninger, W. C. Recreation and mental health. *Recreation*, 1948, **42**, 340–346.

Merton, R. K. *Social theory and social structure.* (Rev. ed.) New York: Free Press, 1957.

Miller, D. R., & Swanson, G. E. The study of conflict. In M. R. Jones (Ed.), *Nebraska symposium on motivation*, 1956. Lincoln, Nebr.: Univer. of Nebr. Press, 1956.

Miller, D. R., & Swanson, G. E. *Inner conflict and defense.* New York: Holt, Rinehart & Winston, 1960.

Miller, N. E. The frustration-aggression hypothesis. *Psychol. Rev.*, 1941, **48**, 337–342.

Miller, N. E. Theory and experiment relating psychoanalytic displacement to stimulus-response generalization. *J. abnorm. soc. Psychol.*, 1948, **43**, 155–178.

Miller, N. E. Comments on theoretical models illustrated by the development of a theory of conflict. *J. Pers.*, 1951, **20**, 82–100.

Miller, N. E. Experiments on motivation. *Science*, 1957, **126**, 1271–1278.

Miller, N. E. Liberalization of basic S-R concepts: extensions to conflict behavior, motivation, and social learning. In S. Koch (Ed.), *Psychology: a study of a science.* Vol. 2. New York: McGraw-Hill, 1959.

Miller, N. E., & Bugelski, R. Minor studies in aggression: the influence of frustrations imposed by the in-group on attitudes expressed toward out-groups. *J. Psychol.*, 1948, **25**, 437–442.

Mintz, A. A re-examination of correlations between lynchings and economic indices. *J. abnorm. soc. Psychol.*, 1946, **41**, 154–160.

Mintz, A. Nonadaptive group behavior. In Eleanor Maccoby, T. M. Newcomb, & E. L. Hartley (Eds.), *Readings in social psychology.* (3rd ed.) New York: Holt, Rinehart & Winston, 1958.

Mischel, W. Preference for delayed reinforcement and social responsibility. *J. abnorm. soc. Psychol.*, 1961, **62**, 1–7.

Montgomery, K. C. The role of the exploratory drive in learning. *J. comp. physiol. Psychol.*, 1954, **47**, 60–64.

Morlan, G. K. A note on the frustration-aggression theories of Dollard and his associates. *Psychol. Rev.*, 1949, **56**, 1–8.

Mowrer, O. H. *Learning theory and behavior.* New York: Wiley, 1960.

Murney, R. G. *An application of the principle of stimulus generalization to the prediction of object displacement.* Washington: Catholic Univer. of America Press, 1955.

Murphy, Lois B. *Social behavior and child personality; an exploratory study of some roots of sympathy.* New York: Columbia, 1937.

Murray, H. A. *Explorations in personality.* New York: Oxford, 1938.

Mussen, P. H. Some personality and social factors related to changes in children's attitudes toward Negroes. *J. abnorm. soc. Psychol.*, 1950, **45**, 423–441.

Mussen, P. H., & Hones, Mary C. The behavior-inferred motivations of late- and early-maturing boys. *Child Develpm.*, 1958, **29**, 61–67.

Mussen, P. H., & Naylor, H. K. The relationships between overt and fantasy aggression. *J. abnorm. soc. Psychol.*, 1954, **49**, 235–240.

Mussen, P. H., & Rutherford, E. Effects of aggressive cartoons on children's aggressive play. *J. abnorm. soc. Psychol.*, 1961, **62**, 461–464.

Needler, M. Hitler's anti-Semitism: a political appraisal. *Publ. Opin. Quart.*, 1960, **24**, 665–669.

Nettler, G. Antisocial sentiment and criminality. *Amer. sociol. Rev.*, 1959, **24**, 202–208.

Newcomb, T. M. Autistic hostility and social reality. *Hum. Relat.*, 1947, **1**, 3–20.

Newcomb, T. M. Individual systems of orientation. In S. Koch (Ed.), *Psychology: a study of a science*. Vol. 3. New York: McGraw-Hill, 1959.

Olds, J., & Milner, P. Positive reinforcement produced by electrical stimulation of septal area and other regions of the rat brain. *J. comp. physiol. Psychol.*, 1954, **47**, 419–427.

Osgood, C. E. Cognitive dynamics in the conduct of human affairs. *Publ. Opin. Quart.*, 1960, **24**, 341–365.

Otis, N. B., & McCandless, B. Responses to repeated frustrations of young children differentiated according to need area. *J. abnorm. soc. Psychol.*, 1955, **50**, 349–353.

Palmer, S. Frustration, aggression, and murder. *J. abnorm. soc. Psychol.*, 1960, **60**, 430–432.

Parsons, T. *The social system*. New York: Free Press, 1951.

Pastore, N. The role of arbitrariness in the frustration-aggression hypothesis. *J. abnorm. soc. Psychol.*, 1952, **47**, 728–731.

Peak, Helen. Psychological structure and psychological activity. *Psychol. Rev.*, 1958, **65**, 325–347.

Peck, R. F. Family patterns correlated with adolescent personality structure. *J. abnorm. soc. Psychol.*, 1958, **57**, 347–350.

Pelz, Edith B. Some factors in "group decision." In Eleanor Maccoby, T. M. Newcomb, & E. L. Hartley (Eds.), *Readings in social psychology*. (3rd ed.) New York: Holt, Rinehart & Winston, 1958.

Pepitone, A., & Kleiner, R. The effect of threat and frustration on group cohesiveness. *J. abnorm. soc. Psychol.*, 1957, **54**, 192–199.

Pepitone, A., & Reichling, G. Group cohesiveness and the expression of hostility. *Hum. Relat.*, 1955, **8**, 327–337.

Peterson, D. R., Quay, H. C., & Cameron, G. R. Personality and background factors in juvenile delinquency as inferred from questionnaire responses. *J. consult. Psychol.*, 1959, **23**, 395–399.

Peterson, Ruth C., & Thurstone, L. L. *Motion pictures and the social attitudes of children*. New York: Macmillan, 1933.

Pettigrew, T. F. Regional differences in anti-Negro prejudice. *J. abnorm. soc. Psychol.*, 1959, **59**, 28–36.

Pettigrew, T. F., & Campbell, E. Q. Faubus and segregation: an analysis of Arkansas voting. *Publ. Opin. Quart.*, 1960, **24**, 436–447.

Pettigrew, T. F., & Cramer, M. R. The demography of desegregation. *J. soc. Issues*, 1959, **15**, 61–71.

Radke, Marion J. The relation of parental authority to children's behavior and attitudes. *Univer. Minn. Inst. Child Welf. Monogr. Ser.*, 1946, No 22.

Raper, A. F. *The tragedy of lynching*. Chapel Hill: Univer. of N. Carolina Press, 1933.

Reckless, W. C., Dinitz, S., & Kay, Barbara. The self component in potential delinquency and potential nondelinquency. *Amer. sociol. Rev.*, 1957, **22**, 566–570.

Redl, F., & Wineman, D. *The aggressive child*. New York: Free Press, 1957.

Riley, Matilda W., & Riley, J. W., Jr. A sociological approach to communication. In W. Schramm (Ed.), *The process and effects of mass communication.* Urbana, Ill.: Univer. of Ill. Press, 1954.

Rogers, C. R. *The clinical treatment of the problem child.* Boston: Houghton Mifflin, 1939.

Rokeach, M. *The open and closed mind.* New York: Basic Books, 1960.

Rose, A. M. *Sociology: the study of human relations.* New York: Knopf, 1956.

Rosenbaum, M. E., & deCharms, R. Direct and vicarious reduction of hostility. *J. abnorm. soc. Psychol.,* 1960, **60**, 105–111.

Rosenzweig, S. The experimental measurement of types of reactions to frustration. In H. A. Murray (Ed.), *Explorations in personality.* New York: Oxford, 1939.

Rosenzweig, S. An outline of frustration theory. In J. McV. Hunt (Ed.), *Personality and the behavior disorders.* New York: Ronald, 1944.

Rosenzweig, S., & Rosenzweig, L. Aggression in problem children and normals as evaluated by the Rosenzweig P-F Study. *J. abnorm. soc. Psychol.,* 1952, **47**, 683–687.

Rothaus, P., & Worchel, P. The inhibition of aggression under nonarbitrary frustration. *J. Pers.,* 1960, **28**, 108–117.

Rotter, J. B., & Wickens, D. D. The consistency and generality of ratings of "social aggressiveness" made from observation of role playing situations. *Amer. Psychologist,* 1947, **2**, 333.

Sargent, S. S. Reaction to frustration—a critique and hypothesis. *Psychol. Rev.,* 1948, **55**, 108–114.

Saul, L. J. *The hostile mind.* New York: Random House, 1956.

Schachter, J. Pain, fear, and anger in hypertensives and normotensives: a psychophysiological study. *Psychosom. Med.,* 1957, **19**, 17–29.

Schachter, S., & Singer, J. E. Cognitive, social, and physiological determinants of emotional state. Mimeographed report, 1962.

Schaefer, E. S., & Bayley, Nancy. Consistency of maternal behavior from infancy to preadolescence. *J. abnorm. soc. Psychol.,* 1960, **61**, 1–6.

Schmidt, H. D. Bigotry in schoolchildren. *Commentary,* 1960, **29**, 253–257.

Schramm, W., Lyle, J., & Parker, E. B. *Television in the lives of our children.* Stanford, Cal.: Stanford, 1961.

Scott, J. P. Dominance and the frustration-aggression hypothesis. *Physiol. Zool.,* 1948, **21**, 31–39.

Scott, J. P. *Aggression.* Chicago: Univer. of Chicago Press, 1958. (a)

Scott, J. P. *Animal behavior.* Chicago: Univer. of Chicago Press, 1958. (b)

Scott, J. P., & Fredericson, E. The causes of fighting in mice and rats. *Physiol. Zool.,* 1951, **24**, 273–309.

Sears, Pauline S. Doll play aggression in normal young children: influence of sex, age, sibling status, father's absence. *Psychol. Monogr.,* 1951, **65**, No. 323.

Sears, R. R. Nonaggressive reactions to frustration. *Psychol. Rev.,* 1941, **48**, 343–346.

Sears, R. R. Relation of fantasy aggression to interpersonal aggression. *Child Develpm.,* 1950, **21**, 5–6.

Sears, R. R. Effects of frustration and anxiety on fantasy aggression. *Amer. J. Orthopsychiat.*, 1951, **21**, 498–505. (a)

Sears, R. R. A theoretical framework for personality and social behavior. *Amer. Psychologist*, 1951, **6**, 476–483. (b)

Sears, R. R. Relation of early socialization experiences to aggression in middle childhood. *J. abnorm. soc. Psychol.*, 1961, **63**, 461–465.

Sears, R. R., Maccoby, Eleanor E., & Levin, H. *Patterns of child rearing.* Evanston, Ill.: Row, Peterson, 1957.

Sears, R. R., Pintler, Margaret H., & Sears, Pauline S. Effect of father separation on preschool children's doll play aggression. *Child Develpm.*, 1946, **17**, 219–243.

Sears, R. R., Whiting, J. W. M., Nowlis, V., & Sears, Pauline S. Some child-rearing antecedents of aggression and dependency in young children. *Genet. Psychol. Monogr.*, 1953, **47**, 135–234.

Seward, J. P. Aggressive behavior in the rat: I. General characteristics; age and sex differences. *J. comp. Psychol.*, 1945, **38**, 175–197. (a)

Seward, J. P. Aggressive behavior in the rat. III. The role of frustration. *J. comp. Psychol.*, 1945, **38**, 225–238. (b)

Seward, J. P. Aggressive behavior in the rat. IV. Submission as determined by conditioning, extinction, and disuse. *J. comp. Psychol.*, 1946, **39**, 51–76.

Shapiro, D. S. Perceptions of significant family and environmental relationships in aggressive and withdrawn children. *J. consult. Psychol.*, 1957, **21**, 381–385.

Shaw, C. R., & McKay, H. D. *Juvenile delinquency and urban areas.* Chicago: Univer. of Chicago Press, 1942.

Sheffield, F. D. A drive induction theory of reinforcement. Paper read at Psychol. Colloquium, Brown University, November, 1954.

Sheffield, F. D., Wulff, J. J., & Backer, R. Reward value of copulation without sex-drive reduction. *J. comp. physiol. Psychol.*, 1951, **44**, 3–8.

Sheldon, W. H., & Stevens, S. S. *The varieties of temperament.* New York: Harper, 1942.

Sherif, M., & Sherif, Carolyn W. *Groups in harmony and tension.* New York: Harper, 1953.

Sherif, M., & Sherif, Carolyn W. *An outline of social psychology.* (Rev. ed.) New York: Harper, 1956.

Shneidman, E. S., & Farberow, N. L. *Clues to suicide.* New York: McGraw-Hill, 1957.

Shuttleworth, F. K., & May, M. A. *The social conduct and attitudes of movie fans.* New York: Macmillan, 1933.

Shuval, Judith T. The role of class instructing inter-group hostility. *Hum. Relat.*, 1957, **10**, 61–75.

Siegel, Alberta E. Film-mediated fantasy aggression and strength of aggressive drive. *Child Develpm.*, 1956, **27**, 365–378.

Siegel, Alberta E. Aggressive behavior of young children in the absence of an adult. *Child Develpm.*, 1957, **28**, 371–378.

Siegel, Alberta E. The influence of violence in the mass media upon children's role expectations. *Child Develpm.*, 1958, **29**, 35–56.

Siegel, Alberta E., & Kohn, Lynette G. Permissiveness, permission, and aggression: The effect of adult presence or absence on aggression in children's play. *Child Develpm.*, 1959, **30**, 131–141.

Siegel, S. The relationship of hostility to authoritarianism. *J. abnorm. soc. Psychol.*, 1956, **52**, 368–372.

Slavson, S. R. *Analytic group psychotherapy.* New York: Columbia, 1951.

Smock, C. D. The influence of stress on the "intolerance of ambiguity." *J. abnorm. soc. Psychol.*, 1955, **50**, 177–182.

Stagner, R. Studies of aggressive social attitudes: I. Measurement and interrelation of selected attitudes. *J. soc. Psychol.*, 1944, **20**, 109–120.

Stagner, R., & Congdon, C. S. Another failure to demonstrate displacement of aggression. *J. abnorm. soc. Psychol.*, 1955, **51**, 695–696.

Stone, A. A. The effect of sanctioned overt aggression on total instigation to aggressive responses. Unpublished honors thesis, Harvard Univer., 1950. Cited in D. McClelland, *Personality.* New York: Holt, Rinehart & Winston, 1951.

Stotland, E. Peer groups and reactions to power figures. In D. Cartwright (Ed.), *Studies in social power.* Ann Arbor: Inst. for soc. Res., 1959.

Strickland, L. H., Jones, E. E., & Smith, W. P. Effects of group support on the evaluation of an antagonist. *J. abnorm. soc. Psychol.*, 1960, **61**, 73–81.

Sutherland, E. H., & Cressey, D. R. *Principles of criminology.* (6th ed.) Philadelphia: Lippincott, 1960.

Tappan, P. W. *Crime, justice, and correction.* New York: McGraw-Hill, 1960.

Taylor, Janet A. Drive theory and manifest anxiety. *Psychol. Bull.*, 1956, **53**, 303–320.

Thibaut, J. W. An experimental study of the cohesiveness of underprivileged groups. *Hum. Relat.*, 1950, **3**, 251–278.

Thibaut, J. W., & Coules, J. The role of communication in the reduction of interpersonal hostility. *J. abnorm. soc. Psychol.*, 1952, **47**, 770–777.

Thibaut, J. W., & Kelley, H. H. *The social psychology of groups.* New York: Wiley, 1959.

Thibaut, J. W., & Riecken, H. W. Authoritarianism, status, and the communication of aggression. *Hum. Relat.*, 1955, **8**, 95–120.

Thomas, E. Effects of facilitative role interdependence on group functioning. *Hum. Relat.*, 1957, **10**, 347–366.

Thompson, Clara. *Psychoanalysis: evolution and development.* New York: Hermitage House, 1950.

Thorpe, W. H. *Learning and instinct in animals.* Cambridge, Mass.: Harvard, 1956.

Thrasher, F. M. *The gang.* Chicago: Univer. of Chicago Press, 1936.

Tinbergen, N. *The study of instinct.* London: Oxford, 1951.

Tinbergen, N. Fighting and threat in animals. In *Penguin new biology*, April, 1953. Cited in R. Fletcher, *Instinct in man, in the light of recent work in comparative psychology.* London: G. Allen, 1957.

Toby, J. The differential impact of family disorganization. *Amer. sociol. Rev.*, 1957, **22**, 505–512.

United States Senate Committee on the Judiciary. *Television programs and juvenile delinquency: hearings before the Subcommmittee to Investigate Juvenile Delinquency, 84th Congress, First Session.* 1955.

Vandenbergh, J. G. Eosinophil response to aggressive behavior in CFW albino mice. *Anim. Behav.*, 1960, **8**, 13–18.

von Holst, E. & von St. Paul, Ursula. Electrically controlled behavior. *Scientific Amer.*, 1962, **206**, 50–59.

Weatherley, D. Anti-Semitism and the expression of fantasy aggression. *J. abnorm. soc. Psychol.*, 1961, **62**, 454–457.

Weatherley, D. Maternal permissiveness toward aggression and subsequent fantasy aggression. *J. abnorm. soc. Psychol.*, 1962, in press.

Weiss, W., & Fine, B. J. The effect of induced aggressiveness on opinion change. *J. abnorm. soc. Psychol.*, 1956, **52**, 109–114.

Wertham, F. C. *Seduction of the innocent.* New York: Holt, Rinehart & Winston, 1954.

White, R. K., & Lippitt, R. *Autocracy and democracy: an experimental inquiry.* New York: Harper, 1960.

White, R. W. Motivation reconsidered: the concept of competence. *Psychol. Rev.*, 1959, **66**, 297–333.

Whiting, J. M. W. The frustration complex in Kwoma society. *Man*, 1944, **44**, 140–144.

Williams, R. M., Jr., *The reduction of intergroup tensions.* SSRC Bull. No. 57. New York: soc. Sci. Res. Council, 1947.

Wolfgang, M. E. *Patterns in criminal homicide.* Philadelphia: Univer. of Pennsylvania, 1958.

Wood, A. L. A socio-structural analysis of murder, suicide, and economic crime in Ceylon. *Amer. sociol. Rev.*, 1961, **26**, 744–753.

Worchel, P. Catharsis and the relief of hostility. *J. abnorm. soc. Psychol.*, 1957, **55**, 238–243.

Worchel, P. Hostility: theory and experimental investigation. In D. Willner (Ed.), *Decisions, values and groups.* Vol. I. New York: Pergamon Press, 1960.

Wright, G. O. Projection and displacement: a cross-cultural study of folk-tale aggression. *J. abnorm. soc. Psychol.*, 1954, **49**, 523–528.

Wright, M. E. The influence of frustration upon the social relations of young children. *Charac. & Pers.*, 1943, **12**, 111–122.

Wright, Q. *A study of war.* Chicago: Univer. of Chicago Press, 1942.

Wurtz, K. R. Some theory and data concerning the attenuation of aggression. *J. abnorm. soc. Psychol.*, 1960, **60**, 134–136.

Yarrow, L. J. The effect of antecedent frustration on projective play. *Psychol. Monogr.*, 1948, **62**, No. 293.

Zajonc, R. Aggressive attitudes of the "stranger" as a function of conformity pressures. *Hum. Relat.*, 1952, **5**, 205–216.

Zajonc, R. Some effects of the "space" serials. *Publ. Opin. Quart.*, 1954, **18**, 367–374.

Zander, A. A study of experimental frustration. *Psychol. Monogr.*, 1944, **56,** No. 256.

Zander, A. Group membership and individual security. *Hum. Relat.*, 1958, **11,** 99–111.

Zawadski, B. Limitations of the scapegoat theory of prejudice. *J. abnorm. soc. Psychol.*, 1948, **43,** 127–141.

Zilboorg, G. Introduction. In S. Freud, *Beyond the pleasure principle.* New York: Bantam, 1959.

Zimbardo, P. G. Involvement and communication discrepancy as determinants of opinion conformity. *J. abnorm. soc. Psychol.*, 1960, **60,** 86–94.

Zuckerman, M. The effect of frustration on the perception of neutral and aggressive words. *J. Pers.*, 1954, **23,** 407–422.

Zuckerman, S. *The social life of monkeys and apes.* New York: Harcourt, Brace & World, 1932.

# Name Index

# Subject Index